THE AMERICAN ADRENALINE NARRATIVE

THE AMERICAN ADRENALINE NARRATIVE

KRISTIN J. JACOBSON

THE UNIVERSITY OF
GEORGIA PRESS
ATHENS

© 2020 by the University of Georgia Press
Athens, Georgia 30602
www.ugapress.org
All rights reserved
Designed by Kaelin Chappell Broaddus
Set in by 9.5/13 Skolar Latin by Kaelin Chappell Broaddus

Most University of Georgia Press titles are
available from popular e-book vendors.

Printed digitally

Library of Congress Control Number: 2019044474
ISBN: 9780820356990 (hardback: alk. paper)
ISBN: 9780820357188 (paperback: alk. paper)
ISBN: 9780820356983 (ebook)

TO MY PARENTS,
BEV & PAUL,
FOR ALWAYS
SUPPORTING
MY ADVENTURES.

CONTENTS

Acknowledgments ix

1. DESIRING NATURES 1

2. CONQUERING NATURES 40

3. SPIRITUAL NATURES 87

4. EROTIC NATURES 121

5. RISKY NATURES 168

6. RESTORATIVE NATURES 214

Appendix. List of Contemporary
American Adrenaline Narratives 233

Notes 239

Bibliography 271

Index 291

ACKNOWLEDGMENTS

My formal academic work on this project began as a graduate student in the English department at Penn State University. My final paper in Bob Burkholder's "Nature Writing/Ecocriticism" class, which I later workshopped in Kit Hume's summer graduate course, eventually became my first published article. Their initial guidance along with feedback from my peers in both classes planted the seed for this book.

I greatly appreciate the support of my colleagues and the administration at Stockton University, where I received research support to attend conferences to develop this project as well as sabbatical release time to complete the final writing and editing. In 2015, Stockton University also supported my attendance at the American Association of State Colleges and Universities American Democracy Project's "Stewardship of Public Lands" seminar in Yellowstone National Park. Additionally, in 2011, I participated in the National Endowment for the Humanities Summer Seminar, "Rethinking the Land Ethic: Sustainability and the Humanities" (Flagstaff, Ariz.), led by Joan McGregor and Dan Shilling. These seminars provided crucial foundational knowledge in the environmental humanities and an amazing network of interdisciplinary scholars. The Faculty Resource Network at New York University also provided access to essential research materials during a summer 2012 scholar-in-residence program. And my time teaching American environmental literature and sharing my research with diverse audiences as a Fulbright Greece Scholar at Aristotle University in Thessaloniki also helped me identify both the uniquely American and more universal qualities of the adrenaline narrative. Ευχαριστώ, especially to Tatiani Rapatzikou, who arranged for me to share my research during my time in Greece.

Stockton undergraduate Danielle (Nobilucci) Chiz organized a library of primary and secondary resources. Working with her that semester remains among my favorite teaching experiences. Zachary St. George, who was my American studies graduate assistant for one term, also contributed research assistance. I also want to acknowledge Shana Loshbaugh, Dale Goble, Ray J. Sapirstein, Janis Edwards, Thomas Ruys Smith, and Karen Dunak, who all responded to my H-NET American Studies query for suggestions about adrenaline narratives written by racial and ethnic minorities. Stockton University's Interlibrary Loan staff, in turn, efficiently filled numerous article and book requests. Thank you.

A heartfelt thank you goes to Beth Widmaier Capo, who read much of the draft manuscript and provided just the right mix of encouraging and critical feedback. Vorris Nunley's steadfast and enthusiastic support took many forms, from brainstorming ideas to sending cookies. Numerous friends, family, students, and colleagues over the years have shared articles and other media related to this topic. My work is richer for their thoughtful attention. I am especially grateful for campus invitations to share my research: this feedback from faculty and students at the University of Alabama in Huntsville, SUNY Fredonia, the University of Wisconsin–Stout, the University of Wisconsin–La Crosse, Miami University Middletown, and Penn State University proved invaluable as I completed the manuscript. I also want to express my gratitude to the staff and editors at the University of Georgia Press for their careful attention to my work. In particular, I wish to thank my anonymous readers: their insightful feedback improved the text considerably.

My less formal exploration of adrenaline narratives began much earlier than my graduate work at PSU, with family camping trips, with sharing books with my father, with soaking up Colorado's adventurous climate while a graduate student at the University of Colorado, with teaching in China and traveling through Tibet, and with an undergraduate January-term backcountry backpacking trip to Big Bend National Park. While reviewing texts on my bookshelf I was reminded that in 1989 adventurer Will Steger presented me with the Girl Scout Gold Award and a signed copy of his book. This research adventure's beginnings are multiple and have taken me to unexpected places. I hope this book will similarly lead you forward—toward a better understanding of the American origins of our adventurous desires and our environmental future.

Portions of the chapters are revised and expanded from the previously published article "Desiring Natures: The American Adrenaline Narrative," *Genre* 35, no. 2 (Summer 2002): 355–82, reprinted in *Contemporary Literary Criticism*, vol. 248 (CLC-248), edited by Jeff Hunter (Detroit: Gale, 2008).

THE
AMERICAN
ADRENALINE
NARRATIVE

CHAPTER 1
DESIRING
NATURES

The Jia Tsuo La pass in Tibet (also called Lhakpa La and Gyatso La), at 17,126 feet (5,220 meters), marks the highest I have ever traveled without leaving the ground. Amazingly, at least from my perspective, I was still over 10,000 feet short of the highest point on earth, Mount Everest—or Chomolungma ("Holy Mother") in Tibetan and Sagarmāthā in Nepali.[1] However, as an American I was not surprised that you could drive your car, or in my case take a tour bus, to the top of the Jia Tsuo La pass.[2] At the peak of my Tibetan travels, I reflected on what desires pushed me to catch a glimpse of Everest from a tour bus. I wondered, if I had not read about twelve people losing their lives on Everest in 1996, if Jon Krakauer had not been one of the climbers that spring to summit, survive, and tell the tale, whether I would have found myself experiencing my own modified extreme adventure three years later. I continue today to consume accounts of perilous outdoor adventures. And I am not alone.

We live in an age where the marketing and consumption of extreme adventure is all around us in ways we might variously label both natural and unnatural: expedition jackets often see far more concrete sidewalks than rock faces, energy drinks and bars fuel work marathons or simply provide a quick meal on the go, and dispatches from climbing teams on Everest occur on the morning news along with advertising for extreme laundry detergent, reports about severe global warming, bulletins announcing excessive financial meltdowns and upturns, and the latest thrilling celebrity gossip. Our electronic as well as print media invite us to purchase a variety of products associated with an adventurous life. For instance, the Sundance clothing company, which narrates its founding as a connection between artistic and environmental pursuits, boasted "Adventure Ready Styles for Fall" in a 2012 email advertisement campaign.[3] Unlike typical North Face or Patagonia ads, which often feature the newest advancements in fabric technology with a model or tent clinging to the side of a rugged cliff, the Sundance campaign engaged an adventure-lite motif: a rustic camp with an old-fashioned canvas tent provided the backdrop for the model, who looked dressed for the city rather than a hike. Cities are even using extreme sports as a means to market to millennial residents.[4] Yet while such marketing campaigns differ in degree, they all rely on the appeal created by connecting adventure and nature: a desire that is fundamental to American identity and that taps into our contemporary fascination with another set of related extremes—apocalypse and survival.

The attempt to understand the desires related to radical, risky acts like climbing to 29,029 feet as well as the everyday participation in and fascination with extreme lifestyles lies at the heart of this book and the extreme adventure narratives it studies.[5] *The American Adrenaline Narrative* identifies and examines such stories' desiring natures and considers how perilous outdoor adventure tales, what I term "adrenaline narratives," simultaneously promote and hinder ecological sustainability. This chapter specifically outlines the narrative's historical roots, the forces that contribute to its late twentieth-century mainstream popularity, the methodology used to understand these stories, and how this understanding contributes to contemporary environmentalism. I go on to outline the narrative's unique characteristics and the chapters that follow, which focus on the five primary desires or attitudes toward nature that adrenaline narratives exhibit.

In brief, to explore these interdepended desires, *The American Adrenaline Narrative* defines and compares adrenaline narratives by a range of American authors writing after the first Earth Day in 1970, selected as a crucial watershed for the contemporary American environmental movement and for cultures of the extreme.[6] In fact, the vast majority of the narratives selected for study are post-1990, when the popular mainstreaming of extreme cultures in the United States hit its stride. Yet the adrenaline narrative—like the American environmental movement—does not begin here (1970 or 1990). The adrenaline narrative's roots are deep and broad, tapping into archetypal journeys and heroic character traits as well as culturally specific American texts and contexts.

ROOTS OF THE CONTEMPORARY AMERICAN ADRENALINE NARRATIVE

Despite key differences in historical and cultural contexts, the term "adrenaline narrative" may be applicable to and useful for pre-1970s adventure/travel nonfiction and texts written by and/or about non-U.S. adventurers.[7] Anne C. McCarthy, for example, traces the origins of what she calls "the Red Bull sublime," or a "sublime [that] rejects the ideology of nature as other," to the Romantic poets Samuel Taylor Coleridge and John Keats.[8] Some framing of the adrenaline narrative's origins may seem anachronistic, such as the *Outside* magazine story about Native American relay racing that labeled it as "America's first extreme sport."[9] Yet extreme sport's heroic masculinity is defined by physical risk and challenge: tests that more ordinary men (and women) fail.

These are not pursuits invented by today's extreme athletes. Rather, the adrenaline narrative traces its roots to ancient Western and non-Western myths that chronicle heroic and tragic feats, including Native American and other Indigenous storytelling and practices that include extreme physical challenge in nature. Later in the chapter I highlight the contemporary adrenaline narrative's connection with classical Greek tragedy. One measure of Native American impact on the adrenaline narrative, and white American masculinity specifically, is that by the end of the nineteenth century Native American "tokens" adorned "the walls [of middle-class American homes] as symbols of masculinity."[10] No longer a "military threat," Native Americans were rendered into symbols in order to "turn a room into a masculine and rugged retreat from the industrial, urban, and overcivilized 'white' world. And yet, of course, this rugged world was safe, since it symbolized a nature under the control of white culture."[11] The appropriated symbolism extracted Native American heroic masculinity without directly threatening domestic tranquility. Such popular commercialization of the adrenaline narrative, specifically its heroic aspects, may also be seen in mountaineering.

One of the first key turns in the adrenaline narrative's modern Western development occurs in the mid-1700s. British writer Robert Macfarlane points out that by the mid-1700s "people started for the first time to travel to mountains out of a spirit other than necessity."[12] This shift changes both the adventurer and adventure. As Macfarlane explains in the film *Mountain* (2017), "adventure replaced reverence," and imperialism increasingly sought to conquer all peaks, including Everest: "This was the moment that mountaineering as adventure entered the popular imagination."[13] Macfarlane describes the explorers as "the film-stars of their age; at once glamorous and notorious."[14] Their accounts were best sellers and fans even "mobbed" them in the street.[15] Thus, armchair and amateur popular captivation with adventure also has a long history that predates our contemporary moment.

In terms of the adrenaline narrative's American origins, we can see early versions and aspects of the genre's characteristics in travel narratives as well as colonial and nineteenth-century (auto)biographies, letters, and diaries that focus on exploration and discovery in the "New World." Precolonial and colonial travel writing such as Álvar Núñez Cabeza de Vaca's *La Relación y Comentarios* (1542), John Smith's *A Description of New England* (1616), and J. Hector St. John de Crèvecoeur's *Letters from an American Farmer* (1782) all help to establish the Americas as a site for adventurous self-fashioning. Hester Blum's work, additionally, on both early American sailors' literary culture and polar expeditions' global print culture provides a "history of exploration" that is also "a history of death. There is the vast colonial violence of the usual practices of imperial ventures."[16] Autobiographical early national (Benjamin Franklin) and nineteenth-century (Walt Whitman) American literature often solidified core American myths related to this imperialism, such as individualism and exceptionalism.

Other American narratives complicate, if not outright object to, manifest destiny and its adventurous conquering desires. Freedom or slave narratives such as Olaudah Equiano's *The Interesting Narrative* (1789), Solomon Northup's *Twelve Years a Slave* (1853), and Harriet E. Wilson's autobiographical novel *Our Nig* (1859) and Native American writing such as Sarah Winnemucca's *Life among the Paiutes: Their Wrongs and Claims* (1883) appropriate spine-tingling narrative constructions while depicting (white) American adventure's consequences for African and Native Americans. Such narratives forge heroic (American) identity out of adversity as a result of racism and, like their white peers, risky environmental challenges.

The popularity of these earlier adrenaline tales remains, as seen in the recent film adaptations of *12 Years a Slave* (2013) and *The Revenant* (2015). Hugh Glass's story (based on events that may have happened in the early nineteenth century) inspired the 2015 film as well as numerous other earlier adaptations, including a 1971 film (*Man in the Wilderness*), a 2002 novel by Michael Punke, and a 1915 poem by John G. Neihardt. Their depiction of an arguably unique rugged American identity accounts, at least in part, for their perennial success. Additionally, their narrative structure exhibits similarities to contemporary adrenaline narratives.

Like their contemporary counterparts, these earlier narratives often blur genres—between fact and fiction as well as travel, nature, and adventure writing. Writing about nineteenth-century American travel writing, for example, William W. Stowe asserts its strong resemblance to religious writing: "Like spiritual autobiographies and saints' lives, travel chronicles attest to certain nonordinary events, reformulate them to match approved cultural patterns, and depict their protagonists as ideal incarnations of respectable models."[17] Thus, the American adrenaline narrative's shared narrative pathways with religious and travel writing can be seen in these earlier forms as well.

This cursory introduction to (pre)colonial, early national, and nineteenth-century American literature of the extreme reveals the stories often focused on exploration—for personal and national trade, recognition, freedom, and land and other natural resources as well as scientific knowledge. Risky exploration's benefits and hazards were material and also provided the foundation upon which American legends were made. Such narratives carry into the early twentieth century, even as the frontier landscape upon which American heroic masculinity depends is deemed closed.

The organization of the National Archives' American West Photographs site, for example, tells its own extreme story of this crucial turning point in American culture, especially where adventure and exploration are concerned. The U.S. Census Bureau announced the frontier as closed in 1890, and these archived images straddle this temporal border. Significantly, the image categories tell a familiar story of exploration, extreme living conditions, and natural bounty, including images of "Disinherited" Native Americans as well as photographs of "Bonanzas from the Earth" and "Surveys and Expeditions."[18] This archive represents and tells through its named categories the dominant western frontier history and mythology that outlast the closing of the American frontier.

The African American polar explorer Matthew Alexander Henson (1866–1955) provides another case in point, further fleshing out the adrenaline narrative's long imperial heritage and the role race has long played in defining elite heroic masculinity. While Henson wrote an account of his role in the exploration of the North Pole (*A Negro Explorer at the North Pole*), Admiral Peary's own account suggests Henson's participation was less than that of the European expedition members. Peary specifically mentions

Henson's "racial inheritance" and his temperamental unfitness.[19] According to S. Allen Counter, author of *North Pole Legacy: Black, White, and Eskimo*, some explain Peary's racist remarks as attempts to placate critics upset about his choice of the black Henson as codiscoverer; others suggest "the reason Peary chose Henson in the first place was because he knew a black man would never be accorded equal recognition for discovery of the North Pole."[20] James Edward Mills argues that "it's fair to suggest that much of Peary's success was the result of Henson's expertise." Mills goes on to explain, "the racially divisive climate of the time would not permit an African American man the same standing in the public eye for such a monumental feat of human achievement. So Peary was recognized as the first to reach the North Pole, while Henson was relegated to the role of sidekick."[21] While the publication of Sherpa accounts suggests "auxiliary" expedition members are finally being recognized for their equal contributions, the adrenaline narrative's history and current telling remains focused on and dominated by elite white males.[22]

Macfarlane's research about and fascination with mountaineering and its hold on the Western imagination as well as the American frontier's perennial popularity demonstrate that we continue in the twentieth and twenty-first centuries to see all of the motivations that characterize the initial mid-1700 and late nineteenth-century American shifts. Macfarlane notes, "today, the emotions and attitudes which impelled the early mountaineers still prosper in the Western imagination.... An estimated 10 million Americans go mountaineering annually, and 50 million go hiking."[23] With official exploration no longer the primary motivator, twentieth-century adrenaline narratives began to justify extreme adventuring, as George Mallory famously explained in 1923, "because it's there."[24] Thus, in the twentieth century the archive continues to grow, even as extreme adventure shifts from an intrepid occupation to an extreme form of leisure.

The archive of these twentieth-century adrenaline narratives includes the articles found in mountaineering journals, such as *Summit* (1955–96), *American Alpine Journal* (1966–), and *The Mountaineer* (1907–1966), as well as titles published prior to 1970 by Mountaineers Books. The Robert H. Bates Mountaineering Collection in the Phillips Exeter Academy Library documents mountaineering history over the past two centuries: it includes an extensive archive of over five hundred titles as well as mountaineer Robert H. Bates's papers (1911–2007). These archives demonstrate how much has changed, as Macfarlane notes, since that initial shift. Whereas "three centuries ago, risking one's life to climb a mountain would have been considered tantamount to lunacy" and wild landscapes were feared and revered from a distance, extreme landscapes underwent a "tremendous revolution of perception...in the West."²⁵ While mountaineering and hiking remain key sports in post-1970s extreme adventures, other risky landscapes and sports also come to the fore.

In this regard, the archive provided by *Surfing Magazine* (1964-2017), as well as regional U.S. archives such as the Cape Fear Surfing Archive, the Appalachian Mountain Club Library and Archives, and the Canebrake Archive (Jim McCafferty's personal online archive of the "Historical Outdoor South"), are also important for understanding the time leading up to as well as during the resurgence of attention to extreme sports in the late twentieth century.²⁶ The National Archives also include additional resources related to "Exploration and Westward Expansion" as well as the national parks and related clubs, such as the "Smoky Mountain Hiking Club—Bulletins & Correspondence" (1931-1938), which is available at the National Archives in Atlanta.²⁷ The history and development of such regional and national clubs help tell the story of how adventure shifted from work to leisure.

Thus, while the genre, like the American environmental movement, by no means starts in 1970, another key shift occurs in the late twentieth century where my study begins: the adrenaline narrative goes mainstream in ways it arguably never had before. While still—for all practical purposes—an elite sport, extreme adventure floods American popular culture. The context of this participation and fascination additionally changes: social justice and environmental movements play a key role in altering the ways we view and interact with nature even as we continue to struggle with longstanding ethical and environmental problems associated with outdoor adventure. Social justice movements, furthermore, shift ideas about the adrenaline narrative's heroic subjects and conquering narratives. As Sean Ryan points out, "since the 1960s" both the environmental movement and outdoor recreation have experienced significant growth."²⁸ This combination of factors results in a new era for the American adrenaline narrative.

MAINSTREAMING OF THE POST-1970
AMERICAN ADRENALINE NARRATIVE

The forty-plus years since the first Earth Day mark the rise in the popularity and marketing of all things extreme—including sports, jobs, travel, beverages, gum, makeovers, laundry detergent, and even the environmental movement itself. While it is difficult to pinpoint the exact moment when cultures of the extreme began to go mainstream in American culture, according to a draft 2002 addition for "extreme" in the *Oxford English Dictionary* the first citation of "extreme" in relation to sports occurred in 1974 in Italian mountaineer Reinhold Messner's book *The Seventh Grade: Most Extreme Climbing*.[29] Extreme cultures and sports grow exponentially from this point and gain mainstream attention and popularity. Without a doubt, cultures of the extreme help define the late twentieth and early twenty-first centuries in America.

By 1997, when author and environmentalist Bill McKibben decides to live strenuously for a year, such extreme athletes are part of the day's "Zeitgeist."[30] Barbara Humberstone, in "The 'Outdoor Industry' as Social and Educational Phenomena," cites "statistical evidence" that supports "the trend in the rapid growth in demand for countryside and water-based 'adventurous and glamorous pursuits.'"[31] There is an increasing global demand for extreme experiences and products. Eric Brymer also notes, "over the past two decades, participation rates in extreme sports have grown exponentially[,] far outstripping the growth rates of any other sporting activity."[32] Kyle Kusz, in "Extreme America: The Cultural Politics of Extreme Sports in 1990s America," cites *U.S. News and World Report* and *Time* cover stories (30 June 1997 and 6 December 1999, respectively) to note the mainstream recognition of extreme sports as well as a concomitant redefinition of extreme sports from atypical activities to exemplifying American identity and ideals.[33] A few years earlier, *Skiing* magazine similarly explained "extreme skiing: its roots, its meaning, its devotees" to its readers.[34] Todd Balf likewise observes "America's late-twentieth-century fascination with fatal adventures" in *The Last River*.[35]

As the litany of examples begins to attest, this popular fascination with the extreme saturates contemporary American culture and media. *National Geographic* posted a weekly "extreme photo" for several years and *60 Minutes Presents* devoted an episode in 2012 to "Going to Extremes."[36] Today, television shows such as *Survivor*, *Survivorman*, *Out of the Wild*, *Doomsday Preppers*, *Dual Survival*, and *Man, Woman, Wild* have proliferated alongside feature-length adventure films. Mainstream-release films of bestselling books such as Jon Krakauer's *Into the Wild* (Paramount Vantage, 2007), Cheryl Strayed's *Wild* (Fox Searchlight Pictures, 2014), and Bill Bryson's *A Walk in the Woods* (Broad Green Pictures, 2015), and more limited-release adventure documentaries such as *180° South* (Magnolia Pictures, 2010) and *Into the Cold* (Vision Films, 2010), present adventure in its serious, humorous, and sometimes tragic respects. The above examples are a small sample of an established range of specialized, mainstream, and counterculture print and other media devoted to the reporting, promotion, and analysis of extreme sports, wilderness survival, and adventure.[37]

Since the 1970s, furthermore, the environmental movement has undergone its own set of extreme developments, most notably the emergence of direct-action environmental organizations such as Earth First! (founded 1980) and Greenpeace (Greenpeace USA founded 1975). The terms eco-raider, eco-terrorist(ism), eco-catastrophe (as well as eco-disaster and eco-crisis), eco-activist(ism), eco-freak/nut, eco-adventure, ecotravel, eco-novel/art/documentary/opera/thriller, eco-consciousness, and eco-sabotage (or ecotage)—among others—enter the popular lexicon.[38] The proliferation of "eco" terms reminds us of the contemporary environmental movement's impact and controversy. During this same period a fascination with extreme weather develops alongside debates about whether or not such climate extremes are the result of global warming.

Consumers during this same period also increasingly consider a wide range of consumable and durable products that signify the degree of their environmental awareness and commitment: local, organic, fair trade, free range, grass-fed, made in the USA, PBA-free, single source, no hormones, made from recycled products, green, sustainably grown/produced, not tested on animals, all-natural, no artificial flavors or ingredients, no artificial dyes, no high-fructose syrup, not genetically modified, vegetarian, vegan. The confluence of these products and ideas contribute to the idea of "extreme environmentalism," which becomes a buzzword among global warming skeptics and others that disagree with a variety of environmental groups, practices, and philosophies. Even committed environmentalists such as David Gessner are looking for a "new environmentalism" that is less apocalyptic and "more human and wild [in] form, a more commonsense form."[39] Whereas extreme is often used as a critique of the era's feminist, civil rights, and environmental movements, extreme also offers the legitimizing features of these adventurous, adrenaline-fueled sports. So-called "extreme" feminism, for example, dangerously goes beyond "natural" gender roles, whereas extreme sports excitingly push normal endurance and risk limits. The parallel rise of extreme sports and cultures presents the opportunity to explore the factors that give rise to these movements that explore "natural" extremes.

UNDERSTANDING CONTEMPORARY ADRENALINE MADNESS

A variety of explanations may be posited for the late twentieth-century and twenty-first-century development and appeal of extreme cultures. Notably, whatever the appeal, the development of extreme cultures in America is not apolitical. As I will discuss in the following chapters, for some participants and observers extreme adventure sports and environmentalism provide solace from and a solution to an environmentally and spiritually diminished culture. In the words of Luis A. Vivanco, "there is an influential strain in Euro-American environmental thought, including writers and activists from John Muir and Aldo Leopold to latter-day deep ecologists and wilderness poets like Gary Snyder, that emphasizes that at the heart of modern environmental degradation and social anomie is the denial of the human connection to the wild."[40] To follow Roderick Nash, a significant paradox results as adventurers lead us into the wilderness: "Wilderness recreation is also a game that cannot be played at any one time and place by more than a few people. Solitude is not easily shared."[41] In short, an increasingly polluted world combined with an increasingly popular penchant for adventure requires greater and greater extremes if one is to find solitude in and connection with nature.

Wild places more often than not provide the preferred setting for this (re)connection. In fact, the cure for this modern ill, as Vivanco suggests in "The Work of Environmentalism in An Age of Televisual Adventures," often involves adventure in the wild: "environmentalism itself relies on and draws from the imaginations and practices of adventure."[42] The memoir *Monkey Dancing*, for example, chronicles a divorced father and his two children's travel around the world "to visit a few of the planet's great ecological wonders that were in danger of disappearing as the consequence of human development."[43] The narrative layers wild, vanishing places and a disappearing, end-of-times world with personal and environmental salvation. Whether one visits them or not, extreme wilderness environments may evoke a comforting nostalgia for the iconic American frontier as well as spiritually reconnect (armchair) adventurers to the natural world. As Susan R. Schrepfer observes, American "wilderness has been the crucible in which identities—national, class, gendered, and racial—have been formed, for better or for worse."[44] This connection—whether presented via a high-octane, white-knuckled edge or an off-the-grid frontier—defines the contemporary age's desire for and production of a zealous nature.

Significantly in this regard, the impetus for Daniel Glick's travel in *Monkey Dancing* is twofold: escape and spiritual transformation. Glick seeks travel for himself and for his children after his brother dies and his wife leaves the marriage for a relationship with a woman. He also worries that while nature is part of his "spiritual core," his children's wired lives have meant that they have failed to make such connections.[45] When Glick set out he "couldn't predict what the wild and unfamiliar might do for my two kids in their shell-shocked state," but he knew that "hitting the road had always served me in times of transition as an entrée into a reflective trance, as a tool of personal reinvention, as literal and metaphorical escape."[46] Glick, like many travel writers, connects adventure and encounter with the strange and wild as key to "personal reinvention" as well as to (re)establishing a primal connection with nature. He describes his adventure, in fact, as simply a more extreme version of going to the zoo or a national park.

Glick posits that "we 'civilized' humans spend gazillions of dollars on zoos, safaris, animal parks, menageries, and even exotic pets" because "deep inside, we must recognize a missing connection that we need to recapture. Something, or a combination of things, about our modern existence has forced us to neglect that connection."[47] This tension between a fundamental need and our everyday disconnected lives cause Glick to question, "but why, then, is there such an insufferably huge gap between this theoretical deep-seated engagement with the natural world and the worldwide human behavior that destroys so many of the planet's inhabitants?"[48] He suggests that "we're now discovering, at least some of us are, that there is something archetypal and *necessary* about wildness."[49] While this "discovery," as Greg Garrard reminds us in *Ecocriticism*, is not new, its resurgence in the late twentieth century indicates such intense sensation seeking may also be a product of our current "unnatural" environment.[50]

The fascination with extreme risk in American culture may also be a by-product of living in a relatively risk-free modern society: "in opposition to declining risks in everyday life, the prevalence of apparent risk-taking in our leisure pursuits seems to be only increasing."[51] Of course, a sense of risk depends on many factors, influenced by nationality, class, gender, race/ethnicity, physical ability, age, and sexual orientation. As a result, the status of white American masculinity provides another suggestive impetus for the development of extreme cultures in the late twentieth century, especially in the United States. As Kyle Kusz points out, the rise of the mainstream recognition and popularity of extreme sports in America in the 1990s corresponds with what has widely been dubbed a "crisis" in white masculinity.[52] These contexts, explored more fully in the chapters that follow, provide important touchstones for understanding the adrenaline narrative's explosive popularity in the late twentieth century and its links to the contemporary environmental movement and crisis.

CLASSIFYING AMERICAN CULTURES OF THE EXTREME

This book and the term "adrenaline narrative" provide a classification for and analysis of a rapidly growing and wildly popular collection of narratives—primarily nonfiction, autobiographical, or biographical accounts—focused on extreme sports, lifestyle, and travel. The stories emerge into the popular consciousness during a time of environmental activism that, like the adrenaline narratives themselves, ranges from conservative to radical acts. While at first glance defining a genre may have limited interest to readers outside literary studies, in this case, attention to narrative form plays a key role in understanding the age's powerful ecological messages and the ways the accounts deftly exploit form to craft suspenseful, page-turning exploits. Like Erin James, I see adrenaline narratives as key to "help[ing] bridge imaginative gaps," and I also share an attention to "the ways in which literary forms can encode environmental meaning."[53] American adrenaline narratives demand our attention because of what they reveal about the "environmental imagination," or the ways in which they disclose "the pathologies that bedevil society at large and some of the alternative paths that it might consider."[54] What we learn from this literature takes us along expected paths and introduces us to new territory.

Narrative and the humanities more broadly offer crucial insight into the environmental crisis. There must, as Barry Lopez suggests in *Arctic Dreams*, be "provisions" for poets, painters, musicians, novelists, and historians among the biologists, geologists, ornithologists, paleontologists, and ichthyologists.[55] We must understand the stories embedded in our landscapes as well as the science. Recognizing narrative patterns complements our understanding of ecological ones. While "the mountains one gazes at, reads about, dreams of and desires are not the mountains one climbs," our imaginative construction of the environment plays a key role in its material reality and use, for better or worse.[56] This book joins a chorus of environmental humanists who argue the "environmental crisis involves a *crisis of the imagination*."[57] More specifically, this book embraces ecocritic Glen Love's notion of engaged literary scholarship: "the most important function of literature today is to redirect human consciousness to a full consideration of its place in a threatened natural world."[58] Adrenaline narratives play a crucial role in this consciousness raising.

If you are reading this book, you probably—like me—have read and enjoyed, if not participated directly in, the American adrenaline narrative. This book aims to foster a critical frame for thinking about direct and indirect participation in this narrative, especially as it relates to environmentalism. It challenges adventurers to take a critical look at their passion and readers to consider the nature of their reading pleasure. This book focuses "locally"—on texts authored by Americans that consciously or unconsciously engage with American nature and adventure, or what Lawrence Buell labels the tradition of "literary nonfiction from St. John de Crèvecoeur and William Bartram to the present."[59] In the chapters that follow we will examine how the adrenaline narrative contributes to this American tradition and to "imaging nature and humanity's relation to it."[60] America is defined, in part, by the wild adventurous spirit and settings these stories exploit. At the same time, we will consider these stories and their American representations of nature within a global context. Accordingly, while our focus is American, neither the adrenaline narrative genre nor the environmental crisis is limited to the United States. Understanding these global and American stories offers insight into ourselves and the larger culture in which we live.

By no means an exclusively American tradition, the adrenaline narrative's national context nevertheless provides a key framework for understanding the literature and its ecological implications, even as texts, authors, adventurers, and readers inhabit global lives. Adrenaline narratives offer opportunities to analyze the environmental crisis in modes that sometimes share in and sometimes conflict with the arguably uniquely American Thoreauvian tradition Lawrence Buell outlines in *The Environmental Imagination* or what Alvah Simon describes in *North to the Night* as "'authentic adventure'" experiences involving "solitude, deprivation, and danger."[61] In Thoreauvian fashion, Simon agonizes during the early stages of his journey about crafting an experience that constitutes an "'authentic adventure.'"

Simon, for example, wonders about the communication system on his boat: "I had to ask myself, what was it *really* that made me so hesitant to establish contact and communication? Was it that my predecessors and heroes did not have this equipment? Did this gadgetry disqualify this as true adventure?"[62] "In modern times," as Gabriela Nouzeilles argues, "reality and authenticity are thought to be elsewhere, in other eras and other cultures."[63] And, as Simon suggests, with other, slower, and less connected technologies. As a result, "the search for authenticity pushes the alternative traveller deeper and deeper into the wild, into extreme landscapes in which nature's overwhelming power is on full display."[64] Thus, even when American adventurers leave the geographic boundaries of the United States, they bring with them the desire for "authentic adventure." Mapping the United States' national eco-imaginary via the adrenaline narrative offers important—and sometimes overlooked—insights into the disparities found among nations' ecological footprints and environmental practices and ethics.

Andrew K. Jorgenson explains in "Consumption and Environmental Degradation: A Cross-National Analysis of the Ecological Footprint" that a nation's ecological footprint, or per capita consumption, is largely determined by the following factors: its world-system placement and levels of domestic inequality, urbanization, and literacy.[65] *The American Adrenaline Narrative* furthers such scientific research by exploring what a nation's ecological imagination, specifically the United States' eco-imaginary, may also reveal about the ethics and practices that inform individual and community consumption and relationships to the environment. American adrenaline narratives thus provide one measure of our eco-imaginary and its impact on our (un)sustainable behaviors.

MAPPING THE AMERICAN ENVIRONMENTAL IMAGINATION—EXTREME EDITION

These extreme narratives distill how to negotiate environmental risks, a key skill for living in the Anthropocene. As a result, I aim to move beyond a literary specialist's argument to define the genre. Rather, identifying the adrenaline narrative's landmarks initiates the exploration of the genre's ecological dangers and potential and provides important insight into the American environmental imagination's connection to masculinity and adventure. My disciplinary and interdisciplinary methods to map the American eco-imaginary via adrenaline narratives are grounded in the traditional literary practice of close reading analysis and in ecofeminism. Of note, although I call my reading of these texts and by extension myself ecofeminist, I reject as well as accept some characteristics generally thought to be ecofeminist.

My methodology rejects essentialist arguments that women are naturally closer to nature than men. I rely instead on the feminist notion developed by Kimberlé Crenshaw that modes of oppression are not distinct: they intersect. That is, this study grounds itself in, as ecofeminist Chris Cuomo describes it, "the belief that values, notions of reality, and social practices are related, and that forms of oppression and domination, however historically and culturally distinct, are interlocked and enmeshed."[66] Such intersectional consciousness about the adrenaline narrative's structure and themes holds potential for intervening in the environmental crisis: if we understand the stories we tell about the environment, it follows that we will understand better how and why we treat the environment as we do. These key stories shape our reality as much as reality shapes them. Laurence Gonzales emphasizes the important role emotions, especially fear, play in understanding reality and truth: "We think we believe what we know, but we only truly believe what we feel."[67] Adrenaline narratives play an important role in shaping and reflecting the "truth" of our current environmental situation.

The texts selected aim to provide a representative sample of this truth. I survey a range of popular and lesser-known texts by American authors, including bestselling books—such as Jon Krakauer's *Into Thin Air* and Aron Ralston's *Between a Rock and a Hard Place*—and lesser-known and lesser-read texts—such as Patricia C. McCairen's *Canyon Solitude*, Eddy L. Harris's *Mississippi Solo*, and Stacy Allison's *Beyond the Limits*. For the purposes of comparison, book-length nonfiction narratives constitute the primary focus; however, adrenaline narratives may also be found in print and online articles and magazines, feature-length and short films, television shows, amateur videos, social networking site posts, fiction, advertising, and blogs. These stories—whatever their format—comprise a distinct genre because—unlike traditional nature, travel, and sports writing—adrenaline narratives incorporate heightened risk or the element of the "extreme" within a natural setting. The chapter's remaining sections define the genre's unique characteristics and contexts in greater detail.

FOOTPRINT OF THE ADRENALINE NARRATIVE

Currently a term does not exist that adequately describes the unique character of the collection of texts this book seeks to analyze.[68] An excursion to your local bookstore reveals that Jon Krakauer's *Into Thin Air*, arguably the adrenaline narrative's most recognized twentieth-century text, may be shelved under the broad category of "Sports Writing" or more specifically under "Mountaineering Literature." The mass-market paperback book jacket suggests it should be classified as "Nonfiction/Adventure." The drawback of the more general classifications such as "Adventure Nonfiction" or "Travel and Adventure" is that they encompass books about life-threatening expeditions as well as travel essays about "exotic" locations and modes of travel, activities that do not cultivate peril. Anthologies like *Wild Stories: The Best of Men's Journal* and *Women in the Wild: True Stories of Adventure and Connection* fit under the broader category of "Travel Writing" or "Adventure Narrative" or even "Adventure Travel Nonfiction." However, not all of the works included within these anthologies are about experiences that push the limits of human endurance. In literary terms, these broad generic categories fail to sufficiently separate texts with vastly different content. In cultural terms, an unrecognized or poorly defined story risks blindness: the inability to see key organizational patterns that shape our world.

Other, more specific classifications such as "Mountaineering Literature," which arguably dominates the book-length print genre, exist; however, they fail to include other types of extreme sports and activities that follow the adrenaline narrative's content, form, and technique conventions.[69] Patricia C. McCairen's book about solo whitewater rafting, *Canyon Solitude*, is one such example. Other watercraft books by American authors that similarly fit this classification include Todd Balf's *The Last River: The Tragic Race for Shangri-La*, Jennifer Hahn's *Spirited Waters: Soloing South through the Inside Passage*, and Joe Kane's *Running the Amazon*. Adrenaline narratives include adventures in a remote natural setting involving *water* (rafting, kayaking, deep-sea diving, surfing), including ice (polar explorations), and *land/air* (mountaineering, rock climbing, base jumping, wingsuit flying, sky diving, backcountry skiing). They also include expeditions involving *long-distance endurance* (running, biking, hiking, swimming) as well as *outdoor survival* or "alone in the wilderness" stories, such as Elizabeth Gilbert's *The Last American Man*, Mark Sundeen's *The Man Who Quit Money*, and Pete Fromm's *Indian Creek Chronicles*. Fromm's book, for instance, covers the months he spent living alone in a tent in Idaho protecting salmon eggs. Eric Blehm's *The Last Season*, a book about the mysterious disappearance of backcountry ranger Randy Morgenson, and Jon Krakauer's *Into the Wild*, a book about the life and death of Chris McCandless, also fall into the "survival" category. Amy Irvine's *Trespass* narrates her experience living off the grid in Utah. Such broadly defined survival narratives often cite the American frontier and wilderness myths as crucial to the alternative, extreme lifestyle documented. Nonfiction accounts of travel to dangerous, remote, and/or ecologically fragile locations may also fall under the adrenaline narrative classification.

As previously mentioned, post-1970 adrenaline narratives share a literary and cultural history with exploration narratives, heroic epics, travel diaries, and the memoir. Their focus on the natural environment also connects them with nature writing. This blending of several genres is a key characteristic of the narrative. However, the adrenaline narrative's distinctive cultural context and unique combination of specific narrative elements—particularly plot structure, setting, tone, and the theme of risk—are key to distinguishing it from related genres such as nature, travel/

exploration, and religious/spiritual writing. A new term is required that identifies the narrative's unique combination of form, content, technique, and context. Just as the adrenaline narrative genre classifies diverse stories into a comprehensible group, the term provides helpful shorthand for a particular type of encounter with and approach to nature.

The term "adrenaline narrative" provides a classification for this genre-bending and -busting collection of stories, largely autobiographical and biographical in nature, focused on outdoor survival, extreme sport, and adventure. Adrenaline narratives may focus on the author's own adventures or a third party's exploits. I coined the term "adrenaline narrative" after thumbing through a book published by Thunder's Mouth Press.[70] This press publishes a series called Adrenaline Classics.[71] Certainly the term "adrenaline" captures the rush the authors/adventurers describe. While the athletes themselves often resist adjectives that emphasize their sports' risks and claim such terms are crass marketing, the term "adrenaline" usefully characterizes and helps distinguish the literature from other forms of (auto)biography, travel, sports, and nature writing as well as less extreme encounters with and in nature. However, the adrenaline narrative differs from the popular understanding of extreme or adrenaline sports in two key ways, setting and plot.

The adrenaline narratives' context and content are distinct from the content and context of the sports included on the Extreme Sports Channel and in ESPN's X Games as well as from several of the books included in the Thunder's Mouth Adrenaline Classics series, which includes anthologies on the mob and the Kennedys as well as on mountaineering.[72] The narratives selected for analysis correspond to the most fully developed and coherent narrative strand of extreme sport: those stories focused on extreme outdoor sport adventures, survival, and radical, "off the grid" lifestyles. An examination of the adrenaline narrative's plot structure and setting helps further distinguish it from related genres and from popular uses of extreme or adrenaline sports.

AN EXTREME SENSE OF PLACE: SETTING AND PLOT

Two related reasons explain why the adrenaline narrative and the broader popular understanding of extreme sports are not completely compatible. First, one of the fundamental characteristics of the adrenaline narrative is its setting. Adrenaline narratives are set in a stereotypically "natural" environment (typically not urban) and involve some element of exploration, telling the story of the trials and triumphs of those who continue to explore and test the boundaries of wild environments and their physical and psychological endurance. Kevin Krein makes a similar definitional argument in clarifying the difference between "adventure sports" and "extreme sports": "I use 'adventure sports' to refer only to sports that take place in powerful natural environments, and involve the possibility of catastrophic accidents leading to the death of participants. The category of extreme sports, on the other hand, includes all of the alternative sports that are seen in ESPN X-games [sic] type venues."[73] While televised extreme sports also involve life-threatening risks, most are not set in a natural landscape, nor do they have a comparable travel component. Skateboarding, bike stunt (BMX), and motocross competitions, for example, follow a closed, designed course. In this sense, they resemble mainstream sports like soccer, football, baseball, and basketball. In other words, "most sport activity takes place in environments that are standardized, controlled, and generally contain right angles."[74] Similarly, while stories about the mob—like those included in Thunder's Mouth Press's Adrenaline Classics series—may have heart-pumping action and danger sequences that rival stories about Everest, they do not narrate an athletic experience or take place in the appropriate setting.

Secondly, whereas the exploration and expedition aspects of the activities considered within the contemporary adrenaline narrative can be related to the established travel and nature writing traditions, other extreme sports do not correspond with this same range of literary traditions. For example, the few books by or about X Games sports and athletes fall under (auto)biography. Even as extreme sport participants and commentators begin to craft a broader narrative tradition in film, video, social media, and books, many of these activities still lack the crucial journey element, a fundamental means of organizing the adrenaline narrative's plot. While X Games and similar athletes travel, moreover, the key component here is travel beyond changing venues for competitions—where travel is part of the risky adventure itself.

However, in time the boundaries between the "unnatural" extreme sports and the more "natural" extreme activities like mountaineering may erode. Certainly, the dichotomy I describe already faces serious challenges. The Primal Quest adventure race, for example, is a multiday expedition-style race (Edition 8 involved five to six days "supported" or up to ten days "unsupported") that involves a large wilderness course where participants run, hike, bike, paddle, climb, and navigate.[75] Everest's established routes and long queues, moreover, perhaps hold more in common with extreme sport's established courses or being guided through an especially extreme run at a ski resort. As a result, the adrenaline narrative pushes the boundaries of this definition.

Currently, autobiographies and biographies of extreme sport personalities, such as skateboarder Tony Hawk (e.g., Tony Hawk with Sean Mortimer, *Hawk: Occupation: Skateboarder*), and histories of the sport dominate the print field (e.g., Jocko Weyland, *The Answer is Never: A Skateboarder's History of the World*). *Between the Boardslides and Burnout: My Notes from the Road* by Tony Hawk presents an interesting exception to this rule, hinting that textual and literary innovations emerging from this field of extreme sports may be found in nontraditional literary forms, such as zines, YouTube videos, social networking sites, and webpages. Designed like a scrapbook, Hawk's book presents an innovative twist on the travel journal—including picture collages, funky text, and lists. The book is a figurative and literal snapshot into Hawk's life on the skateboard circuit. Hawk's book presents an adrenaline lifestyle as much as an adrenaline narrative.

Indeed, as the above examples indicate, the very definition of what constitutes "nature" is eroding—or at least being challenged: "nature is not natural and can never be naturalized, even when human beings are far from the scene. *Nature is unnatural*, if the word 'natural' is meant to describe the status of extant slabs of inert matter."[76] Such challenges to our understanding of nature as separate from culture, as Timothy Morton points out in *Ecology without Nature*, are fundamental to intervening in the ecological crisis. This "dark ecology" asks us to reject "putting something called Nature on a pedestal and admiring it from afar" because this understanding of nature "does for the environment what patriarchy does for the figure of Woman. It is a paradoxical act of sadistic admiration."[77] However, most adrenaline narratives construct nature as a distinct "wilderness" destination, which is also often a markedly gendered product of patriarchal and colonial fantasy.

Because adventurers tend to mark the space where adventure occurs (in nature/wilderness) and those other "everyday" environments (work/home), most narratives do not deconstruct the basic definition of wilderness as outlined in the Wilderness Act of 1964: "A wilderness, in contrast with those areas where man and his own works dominate the landscape, is hereby recognized as an area where the earth and its community of life are untrammeled by man, where man himself is a visitor who does not remain."[78] When the adventurer makes his or her home in the wilderness, the distinction is maintained via the life that others live in "civilization." As a result, most often—at least with adrenaline narratives—a true "dark ecology" approach to nature and wilderness depends more on the reader-critic than on the writer-adventurer; however, I will discuss in chapter 4 examples of what Timothy Morton calls "the mesh" and what Stacy Alaimo identifies as trans-corporeality.

Adrenaline narratives most often assume, in other words, clear distinctions between the vast space and distance from civilization wilderness denotes and the unruly pockets that characterize "wild" places. Scholars helpfully distinguish "wilderness" (location) from "wild" or "wildness" (quality/process). For some, such as William Cronon, wilderness is largely a construct, but for others, as defined by the Wilderness Act, wilderness (also) designates a specific location away from "civilization." As Michael Cohen explains, wilderness confirms "Roderick Nash's distinction, that wilderness is a noun, but acts like an adjective."[79] Cohen goes on to outline the five ways the term "wilderness" functions: (1) as a "noun or adjective," or "what it is"; (2) as an "image, or icon: symbol," or "how it means"; (3) as an "ideology," or "where it fits in a system of values"; (4) as a "representation," or "how its literary or political rhetoric mediates"; and finally (5) as "the Law," or "the Wilderness Act as social convention and tool."[80] Wild, on the other hand, may be seen as the process or quality of nature that wilderness, humanity, or culture more broadly exhibits or shuns. Cheryl Strayed, for example, explains in *Wild* that her father's "failure to love me the way he should have had always been the wildest thing of all" in her life.[81] However, her time on the Pacific Coast Trail teaches her that she does not "have to be amazed by him anymore."[82] A new, more positive sense of wildness replaces her father's abandonment as the "wildest thing."

As the adrenaline narrative's primary setting, wilderness functions in all of these ways—as defined location, symbol, ideology, representation, and law. We also see a range of "wild" processes and qualities, from taking wild or extreme risks to (re)connecting with wild nature, both internally and externally defined. Additionally, some adrenaline narratives are addressing two key problems Greta Gaard identifies with this definition of wilderness. First, the Wilderness Act's definition "seems both androcentric and ethnocentric: it does not describe the ways that women's movements through wilderness affect its definition; nor does it describe the activities and locations of indigenous cultures and their efforts to shape their environments." Additionally, "it is now widely known that no area of the Earth is unaffected by white Western industrialized culture."[83] I discuss in greater detail in chapter 4 that while erotic desire does not always collapse nature/culture boundaries, it does redefine our relationship to wilderness. Nevertheless, contemporary wilderness as represented in the adrenaline narrative largely remains a distinct location and a state of mind fostered by engagement with nonhuman or "wild" nature.

This emphasis on a distinctly wild place and process means adrenaline narratives' content, structure, and technique hold the most in common with travel and nature writing. The travelogue, according to the *Oxford Dictionary of Literary Terms*, is defined as "an account of one's travels: a book, article, or film recording places visited and people encountered."[84] Like travel literature, the adrenaline narrative's plot follows the adventurer's journey away from a specific location, on to a goal, and then perhaps back home again. Whether in essay, film, or book-length format, most adrenaline narratives follow a formula that describes, albeit not always in strict chronological order, the events leading up to the adventure, the narration of the adventure itself that builds to a near-death and sometimes tragic crisis, and then a denouement that discusses the aftermath. Susan Birrell makes a similar observation in her analysis of Everest narratives: "Everest tales, like sport narratives, follow a familiar trajectory from anticipation (the preparation and trek to base camp), to challenge (establishing base camp and all the intermediary camps along the way), to climax (the final push to the summit), to denouement (back to base camp and home again)."[85] As will be discussed in chapter 3, "Spiritual Natures," the genre's journey structure connects it to pilgrimage and ritual.

While Jennifer H. Laing and Geoffrey I. Crouch do not focus exclusively on contemporary American adventure narratives, their essay "Myth, Adventure and Fantasy at the Frontier: Metaphors and Imagery behind an Extraordinary Travel Experience" helps to outline the adrenaline narrative's elements, especially its setting and plot. Laing and Crouch outline seven characteristics key to frontier travel narratives. First, adventure travelers "paint the object of their travels in language reminiscent of a lover," including the virgin and siren metaphors that emphasize nature's allure. Second, Laing and Crouch point out that "frontier journeys may also be described as 'fateful' or the result of kismet or destiny." Links with "mythical constructs" and "retracing historic expeditions or following in the footsteps of famous travellers or explorers" form the third and fourth elements.[86] The fifth characteristic, where travel is described as a dream, bears important connections with the sixth category, which presents nature as a fantasy or fairy world.[87] Finally, "frontier travel may involve an element of the theatrical."[88] The theatrical emphasizes "performance and 'play,'" even as the adventurer "seek[s] a more authentic or 'real' experience."[89] This "performative" feature emphasizes connections between nonfiction adventure's narrative structures and classical drama: "high-risk activities... [are] motivated, to a degree, by a 'dramatic world-view' in Western society, which has its roots in classical Greek theatre and involves conflict and tension-building finally released or solved through 'denouement,' which leads to a purification or release known as 'catharsis.'"[90] A consideration of the gendered, racial, and classed implications of the narrative structures Laing and Crouch describe as they play out in adrenaline narratives quickly reveals their investment in heroic masculinity.

Laing and Crouch stress that the *"performance of adventure"* requires "following in the footsteps of explorers of old and performing a role based on heroic or mythic journeys of the past, as well as aspects of fairytale and fantasy."[91] The documentary film *High and Hallowed: Everest 1963*, for instance, follows several mountaineers' attempts to repeat the 1963 American Mount Everest Expedition.[92] *180° South: Conquerors of the Useless* likewise retraces Yvon Chouinard and Doug Tompkins's road trip from Ventura, California, to Patagonia, Chile.[93] The documentary *Into the Cold* commemorates the centennial of Admiral Robert Peary and Matthew Henson's expedition to the North Pole. Director Sebastian Copeland and his partner in the trek Keith Heger commemorate the centennial because global warming means retracing the journey on foot to the North Pole will not be possible for the bicentennial.[94] Contemporary adventure, in this sense, is often less about exploring new territory than about retracing explorations. This drive to repeat or even best prior adventurers by following a more difficult route or accomplishing a feat in less time places the adventurer in the footsteps of previous—most likely white and male—explorers. Ann Bancroft, for example, explains, "I was a tiny speck on the ice, but at the same time I was conscious of being tied to all the explorers who had come before me, of becoming part of the history of the landscape, joined with the continent in my struggle to cross it."[95] Adventure links the individual to this elite community of mostly white forefathers. Individual struggle and risk gain significance when placed in the context of this elite history.

Jarid Manos in *Ghetto Plainsman* identifies the theme of historical exclusion, noting the dominance of white voices in the American frontier literature he finds in New York City's libraries and bookstores:

> I often went down to the library, or the Strand or at Pageant Books and Prints on 9th. Upstairs at Pageant they had all kinds of old books for sale, tattered copies of paperbacks, musty old hardcovers, some that were first editions, all telling me in hundreds of thousands of words what the Anglo race had experienced and done out West, from First Contact to Conquest and Settlement. I tried hard to find other voices about the West,

American Indian, Spanish, Black, Chinese, Arab, whatever, but found next to nothing, even though all had played some part or other in the whole story.[96]

Manos suggests that it is not that "American Indian, Spanish, Black, Chinese, Arab, whatever" have nothing to say, but that their voices are purposely excluded in the written accounts. The 2015 documentary film *Sherpa* explores a similar gap by examining the 1953 portrayals of Sherpa Tenzing Norgay against the aftermath of an avalanche in 2014 that killed sixteen Sherpas, just a year after a high-altitude brawl between Sherpas and climbers made headlines.[97] The film seeks to raise awareness about the Sherpas' place within Western mountaineering by outlining the Sherpas' distinct contributions to and achievements in the sport.

The "losers" of this history, in other words, do not (often) have a voice.[98] They are more often than not excluded from the adventure archive. In a similar vein, Tashi Sherpa remarks, in an interview published in *Outside* magazine, "even in documentary films like *Into Thin Air* and *Everest*, you don't get to see Sherpas. We have been left out. But we are the ones who, despite the risks and hazards, make sure that all is well on Everest."[99] Thus, even as marginalized voices emerge in the press and literature, they remain largely silenced actors. Their adventure narrative follows a different structure and, as a result, resists easy incorporation into the dominant narrative.

As I have begun to outline here, what makes this literary genre distinctive has cultural implications, particularly in regard to American society's relationship to nature, sustainability, and risk. The adrenaline narrative's five descriptions of the natural environment are a case in point. When we examine the adrenaline narrative as a genre, distinctive environmental messages via these five representations emerge. Jeffrey McCarthy argues, in "Why Climbing Matters," "environmental thinkers can learn from mountain climbers."[100] I extend McCarthy's argument to suggest environmental thinkers can learn much from the full spectrum of these adrenaline lifestyle sports and their narrative forms because—as McCarthy argues specifically in regard to climbing literature—they model the "primary modes for experiencing nature in our culture."[101] Additionally, their engagement with risk specifically offers insight into living with and responding to global climate change. The adrenaline narrative's five representations of nature are part of the genre's defining characteristics and play a key role in the adrenaline narrative's construction of the American environmental imagination.

REPRESENTING EXTREME ENVIRONMENTS: FIVE DESIRING NATURES

American adrenaline narratives exhibit four primary attitudes or desires toward nature: *conquering, spiritual, erotic,* and *risky*.[102] Increasingly, furthermore, narratives exhibit an emerging fifth desire, *restorative*. Where conventional, conquering notions of desire seek to control nature, spiritual constructions of desire rely on transcendental religious discourse to express connections with nature and its transformative potential and effects. An erotic desire founds itself in mutual relationships with nature. Composed of an ecofeminist mix of deep and dark ecology, the erotic views all of nature as interdependent and having inherent worth. Risk pervades conquering, spiritual, and erotic representations of nature, emphasizing a primal fear or awe of the wild. Risk connects adventure and the environment and is a characteristic found in all adrenaline narratives. Finally, restorative desire builds from characteristics found in both restoration ecology and restorative justice. This redemptive attitude focuses on long-term sustainability.

These five attitudes, or artful and persuasive rhetorics, are more than isolated, metaphoric, or personified representations of nature: they form coherent semiotic systems that play crucial roles in shaping and understanding the American environmental imagination and, consequently, our (un)sustainable behaviors. As Jedediah Purdy argues in *After Nature: A Politics for the Anthropocene*, "far from being frivolous make-believe, imagination is intensely practical." That is, "imagination also enables us to do things together politically: a new way of seeing the world can be a way of valuing it—a map of things worth saving, or of a future worth creating."[103] Thus, while individual adrenaline narratives are rooted in the specific politics of their place and sport, the five desires form significant thematic repetitions across the genre's specialized locations and activities. These repetitions both reflect and shape our environmental imagination.

Of note, the five desires are not unique to nor do they originate with contemporary American adrenaline narratives. However, their repeated use within adrenaline narratives and in the context of the contemporary environmental movement helps define the genre and the American environmental imagination. While chapters 2, 3, 4, and 5 isolate each of the four primary desires for sustained discussion and chapter 6 highlights the fifth, emerging desire, the desires often appear together in the texts studied, more interconnected than absolutely distinct. Teasing out their distinctive qualities and noting where one desire takes precedence over another helps us gauge the adrenaline narrative's complex place within and shaping of the American environmental imagination.

ADRENALINE SCALE: EXTREME STYLE AND TONE

In addition to distinctive natural settings, a recognizable journey plot structure, and the five desires, adrenaline narratives have identifiable literary styles and tones. I outline risk's aesthetics and politics in chapter 5. Here I focus on the narrative's adrenaline scale or degree of risk, which defines and distinguishes adrenaline narratives from other adventure stories. Adrenaline narratives range from fairly straightforward nonfiction accounts of the adventurers' exploits to consciously literary, nail-biting thrillers. The most "literary" adrenaline narratives often refer to and quote from other adventure tales as well as employ vivid, descriptive language. Stacy Allison, who was the first American woman to summit Everest, for example, relates an interesting story without the narrative flourishes present in Patricia C. McCairen's and Jon Krakauer's books. Briefly comparing these three authors' styles and books explains these subtle and not so subtle differences.

While McCairen's narrative about her feat as the first woman to raft the Colorado River solo employs chapter epigraphs and literary embellishments, her story lacks the marketing and timeliness that often produce a bestseller. Furthermore, McCairen's publisher, Seal Press, publishes for a niche market, whereas Krakauer's publisher, Anchor Books, is a large publishing house with mass market resources and appeal. Jon Krakauer, a consummate craftsman and arguably the most recognized professional American adrenaline writer, reaps the full benefits of his powerful writing style, his major publishing house, and his book's timeliness amid media attention to the 1996 deaths on Everest. He also likely benefits from the rich literary history associated with mountaineering: as author and *Outside* magazine contributing editor Bruce Barcott puts it, "mountain climbing remains the most literary of all sports."[104] Thus a range of writers and content producers can be found within the genre, from experienced professional writers to first-time authors who may work with ghostwriters or cowriters. To establish their shared ethos with their audience and knowledge of the subject, authors often employ technical language related to their sport and frequent references to their own extreme adventure experience—even if the particular essay or book is not focused on their personal exploits.

Adrenaline narratives are also characterized by their life-threatening, ambition-bursting adventures. Mark Twight's collection of essays *Kiss or Kill* both describes and encourages this sense of conscious peril, which is key to distinguishing adrenaline narratives from other nonfiction adventure and travel writing. He in fact argues that "the risks young alpine climbers take today are justifiable in order to make the artistic statements of the age."[105] The perilous setting or sense of place forms a key trope in adrenaline narratives. Birrell similarly emphasizes that the Everest narrative's "cast of dedicated, adventurous, and capable climbers" crafts "the dominant and preferred narrative of bravery and perseverance in the face of hardship and challenge, and each asserts the importance of the struggle."[106] The adrenaline narrative's perilous and frequently suspenseful and heroic tone distinguishes it from other travel and nature writing.

Unlike, for example, twentieth-century nature writing such as Annie Dillard's *Pilgrim at Tinker Creek* or travel writing such as Bill Bryson's *Lost Continent: Travels in Small-Town America*, adrenaline narratives sustain heightened risk or an element of the "extreme" within this setting. Crudely stated, adrenaline sports and the narratives written about them require at least a few dead adventurers killed by a combination of their own ambition and extreme conditions. As Heidi Howkins writes, "admitting that we are riskmongers or adrenaline junkies is not fashionable, especially after the recent hullabaloo about the 1996 Everest tragedy. Still, there is something essential about the possibility of real loss, even death, and without the presence of danger many climbers would quit."[107] Crouch agrees, clarifying that "there is little honor in certain success, but there is much to be gained from a probable failure," and that "mountains aren't worth dying for, but they are worth risking dying for."[108] The knowledge that adventurers could and sometimes do die as a result of their risky behavior is a fundamental part of the narrative's thrill and suspense.

Just as mountains and rivers can be rated for their degree of difficulty, so too can adrenaline narratives be rated for their degree of adrenaline. Krakauer's *Into Thin Air*, Ralston's *Between a Rock and a Hard Place*, and Balf's *The Last River* rate high on the adrenaline scale, a reflection of the authors' writing styles, the activities and situations they describe, and their representation of the natural environment. In contrast, Pete Fromm's *Indian Creek Chronicles*, Jennifer Hahn's *Spirited Waters*, and Miranda Weiss's *Tide, Feather, Snow* rate lower on the adrenaline scale. Self-consciously invoking Krakauer's title, Jim Malusa's *Into Thick Air* explicitly bills itself as "anti-expedition," in direct contrast to "thin air" stories.[109] Malusa's narrative playfully compares the risks involved with biking to the "bellybutton" (lowest point) of six continents and the risks of climbing Everest or tackling the

Seven Summits (climbing the tallest mountains on all seven continents).[110] Malusa explains, "nobody, so far as I knew, had ever reached all the world's depressions—or at least they weren't talking about it. The idea of climbing the Seven Summits, highest on each continent, inspired a race to the top of the world. The Six Sumps were forsaken, the opposite of success, and it was easy to understand why. Take your choice: climber or lowlife."[111] Malusa "reverses the traditional valuations of ascent and descent" "by making descent the central object of visual and narrative interest."[112] While Malusa elects the "lowlife" lifestyle, he still "suffer[s] voluntarily" and in ways "as absurd as peeing into a water bottle at 20,000 feet because you'll freeze if you leave your tent."[113] As I will discuss in the following chapters, these muted adrenaline narratives by authors such as Malusa, Hahn, and Weiss often work more against than with conquering desire, emphasizing spiritual and/or erotic desires.

Miranda Weiss's narrative, for example, chronicles her move to Alaska. Her book beautifully details Alaska's extreme landscape and the challenges it poses. For example, Weiss stresses, "it was clear from the beginning: If you didn't know the place well, know it intimately, you would starve or have to go somewhere else."[114] Weiss spends much of the book describing her acclimation to Alaska's unique climate and culture; however, she resides in relative comfort and security in rental houses. Still, as Richard Nelson points out, in Alaska warnings such as "no one should ever leave home without preparing to be stranded" must be taken seriously.[115] Weiss's survival story is very different from the one Jon Krakauer describes in *Into the Wild*, which investigates the events that led to Chris McCandless's death in the Alaskan wilderness. Nevertheless, even for Weiss, Alaska, and winter, in particular, "invited disaster." Weiss notes, "there was nearly one death a week from snowmachine accidents alone."[116] Alaskan writer and wilderness rower Jill Fredston similarly notes Alaska's "uncompromising" environment, which has resulted in "a lot of death. I need more than the fingers on both hands to count the number of good friends close to my age who have died in mountaineering, avalanche, fishing, and airplane accidents."[117] Weiss describes her life as "survival and leisure commingled," which is an apt description for all adrenaline narratives.[118]

Cindy Ross's account of her family's hiking adventures in *Scraping Heaven: A Family's Journey along the Continental Divide* offers another relatively muted adrenaline tale. Her "adventurous life" may seem more or less imprudent given that her outdoor adventures involve her small children.[119] Yet despite their varying degree of adrenaline, the muted and full-throttle adrenaline narratives share common insights about risk. For example, after a particularly rough and dangerous day on the trail, Ross's son "Bryce asked if we were going to die." Ross concurs with a family friend, Bob, who is also on this section of the hike, that "'This is really living.' Yes, sir. We know we're alive on a day like this. No doubt in our minds."[120] This sense of feeling most alive during moments of physical risk is shared among the more extreme and more subdued adrenaline adventurers and tales. Ruth Anne Kocour similarly describes climbing in high alpine environments as something that "energizes and makes me feel more alive than at any other time in my life."[121] Varying levels of risk ultimately produce similar conclusions among adventurers—whether they are climbing Everest, rafting extreme rapids, sailing around the world, seeking adventure in Alaska, walking the Continental Divide, living off the grid in Utah, or biking to the lowest points on earth. The following chapters survey the genre's high- and low-octane narratives to provide the fullest picture of the genre's range, depth, and ecological imaginations.

Adrenaline narratives of all persuasions often boost their intensity by focusing on fatal exploits as well as death-defying first or exemplary achievements, such as Lynn Hill's first free climb of the "nose" of El Capitan in Yosemite National Park or Weiss's more subtle reminders about how "even small things could spell death in winter."[122] These bold adventures, as the book jacket to a paperback edition of Jon Krakauer's *Into Thin Air* attests, both "thrill and terrify" readers. Perhaps the simplest way to identify an adrenaline narrative is that it tells of a spine-tingling outdoor adventure the "normal" American will never undertake.

German sociologist George Simmel's description of the adventurer is helpful in characterizing the adrenaline narrative's adventurers and narratives about their exploits. Vivanco summarizes Simmel's definition as follows: "The adventurer is defined by his or her engagement with the exotic and the unknown, and so the search for adventure can entail a deliberate and self-conscious attempt to reveal and revel in the Other—peoples, landscapes, states of mind, spiritualities, animals, and so on. Danger and risk are also typically at the center of adventure's distinction and significance, as are notions of deviance and liminality."[123] Simmel's definition and its focus on "exotic," "unknown" social and physical environments, "deviance," and "liminality" stress adventure's colonial and countercultural roots. Adventure's connection with conquest and danger is juxtaposed, in our contemporary context, with the erasure of "the line between risky, aberrant behaviors and normality."[124] We live in an age where weekend warriors can purchase a place on an Everest expedition and extreme and survival situations are airing on television and the Internet at any given moment. Individuals can experience their own personal, everyday extreme by drinking a soda or energy drink or wearing adventure clothing.

We live, in other words, in what Michaelis Lianos and Mary Douglas refer to as a "dangerized" world that "encourage[s] us to redefine and dread the Other."[125] Adventure, or "a self-conscious experiential engagement with danger and risk," as Vivanco puts it, as a result "represents an acceptable and increasingly significant, even ubiquitous, interpretive framework for social interaction."[126] Extreme adventure also reflects an increasingly "dangerized" view of nature—whether expressed in a fascination for extreme weather or, as in Slavoj Žižek's words, "Mother Nature is not good—it's a crazy bitch."[127] Armchair adventurers feed off the stories that describe such extreme adventures, natures, and their attendant powerful desires. As a result, risk not only characterizes the adrenaline narrative's setting and tone, it also appears as an aesthetic and reoccurring theme, as I discuss in more detail in chapter 5. Trends in who performs and writes about these feats also play a key role in characterizing the genre and its dominant desires toward environmental politics.

ADVENTURE'S IDENTITY POLITICS:
AUTHORSHIP AND PROTAGONISTS

Another important feature of the genre is that the vast majority of American adrenaline writers and adventurers are white males. The environmental diversity initiative Green 2.0 quantifies similar racial and gender inequities among American environmental organizations, reporting in 2014 that "despite increasing racial diversity in the United States, the racial composition in environmental organizations and agencies has not broken the 12% to 16% 'green ceiling' that has been in place for decades."[128] As a result, the American environmental imagination is skewed to present white masculinity as the normative position. To put the racial implications in a more specific context, only recently, in May 2006, was Sophia Danenberg the first African American to summit Everest. To date, no African American male has summited Everest; however, Philip Henderson attempted to summit during the 2012 season and an all-African American expedition team is also organizing a Seven Summits bid, which includes Everest.[129] A documentary film of the all-African American expedition to Denali, *An American Ascent*, was released in 2016.[130] Notably, only one book-length published account exists by an African American (adventurer and writer James Edward Mills) that documents a summit attempt of a major peak (Denali).

In contrast, at least three disabled climbers—all white—have written accounts of their climbs of Everest.[131] While these "Supercrip" exceptions exist, they prove the general rule: the largely first-person extreme adventure archive is ableist as well as skewed toward white males. As Elizabeth A. Wheeler points out, "there is a pitfall, however, in relying on first-person memoirs to elaborate environmental consciousness. Thinking through one's own able body can reproduce normate assumptions about other people's bodies."[132] The same holds true for other adventure sports and for long-form wilderness survival narratives; only a very small number are penned by or about minority adventurers and all of those are male. While this study relies on (auto)biography to uncover "environmental consciousness," it does so in order to define "normate assumptions" and amplify a range of voices that may or may not meet conventional expectations.

James Edward Mills labels the larger phenomenon reflected in the absences and silences the "adventure gap," or the "racial divide between those who participate in outdoor activities and those who don't."[133] Mills's *The Adventure Gap* explores this disparity while documenting the first African American summit attempt of Denali and profiling the team members and other significant African American extreme athletes. His media organization, the Joy Trip Project, likewise promotes and monitors sustainability and diversity.

Mat Johnson's satirical, fantastical novel *Pym* (2011) exploits racial stereotypes in its portrayal of an all-black expedition to Antarctica and the protagonist's search for "Tsalal, the great undiscovered African Diasporan homeland."[134] The characters include "Afrocentrics who loved... adventure. It was an eccentricity that they... were very proud of. Theirs was a type of pride peculiar to our ethnic group. It said, 'Look, I'm black and I'm taking pleasure in something I'm not expected to.'"[135] Where nonfiction (largely) lacks this narrative perspective, Johnson's fictional *Pym* fills the gap. The Funny or Die video, *Black Hiker with Blair Underwood*, also exploits this stereotype by depicting the reactions of several white hikers, black media, and park rangers when they encounter a black hiker on the trail.[136] The genre's whiteness, as I will explore in the next chapter, is not an accident but rather an imperial and patriarchal legacy.[137]

Gender provides another key lens into the adrenaline narrative and the picture of the American environmental imagination it portrays. Men dominate extreme sports and related activities—a fact also reflected in the genre. Tellingly, the *New York Times* and other major media outlets did not cover Sophia Danenberg's summit.[138] No book-length and few article-length accounts of her accomplishments exist. Despite the popularity of adrenaline narratives, her story has, for the most part, not been told. In the Adrenaline

Classics anthology *High: Stories of Survival from Everest and K2*, furthermore, a woman wrote only one of the sixteen essays included. Significantly, the author Maria Coffey, a professional sea-kayaking and trekking guide, is the partner of Joe Tasker, who disappeared on Everest's northeast ridge in 1982. While there are increasingly more adrenaline narratives authored by and about white women adventurers, we are still anticipating the first book-length narrative penned by or focused on a contemporary (published post-1970) American woman who is also a racial or ethnic minority. The Appalachian through-hiker Rahawa Haile signed with Harper to publish a memoir recounting her 2016 experience.[139] This disparity speaks volumes on how American culture shapes and understands adventure's "appropriate" subjects and objects.

The genre's heteronormative characteristics are key to point out as well. I did not find an American adrenaline narrative about or by an openly gay male adventurer; however, you can follow Cason Crane on social media. Crane is "the first openly LGBT and fifth youngest person to climb Mt. Everest and the Seven Summits."[140] Both Ann Bancroft and Lucy Jane Bledsoe talk about their partners in their writing. Bledsoe has been a Lambda Literary Award finalist. Blaire Braverman includes discussion of her transgender partner. Eli Clare's memoir *Exile and Pride: Disability, Queerness, and Liberation* "crips and queers conventional mountain climbing narratives."[141] As I discuss in chapter 2, heterosexual female adventurers sometimes express anxiety about not finding love because of the ways their sport defies conventional gender expectations. Like the absence of minority men, such participation gaps raise questions about social and economic access and whether adventure, as implied in Simmel's description, is always already patriarchal and imperial.

The high proportion of heteronormative white men who write within this genre in part explains why conquering representations dominate the genre: in conquering, they perform and embody a dominant form of masculinity. Women, gay men, and racial and ethnic minorities face special challenges when entering sports founded on the exploration of "unknown" regions and the conquering of mountains for national or individual prestige. Lynn Hill, a pioneering female rock climber, notes the sport in the 1970s "was directed by a fraternity of men."[142] Along similar lines, mountaineer Heidi Howkins explains in her prologue, "I was the only female climber on each team, in most cases the only woman on the mountain. Sometimes more, sometimes less of a woman; as a woman in a world of male climbers, you have to either lose or use your femininity to stabilize the gender tensions."[143] Howkins's description is key to understanding adrenaline sports' gender dynamics. Women, especially those that pioneered involvement in traditionally male sports, either had to emphasize their femininity or become one of the boys. This behavior suggests gender performance is an important means of keeping peace among adventurers. Pioneering female athletes like Hill and Howkins frequently note in their biographies the distinct challenges they faced as women.

While sexist and racist attitudes regarding women's and minorities' physical and mental capacities have changed, the legacies of their traditional roles continue to haunt these sports and the genre. For example, while he notes exceptions, extreme kayaker Tao Berman accounts for the lack of women in his sport and other extreme sports as a result of biological disposition. Berman claims, "as is true with other extreme sports, there aren't a lot of girls. I chalk this up to the fact that girls tend to have a stronger 'self-preservation gene' and prefer not to spend as much of their lives injured."[144] Sexist and racist stereotypes persist. Dominant forms of masculinity that reward men for taking risks, furthermore, depend on such cultural stereotypes as tools to recruit men to enter a range of dangerous professions, from working in a coal mine to joining the military or becoming a firefighter. The U.S. Navy, for example, began using "Navy. It's Not Just a Job. It's an Adventure" in 1976.[145] While Berman suggests risk-taking is genetic, the adrenaline narrative points to the range of cultural narratives that promote risky masculinities.

Social and economic class also plays a role in understanding the adrenaline narrative's authors and protagonists. Today's career, elite adrenaline adventurers support themselves through sponsorships, writing, films, photography, and other media and event appearances. Weekend warriors and "dirt bags" (the extreme adventurer's version of a "starving artist") fuel their extreme leisure pursuits largely through other sources of income. Risky professions, such as the military, connect risk and adventure as a means to recruit. Thus, the modern era repackages individual adventure and risk while maintaining its connection to national identity. Such historical and narrative legacies in part account for the genre's masculinist, Anglocentric, heteronormative tropes and the unique challenges encountered by individuals who wish to participate in a sport and genre so long defined by conquering, white masculinity. A fuller discussion of the adrenaline narrative's patriarchal and imperial roots follows in the next chapter, "Conquering Natures."

The adrenaline narrative's popularity, because of or despite these patriarchal and imperial legacies, speaks to American fascination with cultures of the extreme more broadly, and to how dominant presentations of the

American environmental imagination are defined by a powerful elite white masculinity. The pull of extreme outdoor adventure—whether for the adventurer him/herself or for the armchair adventurer consuming the text—presents a curiously conservative picture of the American environmental imagination in the current ecological crisis. The adrenaline narrative's "alternative" lifestyle often appears as a repackaging of mainstream patriarchal white masculinity. What draws audiences to these narratives now?

EXTREME AUDIENCES, AMERICAN DREAMS: READERS

At the other end of the adrenaline madness equation is the audience enthralled with these risk takers and the environments they describe. What accounts for America's fascination with these stories? What attracts readers and viewers to the highs and lows of extreme adventure? As discussed previously, the narratives provide a connection to wildness, if not wilderness, for an audience largely disconnected from nature. The narratives also promote a familiar American masculinity that, as Elizabeth Gilbert explains, keeps the American dream alive. Gilbert declaims, "because, at some deep emotional level,... somehow it's still true, that we Americans are, against all other available evidence, a nation where people grow free and wild and strong and brave and willful, instead of lazy and fat and boring and unmotivated."[146] In this sense, Americans—in particular—are culturally disposed to find adrenaline narratives appealing. Adrenaline narratives tap into foundational American myths.

Crucial to the appeal are the ways the adrenaline narrative simultaneously invokes America's grand frontier narrative and a foolish elitism. John Trombold's article "High and Low in the Himalayas: Jon Krakauer's *Into Thin Air*" suggests the narrative's critique of "the hubris of social class" in part accounts for the popularity of Krakauer's and other narratives about adventurous deaths.[147] This reading also helps explain why nonelite participants remain largely absent from adrenaline narrative texts: readers, according to this logic, would not be able to mine these same tensions and enjoy the resulting self-satisfaction should nonelite Sherpas, for example, play a larger narrative role. Trombold argues, "*Into Thin Air* is a treatise exposing the social tensions inherent in a culture with unequal access to leisure and prestige and... in which the purported transcendence of commercial relations is a mark of extreme privilege."[148] Trombold suggests *Into Thin Air*'s "audience seems prepared to believe that the moral failings precipitated by social elitism and consumer culture caused the deaths on Everest."[149] Tragic catharsis results in a feeling of superiority. This moral reading, furthermore, distinguishes "pure" climbers from commercial ones. Pure climbers or adventurers—those free of commercialism and an overreliance on technology—are deemed tragic heroes whereas those steeped in commercialism are vilified or seen as unworthy.

Morality tales help us account for the popularity of tragic adrenaline narratives, but what accounts for the popularity of those stories that narrate successful feats? John Dufresne argues that nostalgia plays a role in our contemporary love of travel writing. According to Dufresne, "our current affection for travel essays is part nostalgic longing for the mystery and excitement of the pre-jumbo jet days of an unravaged earth. The world withers and whimpers and we wave goodbye, as it were."[150] Adrenaline narratives contribute to a narrative that one must travel to the ends of the earth because such pristine or extreme wilderness spaces no longer exist at or near home. In reality, unsullied wilderness no longer exists even at the top of the world. Lacking a true wilderness, as Dufresne notes earlier in the essay, the armchair adventurer returns to an earlier age of travel literature. At the time Dufresne's essay was published (1991), publishers "scrambled to find and to reissue the great travel journals of the 19th century."[151] A similar escape to an idealized virgin wilderness can also be found in many contemporary adrenaline narratives that exploit descriptions of unspoiled, wild settings.

The adrenaline narratives' popularity also suggests that American culture lacks necessary rituals and a sensory connection to nature. As Jeffrey McCarthy writes, "the fundamental environmental issue for our society is our estrangement from the natural world."[152] This lack drives adventurers like Allison and McCairen to seek solace in extreme feats and environments. Armchair adventurers empathize and vicariously participate in their cathartic journeys and some readers are even inspired to join them on the trail. Krakauer highlights in *Into the Wild* risk's deep ritual significance, especially for young men. Krakauer explains, "it is hardly unusual for a young man to be drawn to a pursuit considered reckless by his elders; engaging in risky behavior is a rite of passage in our culture no less than in most others."[153] Americans, therefore, seek in adrenaline narratives what we used to find in cultural rituals. Paul Shepard's notion of a "madness" produced by the abandonment of "the ceremonies of adolescent initiation that affirm the metaphoric, mysterious, and poetic quality of nature" likewise suggests our modern technological and secular age cannot fulfill our "natural" desires, and so we turn to the extreme.[154]

Shepard explains in his psychohistory that the gradual alienation from the natural world produces Western society's adolescent regression, a kind of "madness" that gives rise to our paradoxical relationship with nature.

> The alternatives open to a society intervening in ontogeny in this way simply play out the opposition that remains unresolved by extrapolating from either the perverse, infantile, erotic pleasure of self-attention or the prudish, horrified distaste for any natural gratifications: thus Protestant culture in North America produces the world's most devoted protectors of wildlife, its greatest leaders in conservation, its most romantic wilderness literature, the first national parks, and the angriest opponents of the soiling of air and water... and it produces an ecological holocaust, the raping of a whole continent of forests and rich soils by uncomprehending destroyers, wrapped in patriotism, humanism, progress, and other slogans in which they profoundly believe.[155]

Shepard describes a paradoxical adrenaline madness: individual pleasures resulting from risky behavior are tied to remote and frequently endangered landscapes.

His words echo Jane Jacobs, who similarly points out America's "schizophrenic attitude" toward the environment.[156] Diane Ackerman in *Deep Play* also places the "madness" for extreme adventures in a late twentieth-century perspective. In the chapter "The Gospel According to This Moment," Ackerman addresses the baby boomer's search for spirituality, arguing that the lack created by many baby boomers' rejection of organized religion is being filled by "deep play of one sort or another." God may be dead, in other words, but Ackerman asserts, "the need for transcendence, communion, ritual, and revelation" lives on.[157] In this light, adrenaline narratives attempt to reconcile lack. The risk society Ulrich Beck describes "is characterized essentially by a *lack*: the impossibility of an *external* attribution of hazards."[158] These are climate change's human-produced wicked problems that paradoxically refuse easy acceptance as scientific fact.

This overview of the genre and its audience appeal reveals America's "schizophrenic" relationship, to echo Jacobs, with the natural world. Adrenaline narratives articulate our desire both to conquer and to protect the natural environment. Krakauer's decision to open *Into Thin Air* with the following quotation by José Ortega y Gasset further attests to the intimate connections between extreme adventures' appeal and Shepard's notion of madness: "Men play at tragedy because they do not believe in the reality of the tragedy which is actually being staged in the civilized world." Adrenaline readers "play" with the tragedies or near tragedies around which the texts build their plots, subsequently forgetting or displacing the real tragedy: our environment's extreme destruction. As I type, in fact, a notification appears on my screen about how the amphibian "apocalypse" is even worse than previously thought.[159]

Adrenaline narratives provide interesting terrain for exploration because they map five telling American attitudes toward nature. These texts provide further evidence of America's inconsistent, paradoxical relationship with nature. Certainly, the sustained and overwhelming popularity of adventure books like *Into Thin Air* attests more to our continued "madness" than a clear sign that we are traveling on the road to recovery. As ecofeminists have been arguing since the early 1970s, conquering reifies the domination of not only nature but also women and other marginalized groups. Spiritual desire, conversely, holds both positive and negative potential. If nature serves only as a vessel for transcendence, it limits our ability to reduce our alienation from the land. Where a spiritual encounter with nature may result in fruitful growth for the individual, the benefits reaped for the larger community and for the natural environment as a whole are not as prominent, if evident at all. Thus, the erotic recognition that "the lightning we witness crack and charge a night sky in the desert is the same electricity we feel in ourselves whenever we dare to touch flesh, rock, body, and earth" potentially serves to benefit the natural world by forging mutual, organic connections with nature.[160] Risk, in turn, amplifies the stakes for both the adventurer and the environment. And restorative desire seeks "sustainable play," offering restorative environmentalism and sustainable social justice. The following chapters, outlined briefly below, explore these desiring natures and their implications for the American environmental imagination in greater depth.

THE TERRITORY AHEAD: CHAPTER OVERVIEWS

To unpack further the significance of the adrenaline narrative's representations of nature, the following chapters turn to key passages found in a range of adrenaline narratives by a variety of authors. Krakauer's popular writing opens each of the chapters that follow, offering a touchstone and reminder about the ways these desires are connected. As the following chapters will argue, erotic desire, the formation most often championed by ecofeminists, illustrates the greatest potential for an ecologically grounded environmental imagination. How participants manage risk, additionally, offers representative individual methods for and consequences of dealing with extreme risks, such as those associated with global climate change. The fifth desire, restorative desire, builds on these principles by emphasizing environmentalism in the Anthropocene, which requires attention to environmental and social justice. However, we will begin with the dominant and traditionally defining representations within American adrenaline narratives: conquering and spiritual.

Chapter 2, "Conquering Natures," examines various representations of conquering desire, where nature is presented as an object of domination and control. (Post)colonialism and its implications for American exploration, adventure, and travel in the late twentieth and early twenty-first centuries provide the chapter's historical and cultural context. A range of primary texts are discussed in this chapter, including Jon Krakauer's adventure books, Andrew Pham's *Catfish and Mandala: A Two-Wheeled Voyage through the Landscape and Memory of Vietnam*, Gregory Crouch's *Enduring Patagonia*, Ruth Anne Kocour's *Facing the Extreme: One Woman's Tale of True Courage, Death-Defying Survival and Her Quest for the Summit*, and William Least Heat-Moon's *River-Horse: The Logbook of a Boat across America*.

"Spiritual Natures," chapter 3, juxtaposes various authors' spiritual representations of nature, where nature is represented as a vehicle for personal and sometimes environmental transformation. Bron Taylor's *Dark Green Religion: Nature Spirituality and the Planetary Future* provides the theoretical framework for understanding sacred representations of nature within the context of a largely bankrupt ecology. Key primary texts discussed in this chapter include Jill Fredston's *Rowing to Latitude: Journeys along the Arctic's Edge*, Aron Ralston's *Between a Rock and a Hard Place*, Steven Callahan's *Adrift: Seventy-Six Days Lost at Sea*, and Alvah Simon's *North to the Night: A Spiritual Odyssey in the Arctic*.

The fourth chapter, "Erotic Natures," examines narratives consciously engaged in writing a different type of adventure narrative, one not based on objectifying nature. Building on ecofeminist and postcolonialist debates about the representation of nature as other, the chapter focuses on erotic presentations of nature, where nature is presented in mutual and reciprocal rather than hierarchical and objectifying relationships. Important primary texts analyzed in this chapter include Eddy Harris's *Mississippi Solo: A River Quest*, Sherry Simpson's *The Accidental Explorer: Wayfinding in Alaska*, Suzanne Roberts's *Almost Somewhere: Twenty-Eight Days on the John Muir Trail*, Jill Fredston's *Rowing to Latitude: Journeys along the Arctic's Edge*, Patricia McCairen's *Canyon Solitude: A Woman's Solo River Journey through the Grand Canyon*, and Jennifer Hahn's *Spirited Waters: Soloing South through the Inside Passage*.

Chapter 5 highlights the fourth primary desire found in adrenaline narratives and the contemporary environmental movement: extreme risk. "Risky Natures" explores these connected stories and their collective risky desires. This chapter places the development of both extreme adventure and the radical environmental movement within the context of what Ulrich Beck describes as "risk society." To explore the roles risk plays in the American environmental imagination, the chapter defines the risk aesthetic that carries across all adrenaline narratives—conquering, spiritual, erotic, as well as the emerging restorative desire. The chapter discusses a range of narrative examples from American literature and popular culture, including Rahawa Haile's "How Black Books Lit My Way along the Appalachian Trail," Elizabeth Gilbert's *The Last American Man*, Gail D. Storey's *I Promise Not to Suffer: A Fool for Love Hikes the Pacific Crest Trail*, Nick Jans's *The Grizzly Maze: Timothy Treadwell's Fatal Obsession with Alaskan Bears*, Blair Braverman's *Welcome to the Goddamn Ice Cube: Chasing Fear and Finding Home in the Great White North*, and Tao Berman's *Going Vertical: The Life of an Extreme Kayaker*. The chapter highlights what we can learn about climate change from risky nature's environmental messages and methods.

Finally, chapter 5 underscores the adrenaline narrative's place within contemporary American literary and cultural history, outlining how the Anthropocene, or "the era of geological time during which human activity is considered to be the dominant influence on the environment, climate, and ecology of the earth," impacts the adrenaline narrative.[161] The adrenaline narrative's narration of the Anthropocene may incorporate (radical) environmental activism as well as greenwashing. Wilderness's role in the Anthropocene suggests both change and resistance to change. The possibilities define the emerging fifth desire, restorative.

At stake is whether wilderness—nature's wildest forms—can or even should be "conserved." Jedediah Purdy suggests in *After Nature: A Politics for the Anthropocene* that wilderness cannot hold a central place in the contemporary environmental imagination if we hope to intervene successfully in the environmental crises that define the Anthropocene. Purdy argues, "the abstention from use that wilderness represents deserves a place in Anthropocene environmental imagination, but it cannot be at the center. An Anthropocene attitude must also take account of the work that people do, the landscapes they create by living, and the things that they destroy."[162]

The use extreme adventure makes of wilderness bridges this divide, but it remains an open question whether the adrenaline narrative can "re-wild" our everyday lives in ways that build a more ecologically sustainable future. Chapter 5 considers the extent to which the "end of nature" demands the end of extreme adventure and the adrenaline narrative.

CHAPTER 2
CONQUERING
NATURES

Into Thin Air's narrative proper begins in chapter 1 with Jon Krakauer "straddling the top of the world, one foot in China and the other in Nepal."[1] This iconic image of the heroic adventurer presents a stereotypical sexual and conquering stance. Standing with the world between his legs feminizes nature and accentuates Krakauer's individual, albeit transitory, dominance over a beguiling and tempestuous Everest. Literally and figuratively on "the top of the world," Krakauer tellingly maps his position as half in Nepal and half in China—not Tibet. However, the narrative quickly undercuts this conventional colonial and patriarchal image of the triumphant heroic adventurer when Krakauer reveals he "just couldn't summon the energy to care."[2] Krakauer's peak-performance problem—his inability to muster a sublime, transformative moment for himself and his readers—begins to suggest the ways conquering remains fundamentally central to and an increasingly problematic part of the post-1970s adrenaline narrative.

Spiritual desire also plays a significant role in *Into Thin Air*. In fact, *Into Thin Air*'s introduction begins with Krakauer's soul-searching.[3] As is characteristic of adrenaline narratives, the desires toward nature often overlap: the opening presents both conquering and spiritual desires. For the moment, however, I will focus on the ways in which conquering desire emerges in Krakauer's writing to provide a template of this attitude. There are several ways to read Krakauer's summit letdown and why he begins his narrative proper here: at a moment that is both the climax and anticlimactic.

Krakauer may be expressing the heroic angst or melancholy that accompanies the achievement of a hard-won goal: this inherent lack provides the impetus for the next adventure. Or, Krakauer may be pointing to conquering's intrinsic problems for the contemporary adrenaline narrative: any domination of nature is transitory, unsustainable, and fraught with echoes of, if not direct, colonialism. Peter L. Bayers explains "Krakauer's guilt" as a result of "his recognition of heroic masculinity's imperialist underpinnings," and, thereby, that Krakauer "represents a new version of masculinity that through guilt tries to absolve imperial masculinity of its sins."[4] If this is the case, whether or not guilt fosters a sustainable adventurous masculinity remains to be seen. Perhaps, given the tragic nature of that season on Everest, a victorious summit image feels disrespectful. Krakauer avoids this by emphasizing his weakness rather than strength, assuming an antiheroic psychological state that contrasts with his conquering, heroic straddle.

Men and women's ability to purchase slots for summit attempts, furthermore, tarnishes the heroic masculinity Krakauer is not quite able to perform. Bayers also understands "Krakauer's anxieties" as "result[ing] in part from his insecurity and guilt about his decentered postmodern 'heroic' masculinity, for he is 'feminized' as a dependent to his guides and the Sherpas."[5] The large, supported expedition, in other words, does not allow Krakauer to claim unqualified individual success. Of course, Krakauer simply may be exhausted and experiencing the mental and physical side effects of high altitude. He describes his diminished physical and mental state as akin to that of "a slow child."[6] By beginning his narrative from this shaky summit, Krakauer points to the other readings as well.[7]

This chapter examines the ways authors invoke and sometimes problematize heroic masculinity and its related conquering desire toward nature, where nature is presented as an object for domination and control. I explore conquering desire's continued potency and intermittent impotence to embody the adventurer's understanding and experience of nature. Patriarchy's gendered hierarchies as well as (post)colonialism and its implications for American exploration, adventure, and travel in the late twentieth and early twenty-first centuries provide the chapter's historical and cultural contexts. Ecofeminist and postcolonial critiques of nature, gender, and race reveal how conquering desire's representations of nature work in tandem with a mythic and historically specific heroic masculinity associated with post-1970 adrenaline sports and adventures. Contemporary American adrenaline narratives demonstrate how conquering desire works by masculinizing adventure and feminizing nature. Narratives that deconstruct conquering desire challenge us to consider the extent to which gender, especially heroic masculinity, has and can be (re)conceived in non-patriarchal ways. The following sections outline the three primary areas conquering desire seeks to control: nature itself, the adventurers' bodies, and adventure's goals. First, though, I explain the concept of heroic masculinity, which permeates all of these areas as well as defines the adrenaline narrative's conquering structure.

HEROIC MASCULINITY:
EXTREME ADVENTURE'S CONQUERORS

Into Thin Air's opening illustrates how desires in contemporary American adrenaline narratives follow worn paths created by invasive (or hegemonic) masculinity while occasionally revealing queer routes that trouble heroic masculinity's tenacious footings. What is meant when scholars and journalists critique or applaud this form of masculinity? How do they define it? Hegemonic masculinity (a term I will use interchangeably with heroic and patriarchal masculinity) reveals the "gender politics within masculinity."[8] As Belinda Wheaton points out, the "concept of 'hegemonic masculinity' helps to determine how particular groups of men, and dominant versions of masculinity, occupy and sustain their positions of power over other forms of masculinities as well as over women."[9] Masculinity is not one "thing." Rather, hegemonic masculinity pushes all masculinities into one form rewarded over other forms. In terms of the "prevailing cultural messages through sport," hegemonic masculinity "celebrate[s] the idealised form of masculinity at the same time as inferiorising the 'other'; women and forms of masculinity that do not conform."[10] In addition to skill-based measures, in other words, hegemonic masculinity uses exclusionary practices such as homophobia and misogyny to separate elite athletes from the others.

This particular form of elite, patriarchal heroic masculinity thrives in sport and adventure cultures. R. W. Connell notes the extreme sport athlete often offers "an exemplary version of hegemonic masculinity."[11] For example, as Nick Ford and David Brown point out in regard to contemporary big-wave surfing, "heroic masculinity" separates "the hegemonic masculine male surfer and the 'Other' (i.e. the females and all the other men)."[12] Even when not overtly racist, sexist, or homophobic, the values associated with the elite athlete's physical or merit-based qualities tend to reward only one specific narrative of masculinity, which translates into one model of success. These "recurring constructions of masculinity...suture tropes of adventure closely with white masculine unfettered mobility, colonialist desire, elite athleticism, and male fraternity."[13] Thus, hegemonic masculinity assumes access to freedom, power, strength, and brotherhood. White heroic masculinity provides the de facto adventurous subject position.

As Krakauer illustrates, this does not mean that heroic masculinity is easily embodied. Being white and male is not sufficient. Rather, hegemonic masculinity reveals assumptions and stereotypes that individuals must negotiate: certain situations and environments heighten the stakes. A clear distinction, for example, between heroes and others is increasingly important for this conquering desire in the contemporary period, as wealth, opportunity, and technology open extreme sports to a broader range of audiences and adventurers. As mentioned in the previous chapter, extreme sports and adventure tellingly undergo increased popularity and mainstream exposure following important gains by the civil rights and feminist movements. Kyle Kusz, as a result, argues extreme sports' rise in popularity stems in part from white anxiety about changing gendered and racial roles: the "masculinized and patriotic representation of extreme sports can be read as a symptom and imagined solution to this post-1960s perceived crisis of white masculinity."[14] Extreme sports provide an outlet to express conventional heroic masculinity. Because, Kusz persuasively argues, extreme sports become firmly associated with "a fraternity of American masculine icons and the American mythology of the frontier," they offer an outlet for the reassertion of conquering desire.[15] Anxiety about changing gender and race hierarchies, moreover, fosters a narrow version of heroic masculinity.

Conquering desire fuses American identity with heroic masculinity and manifest destiny. The resulting "narrative constructs an unmistakable whitened, male-centered national genealogy which begins with our country's founding fathers and extends to the extreme sport practitioner."[16] Maria Coffey likewise notes, in *Where the Mountain Casts its Shadow*, "the stories of mountaineers are new versions of old myths."[17] Thus, what makes these adventures and their protagonists American is a combination of the adventurers' nationality and adherence to a specifically frontier heroic masculinity. Such heroic American men (still) conquer, and rugged masculinity can be unapologetically expressed. Or at least they *should* have this freedom.

Contemporary advocates of heroic masculinity emphasize its vilification by "complaint feminists." In truth, they argue, "we all must prove we are strong before people assume we are. This goes for everything in life, not just climbing. Show your strengths, have grit, and earn respect."[18] Heroic masculinity provides the solution as well as the (alleged) problem: whatever your gender or race, demonstrate your heroic strength and endurance to achieve success. Groundbreaking (white) women athletes have often followed this model in order to achieve success. For example, Dianne Chisholm argues "[climber Lynn] Hill's lived female body is ever situated within a territory and history of masculine domination and the key that she offers for transcending/ascending the crux of each situation is to rely on the 'natural intelligence of the body' to move through it."[19] Significantly, Chisholm does not gender the "natural bodily intelligence" she ascribes to Hill. While Hill's female body cannot escape novelty in a male-dominated space, her physical ability and elite climbing performance quiets critiques that she does not belong simply because she is female. Chisholm argues that Hill serves as an example of how "the situation has changed since 1977, when [Iris Marion] Young first presented her paper" ["Throwing Like a Girl"]: "Hill's free climbing presents a contemporary and kinetic counterexample to Young's dated and static 'throwing example.'"[20] Physical ability quiets critics as well as suggestions that the model for success is rigged.

Heroic masculinity (sometimes called grit) aligns with the Protestant work ethic and sense that those who work hard will be rewarded. This American bootstrap mentality points to "actions by individual people" that "do not reflect systematic oppression" or exclusion. Heroic masculinity in "our politically correct culture" must contend with cries of sexism or racism when people are simply being "rude," resulting in mistrust and miscommunication.[21] As a result, heroic masculinity is especially difficult to critique or alter in an American context, as it provides the model by which both adventurous and American success are determined.

History reinforces this model. As mentioned in the previous chapter, contemporary adventurers follow—often literally by repeating the same route—previous adventures. This repetition often reinforces iconic white male trailblazers while ignoring or silencing others. Laing and Crouch conclude that the "narrative or myth of adventure is then used by the traveller to enact and interpret their experiences at the frontier. Once home, the triumph of the returning hero is celebrated in print and in person, through public presentations and documentaries."[22] Thus, to participate in, repeat, or even rework these narrative structures requires engagement with a public, patriarchal form of white masculinity, one that historically views nature as a feminine virgin or siren and depends on leaving home to pursue adventure. As such, any narrative that does not reproduce these forms would be hard-pressed to identify as adventure.

Rather than neutral terrain, the adrenaline narrative's tropes and structure map elite white masculinity. This combination of elite white male privilege and extreme wilderness adventure defines the adrenaline narrative's hegemonic masculinity and subsequently equally dominating conquering desire. The public celebration described by Laing and Crouch, moreover, is increasingly connected to sponsorship dollars for the contemporary elite adventurer. An examination of class in post-1970 adrenaline narratives reveals similar struggles between hegemonic masculinity's pull and new forms and narratives.

HEROIC MASCULINITY:
CLASS AND AUTHENTIC ADVENTURE

The adventurers' class status plays a vital role in conquering desire and defining heroic masculinity because the adventurers' social class connects to individual accomplishments and exploits. Even a relatively inexpensive hiking trip may highlight class privilege. Suzanne Roberts, for example, admits, "here I was, in the developed world, creating problems for myself because my life, in reality, was too easy." She later elaborates, "there were people in the world, after all, with real problems." Roberts later realizes that "what we had been doing was closer to 'real' than what we usually did."[23] This realization results from her disconnection from consumer culture while on the trail. Her remarks indicate self-consciousness, if not outright guilt, about the privileges associated with consumer culture as well as the leisure time required to embark on a long hike.[24] Placing these hardcore author-adventurers within economic class categories, however, becomes a difficult task because, like starving artists, the writers-adventurers often assume debt and/or pursue less financially profitable employment in order to train for and go on adventures. They sacrifice wealth for their "art."

Regardless of the amount of financial capital individual American adventurers possess, they certainly are among a culturally elite group because of the specialized skills they enjoy and the leisure time required to develop those skills. They create, as Susan Kollin describes, "a different kind of class expansion." Building on Michael Nerlich's "ideology of adventure," Kollin posits that "the desire to survive extreme natures explains how new forms of adventure currently enable a different kind of class expansion." Adventurers who employ Indigenous guides especially highlight class and racial dynamics that follow longstanding imperial codes, highlighting how this "class expansion" follows familiar, albeit "neo-imperialist" paths.[25] For example, consider the pay disparity between white guides and Sherpas. Krakauer notes in 1996 that white guides earn anywhere from $10,000 to $15,000 per expedition, whereas Sherpas are paid only $1,400 to $2,500.[26]

Wealthy novice adventurers and corporate sponsors, moreover, can increasingly buy their way to the top of summits and through dangerous river gorges, a class issue Krakauer addresses in *Into Thin Air*. Krakauer's derogatory description of the millionaire socialite Sandy Hill Pittman, who was also climbing Everest in 1996, is one such example.[27] Additionally, as seen in Krakauer's summit letdown, contemporary adventure's economic realities impact heroic masculinity, especially its emphasis on pursuing "authentic adventure." Corporate sponsorship provides the large capital necessary to finance technologically sophisticated expeditions. Small and especially large trips put big money from corporate sponsors or clients on the line—Krakauer reports clients paid Rob Hall $65,000 in 1996 for a shot at climbing Everest.[28] By the publication of Graham Bowley's *No Way Down: Life and Death on K2* in 2010, writers and climbers were characterizing Everest as "overrun by a circus of commercial expeditions, by people who paid to be hoisted up the slopes."[29] This problem soon plagues K2 as well: "But there was the beginning of the trend on K2 that had afflicted Everest decades ago. Unqualified climbers paying big money to come to a mountain they had no business attempting. With just a click on the Internet you got a place on a trip."[30] Key here is that a "true" climber/adventurer earns his or her way to the summit by means other than paying a fee. Authentic adventurers do not buy a slot on an expedition; yet the financial realities of contemporary adrenaline adventure mean that few expeditions—even small ones—are possible on shoestring budgets.

Costly gear and leisure time aside, the realities of any climbing or extreme adventure endeavor that comes with a $10,000 permit price preclude any notion of "pure adventure" outside commercial considerations.[31] Todd Balf suggests in *The Last River*, a book about a fatal river expedition on the Yarlung Tsangpo, that "corporate expeditioning" has forever changed modern expeditions, and not necessarily for the better.[32] As a result, some elite athletes reject the increased reliance on technology, corporate sponsorship, and large expedition-style adventures. Lynn Hill explains this philosophy of "authentic" adventure: "This was 'alpine-style' climbing at its boldest. This way of climbing mountains had become the more respected style of mountaineering in the 1970s, largely due to the example of Reinhold Messner, a brilliant climber who espoused climbing mountains 'by fair means.' Messner pooh-poohed the grand old style of big expeditions. Confronting the mountains in this lightweight manner was more adventuresome and more spiritually connected to the mountain, yet more risky and less certain of success. It was a style befitting only elite climbers."[33] Hill marks out the rightful, more "adventuresome" (conquering) and spiritual claims held by those that follow "pure" or noncommercial and less technology-dependent methods. Krakauer similarly notes in *Into Thin Air*, "nobody was admired more than so-called free soloists: visionaries who ascended alone, without rope or hardware."[34] Both Hill and Krakauer suggest that "pure" climbers are more heroic as well as spiritually closer to the environment, members of an elite untainted by consumerism and technology.

One of the best contemporary examples of such an athlete is American free solo climber Alex Honnold, who also arguably represents an alternative heroic masculine form for the ways he combines extreme risk, pure form, and humble-bragging, as opposed to hand-wringing guilt. However, as Erin Monahan points out, Honnold's "Peter Pan" version is more of the same: "When you fit the Disney standard trope of the hero, cis white male, you can do no wrong. Being exalted as an 'overgrown boy,' permits Alex Honnold innocence."[35] Sender Film's *Alone on the Wall* exploits Honnold's "dorky, awkward, goofy" demeanor and bare-bones, "dirtbag" van lifestyle against his graceful, breathtaking big-wall free solo climbing, which is an elite form of rock climbing without ropes.[36] One error or slip without rope protection means death. To emphasize the purity of Honnold's style and the extreme risk, parts of the film contain images of Honnold climbing with his breathing and the wind rustling as the only audio. Fellow climbers attest to Honnold's "sick" climbs, but the documentary emphasizes his unassuming, minimalist approach to solo climbing by filming the testimonies separately from Honnold's climbing, as if to suggest that no one is watching (or sponsoring) his climbs.[37]

In *Alone on the Wall*, Honnold and other climbers narrate over scenes of him climbing, but the voice-overs and images suggest Honnold is "alone on the wall." There are a couple of exceptions to this format, one of which takes place about twenty minutes into the twenty-four-minute film. A sequence featuring silent climb shots (again, the only audio is the wind and Honnold's breathing) is interrupted with Honnold reflecting on and then shown having a "moment of panic" and a brief exchange with the cinematographer. The cinematographer tells Honnold to "just come back, if you're not feeling it."[38] Honnold breaks out of his "little prison" and continues with the climb. Another key moment appears earlier, as Honnold nears the end of free soloing Moonlight Buttress.[39] This moment of celebration contrasts with the moment of panic and then return to control on Half Dome. Both scenes on Moonlight Buttress and Half Dome break the fourth wall with the cinematographer.

The 2018 film featuring Honnold, *Free Solo*, likewise emphasizes his pure form, isolation, and dorky vulnerability while also highlighting the intense marketing work required to support his career and Honnold's nonprofit environmental work. We see all of these aspects within the film's first twenty minutes. Later in the film the cinematographers and fellow climbers discuss the additional pressure their presence potentially puts on Honnold and their fear about participating in a free solo filming project.[40] Honnold seems to be largely immune to such pressure—his brain, in fact, may not be wired for fear or has been trained to require greater stimuli to register anxiety.[41] Whether a result of his training or his biology or some combination of both, Honnold's extreme tolerance for risk and lack of technical equipment place him among the purest of the purists.

If Honnold's free solo climbing is "high art," the Discovery Channel show *Naked and Afraid* is the pop culture counterpart. The show likewise exploits ideas of authentic or pure adventure, but for entertainment purposes rather than the individual pursuit of an elite art. The show places "two complete strangers—sans clothes—in some of the most extreme environments on Earth": "Each male-female duo is left with no food, no water, no clothes, and only one survival item each as they attempt to survive on their own."[42] Their nakedness emphasizes their extreme exposure and lack of technological assistance, despite cameras capturing their every move. Like Krakauer's narrative, *Naked and Afraid* highlights the myth of a "noble autonomy from market forces."[43] The fit yet vulnerable bodies combined with the possibility of sexual tension between the participants arrests our attention and results in commercial success.

Athletes who wish to be associated with "pure" adventure and heroic masculinity must continually separate themselves from other, nonelite adventurers. Referring to a poster of two climbers commemorating an "'important new route,'" Gregory Crouch, for example, prefers "the quiet respect of my peers."[44] Crouch also notes, "but no place on earth sells what I took away from Patagonia. No money buys the friendship and respect of an Alex Hall, a Charlie Fowler, a Stefan Hiermaier, or a Jim Donini. I had not been found wanting, and I had seen the heart of the sunrise. I left Patagonia a rich man."[45] Crouch's nonmaterial wealth pays dividends in the private respect he has earned from his male peers and from his pure connection with nature: "I had seen the heart of the sunrise." The fact that Crouch is "not...found wanting" also emphasizes the heroic nature of such authentic adventure. Heroic masculinity demands that the adventurer not take the easy route.[46] It continues the American "self-reliance" tradition and Protestant work ethic.

Claims of authenticity and difficulty are further complicated when one considers how gender influences extreme adventure's economics and access to heroic masculinity. Jennifer Jordan, for example, critiques Jon Krakauer's portrayal of Sandy Hill Pittman in *Into Thin Air*: "In my reading of Jon Krakauer's brilliantly told story, I sensed a certain bias, an agenda, concerning the women on the mountain that year, particularly Sandy Hill Pittman, whose wealth and personality he spent a lot of ink chastising, as if being arrogant and rich somehow made her less of a climber."[47] Jordan highlights how certain kinds of strengths (wealth, confidence) are attractive in a man but a liability for a woman.

Moreover, whether deemed pure or commercial extreme athletes, there are great inequities in the financial support for men's and women's adrenaline activities. Climber Lynn Hill, for example, notes the inequity between prize money for men's first prize ($15,000) and women's first prize ($5,000) in the 1980 Survival of the Fittest competition.[48] Hill also notes that after she objected to the prize disparity, the organizers promised to raise the prize money for women the next year: "True to their word, the producers raised first prize for the women to ten thousand dollars."[49] While Hill experienced fairly swift changes as a result of her objections, pay disparity remains an issue in women's professional sports. As I write, players from the U.S. Women's National Team have a pending gender discrimination lawsuit against the U.S. Soccer Federation related to pay disparity. Change, if it happens at all, more often comes at a much slower pace than Hill describes about her experience in 1980. The World Surf League, for instance, announced in September 2018 that it will begin awarding the same prize money to men and women starting in 2019.

Sponsorship money is an especially key issue for extreme athletes and their ability to hone their craft. Most female adventurers note in their narratives that it remains more difficult for women to raise funds for expeditions and secure sponsors: Ann Bancroft, for example, took on $450,000 of personal debt for her American Women's Expedition (AWE): "Part of what I came to understand after that first trip is the extent to which economics is a barrier for women to live out our potential, doing what we were meant to do in our work."[50] What the wage gap attempts to quantify on the quotidian scale, the funding gap for expeditions illustrates on the extreme scale. Both address the material effects of institutional sexism.

These inequalities have nothing to do with the purity of the adventurers' approach to their sports. Bancroft goes on to clarify that people with sexist "attitudes controlled the money, it affected our ability even to have a chance at making the journey. I finally understood that the economic barrier was far greater than any of the other biases we had encountered."[51] Bancroft, as a result of the personal debt she incurred, set a goal "to come up with a better model for expedition funding" and to "break the way for women who would come after."[52] She needed to raise $1.5 million for the expedition.[53] As Anne Atwood, who helped fundraise, puts it, this was a chance to shift "the way women are viewed by the world."[54] The funding and prize disparities reflect women's place within the elite adventure hierarchy and their assumed lack of commercial public appeal. Access barriers such as less funding help assure these obstacles and narrative patterns are not broken.

HEROIC MASCULINITY: RACE AND AUTHENTIC ADVENTURE

Others are not accorded the same recognition. Increasing tension between the largely white Western expedition leaders and Sherpas can be seen in the widely publicized 27 April 2013 brawl on Everest between several Sherpas and climbers Simone Moro and Ueli Steck as well as in the 2014 shutdown of Everest after an avalanche killed thirteen Sherpas. Numerous media outlets covered the closing of the 2014 Everest climbing season. The *New York Times*, for example, reported that "this was the year that frustration boiled over. The avalanche that killed at least 13 Sherpas last Friday has prompted an extraordinary labor dispute, as Mount Everest's quiet workhorses took steps on Tuesday to shut down the mountain for the season, demanding that the government share proceeds from what has become a multimillion-dollar business."[55] Perhaps "silenced" rather than "quiet" workhorses would be more accurate. Additionally, in this "labor dispute," the term "workhorses" emphasizes the Sherpas' status as cogs within the machine—rather than skilled, experienced guides or elite athletes.

The few elite African American adventurers—such as the Pioneer Climbing Expedition members, who hope to be the first African American team to climb the Seven Summits, and Captain William Pinkney, who was the first black American and fourth American to sail solo around the world—contend with this dominance. *Los Angeles Times* writer Joe Mozingo suggests that Elliott Boston hopes "to lead minorities into the wildlands the way Tiger Woods has guided them onto the fairways."[56] While an African American woman (Sophia Danenberg) has summited Everest, she has not been positioned to be a minority ambassador for the wild. Tom Hornbein writes in his foreword to Maria Coffey's *Where the Mountain Casts its Shadow: The Dark Side of Extreme Adventure*, "note that as we begin the twenty-first century, most mountaineers are male, most partners female."[57]

Hornbein's claim is further supported and explained by marketing research looking at the roles of gender and race in outdoor recreation advertising. Derek Christopher Martin's "Apartheid in the Great Outdoors: American Advertising and the Reproduction of a Racialized Outdoor Leisure Identity" is a case in point. Martin examined advertising in *Time*, *Ebony*, and *Outside* (time span 1985-2000) to demonstrate the presence of "a stereotyped leisure identity that is associated with wildland leisure activities that results in fewer Black Americans participating in outdoor recreation."[58] As I discuss in more detail shortly, fears of racial violence appear to hinder African American participation in the outdoors.

HEROIC MASCULINITY:
GENDER AND AUTHENTIC ADVENTURE

While Martin focuses on race, his analysis correlates to gender as well. In terms of gender, research suggests that there is a gap between women's increased overall participation in sports since Title IX and participation in outdoor adventure, specifically, during the same period. McNiel, Harris, and Fondren point out in their 2012 article, "Women and the Wild: Gender Socialization in Wilderness Recreation Advertising," that despite women's increased participation in organized sports and in organizations such as the Girl Scouts that encourage outdoor recreation, women continue to be "underrepresented in wilderness recreation."[59] Women's relative lack of representation in advertising in magazines such as *Backpacker* and *Outside* may contribute to their lower participation rates.[60] They go on to explain, "this contradiction suggests that wilderness recreation activities are not viewed in the same way as other forms of leisure and that activities situated in the 'wild' may have particular meanings for women that dissuade them from participating. Such findings reinforce the notion that gender socialization regarding wilderness recreation is also shaped by structural constraints, such as cultural beliefs about women's 'places' that can lead to overt or subtle gender bias that constrains some women's participation in these activities."[61] While statistics on domestic violence and sexual assault recognize a woman's greatest risk for violence is in the home, a woman's fear for her safety outside the home often amplifies perceived risk, especially among nonadventurers. Sarah Grothjan writes against this stereotype in her essay, "Backpacking is My Respite from Sexual Harassment," emphasizing "I shouldn't feel safer summitting an icy peak than I do in my own home."[62] As an October 2015 *Backpacker* article, "Why Women Shouldn't Worry about Hiking Alone," emphasizes, "public lands are overwhelmingly safer places than the rest of the country—for men *and* women."[63] Patriarchal norms that stress reverence for and protection of the (feminized) landscape condemn a violent, perverse masculinity that would symbolically or physically rape nature/women.

New research out of the climbing community, however, suggests the outdoors may be no safer than anywhere else: sexual harassment and sexual assault (SHSA) "is a problem in the climbing community, just as it is in the rest of society: nearly half of all women, 1 in 6 men reported having experienced some form of behavior classified as SHSA" while climbing.[64] Additionally, as the exposé related to sexual harassment in the national parks, "Out Here, No One Can Hear You Scream," suggests, wilderness environments may also breed a culture of normalized sexual violence.[65]

Extreme adventure's hypermasculine landscape might make female adventurers feel especially vulnerable. In *Born to Run*, for example, Christopher McDougall describes a situation where an American woman was surrounded by a "band of thugs who—being womanless in the wilderness—were drunk and dangerously lusty. One of the thugs grabbed the American woman."[66] Adrenaline narratives do not uniformly emphasize this fear or potential danger: while women often address the "boys' club" mentality that pervades extreme landscapes and sports, they also often emphasize that a culture of trust pervades extreme adventure. Jennifer Pharr Davis, for example, explains, "maybe it's related to the lack of women on the trail, but throughout all my home stays along the trail, I felt myself connecting very intensely with the women I encountered. They were individually and collectively redefining what I thought a woman could or should be."[67] Davis also confesses, "I was frightened to be the only one in the shelter. I no longer feared solo-camping in my tent, but in a shelter I never knew who might show up and join me. I wasn't specifically worried about other hikers, but I think most women have a fear of waking up next to a strange man and not knowing how he got there."[68] This generalized fear demonstrates how women cannot escape rape culture. I discuss in greater detail in chapter 5 how rape culture polices women by suggesting that they should not adventure (alone).

DIVERSIFYING HEROIC MASCULINITY: ADDRESSING THE ADVENTURE GAP

Without a doubt, as we have begun to see, race, gender, and class, and more specifically their implied cultural values, significantly shape the genre. Thus, while some ripples indicate change within the sport and genre, an elite, heroic male whiteness continues to dominate the scene. Anaheed Saatchi argues in a 2019 Melanin Base Camp blog post entitled "Stop Making Movies about White Guys Doing Cool Shit," "it's time to make room for other narratives, for success to take on different shapes and hues." She challenges extreme sports and climbing in particular to "redefine what groundbreaking actually looks like."[69] In essence, Saatchi is not asking for this particular form of masculinity to disappear, but for it to cease being the only (or hegemonic) heroic form.

The few adrenaline narratives by racial/ethnic minorities begin to address these gaps. African American Eddy L. Harris in *Mississippi Solo: A River Quest* questions, for example, why blacks do not inhabit or go to particular places: is it because of personal taste or due to an unwelcoming environment? In other words, "is the exclusion self-imposed or by hints both subtle and overt?"[70] In his narrative Harris addresses extreme adventure's racial codes, mapping his own growing awareness that "it is perhaps startling to realize that there are places blacks don't much go to."[71] While talking with a friend and planning his canoeing trip from the Mississippi's source to New Orleans, Harris becomes conscious of potential dangers for a "black man alone and exposed and vulnerable": "But suddenly being black, as well as being tall, took on new meaning. Being tall because of the long journey ahead with me sitting cross-legged in a canoe. Being black because of how I would perceive and be perceived."[72] Harris implies that black people do not enter the wilderness, particularly the Southern wilderness, because it has historically been and remains a site of black vulnerability and racial violence. Of course, the same threat of violence is felt in urban and especially suburban America, too.

Andrew Pham provides further insight into the legacy of colonialism for the (post)colonial adventurer in *Catfish and Mandala: A Two-Wheeled Voyage through the Landscape and Memory of Vietnam*. Early in the narrative Pham explains that his father told him a different kind of heroic adventure story: "The adventure stories he had told me as a boy on his knee were replaced by his death-camp saga."[73] Pham's personal family history reveals that one's sense of risk as a leisure activity demands certain privileges. His father's extreme survival and escape from the death camp and how the family survived and eventually raised the funds to flee Vietnam (by running a brothel) is a very different path to retrace in his own biking adventure through Vietnam. Pham is implicated as both a patriarchal, if not an imperial, power and the victim of imperialism. As a result, his adventure is a complex mix to confirm both his Vietnamese and American identities.

In the narrative, Pham shifts between more fully realizing his American identity, which requires a frontier adventure, and discovering his Vietnamese identity: "It appeals to me. Riding out my front door on a bicycle for the defining event of my life. It is so American, pioneering, courageous, romantic, self-indulgent."[74] However, Pham is told that as a Vietnamese he lacks the stamina required for this adventure. Binh, a friend of Pham's cousin, tells him, "'you won't make it. Trust me, I've been around a long time. Vietnamese just don't have that sort of physical endurance and mental stamina. We are weak. Only Westerners can do it. They are stronger and better than us.'"[75] Binh's remarks underscore the racial and gendered components of Western (and specifically American) adventurous masculinity: it connects women and nonwhite others to nature and deems them unfit to master the natural world.

Terrain also plays a key role in how American adventurous masculinity is mapped and limits more diverse accounts from being incorporated into heroic masculinity. For example, Jarid Manos's urban extreme adventure focuses less on nature's dangers and challenges and more on the cultural dangers posed by his dark skin, risky drug-dealing work, and precarious urban housing. When Manos addresses his drug dealing, he rhetorically questions the other options available to support his environmental work: "But aside from dealing, what are my options? There's a war going on against the Earth herself that's much bigger than the one in the Persian Gulf. And that's bad enough. I need to at least get on a playing field, even if it's never level."[76] The precarious financial foothold drug dealing provides is not only a means for Manos to fund his environmental work, but it also provides the bare basics to survive. His survival strategies are not something done away from home or as a means to return home, but rather to try to achieve a place Manos might describe as home. In this light, he risks for a greater sense of security. His illegal drug trafficking, furthermore, hinders easy inclusion in heroic masculinity and prohibits public tribute.

While Manos breaks new narrative ground, minority adventurers—like their white counterparts—also retrace the steps of previous expeditions. Perhaps the best-known minority-led expedition retracing is William Least Heat-Moon's *River-Horse: The Logbook of a Boat across America*. In *River-Horse*, Least Heat-Moon documents his travels from the Atlantic Ocean to the Pacific Ocean, often following routes detailed by American explorers such as Henry Hudson and Lewis and Clark. Least Heat-Moon and his copilot leave the harbor in Newark Bay (Elizabeth, New Jersey) on Earth Day. This "participatory history" connects and interrogates the colonial history with their journey as well as notes the ecological status of the rivers they travel.[77] Thus, Least Heat-Moon's reflective retracing questions as much as it celebrates his white adventuring predecessors.

Least Heat-Moon explicitly considers his journey's "westering" mythos and its connection to and departure from the colonial enterprises before him.

> At times we [Least Heat-Moon and his copilot, Pilotis] talked about explorers, settlers, early travelers, wilderness, of how America perhaps more than any other nation built itself and many of its cherished myths around westering, a concept then and now most evident and the source of the greatest theme in our history: the journey. Westering is only logical from a country whose people all have ancestors from the eastern hemisphere, whose leaders considered Westward ho! a manifest destiny to be executed for the good of humanity—never mind those already dwelling there who sometimes got in the way. The American fate was to drive on to the sea where the sun sets, to take up the land, remake it according to our own images. We, so goes the gospel of our historiography, we descendants of the purported ancient Garden, were foreordained to create a new one. Whether that impulse was noble I leave to others, except to argue that our destiny would look considerably more estimable had our ancestors—and we—conceived the New Eden in terms less those, to keep the biblical context, of Mammon.[78]

While Least Heat-Moon "leave[s] to others" the question of whether the "impulse was noble," the above passage clearly critiques the effects of such (ig)noble impulses. In fact, early in the narrative Least Heat-Moon remarks, "adventure was a putting into motion one's ignorance."[79] This self-deprecating adventurer critically retraces his own and past travelers' views of the land and people encountered.

The risky journeys undertaken by Eddy L. Harris, Jarid Manos, Andrew Pham, and William Least Heat-Moon trouble the centrality of white exploration by centering men of color as the heads of their expeditions and focusing on their personal transformations. They also emphasize the increased danger that results because of their status as minority adventurers. While the standards of white adventurous masculinity are never absent, Harris, Manos, Pham, and Least Heat-Moon expose heroic masculinity's assumptions. Least Heat-Moon, for example, remarks, "I optimistically reckoned that each day of survival, each league of fast education, increased our chances of completing the voyage."[80] He admits, "there's nothing a person of words likes more than an incident of survival."[81] This idea that risk is key to success or "earn[ing] passage" as well as to the narrative of survival also connects to environmental knowledge: "the object isn't just to get to the top but to get there in such a way you learn the nature of the mountain."[82] Such learning requires a test. As a result, their journeys and heroic masculinity do not erase colonialism, but rather explore how nonwhite men forge adventurous masculine identities both within and outside of white cultural norms.

Looking at a wider, more diverse range of adrenaline narratives reveals more clearly that conquering desire genders risk as masculine and nature as feminine. Understanding the nature of conquering desire in post-1970s American adrenaline narratives demands attention to America's entwined patriarchal and colonial practices and narratives. Just as Susan Birrell argues Everest narratives "are implicated in a complex web of power relations," so, too, are all adrenaline narratives implicated: "Four strands in particular are woven throughout the stories—nationality, class, ethnicity, and gender."[83] Conquering desire utilizes double standards in order to promote its ethic of heroic hegemonic masculine control and power. These related discourses about conquering nature form the heart of conquering desire. Nature's representations in adrenaline narratives reveal these patriarchal (conquering) power dynamics at work.

CONTROLLING NATURES:
NATURE AS FEMINIZED OTHER

While women and nonwhite males constitute a minority of adventurers, race, gender, and hyperbole play key roles in the ways conquering desire represents and attempts to control nature. Representations of nature are racialized when patriarchal logic represents (post)colonized peoples as closer to nature and thereby feminized and subject to control. Following mythic and colonial representations, conquering desire may present nature as a mysterious, dark other, which, as ecofeminists and postcolonial critics point out, is often just another way to describe nature as woman or the object of colonial desire. While post-1970s adrenaline narratives continue to feminize nature explicitly, they rarely unambiguously racialize the landscape; however, they also, as I discussed above, rarely include or feature nonwhite adventurers.

The lack of Indigenous peoples and racial/ethnic minorities within extreme landscapes, especially as central actors in the adventure, embodies their secondary or "local color" status within conquering desire's conception of nature and adventure. The adventurer sees through "Orientalist, post-colonial or neo-colonial discourse and frameworks, often where the 'exotic Other' and the 'authentic' are sought at once."[84] Canadian Les Stroud's *Beyond Survival* and its quest to document Indigenous survival skills, as the introduction to the show attests, "before they are gone," is a prime example of such contemporary colonialism.[85] American Matt Walker designs extreme adventure experiences for his clients in order to change their everyday lives. In doing so, he has identified five elements key to adventure, the first of which is "out of the ordinary."[86] The short film about these characteristics, *The Five Elements of Adventure*, opens in Katmandu, highlighting that "all adventures begin this way, traveling somewhere, stepping out of our everyday into something that's unknown, into something out of the ordinary."[87] A sleek new Nissan vehicle weaves through Katmandu's narrow, chaotic streets and other exotic locations to provide visual dissonance and advertising. The film's setting jolts the participants into "a completely different world" while staging their "touristic gaze," which views the local culture as the object of the participants' (and viewers') experience.[88] In Esther Bott's formulation, "Embodied 'Otherness' is required to emphasise the 'adventurousness' of the tourist and his destination to potential consumers of adventures."[89] As local color, residents and landscape collapse into one another.

While nature is not often explicitly racialized as an exotic other in contemporary adrenaline narratives, conquering desire often crafts a vision of nature connected to longstanding chauvinist understandings of the female/feminized body. For example, nature, like woman, is often described dichotomously: as pristine and unpopulated (virgin) or as tempting, mysterious, and/or polluted (whore). Pristine locations are especially key for establishing ownership, a topic I will discuss in greater detail later in the chapter. Joe Kane, in *Running the Amazon*, provides a good illustration: "This river, this forgotten place, was ours now, and ours alone. No towns, no bridges, no roads, no huts, no gold panners, no peasants working postage-stamp fields. A *wild* river."[90] In order to be "ours alone," Kane suggests in this passage that ownership requires the "empty" space of wilderness, which ignores and erases the flora, fauna, and any Indigenous peoples that inhabit this space. In this sense, America's definition of "untrammeled" wilderness (as defined by the Wilderness Act of 1964) depends on conquering.

More explicitly gendered terms and phrases such as "mother earth" and the "rape of the land," where rape is by default a feminizing term, depend on nature's connection to the female/feminized body. Under patriarchal logic, nature's unpredictability (like woman's changeable nature) and status as other provide justification that it rightfully falls under husbandly dominion. This is the (masculine) control that will create order out of (feminine) chaos. The narrative order adrenaline narratives underscore, as Susan Birrell points out in regard to Everest narratives, consciously and unconsciously creates such patriarchal communities.

> Thus the narratives of Everest and the mountain they reference can be conceptualized as part of a ritual process through which community is forged. As we read heroic Everest tales of courage, suffering, deprivation, and perseverance we pay direct homage to Everest explorers and climbers. In so doing we also affirm the values they represent, both the exposed values that form the dominant messages of mountaineering literature—the nobility of heroism, bravery, and suffering—and the values hidden deeper within the narratives—the consolidation of class privilege, the exclusivity of gender, the naturalization of ethnic difference. To the extent that these stories bind the reader to Everest, the values it represents are reaffirmed and reproduced. And to the extent that the process works without our conscious knowledge or consent, the process does ideological work.[91]

As outlined above by Birrell, conquering desire's "ideological work" within adrenaline narratives presents familiar terrain for (eco)feminist critique.

In fact, so familiar is this terrain that the adrenaline narrative's conquering desires would seem at first blush to provide an easy straw man to ecofeminism's more "politically correct" notions of power and identity politics. However, such one-dimensional framing neglects to address questions regarding why and how conquering desire remains such a powerful force within American culture and our environmental imagination generally and within the adrenaline narrative specifically. If so easily deconstructed, why do conquering (patriarchal) desires appear in a range of narratives by authors/adventurers writing after the critiques of second-wave feminism? Ideological differences among feminists and nonfeminists do not account fully for the persistent hold conquering desire has over our environmental imagination. While some adventurers may fit a backlash model, misogynistically insisting women do not belong in the realm of extreme adventure, this explanation does not provide insight into more nuanced representations of nature's identity politics. Rooting out conquering desire requires continued thinking about the nature of gender, race, and power.

CONTROLLING NATURES:
SEX AND VIOLENCE AND THE USES OF NATURE

When describing his own youthful adventures in nature, Krakauer in *Into the Wild* employs gendered and colonial language. He likens his desire for the extreme to the same "dark mystery" found in women's bodies: "I couldn't resist stealing up to the edge of doom and peering over the brink. The hint of what was concealed in those shadows terrified me, but I caught sight of something in the glimpse, some forbidden and elemental riddle that was no less compelling than the sweet, hidden petals of a woman's sex."[92] To heighten the adventure's drama, conquering desire exploits the nature/culture dichotomy and the related masculine/feminine features of the conquest. The adrenaline narrative's pervasive language of conquest provides additional evidence that the genre's whiteness is not an accident of history but rather an imperial as well as mythic legacy.

After describing his desire for risky adventure as akin to the desire produced by a woman's body, Krakauer goes on to clarify in the next paragraph that this desiring nature is a "very different thing from wanting to die"—a common and seemingly logical assumption made by his readers.[93] Krakauer does not explain, however, what exactly is desired, if not death. Implicitly, Krakauer's sexual metaphor argues that extreme encounters with nature are a form of *jouissance* and *plaisir*: an experience, to use Roland Barthes's terminology, that pleasures the adventurer as well as the reader by describing nature in familiar terms—in this case a desire for the female body.

While masculine heterosexual desire is not inherently dominating, ecofeminists may underscore the implicitly violent nature of Krakauer's sexual metaphor. The conventional terms Krakauer employs in this passage—"dark mystery," for example—draw from rather than explicitly critique or disavow traditional constructions of patriarchal-colonial desire. As a result, while Krakauer's comparison may not be unequivocally dominating, the metaphor's ambivalence advances into this territory. While Krakauer's description ruptures the reader's logical expectations about the suicidal nature of extreme adventure, it confirms the adventure's patriarchal nature by employing the conventional language of sexual conquest and discovery. In this sense, extreme adventures can be understood as a search for a "little death"—an orgasmic experience that necessarily derives pleasure from danger and violence. Barry Blanchard, whom Aron Ralston quotes as an epigraph for chapter 15 of *Between a Rock and a Hard Place*, more crudely states, "it was like having sex with death."[94] The idea that both fear and bliss construct pleasure forms the heart of both Barthes's and Jacques Lacan's definition of *jouissance*, the latter of which, in Catriona Sandilands's formulation, "cohabits the Real with the domain of death and lies within human social existence at the same time as it is unassimilable."[95] Not surprisingly, ecofeminist readings do not mesh well with many American adrenaline narratives because of these patriarchal structures and their reproduction of patriarchal pleasure.

Seen as a form of oppression aimed to justify the exploitation of women, ethnic/racial minorities, and nature, ecofeminists endeavor to disrupt the familiar patriarchal pleasure Krakauer constructs in his sexual metaphor. Ecofeminists argue that such constructions of the other are dangerous because, rather than building egalitarian relationships, nature is defined as an enigmatic entity to be discovered, conquered, and controlled by the adventurer. For example, as part of her critique of the patriarchal discourse surrounding nature, groundbreaking ecofeminist Susan Griffin in *Woman and Nature: The Roaring Inside Her* (1978) addresses the male desire to conquer nature: "He finds the unknown irresistible. He believes what is hidden in this land calls to him.... In facing down danger, he has become more than himself. Thunderstorm. He is conqueror. Lightning. He has pierced the veiling mountains."[96] By mouthing the discourse of the penetration of nature/the female body and then reducing it to a dream or myth, Griffin critiques the patriarchy's false knowledge. Griffin continues, "suddenly he finds he cannot see.... He wanders like a ghost into the land of the forgotten. With each step this place pierces through him to reveal more clearly his desperation."[97] Here the land penetrates the man, revealing his fallacious (or *phallacious*) understanding of it.

Griffin plays with the notion of the sublime and the mythical language often employed when describing the conquering of land/woman. In her discussion of gender and mountaineering literature, Julie Rak points out that prior to the 1970s, "mountaineering became central to ideals about cultural superiority and masculine heroism from the beginning of the nineteenth century to the end of what is called the golden age of high-altitude mountaineering in the 1950s, when all the 8000-metre peaks in the Himalayas had been climbed."[98] Dominated by notions of "cultural superiority and masculine heroism," the "golden age" of climbing taught "readers of these narratives... what it was to be a heroic white man (who wasn't a soldier but an adventurer)." Rak explains, "they also learned how desirable it could be to 'master' an empire by exploring and claiming it vicariously. After World War II, for instance, summiting the highest peaks in the Himalayas became a way to prove to the British public that Britain was still a powerful country in a symbolic sense even as its empire began to shrink."[99] While the counterculture movement of the following decade changed mountaineering and its literature, we continue, as evidenced in Krakauer's writing, to see patriarchal-colonial narrative structures in post-1970s narratives.

In the 1970s, mountaineering culture transforms into what Sherry B. Ortner describes as the "countercultural" style.[100] As Rak presents it, "countercultural ideology meant that leadership styles became more egalitarian and collective decision-making was used far more."[101] Rak explains, "during this time, the Romanticism of the Heroic era gave way to the Romanticism of the countercultural movement.... These climbers had a new goal: individual self-realization.... However, most gendered assumptions about climbing did not change very much."[102] Extreme sports' counterculture lifestyle likewise does not shift most gendered expectations. The use of sexual metaphors to describe nature is a case in point.

My reading of Krakauer's uses of sexual imagery to describe the adventurer's experience in and with nature is enhanced by placing it in conversation with other writers who use sexual metaphors in their writing about nature and other critics who address these metaphors. Kevin Krein's reading of a passage by mountain biker Lee Bridgers notes both the promise and the predicament of using the analogy of heterosexual sex—where a male adventurer likens his experience with nature to sex with a woman—in adrenaline narratives.[103] Bridgers writes in the essay "Out of the Gene Pool and into the Food Chain," "the single most important draw of riding a mountain bike is NATURE—not the environmentalist, tree-hugging, untouchable nature of Sierra Club twits who try to make themselves look like caring people by keeping you off the grass so they can buy a three-million-dollar home and have the mountains untouched in their picture window—but the nature that you can just dive into and have sex with. The challenge is to treat her right."[104] Interestingly, Bridgers places environmentalists—specifically the Sierra Club—as paternalistic, if not patriarchal, controllers of nature: those who wish nature to stay virginal, untouched—except by their own elite touch. Jedediah Purdy in *After Nature* likewise connects "some of the strongest conservationists" with imperialism rather than democracy.[105] Purdy also critiques the Sierra Club for "making a hasty peace with a consumerist relation to nature."[106] Bridgers and Purdy help outline two extremes: those who wish to observe and those who wish to play.

These contrasting representations suggest two environmental modes of thinking: preservation for light or no human use and conservation that plans for a range of human interactions with the environment. Bridgers advocates for a more intimate, dirty experience: he desires what Kevin Krein points to as "the opportunity for an intimate connection with nature...something many human beings desire." Krein goes on to explain what he finds "interesting about Bridger's [sic] use of the metaphor of sex" and its implication that "in its most common instantiation, two partners play active roles. In successful sexual activity, partners interact with, and react to, each other. A good game is one that is played between two competitors who bring out the best in each other, who force each other to react to unpredictable maneuvers, and who ultimately work together to create a beautiful and dramatic interaction."[107] Krein's curious description of "*successful* sexual activity" (emphasis added) is what feminists would understand as noncoerced, consensual sex. Ecofeminists, as I will detail in chapter 4, label this type of interaction with nature erotic due to its emphasis on mutuality. Bridgers's use of "sex with" implies such mutuality. His description of "untouchable" nature, by contrast, suggests a prohibitive, greedy violence is being done to nature by those who would label mountain biking as a spoiling or even a violent rape of the land.

While Bridgers's word choice of "sex with" is key, his reworking of this metaphor cannot fully escape its historical connotations, especially when his essay also deploys nature as a tempting seductress. Bridgers goes on to describe a trail site, Prostitute Butte, as "a rare gem—a gigantic rude stone formation that resembles a naked lady beckoning a bit of sodomy."[108] The description of the rock formation shifts from precious stone ("rare gem") to a monstrous woman ("gigantic rude stone formation") who desires a sex act historically (and often presently) considered deviant. The formation is both "prostitute" and "lady," "rude" and "beckoning." Her name, "Prostitute Butte," in this sense is a bit of a misnomer, as there is no mention of payment exacted for this seduction. These word combinations shift between virgin and whore representations.

The "successful," to borrow Krein's terminology, use of sexual metaphors in adrenaline narratives seems complicated by the fact that sexual metaphors post-1970 operate in an age that promotes mutual, enthusiastic consent. Sexual equality demands noncoerced consent. Krein notes the "limitations to the [sex] analogy" as follows: "In traditional sports (as well as sex), hopefully, both partners are active and aware of each other. In the case of adventure sports, the relationship is noticeably one-sided. Mountains do not care whether they are skied or climbed and waves do not change their course for surfers."[109] Krein hints that human interactions with nature will always occur in the absence of verbal or explicit consent. He explains, "while not a conscious participant, the natural world can take on the role of a partner with which one must interact. This is true whether or not one experiences that situation as being one of combat against, or harmonizing with, one's environment."[110] Krein emphasizes that nature's indifference or—differently framed—inability to provide express consent places all demands on the individual, who has the choice to engage nature as a combatant or as a partner in his or her endeavor.

Just as Bayers suggests Krakauer represents a new masculinity in *Into Thin Air*, Karin Wagner points to Lee Bridgers and his essay as an alternative model for masculinity, describing his views of risk, extreme sports, and environmentalism in "Out of the Gene Pool and into the Food Chain" as aligned with a "good guy" who displays a "multidimensional masculinity."[111] Yet Bridgers's essay still invokes the virgin-whore dichotomy. Certainly, he deploys "polluted" nature differently than Crouch does in the following simile: "It's a crack size that climbers shun like venereal disease."[112] As a result, Bridgers's essay is more ambivalent: Bridgers's writing still profits from invoking hegemonic masculinity that demands the policing of women into two categories: virgin or whore. However, his preference for a dirty, slutty nature (its whorish incarnations) troubles a puritanical vision of women, nature, and sustainability.

An examination of the feminized and sexual nature presented in Gregory Crouch's *Enduring Patagonia* helps parse the line between combat and harmony in contemporary (non)patriarchal masculinities. Like Krakauer and Bridgers, Crouch draws upon conventional conquering desires to describe nature. For example, Crouch writes, "yesterday we climbed about 1,200 feet of virgin stone."[113] At the narrative's end, furthermore, Crouch's language invokes both the notion of virgin territory and nature's seductive magic as key to his individual transformation. He observes, "how remarkable, here at the start of the third millennium, to journey into a slice of geographic unknown. I thirst for the undiscovered country. Exactly where the coming voyage will take me, and what it will make me see, I can barely begin to guess. But one thing I do know for certain—I won't be the same man when I come back. Patagonia works its magic."[114] Crouch remythologizes the natural landscape so he can (re)discover it and himself. Crouch's individual transformation—"I won't be the same man when I come back"—depends on a "magical," fantastical setting (Laing and Crouch's sixth characteristic of adventure travel writing). The connection between virginal, magical nature and (re)discovery seems key. A polluted or otherwise used nature would not mirror the adventurer's goals; however, the dichotomy can function only to the extent that the other representation appears.

A dichotomous representation of feminized nature—as both pure and sinister—appears early in Crouch's book.

> The Torre emerges from the storm like an enraged angel, sheathed from head to toe in an armor of shimmering rime ice. Clouds swirl around the peak, and afford us brief glimpses of the summit. She looks so evil. Her rewards are elusive and distant, the gauntlet of fear and suffering ever-present and agonizing. Whenever the Torre comes out of her cauldron of cloud and wind we launch a frenzy of backpack stuffing and last-minute eating, choke down a final cup of coffee, and march like lemmings toward her remote fortress, begging for punishment. It is the most extraordinary case of unrequited love.[115]

The above passage portrays feminized nature as a sadistic, withholding lover. The passage builds by connecting contrasts. It opens with an angry angel, transforms the angel to a warrior encased in "shimmering" armor, and then explicitly genders the summit as an evil female lover that refuses her suitors. Feminized nature is a mythic, god- or demon-like entity in its simultaneous embodiment of angelic and cruel characteristics. Notably, Crouch does not always gender nature, specifically the Patagonian landscape, as female: "The lord of Patagonia, briefly negligent, was now violently awake."[116] This example also maintains sadistic hierarchies that place nature on a higher realm. Patagonia is a "violently awake" ruler, which is similar to the "enraged angel." However, rather than purity, this description contrasts the lord's violent attention with temporary neglect.

Mountaineers and mountain bikers are not the only adventurers to portray nature in these terms. Kayaker Joe Kane similarly describes the Acobamba abyss, a section of the Apurímac River in Peru, as a demonic woman. Kane affirms, "given these changes in mood, in appearance, it was impossible not to think of the river as having a will and intent of her own. In the end, however, it was sound, a voice, that most gave her life—she *roared* as she charged through her canyon. She seemed not only willful but demonic, bent on the simple act of drowning us. You could shout at her, curse her, plead with her, all to the same effect: nothing. She barreled on indifferent, unrelenting."[117] Indifference to human struggle is key to nature's mythic, dual, god-and-demon-like demeanor.

While indifference presents a problem for consensual sex, godlike unresponsiveness depends on the adventurer's faith and ability to do the right things to please or at least not anger god/nature. Jill Fredston in *Rowing to Latitude* similarly emphasizes nature's indifference: "Nature is indifferent to such choices."[118] The purpose of such mythic indifference and the desire to transform it, according to Hans Blumenburg and Sigmund Freud, is to "allay anxiety over the world": "Like Freud, Blumenburg asserts that humans wish the world were nicer than it is."[119] Such indifference frames our dysfunctional relationship with nature: nature becomes a cruel mistress and an unforgiving landscape. Despite the abuse, the adventurer refuses to leave the relationship and expects the same of nature.

While Crouch's mythic nature remains a cruel mistress, reckoning with her provides a crucial testing ground. Crouch emphasizes, "the Patagonian gauntlet of hardship cannot be evaded.... But there are a handful of climbers who find the opposing miseries of the Patagonian Andes irresistible and are repeatedly drawn to this proving ground." This reckoning, or "combat," is violent in nature. He further describes "the mountains" as possessing "no generosity and no justice. They stand unmoved by the human dramas that play out on their flanks, and they give and take with unknowable whim. We have only the dignity of persistence with which to combat this terrible faceless indifference."[120] This is not a pastoral landscape, but the fierce, treacherous ground of survival that links back to the heroic masculinity myths discussed earlier.

Extreme nature here is not a sunny summit, but a violent landscape. Ruth Anne Kocour writes, "I had become a willing participant in an exercise in violence, a mere speck of dust against the teeth of a savage Alaskan storm."[121] Problems occur when one tries to encounter violent nature, as Howkins points out, in the same ways one engages its gentler modes. Howkins explains, "we have no problem feeling a sappy affinity with the natural world, with trees and wildflowers and sunsets, until we confront the truly wild parts of it, the cougars and avalanches and rattlesnakes that challenge our ability to confront death without whimpering, to accept the inevitable. In the presence of the wild, attempting to see beauty, to grasp the meaning of the experience is a little like trying to drink from a fire hydrant."[122] This passage suggests, especially through its fire hydrant simile, that wild nature asks us to confront human insignificance: wild nature reveals that our individual lives and desires mean nothing. There is no gentle beauty, at least for Howkins, in the decidedly unpastoral scene described. Instead of offering a beauty that is easy to drink in, wild nature throttles at full pressure. Not losing control at such moments becomes key: faced with an uncontrollable environment, the only thing the adventurer can control is him/herself by confronting the "inevitable" (pain, death, danger) without sniveling. The control of the adventurer's emotions and body comprises another key aspect of conquering desire.

The key question in these representations of nature, desire, and control is the extent to which they reinforce patriarchal stereotypes or successfully rewrite them. Comparing these male writer-adventurers with Susan Griffin's positive gendering of nature as feminine provides a helpful counterpoint. Later ecofeminists often point out that Griffin's positive gendering of nature as feminine dangerously essentializes women's relationship with nature in much the same ways as discussed above in relation to Krakauer's, Bridgers's, and Crouch's writings.[123] Such ecofeminists claim that, while couched in less overtly oppressive language, Griffin's glorified conflation of women and nature ends up replicating the very confining discourse she critiques. In other words, rather than constructing a different discourse, Griffin uses the tools of patriarchal discourse in order to deconstruct patriarchal ideology. The problem with this tactic is that Griffin can never fully escape patriarchy's trappings. For instance, the land penetrates the man in the previously quoted passage: "Suddenly he finds he cannot see.... He wanders like a ghost into the land of the forgotten. With each step this place pierces through him to reveal more clearly his desperation."[124] Griffin seemingly replicates patriarchal logic.

Chris J. Cuomo, however, disagrees with this reading. Cuomo, author of *Feminism and Ecological Communities: An Ethic of Flourishing*, asserts that Griffin does not "render femininity stereotypically."[125] Griffin does not simply fashion a stereotypical portrayal of femininity but at moments her discourse should be examined for the ways it replicates potentially dangerous discursive structures, a problem later ecofeminists try to avoid. Likewise, given the ambivalence present in Krakauer, Bridgers, and Crouch's narratives, we may also suggest that they do not simply, to paraphrase Cuomo, render elite white masculinity stereotypically. Jarid Manos's personification of nature provides a case in point: "She'd been critically wounded. But she was not dead yet. She was still wild, despite what people had done to her.... Like a wild vine trying to twist itself up into the sky, it—she—was trying to rise up. Fight the power. Shake it off."[126] The environment in this passage is gendered female and tenacious, much like the descriptions that appear in Crouch's narrative. The language of uplift, though, suggests a different power dynamic is at work, one where a weed (a plant considered undesirable by culture) is being beaten back by humanity. The "wild vine" must "fight the power." Wild nature, not the adventurer, must "shake off" the wounds inflicted.

Thus, while some adventurers may want or expect extreme environments to operate as genderless spaces, such spaces do not exist. Ruth Anne Kocour claims she is able to resist gendered frameworks by not "focus[ing] on the fact that I am a woman": "The mountain is not the place to draw gender distinctions, though this was not the first time I had faced down a Spanish inquisition. I choose not to focus on the fact that I am a woman and because I don't, others rarely do—thank goodness."[127] Kocour also writes, "it didn't bother me [being the only woman]. After all, it was part of the challenge that I had bought into, the mountain, the elements, and even being alone with this group of men."[128] Adrenaline narratives—and even Kocour's own remarks—overwhelmingly illustrate that spoken and unspoken gender distinctions are being imposed.

Additionally, the media outlets that present these landscapes for athletes and armchair enthusiasts alike increasingly shape our experience of wilderness and wilderness sports. In his study of skiing media, for example, Stoddart includes a quotation from a skier, Billy: "'The photos of the big mountain skiing in Alaska, and all of that, it's almost like looking at a *Playboy* sometimes.'"[129] Billy collapses the airbrushed, idealized female body and the landscape, describing it as "adventure porn." These visual and verbal codependent representations of heroic adventurers and nature as feminized other have significant implications for our understanding of the American environmental imagination and its influence on the environmental movement and environmental policy.

Nature as other implies an environmental stewardship approach, where humans are the rightful caretakers/husbands/settlers of the natural environment. Understanding nature as other contrasts with Aldo Leopold's idea of "thinking like a mountain" and suggests that nature, particularly wilderness, requires (masculine/paternalistic) control and protection. Of course, the desire to protect the environment and the management of natural resources are key to a range of approaches in the environmental movement. Debate about the methods that best foster sustainability inform the critique of conquering desire as well as arguments that some form of control or management will always be necessary.

Key to this debate is the extent to which any attempt to control or manage nature results in patriarchal practice. The debate raises questions about the environmental risks associated with the other extreme: insisting nature best cares for itself and does not need human interventions. The continued desire to control nature also speaks to the denial or inadequate recognition of the climate crisis: the conquering of remote, fragile environments often privileges human aspirations over ecosystem health. In more quotidian terms, buildings placed and repeatedly rebuilt in flood plains or other areas prone to natural disaster speak to human confidence to overcome nature. In more extreme terms, garbage and dead bodies litter Everest; expeditions carry large carbon footprints.[130] Climber Conrad Anker admits, "I'm particularly guilty of contributing to this mess. I travel in jets. Visiting the Himalaya to climb has a huge carbon footprint. The cams, rope, tents and sleeping bags integral to climbing all have a plastic-based carbon price tag. I consume a stack of resources. I recognize this."[131] Yet we continue to climb. Examples of the adrenaline narrative's conquering desire underscore the significant roles control or lack thereof plays in our understanding and use of the natural environment. Control, especially the policing of the adventurer's gendered body, emerges as another key concept for understanding conquering desire's definition of the wilderness, masculinity, and femininity, as well as of what it means to protect wild habitat and be a (wo)man.

CONTROLLING NATURES:
HYPERBOLE, CONQUEST, AND OWNERSHIP

Conquering desire often uses hyperbolic description to describe nature as a stereotypically overblown enemy, presenting nature as a dangerous, unpredictable force, not an equal. These inflated descriptions, in turn, play off of and enhance the adventurer's performance of heroic masculinity. Gregory Crouch, for example, uses military language to describe Patagonian winds: "I can feel the Lords of Patagonia marshaling their battalions."[132] This pattern is also evident when the adventurer is female. The language of conquest or ownership appears in narratives written by men and women. Ann Bancroft, for example, deploys military language, emphasizing, "we were battling for every inch."[133] Ruth Anne Kocour similarly presents the weather as a formidable enemy, describing a storm as an "out-of-control beast with devilish intentions. It tore across ridges, ripped through crevasses, snatched at anything not securely fastened, and vibrated the ground to which we clung for our lives."[134] Kocour also likens the storm to "an out-of-control locomotive."[135] In these inflated descriptions, nature is a lord going to battle, a devilish beast, and a runaway train—all opponents no ordinary human could control, let alone conquer.

In this vein, Paul Beedie notes in "Legislators and Interpreters: An Examination of Changes in Philosophical Interpretations of 'Being a Mountaineer'" that "mountaineering is usually understood as a battle between human endeavour and wild nature."[136] The adventurer's aim is to overcome successfully the physical and mental challenges nature presents. Jeffrey McCarthy describes in "Why Climbing Matters" this representation of nature as "the conquest model...[where the] active climber overcomes an inanimate world": "This is the vocabulary of conquest, and here the climber's efforts become significant insofar as they succeed in dominating the natural world."[137] The conquest model is not the exclusive domain of climbing narratives. Joe Kane's *Running the Amazon*, for example, explicitly describes an individual's river-running style as militaristic, where nature functions as an enemy to be conquered. Kane relates, "Truran said that Chmielinski attacked the river like a military man. He was brave, and though his kayaking skills were self-taught, he had a superb feel for white water—he refused to let the river's power intimidate him. He felt the river in his bones and respected it the way a general does a worthy enemy: It was something to conquer."[138] While both Beedie and McCarthy frame this battle as a "human endeavor," this style of heroic, risky adventure is decidedly masculine.

Extreme environments evoke mythic heroic frameworks and historically specific national narratives about the American frontier. Conquering language also serves to buttress patriarchal control. At his story's conclusion, for example, African American Eddy L. Harris takes ownership of the river. He declares, "after all I'd been through, all the wonder I'd seen, all the pain, that river was mine. I'd paid for it with sore shoulders and aching knees and a back that will never be right again, with smiles from strangers and good wishes too dear to waste, with two thousand miles of strain, with days of glory, with nights of peace and wonder, and with chipped teeth. This river is mine."[139] Successfully overcoming physical and mental hardships results in ownership.

Aron Ralston, by contrast, emphasizes that his ownership is the result of kinship and knowledge of habitat, not the result of conquering or suffering. Ralston notes, "I felt a sense of ownership of these cold high mountains, these buried alpine tarns, these sound-dampened forests; and a sense of kinship with the elk, deer, beaver, ermines, ptarmigans, and mountain goats. The more I visited their home, the more it felt like mine."[140] Ralston's hard-won ownership comes via observation and increasing familiarity with the flora and fauna and not by the pain suffered by the loss of his arm. As a result, Ralston shifts ownership from acts that stress overcoming physical challenges to mastering knowledge about the environment via careful, thoughtful observation.

The act of listening to nature is key to survival and reveals another side of conquering desire that connects with erotic desire, as I discuss in chapter 4. In *Facing the Extreme* mountaineer Ruth Anne Kocour points out, "those who do not listen to the mountain, or to themselves, are accidents waiting to happen."[141] In fact, adventurers often note that the environment will demand recompense from anyone that does not heed its warnings. Kocour cautions, "the mountain was beginning to exact payment from those who dared not listen to its words of warning—first the Italians, now the Koreans."[142] Reading indifferent, unresponsive nature requires experience and patience. Crouch, for example, genders the delicate balance between driving for a summit and knowing when to resist the urge to do so. Here the control of a feminized desire becomes key to skirting successfully the extreme edge between a calculated risk and a foolish gamble of one's life. Crouch suggests, "you must care completely, and at the same time you can't care at all. You must give yourself over to the she-wolf of desire and strive toward success and the summit with every ounce of strength, every iota of commitment, every fiber of being. But at exactly the same time that you climb with the full power of desire, you must be able to judge the evolving situation as uncontrollable and abandon ascent without hesitation."[143] Crouch's passage draws upon the traditional gendering of emotion as feminine and logic as masculine. Desire is emotion, a "she-wolf," whereas logic—implicitly male—is paired with feminine desire to balance its strength and danger.

While listening to nature is key for everyone's survival, the adrenaline narrative's focus on risky situations tends to elide connections to our everyday lives and situations. We are largely out of tune with our environments because the focus remains on the individual need to survive. This focus tends to transform nature into an other, strategic ownership or knowledge of which results in mastery. Whether earned by sheer grit and survival, the quieter powers of observation and listening, or some combination of them both, the sense of ownership Ralston and other adventurers enjoy creates its own set of problems as well as complicates our understanding of contemporary conquering desire.

By evoking a sense of ownership, furthermore, the adventurer effectively makes a nonproductive act productive. As Julie Rak puts it, "climbing, particularly before the 1970s, was a key way for modern men—and especially middle-class and upper-class white men associated with imperial and colonial regimes—to imagine themselves as men who are socially productive *because* they are engaged in what is essentially an unproductive activity."[144] Possession of nature reflects the adventurer's control over his or her environment and thus constitutes successful, productive labor. Miranda Weiss in *Tide, Feather, Snow: A Life in Alaska* discusses the nature of land ownership in terms of naming: "Naming was one of the many ways to try to own a place." Like Ralston's developing knowledge of the flora and fauna, this process of knowing through classification provides Weiss with a method to establish Alaska as "home." She also recognizes, though, "how so many acts of ownership mean nothing."[145] Weiss—at least in this passage—may be more optimistic than the Alaskan Indigenous populations or even the flora and fauna (could they express such thoughts) about the meaningless, transitional, or ineffectual impact of such acts of ownership.

While sometimes ephemeral, this ownership has, as Weiss notes, left its impact on the land. As she writes in the epilogue, "to live in this place, is, in part, to destroy it; that is the paradox—and the responsibility—we live with every day."[146] Her own "urgent appropriation" of Alaska as home involves death. She finds a dead otter on the beach and learns how to skin it. The pelt provides a talisman of how she "had taken hold, on my own, of this place."[147] Her meditations on ownership explore the implications of self-centered possession. Like Ralston, her ownership comes with intimate knowledge of the land as well as full comprehension of her destructive impact on the environment. As a result, conquering desire—connected to ownership and mastery—in their narratives takes on an altered capacity: their representations of possessed nature account for human violence against the environment. Their reflective accounts of the environmental consequences shift conquering desire away from unqualified celebratory achievement. As noted in this chapter's introduction, Krakauer's ambivalence connects to his exhaustion and—later—regret. Weiss and Ralston also emphasize ambivalence in their achievements because of the environmental costs. Recognition, nevertheless, does not result in significant power shifts.

CONTROLLING NATURES:
POWER

Power relationships in contemporary adrenaline narratives are not easily or simply altered. As the earlier descriptions of life-threatening weather attest, adventurers often have only a tenuous hold over their environment. After weathering a bad storm on Denali, for example, Ruth Anne Kocour describes a sense of having earned the summit through suffering.[148] She acknowledges, "our summiting had been not just the conquering of a mountain. It had been a celebration of survival. We felt like undecorated heroes."[149] While "conquering" and "heroes" suggest power ultimately lies with the climbers, Kocour's personification of the mountain reveals that Denali actually *allowed* the climbers to summit: "Denali...had shown little compassion for those who had attempted to scale her lofty heights so far this year."[150] Denali's "compassion," along with the climbers' suffering, earns the climbers' success: "We had all earned our place in one way or another."[151] Shifting power dynamics once again, Kocour emphasizes that their survival was a choice, not a pure act of nature's compassion. Kocour writes, "I could hardly believe it, after all that we had been through—we hadn't died, we had survived, we had been strong enough to match the mountain. Our survival had been a choice—the right choice."[152] The power gymnastics outlined in these passages reveal conquering desire's slippery, grasping nature: conquering desire pumps up nature's danger while still insisting on its own manifest control. While nature's awesome power must be emphasized and recognized, survival is a result of controlled choice rather than luck or dependence on nature's whims. Chapter 5 explores risk and control in greater detail.

The status of the global within these tales offers another perspective on conquering desire's shifting rather than straightforward power structures. Susan E. Frohlick, for instance, questions "oppositional categories such as 'tourist' and 'local'" in her analysis of the global on Everest.[153] On one hand, the "universal, mobile subject, the mountaineer,...is actually a white, Euro-North American male."[154] Yet "'the global' is negotiated differently in different locales by different—although linked—discourses."[155] The same might be said for the oppositional categories of (male/white) adventurer and (female/nonwhite) nature, especially as more women and nonwhite adventurers are recognized as full expedition participants and as more women and nonwhites participate in extreme adventure sports. Yet even as women and minorities, especially since the 1970s, join the ranks of adrenaline narrative adventurer-authors, their presence has not necessarily radically changed the hegemonic masculinities at play. As in the case of affirmative action, white women have enjoyed the most significant gains in recognition and participation in extreme sports. The paucity of narratives written by nonwhite American males and the lack of nonwhite female author-adventurers speaks to the remaining gaps. Patriarchal heroic masculinity continues to suppress women's and racial/ethnic minorities' full participation by defining adventurous risk as white and masculine.

Contemporary post-1970 adrenaline narratives thus suggest that adventure sports maintain more than they challenge conventional gender performance expectations. Their extreme environments especially highlight the nature of masculinity and femininity. "What it means to be a man or a woman in harsh circumstances," according to Julie Rak, "is central to all of these concerns [nature, bodies, history, and heroism]."[156] Mark Stoddart makes a similar claim in regard to skiing: "Through outdoor sports like skiing, participants embody and perform traits associated with athletic masculinities and femininities."[157] Rak also suggests that examining the subculture of climbing provides insight into "mass cultural formations [of gender] worldwide."[158] An examination of adrenaline narratives suggests that conquering desire often demands the collapse of athletic femininities into hegemonic masculinity.

CONTROLLING ADVENTUROUS BODIES: HIGH-PERFORMANCE GENDER

Conquering desire, as outlined in the first section, requires the orchestrated performance of testosterone-infused behavior by testing and valorizing traditionally masculine traits, such as courage and strength, in a nondomestic setting. We understand (extreme) adventure as masculine in part because of its association with bodily risk outside the domestic sphere. The mythic hero must leave home to test himself. For example, Alvah Simon describes an encounter with a bear away from his domestic base as his adventure's transformative moment: "Here, as if it was etched in the delicate tundra grasses, was my line, my edge, my Ultima Thule, where a man meets his moment, where the fear passes through him and still he stands, open to every consequence of living and dying." Simon imagines the bear telling him, "'I give you back your life. It has been washed pure by your fear. Enjoy it deeply, learn from it daily, and use it wisely, for there is a purpose larger than yourself.'" After he is given his life back by the bear, Simon returns to "wife and home."[159] Likewise, Ruth Anne Kocour—after summiting Denali—wants to return to husband and home. She explains, "though I had made the summit, it was becoming apparent that this mountain of my dreams had laid claim to my soul. I had been to the edge, looked into the void, and stepped back. Now, more than ever, I needed to go home and flee the mountain."[160] Home symbolizes stability and safety, which makes it a poor environment for the fear-purifying, edgy transformations both Simon and Kocour seek.

Not surprisingly, traditional gender roles tying women more closely to the home impact female adventurers' ability to perform heroic masculinity. Patricia McCairen, for example, emphasizes that she is viewed as "peculiar" for adventuring alone. She clarifies, "men, for the most part, have not been labeled peculiar when they go adventuring alone. Rather, they are considered brave and daring. Of course, by keeping women tied to the kitchen and bedroom, a man has someone to come home to, someone to swoon over his heroic deeds." She goes on to say in the next paragraph, "I'm not sure I blame them. I wouldn't mind having someone to return to."[161] Where women are often tied to the home, men feel pressure to leave home as a necessary ritual into or to reaffirm their manhood. Maria Coffey in *Where the Mountain Casts its Shadow* reminds us that adventure may be a masculine "Huck Finn" escape from a domineering domestic femininity: "In writing about the search for the Northwest Passage, Christopher Isherwood said that sometimes extreme adventure is chosen because, despite the dangers and hardships, it is easier to face than the trials of domestic life."[162] Gendered space in adrenaline narratives involves a complex matrix of civilized home (feminine) and risky mobility (masculine) in wild terrain also often gendered female. Nature is feminine in ways distinct from the ways domesticity is feminine; however, both provide surfaces for the projection of hegemonic masculine desire and control. Both men and women may be trapped and empowered by these projections.

These examples expose the myriad ways adventure is a masculine performance and enterprise. Citing Martin Green's 1979 book *Dreams of Adventure, Deeds of Empire*, Richard S. Phillips emphasizes, "adventure, in general, is a 'masculinist' narrative."[163] While both Green and Phillips focus on fictional adventure tales, their observations regarding adventure's masculine stripes hold true for nonfiction narratives, too. Adventure, in this sense, is a specific iteration of risky behavior, where risk outside the home helps define masculine behavior. Phillips points out that the nature of this masculinity, furthermore, is best understood through the lens of intersectional analysis: "Adventure stories chart masculinities contextually, in relation to particular constructions of class, race, sexuality, and other forms of identity and geography."[164] While the object of desire may shift through various identity categories, the stereotypical adventurer is a heterosexual white male, the subject of hegemonic masculinity.

As I have already outlined, the power afforded this position requires strict adherence to a set of behavioral codes. Participation in the risky adventures that constitute adrenaline narratives requires, if not the performance of, then an engagement with, what bell hooks describes in *Feminism is for Everybody* as "white-supremacist-capitalist-patriarchy."[165] Always already masculine, adventure's worn paths direct participants to see nature as an obstacle to be conquered. Not surprisingly, as a result, TV adventurers such as former *Dual Survival* star Cody Lundin find themselves out of work—replaced when they refuse greater physical risks or when even more "extremely" qualified participants are found.[166] The policing of these behavior boundaries, which I will discuss shortly, stabilizes patriarchal hierarchy.

Chapter 4 discusses narratives by men and women "that offer alternate constructions of landscape" and gender performance.[167] Here, however, I am interested in how and why post-1970s adrenaline narratives' representations of nature maintain conquering desires. In this regard, Nick Ford and David Brown's questioning of second-wave feminism's emphasis on inclusion as a means to alter power structures is instructive. Building on Pierre Bourdieu's *Masculine Domination*, Ford and Brown suggest that "women can occupy dominant positions and engage in dominant practices that justify the so-called masculine 'traits' (e.g., managers, politicians, military personnel, and, increasingly, sportswomen to name a few). However, these have arguably done rather less to challenge the symbolic gender order that underpins social life in Western societies than many second-wave feminists may have originally thought."[168] Women's and nonwhite people's inclusion matters, but so, too, do the gendered and raced performances these bodies enact. As the examples discussed above of female and nonwhite adventurers who deploy conquering representations of nature suggest, risky adventure's protocols police the presence of others, just as they do white men, steering all bodies to conform to hegemonic masculinity.

Even when expeditions recruit all-female members and consciously attempt to follow different leadership styles, adventure's patriarchal patterns are hard to break. Arlene Blum, for example, notes leadership problems within her all-female expedition that were not simply solved by eliminating men. She laments, "I'd hoped for cooperation and harmony on our expedition, but I learned that all climbers, regardless of gender, are at the mercy of both nature and human nature. Difficult as it was to admit, women could be as competitive and edgy as men when stretched to their limits in the high, thin air. Although everyone agreed that if anyone reached the top it would be a victory for us all, each climber wanted to be that 'anyone.'"[169] Blum's description suggestively underscores that the performance of patriarchal masculinity remains a "universal" means to engage risky environments: a product of "nature and human nature." Blum's realizations also challenge conventional understandings—whether framed as essentially or culturally based—of women's cooperative nature. Suzanne Roberts describes a similar dynamic in *Almost Somewhere*, writing, "rather than displaying a true sort of girl power, we turned on each other."[170] Their remarks question whether extreme wilderness environments are naturally or socially constructed to privilege hegemonic masculinity.

Scholars engaged in the study of landscape agree it structures and reflects behavior. Derek Gregory states that the modern concept of landscape has "implications of power, domination, and representation."[171] Mark Stoddart similarly points out, in regard to "sportscapes," "the cultural construction of sportscapes often reinforces dominant discourses about gender and sport participation."[172] As a result, "gendered relations of power are not only 'social.' They are inscribed in the physical environments where sport is performed."[173] In literature, all environments are (re)constructed for the reader. The authors of adrenaline narratives more often represent the natural environment as something that they must plan for and react to rather than something that they consciously construct for themselves or something constructed to counteract the inscription of hegemonic masculinity. However, women adventurers sometimes consciously resist the frameworks that position them as helpless outside of the home or that would seek to limit their adventures because they are (potential) mothers.

For example, as McCairen goes further on her trip down the Colorado River, she recognizes the role female dependency plays in her own gender performance. In her words, she "begin[s] to see the bits and pieces of dependency that cling to me. The dependency of wanting to be rescued that goes far beyond the desire to have another person present in the event I hurt myself. I still carry the belief that being dependent is feminine and attractive. That's the catch. I want autonomy, but if I achieve it, I fear I'll be unlovable. I learned early in life to garner attention by being slightly helpless. Just now and then, here and there."[174] Masculine strength connects to feminine dependence and a desire for protection. McCairen reminds us that the environment (re)enforces masculine and feminine performances. Norwegian adventurer Liv Arnesen relates a similar story about how her adventurous life seemed at odds with her romantic one: "I just couldn't seem to find a man who, instead of expecting me to be a homemaker, would be willing to let me be what I needed to become.... I had pretty much resigned myself to remaining single when I met Einar [her husband]."[175] Both women also remind us of the potential consequences of not following these expected performances, especially in a heteronormative context. They risk—or at least fear—not being loved whenever they step outside expected gender roles because, for instance, "in Norway (as in much of the rest of the world), that kind of expedition [referring to Arnesen's expedition across Greenland] was seen as the province of men."[176] Culture reads male and female risky participation very differently, even if women follow hegemonic masculinity's rules.

CONTROLLING ADVENTUROUS BODIES:
POLICING HEROIC MASCULINITY

Conquering desire polices female adventurers in all the familiar ways: when women enter masculine spheres, they are held to double standards; male adventurers gain and protect their own claims to heroic masculinity by policing these boundaries. Rower Tori Murden McClure observes the following about the gendered nature of risk and adventure in *A Pearl in the Storm*: "Men occasionally garner fame out of expeditions. Women do not. Men are sometimes rewarded for their rugged individualism. Women are not. When a woman is too robust or too independent, she gets asked what her boyfriend thinks about it. No one genuinely cares what the boyfriend thinks; they just want to know whether or not she has a boyfriend."[177] McClure highlights the double standards with which female adventurers must contend. As Jennifer Jordan writes, "women have had very different experiences than men in the climbing world."[178] These female author-adventurers imply, if not directly state, that women who accomplish masculine feats are not viewed as (attractive) women. For instance, Arlene Blum explains what the phrase "no real women climbers" means: "'It means that women either aren't good climbers or they aren't real women.'"[179] To be a "real woman" demands dependence on a male. To be a real adventurer demands dependence on no one (or at least demands the understanding that one's survival ultimately rests in one's own hands and not on being rescued by another).

Thus, women cannot be real adventurers and remain women. While men, as Krakauer demonstrates, may feel survivor's guilt for—in retrospect—focusing more on their own survival than assuring the safety of another team member, final responsibility lies within the individual. Or, as Kocour observes, "you cannot act like Mother Teresa on the mountain and expect to live. The best thing mountaineers can do for others is to take care of themselves."[180] Yet women are often socialized to be selfless. Additionally, as Krakauer notes in *Into Thin Air*, large-scale expedition climbing complicates these traditional extreme adventure codes. Guides, for instance, may feel additional responsibility to bring paying clients to summits and, as a result, take risks they normally might not take. Guides or other climbers may also compensate for less-experienced members on a large expedition who they deem incapable or less capable of taking care of themselves. Yet when it comes to evaluating adventurers, women are nevertheless often judged by a different standard.

A fuller examination of this bias appears in Jordan's study of the women of K2 when she contrasts ways the deaths of female and male climbers are publicly commemorated.

> In the weeks after her [Alison Hargreaves's] death climbers, columnists, and social scientists came out of the proverbial woodwork to opine about her "obsession" with climbing K2, about her being "blinkered" by summit fever, about her "selfishness" in choosing the mountain over motherhood. One of those throwing his criticism into the ring was Peter Hillary, who criticized Alison for ignoring the telltale signs of bad weather moving in. When the rebuke of the son of Sir Edmund ran worldwide, the firestorm began, causing Alison to suffer in death the indignity of having her morals and her mental health questioned in a way never suffered by the men who died with her or by the other fathers who have left children behind: Alex Lowe, Scott Fischer, Rob Hall, Paul Nunn, Al Rouse, Maurice Barrard, Nick Estcourt, and so many more.[181]

Jordan points out that where male climbers die heroic deaths—dying doing a sport they loved—women are remembered as bad mothers.

Jordan herself struggled with this realization. She eventually, though, comes to terms with the five women's lives and deaths. Jordan explains, "I finally realized that although I didn't celebrate living at that edge, I couldn't condemn these five women, or the mountains, when they themselves accepted the risks." She also states, "their choice to live and die in the mountains was one of passion, purpose, and talent, not idle arrogance or selfish whim."[182] "Passion, purpose, and talent" matches heroic masculinity's key tenets described above. While Jordan eventually realized these women should not be held to different standards than their male counterparts, the double standard remains ubiquitous.

Arlene Blum points out this same double standard in reference to a 1981 article in the July issue of *Outside*, "Has Women's Climbing Failed?"[183] Blum writes, "at the time, there was an unwritten code that when men die in the mountains, no one is blamed, even in cases of egregious negligence. Apparently the rules were different for women."[184] Heidi Howkins also notes a double standard in how she was viewed. In response to the accusation that she is "obsessed," Howkins explains, "he would call me hard instead of obsessed if I were a male, I said to myself, seething. Why is enduring a little pain considered a sign of strength for a Ukrainian or Polish man, and a sign of neurosis for an American or British woman?"[185] The gendered embodiment of risk is key: women are not only connected to the home, they are (potential) mothers.

Mothers or potential mothers that engage in risk are viewed differently than (potential) fathers. Fear of being labeled a bad mother combined with the old boys' club mentality helps account for why fewer women participate. Ellen Miller researches Everest's female summiteers, who number "a total of seventy-five as of the end of 2002"; she notes "'almost all of them did not have children when they climbed Everest.'"[186] While I was unable to find updated numbers regarding female Everest summiteers and their motherhood status, Maria Coffey notes, "over the past twenty years, the number of female rock climbers has soared. But mountaineering remains a male-dominated activity, with female climbers the caliber of Wanda Rutkiewicz and Steph Davies still a minority. Steph believes it is the mountaineering culture that turns off many women initially."[187] Thus, specific sports and their levels of risk may be more personally and socially acceptable and welcoming. Arnesen and Bancroft similarly note, "polar exploration was one of the few remaining all-boys clubs. Some men still do not want to give it up."[188] I look more closely at the gendered implications of risk in chapter 5.

A woman who risks, especially in ways that may endanger domestic stability, even today is judged much more harshly than the adventurous man. For example, when talking with fellow climber John Hall about her hepatitis diagnosis, which she was suffering from during an expedition, climber Arlene Blum recalls the sexism that framed her experience as a female climber. Hall remarked, "'When you didn't carry your share, I thought you were acting just like a woman. Now I know—'... 'Well, you have to admit that women aren't as strong as men in the mountains.'"[189] Hall's remarks reveal a biological imperative: women are not considered capable of handling the extreme environments without the help of men. His remarks are similar to those expressed by Binh about Pham's "natural" Vietnamese weakness. Of note, men are doing the policing in all of these examples: Binh of Pham, Jon Krakauer of Sandy Hill Pittman, Peter Hillary of Alison Hargreaves, and John Hall of Arlene Blum.

However, women also police themselves, sometimes holding themselves up to an extreme standard of physical endurance to prove they are not in need of being rescued. Jill Fredston reveals in *Rowing to Latitude*, for example, "yet I had a surprisingly hard time giving up the goal....I couldn't quite shake the notion that quitting equaled failure and weakness." Fredston describes Doug, her male partner, as "ever rational and remarkably skilled at separating reality from this ego." Fredston suggests her personality is different than her partner's. Ultimately, they both discover "no one cared that we hadn't reached our goal."[190] However, other women experience gendered backlash once they decide to quit. When Tori Murden McClure, the first woman to row solo across an ocean, is rescued during a hurricane by Captain Lorenson, he tells her, "'You should not have tried to do this. It is lucky that you are a woman. If you had been a man, I would not have stopped this ship to pick you up.'"[191] While he eventually warms up to her, from the captain's initial viewpoint her sex both predicts her failure and assures her rescue.

A woman's physical appearance may play just as large a role as her physical abilities in how she is viewed as an athlete, especially by fellow adventurers. For instance, Jordan discusses the challenges Chantal Mauduit faced as a climber because she was beautiful: her beauty opened her up to more critiques and also resulted in her being underestimated as a climber. Even Jordan questions whether or not Mauduit took advantage of her beauty to push the limits of her experience and skills. Jordan considers, "if Chantal had been a man, they knew she probably wouldn't have gotten a lot of the help she got. Not that a man would have been left for dead, but he wouldn't have been helped *up* past the point of his own power. Expedition gossip that Chantal was reckless spread through the climbing world, and her reputation in it continued to spiral downward."[192] Just as nature's beauty dangerously tempts the male adventurers, so too does a beautiful female on the mountain. And, as in Tori Murden McClure's case, men are obligated to assist and rescue women in ways they are not obligated to men.

As a result, excluding women from expeditions provides a means to avoid the alleged distractions and dangers—not to mention assumed additional burdens—created by female adventurers. In the words of Heidi Howkins, "my mere presence as a female on the mountain, he [an Italian climber on another team] announced to anyone who would listen, was 'ruining the group psychology' of his expedition."[193] Blum similarly explains, "in spite of my excellent qualifications, they had decided that having a woman on the team might adversely affect the 'camaraderie of the heights' and cause a problem in 'excretory situations high on the open ice.' I was being excluded only because I was a woman, and there was nothing I could do about it."[194] Blum also recalls reading in an expedition brochure, "'women are invited to join the party at base and advanced base to assist in the cooking chores. Special rates are available. They will not be admitted on the climb, however.'" The reasons given for this exclusion included: "'Women are not strong enough to carry heavy loads'.... 'And the high altitude. Women aren't emotionally stable enough to handle it.'"[195] Explicit restrictions remained through the late twentieth century in the United States.

Of note, "even American women scientists were not 'allowed' in Antarctica until 1969," as Arnesen and Bancroft remind us. Arnesen and Bancroft explain, "the arguments against the presence of women on the continent in the early 1900s had begun with predictions about the inability of 'the weaker sex' to survive the harsh conditions in Antarctica. More modern objections included the assumption that women would destabilize the male culture of the continent with cat-fighting, nagging, and sexual promiscuity. As recently as the 1970s, the 'lack of facilities' for women was enough reason for some countries to restrict or even forbid women's presence."[196] To the best of my knowledge, explicit gendered pricing and restrictions no longer exist. Yet less overt policing remains. Concerns about women's physical and mental competencies, moreover, fly in the face of the preliminary scientific data that suggests women may actually have certain advantages in extreme environments, such as high altitudes. "Although there has been almost no scientific research on the effects of high altitude on the female body," according to Jordan, "what little data there are actually indicate that women are *better* suited to the rigors of the Death Zone than their male colleagues."[197] The social construction of gender assumes women's dependence rather than their strength.

In the face of such strong opposition against female adventurers, Blum organized her own women's expedition to Annapurna and Liv Arnesen "skied to the South Pole alone simply because I couldn't find anyone to go with me. The men who were planning trips did not want a woman on their teams; and the female sport skiers I talked to were not interested in the extended camping and harsh weather of an Antarctic trip."[198] Consequently, "that slow, uphill battle to prove that women could hold their own in Antarctica explains why, incredibly, Ann and Liv's attempted traverse in 2000-2001 was a first for women."[199] Blum's Annapurna expedition accomplishments, furthermore, were tainted by a letter sent to *National Geographic* claiming the women used sexual favors and alcohol to gain men's assistance, especially from Sherpas.[200] Thus, despite their connection to alternative lifestyles, extreme sports often reinforce conservative patriarchal practices rather than welcome adventure by women and minorities, and thereby encourage traditional masculinities and femininities.

White male adventurers must also police their behavior to conform to conquering desire. For example, when Peter Nichols finds himself stranded in the Atlantic Ocean, he does not see the task ahead as becoming more feminine but more masculine. Nichols states, "I may have more than I bargained for, with the condition of my boat, but all I could have hoped for as a test. I must try to get *Toad* [the name of the boat] safely to land. I must be a man about it. I don't have to commit suicide and go down with the ship if it really sinks; I can try to save myself if the struggle ahead fails despite all my efforts."[201] To "be a man" does not involve a death wish: that is, to "commit suicide" by going down with the ship, which is required in another model of seafaring masculinity.

This form of athletic masculinity requires the endurance to make it through the test, not only by surviving but also by growing as a person: "I am sailing to meet my true self," Nichols writes, "and hoping to find an improved version. I don't want to see myself curling up again."[202] To curl up or assume a fetal position represents the opposite of this transformation into a self-actualized, individual masculinity. Agency, as opposed to feminized passivity, is masculine. As Kocour emphasized about her successful summit bid, "our survival had been a choice—the right choice."[203] Survival is an individual active choice, and, therefore, is gendered masculine. The quality of this survival—how it is obtained—and the adventure's goal beyond individual accomplishment are increasingly more important. Critiques of patriarchal and colonial goals to conquer the other mean adventurers must reframe their goals to reflect more environmentally and socially conscious objectives.

CONQUESTS FOR THE GREATER ENVIRONMENTAL GOOD: NEO-PATRIARCHAL GOALS?

Extreme adventure's risk, which brings one to the brink of death and endurance, tests individuals and rewards them, in its modern version, with the experience of "true self." Stacy Allison explains, "reaching that windswept perch, I decided, would cleanse my spirit and heal my wounds. More than that, it would send me home with a title: The First American Woman to Climb Everest."[204] Similar to Krakauer's passage that opened this chapter, Allison anticipates the summit will bring about transformation and clarity. She also expresses her desire to conquer, to come home with a title. Krakauer in *Into Thin Air* similarly points out, "the culture of ascent was characterized by intense competition and undiluted machismo, but for the most part, its constituents were concerned with impressing only one another." As a result, "getting to the top of any given mountain was considered much less important than *how* one got there."[205] As I discussed above, if a climber—male or female—summits Everest but uses supplemental oxygen and/or extensive help from Sherpas and/or expedition leaders, then that climber's accomplishment is not viewed the same as one who climbs more "purely." Just like the distinctions made in surfing mentioned at the outset of this chapter, extreme athletes insist on elite status as an important marker of authenticity.[206]

The intense focus on individual ability, responsibility, and transformation is connected to extreme adventure's decreasing use as a technique of national soft power. All extreme sports have largely—at least in an American context—shifted from national projects to individual feats. According to Graham Bowley, "in the modern mountaineering age, the Western expeditions no longer climbed for their country—that belonged to a different, old-fashioned era. Their teams were sometimes organized along national lines but more than ever they were a loose multinational collection of friends."[207] Even Crouch, who uses conquering desire throughout his narrative to frame his encounter with nature, finds national feats "meaningless" in the current climate of extreme adventure. Crouch complains, "the first American ascent of this, the first British ascent of that, those strike me as meaningless distinctions. Nationalism is one of the stupidest forces in mountaineering."[208] Gone are the days when one conquered a peak, river, or territory for country. Maria Coffey notes, in *Where the Mountain Casts its Shadow*, "with all the great peaks of the world claimed, the days of climbing mountains for the sake of one's country are largely over, but mountaineers continue to be celebrated." Coffey summarizes the honors bestowed on various contemporary climbers and then asks, "what is it about mountain climbing that transforms a fundamentally useless, selfish activity into a heroic act?"[209]

The language and goal of conquest remains. Climber Lynn Hill reflects on the residual conquering language in her autobiography: "Certainly we do not 'conquer' anything by climbing to the top of a rock or peak. Perhaps forty or a hundred years ago getting to the top of a mountain and surviving the harsh conditions of the alpine environment was perceived as a triumph of man against nature. Today modern technology and extensive exploration of nearly every corner of the earth has changed our interaction with the world, but it seems that the spirit that drives us to search remains the same."[210] Hill suggests that technology combined with the lack of unexplored territory has made extreme sports less dangerous and, as a result, less about "a triumph of man against nature." Heidi Howkins clarifies, "adventures today are about exploring the unpredictable, not the unknown."[211] The declining appeal of national claims and lack of unconquered, unknown territory means adventurers must repeat or find original routes to justify their expeditions. They devise new, purer, and/or riskier methods to complete old accomplishments. In this way, an equally powerful conquering desire to be an innovator, or accomplish a feat in new or record fashion, is replacing national accomplishment.

Perhaps uncomfortable with purely "useless," selfish pursuits, adventurers also increasingly connect the expedition's goals with larger, educational purposes, such as raising environmental awareness or building self-esteem among children. Ann Bancroft, for example, emphasizes the desire to make history and a difference: "I didn't just want to make history as the first two women to cross the continent; I wanted to do my bit to change the world, too."[212] Bancroft references an online curriculum developed for school children about pursing their dreams. The curriculum was key for Bancroft's participation: "The emptiness came from not having a full purpose beyond my own ambition. That's when I swore that if I ever did another expedition, I would figure out a way to bring the kids with me."[213] Similarly, the French-born long-distance swimmer Benoît Lecomte, who now calls Texas home, swam across the Atlantic Ocean to raise money for cancer research (1998) and dedicated his Pacific Ocean swim (2018) to ocean pollution. Making a difference provides an altruistic narrative frame for the otherwise selfishly ambitious endeavor.

Some adventurers use making a difference as part of their extreme physical challenge as well as narrative frame. For example, Rob Greenfield's *Dude Making a Difference: Bamboo Bikes, Dumpster Dives and Other Extreme Adventures across America* tells the story of his "off the grid" 4,700-mile bicycle ride across the United States.[214] He set a goal to raise ten thousand dollars to benefit several charities focused on environmental sustainability, donates a hundred percent of his book proceeds to "One Percent for the Planet nonprofits," and has "vowed to donate 90 percent of my earnings from media to good causes and to keep no more than $15,000 per year for myself."[215] Ken Ilgunas similarly hiked the Keystone XL Pipeline to raise awareness about global warming. While the hike failed to stop the pipeline or climate change, "the trip helped bring more awareness of the XL to a few people who otherwise wouldn't have become acquainted with it."[216] Planning, execution, and activities beyond the adventure itself combine extreme sustainable living and adventure in order to achieve social and/or environmental justice.

Connecting expeditions to a purpose or purposes beyond individual ambition, as Maria Coffey points out in *Where the Mountain Casts its Shadow*, is not only key for the athletes but also for the sponsors. Coffey explains, "the corporate world, eager to maintain the efficiency and enthusiasm of their employees, has created yet another type of hero—the motivating mountaineer."[217] The modern adventurer inspires individuals to pursue their dreams: as Tania Aebi tells us, "I was giving a few people the inspiration that if I, a complete ninny, could do this [sail around the world solo at eighteen] and survive, someday they could live out their dreams, too."[218] Sponsors profit from their adventurous role models. Greenfield thanks a range of corporate, individual, and nonprofit sponsors in his acknowledgments.[219] Sponsors hitch along, "trusting" Greenfield "to represent [their] organization and...supplying...gear to spread the message of sustainability."[220] The conquering of an altruistic goal alongside the successful completion of an adventure offers a new spin on the hero's path, even as adventurers retrace expeditions.

CONQUERING HEROIC AMERICAN DREAMS

Hegemonic heroic masculinity survives, in part, because it is entwined with American identity's mythological essence. Hypermasculinity cannot be underestimated because, as Elizabeth Gilbert explains, it keeps the American dream alive. This mythological and historical frontier narrative, moreover, requires women's subordinate role, demanding they keep the home fires burning. Gilbert notes, "women are for rescuing and also for tipping your hat to as you ride off into the sunset without them."[221] Distinct gender roles play a vital part in keeping the American dream alive. Furthermore, those women and nonwhite males that jump a horse and ride off into the sunset often do more to perpetuate the myths than to complicate this history.

Conquering desire presents a fantasy about masculinity, which is, in turn, a fantasy about America. Conquering desires, as a result, remain because adrenaline narratives rehearse the familiar notes necessary to keep the myth alive. According to Coffey, "despite the cost, society needs its risk takers, those who dare to make huge leaps into the unknown, stretching the imagination of the time beyond its previous limits.... Extreme climbers venture to the edge of existence, discovering new physical, mental and spiritual territories. Their mythic stories give us a window into our deepest concerns and point toward the potential of human experience. They tap into what Joseph Campbell calls 'the inconvenient or resisted psychological powers that we have not thought or dared to integrate into our lives.'"[222] Patriarchal heroism demands that masculine power trump feminine weakness: "And the frontier vocabulary has outlived our actual frontier," according to Gilbert, "because we've based our American masculine identity on that brief age of exploration and romantic independence and westward settlement."[223] Adrenaline narratives indicate the extreme challenge to shift adventure's, America's, and masculinity's fundamentally connected structures.

Addressing the question about whether or not encounters with nature are always already framed according to conquering desires, Crouch explains that a climber generally describes nature in one of two ways:

> Climbing discussions usually fall into one of two camps: the one of conquests and triumphs, and the one of harmony with the natural world. The truth, like most truths, lies between. In the conquest and triumph stories, you almost expect a brass band to appear as the heroes approach the summit. I've never felt that kind of climax. Satisfaction grows as my fear and agony fade with time. And as for climbers always moving in a constant state of harmony with the alpine world, it may tell well, but it happens like that for me only in a few exceptional moments. My truth allows me moments when I soar, and a lot of trench warfare in-between.[224]

Crouch suggests that Krakauer's summit description that opened this chapter is truer than what other accounts may lead us to believe. He further emphasizes that the adventurer rarely experiences a heroic conquering, nor does s/he feel complete harmony.

The truth conquering representations must also contend with is that such desires for and of the land threaten the environment in, if not unprecedented, then certainty increasingly irreversible ways. As Miranda Weiss writes about Alaska, "people who are paying attention say that these desires—for money, oil, gold, and a life away from it all—are threatening Alaska as it has never been threatened before. Our hankerings make us restless—so we move often; our ambitions transform the land and sea. Today, Alaska is warming, melting, and shrinking."[225] The conquering desires Weiss identifies, "for money, gold, and a life away from it all," extract natural resources in the pursuit of individual "hankerings." The consequences of these desires—"warming, melting, and shrinking"—are already impacting the land. It is only a matter of time before "the riches we've come to depend on here" disappear.[226] This realization troubles contemporary representations of nature—often limiting a full or unequivocal expression of conquering desire. In contrast, the connected desire for more—for some larger meaning to be extracted from risk, suffering, and destruction—forms the heart of spiritual desire, the next representation of nature under discussion.

CHAPTER 3

SPIRITUAL

NATURES

Taking a moment to counter the argument that people who climb mountains are simply "adrenaline junkies," Jon Krakauer in *Into Thin Air* emphasizes mountain climbing's physical and mental tedium, likening it to a "Calvinistic undertaking": "I quickly came to understand that climbing Everest was primarily about enduring pain. And in subjecting ourselves to week after week of toil, tedium, and suffering, it struck me that most of us were probably seeking, above all else, something like a state of grace."[1] Like a religious ascetic, Krakauer argues the bodily punishment and endurance required in climbing are forms of discipline and zealous penance that result in transcendence. Furthermore, Krakauer explains in the introduction that writing his narrative was "an act of catharsis."[2] The passages from Krakauer suggest the religious or spiritual tone often found in nature and travel writing pervades adrenaline narratives as well. Maria Coffey contends that "reaching a spiritual state of being is the principal lure of extreme adventure."[3] Extreme nature often elicits some form of piety even among agnostic travelers.

The spiritual natures found in adrenaline narratives include themes that connect physical and mental endurance with personal transformation as well as a pilgrimage structure, which frequently organizes the adrenaline narrative's plot. Epiphany, furthermore, often plays a key role in the adventurer's internal quest. Spirituality thus refers to a continuum that includes, in some instances, specific (organized) religious beliefs held by the adventurer as well as a secular reverence for nature. The qualities Bron Taylor describes as foundational to "dark green religion" are shared by the "dark green" spiritual nature adrenaline adventurers seek and describe: each "considers nature to be sacred, imbued with intrinsic value, and worthy of reverent care."[4] Extreme spiritual nature also has a "shadow side" that "might mislead and deceive; it could even precipitate or exacerbate violence."[5] Extreme spiritual odysseys, as a result, may be seen to objectify nature in ecologically suspect ways.

Personal transformation, in such cases, trumps trespass over ecologically sensitive terrain. This view furthers Lynn White's controversial thesis that Western religions—or, in this case, green spiritualities—have played a key role in the environment's destruction. They also tap into, as Dorceta E. Taylor points out, fundamental American ideas. Taylor explains, "transcendentalists placed a premium on individual autonomy and freedom. They also believed the best route to social reform was through individual or personal reform."[6] Likewise, spiritual desire in adrenaline narratives heightens attention to sublime landscapes to facilitate personal transformation. Spiritual desire may focus on divinity, emphasizing its transcendental roots, or it may, in the romantic tradition, focus more on strong emotion as a guiding principle. Adventurous spirituality may also appropriate the religions of Indigenous, non-Western peoples, who—as Bron Taylor notes—are often perceived as being "socially and ecologically superior to 'civilized' peoples and from whom civilized people [have] much to learn."[7] Such appropriations may further (post)colonial practices and connect with conquering desire or, on the other hand, facilitate greater cultural and environmental understanding and connection with erotic desire. Adrenaline narratives suggest that spiritual connections with nature can have profoundly positive impacts, for the individual adventurer as well as a larger audience and the environment: "it could be argued that one of the most powerful forces for cultural and values change is spirituality."[8] Adventurers, for example, often shun, if not altogether eliminate, disposable consumer culture and use their narratives to promote awareness of environmental destruction and its consequences.

These contradictions and appropriations further suggest, to use Jane Jacobs's term, a "schizophrenic" relationship with the natural world.[9] They articulate a desire to exploit *and* to protect the natural environment as well as its inhabitants. This contradictory quality forms the essence of the adrenaline narrative's spiritual representations and reveals spirituality's indelible power within the American environmental imagination. To explore the adrenaline narrative's spiritual natures, this chapter first outlines their pilgrimage structure and then follows with an analysis of their use of epiphany, sacred language, and sublime settings. The chapter concludes by examining how pollution (literal and figurative) impacts spiritual desire.

EXTREME PILGRIMAGES: SEEKING HIGHER GROUND

A pilgrimage is a devout and frequently arduous journey. Gregory Crouch explicitly describes each visit to Patagonia as a pilgrimage: "Seven times I've made the pilgrimage. And I will go back, for the times that I spend in those mountains are the most charged moments of my life. In the mountains, life sings. Normal life can be such drudgery; little seems important. But in the mountains, all is different, for the alpine life is a life of consequence."[10] Crouch's description suggests that, while each journey is unique, the "Everyman" chronicler shapes his or her extraordinary and transformative adventures in order to make his or her rite of passage a shared transformative experience with the reader. This translation by the writer-adventurer as pilgrim to his/her reader is key. The adventure makes lives of "consequence" possible: heightening the meaning and, at times, life-or-death consequences of even small choices and actions. The reader by extension experiences at least a shadow of this catharsis as he or she reexperiences the adventure through the narrator's description. Extreme pilgrimages combine vicarious connection with nature, adventure, and personal transformation for a population increasingly disconnected both spiritually and materially from nature.

Adventurers often describe two journeys: one external and another internal. For example, Stacy Allison, the first American woman to climb Everest, focuses on her "internal adventure." For Allison, the desire to climb mountains is best expressed in psychological and spiritual terms; she seeks self-knowledge. Allison reveals, "climbing has always been more than a physical pursuit for me. Each mountain I face is another pinnacle in an internal adventure. An exploration of myself, an expression of my spirit."[11] In fact, an abusive husband contributed to Allison's decision to climb Everest. She explains, "when my life turned sour, the tip of Everest gained significance.... Reaching the windswept perch, I decided, would cleanse my spirit and heal my wounds. More than that, it would send me home with a title: The First American Woman to Climb Everest."[12] Allison's internal journey promises both spiritual catharsis and a conquering title. The title's healing prestige connects conquering and spiritual desires.

Numerous other adventurers mention some form of internal journey or transformation as a result of their involvement with extreme sports. Rock climber Lynn Hill, for example, notes "climbing is a form of exploration that inspires me to confront my own inner nature within nature."[13] Hill connects her inner self or "nature" with her outer environment. Likewise, Jennifer Hahn connects her internal and external journeys: "It is the story of my own inside passage amid the animals, plants, people, and oceanography of the Inside Passage. I set out on this journey and no other because I wanted to live in nature. I wanted the ocean, tides, trees, and sea stars to be my teachers."[14] Hahn emphasizes how nature will teach her what her formal university education could not. She writes, "I'd done my time at a university studying natural history and ecology, and now I wanted to have rooted, winged, furred and feathered teachers. I wanted to live wildly, to be an apprentice to the ocean."[15] The nature apprenticeship is key to the next stage in her education and discovering her "own inside passage." Additionally, a friend reminds Hahn, "your journey isn't about miles. It's about learning to love yourself out there...to accept help when you need it."[16] Additionally, Hahn's friend Whitebear, by emphasizing that the physical miles are less significant than her interior growth and that she will likely require assistance in some form, implicitly advocates against traditional heroic masculinity, which would demand Hahn not ask for help. Self-discovery, specifically "a reminder to love yourself," rather than conquest sets Hahn "on a new path."[17]

As the above examples suggest, self-discovery has replaced, to a certain extent, the traditional, patriarchal, conquering role of physical exploration and discovery in the modern adventure narrative. Ann Bancroft, for example, explains that she skied across Antarctica both as a result of historical inspiration and for the chance to "journey inside": Ernest Shackleton's "inspiring drama, played out decades ago on this frigid, icy stage, had led me to seek out the same path—not to explore, as this continent was discovered long ago—but to journey inside myself. To see what I had to offer in this incredible test of mental strength and physical skill."[18] Like a religious pilgrimage, extreme adventure uses physical challenges as tests and a route for inner discovery.[19]

The internal journey is not often linear: adventurers describe roadblocks, backtracks, surprise turns in the road, and repeated patterns of self-discovery. Ruth Anne Kocour describes her journey for self-knowledge as circular.

> To paraphrase T. S. Eliot, no matter how much time I spend exploring faraway places, the result will be to end up where I started, at the beginning, seeing my life with new understanding. That, for me, sums up the worth of the pursuit of rarefied air and mountain summits. As hard as the experience gets, it's never just the summit. It's each step along the way and the sights seen and the lessons learned that make the ten minutes on the summit so special. Yet even without the summit, other, "internal" summits are climbed, so in many ways, mountaineering is, for me, more about the journey than anything else.[20]

While the title of her book might initially appear to suggest otherwise—*Facing the Extreme: One Woman's Tale of True Courage, Death-Defying Survival and Her Quest for the Summit*—Kocour insists on process over result. She is, after all, on a "*quest* for the summit" and not simply peak bagging. She also hints in the title that the summit may be a psychological (an internal journey requiring "true courage") as well as a physical (external) challenge.

Kocour's "true courage" is one that results in greater personal understanding, connecting risk and personal transformation. Furthermore, the title and the above passage highlight the quest or journey rather than a successful or failed summit bid. Kocour also hints that returning back to her life (coming back alive) is more important than reaching the summit. Nevertheless, Kocour writes, "as miserable as we felt at this moment, to me, the summit offered essential meaning to our effort. Without the summit, what we had experienced and were experiencing now would be nothing more than an exercise in futility."[21] She later clarifies, "'Climbing and summiting are two entirely different things'.... There is no way you can ever equate the destination with the journey. Both are important, but both are also different."[22] Whether the adventurer stresses the goal or the journey offers insight into whether their approach is primarily conquering or spiritual or a combination of both.

For many adventurers, a continuous tension exists between the journey (process) and the successful bid for the destination or goal. Kocour recognizes this, too, emphasizing that this view requires a shift from conquering to spiritual desire. She explains, "at its best, high-elevation mountaineering offers accomplishment for the sake of growth as well as sport without competition where the concept of winning doesn't necessarily mean coming in first. The mountain becomes the means to improve the person, which works so long as the person involved doesn't have deluded ideas about 'conquering' the mountain."[23] To this end, knowing when to push on and when to turn back is key and is as much about the mental journey as it is about a physical one. Kocour stresses spiritual desire over "conquering." Of course, sometimes adventurers do not have the choice simply to turn back in order to survive. Rather than conquering a mountain, such adventurers may also depict their suffering as key to their individual transformations.

Rock climber Aron Ralston, who cut off his own arm to order to save his life, provides a defense of extreme sport's higher calling and, like Kocour, advances a spiritual rhetoric instead of a conquering one. Like Krakauer, Ralston counters accusations of brute adrenaline with controlled "cathartic suffering."

> I think some people would consider these the thoughts of an adrenaline junkie, but I relished more the *control* of my adrenaline than the ride it would give me if I unleashed it.... I pushed my limits for endurance, engaging in prolonged experiences of cathartic suffering to break down my interior walls, to cleanse my spirit for purer emotions than boredom or stress, and to surpass myself. Periodically, I would have a euphoric realization taking me beyond the filters of my brain, in which I understood that the fear and the pain existed only in the gap between a pair of neurons. I called it getting over myself.[24]

Both Krakauer and Ralston emphasize how extreme adventure's physical challenges result in individual transformative purification. Rather than offer an ego trip, risky adventure allows the athlete-esthete to "get over" him- or herself. This mental or emotional pursuit requires physical discomfort. In Heidi Howkins's words, "in our quest for physical comfort, we often neglect our spiritual need to honestly and openly confront both our own mortality and the fragility of our world."[25] In this sense, the ends justify the means. The adventurers emphasize how physical challenge in nature tones the body, mind, and spirit.

Similarly, rower Jill Fredston describes her sport as something more than a mere profession. Fredston maintains, "wilderness rowing is far more than sport to me; it has been a conduit to knowing and trusting myself. It is my way of being, of thinking, of seeing. My rowing has taken me north and pushed me to explore my own horizons. In the process, rowing has evolved from something I do to some way that I am."[26] The idea of extreme sports as a calling and way of life also likens adventure to religious-spiritual experience. Adrenaline narratives generally reserve this spiritual experience for the primary, active adventurers. While the individual adventurer remains the main focus, Arnesen and Bancroft also emphasize that their expedition support team experienced a "personal internal journey."[27] Likewise, readers may also benefit through their oblique engagement with the physical and spiritual narrative. Thus, direct and indirect participants in the adventure can experience its transformative benefits.

The adventurers also emphasize that the physically arduous journey is as important as, if not more important than, the actual destination or the successful completion of the goal. Runner Cami Ostman notes that she "needed a quest." She describes how "some women climb mountains" and others travel to "sacred sites" or view "important works of art."[28] For Ostman, running a marathon on seven continents becomes her "midlife quest." In doing so, she comes "face-to-face with my inner self," which includes her "Inner Wisdom" and "Inner Bitch."[29] Her "spiritual quest was meant to be punctuated by trials."[30] The physical act of running provides her with "a natural way to do personal-growth work."[31] Ruth Anne Kocour also describes her near-death experience on Denali as "a necessary rite of passage, a collection of lessons that would equip me for every day of the rest of my life."[32] For Kocour, "the mountain was God, and I would carry this moment forever." The mountain provides religious experience, setting, and instruction: "Almost as suddenly as the silence had fallen over us, like a call to prayer, we snapped out of it and our little mountain congregation began to minister among ourselves."[33] The mountain is God and church. Furthermore, as a result of her experience, Kocour "felt an integral part of nature and all its elements. I had begun to feel whole and complete as never before."[34] Sustained physical challenge connects the adventurer to a godlike nature and offers a transformative perspective that outlasts exploring a risky environment.

In some cases, the description of the physical journey shifts from conquering to spiritual desire. For example, Tori Murden McClure in *A Pearl in the Storm* initially embarks on her extreme adventure to cure herself of "helplessness." Her journey initially adopted a conquering understanding, which demanded that she conquer nature/her own weakness as a means to transform herself. McClure explains, "in the beginning, I thought I could not be worthy of love until I had beaten helplessness."[35] Interestingly, McClure feels the opposite of McCairen, who I discussed in chapter 2. McCairen, recall, identified helplessness as key to her feminine attractiveness. She thinks, "that's the catch. I want autonomy, but if I achieve it, I fear I'll be unlovable."[36] While the women view helplessness differently in terms of being loved by men, both women identify conquering helplessness as key to their journey's success.

By the end of her journey, McClure has learned that vulnerability is key to humanity. She reveals, "in the end, I learned that my humanity is grounded in helplessness, and it is that very humanity that makes me lovable. I had expected to find enlightenment with my head, and in the end, I found all the enlightenment I need in my heart."[37] By opening her heart rather than focusing solely on logic, McClure finds "enlightenment." McClure also implicitly challenges gendered assumptions about helplessness. Rather than identify helplessness with femininity and weakness, McClure recognizes that vulnerability is shared by all humanity. In this way, the spiritual journey is distinct from the conquering one because of its emphasis on personal transformation rather than conquering nature or achieving fame or fortune.

Yet sometimes the line between conquering and spiritual desire is difficult to find. Julie Rak discusses, for example, adventure's (patriarchal) homosocial aspects in relation to the 1950 Annapurna climb by a French team. Rak states, "although he [Maurice Herzog] ostensibly talks about leadership and duty, his rhetoric of sacrifice and his reference to the trust between men makes the moment homosocial, giving it spiritual overtones and establishing an emotional basis for the relationship between men which exceeds ordinary friendship."[38] Rak suggests that the spiritual acts as a beard for homosocial desire. Male adventurers may use spiritual desire toward nature to express same-sex close friendships. This desire for male bonding may also help explain some men's reluctance to have women on expeditions and vice-versa: same-sex spaces can nurture homosocial desire's intense camaraderie. Nature—rather than the opposite sex—becomes the shared love or object of desire, but the action remains focused on the relationships built and shared among the adventurers.

One succinct way of distinguishing conquering and spiritual journeys is to draw upon the difference between seekers and explorers. Alvah Simon describes Knud Rasmussen and Peter Freuchen as seekers rather than explorers: "They were seekers, and that is a different thing. They sought that spot from which in every direction lay one of the essentials of self-knowledge—uncertainty."[39] Explorers are patriarchal (conquering) whereas seekers are spiritual. Jill Fredston's description of her spiritual journeys further explains the difference. Fredston posits, "our journeys are food for our spirits, clean air for our souls. We don't care if they are firsts or farthest; we don't seek sponsors. They are neither a vacation nor an escape, they are a way of life."[40] The "pure" adventure Fredston describes, however, cannot be completely separated from the heroic masculinity discussed in chapter 2. Fredston's language encompasses spiritual and conquering desires: the journey is "food" for "our spirits,...our souls" and the "pure" mode of her adventure, which eschews corporate sponsors or any taint of commercialism, connects it to an elite heroic masculinity as well as a minimalist, spiritual "way of life."

Notably, many of the adventurers quoted thus far have been female. So prevalent is the stereotype and the narrative that *The Onion* recently spoofed it in the article "Woman's Solo Hiking Trip Shockingly Doesn't Have to Do with Inner Journey or Anything."[41] Perhaps women emphasize their internal adventures in their adrenaline narratives because "it would have been easier to follow the thread of the hero path if I'd been born male."[42] McClure goes on to explain, "where men tend to be defined by their actions, women tend to be defined by their relationships. It is perfectly acceptable for a woman to follow her husband into the unknown.... When these women suffered, we saw them as victims of circumstance, innocent victims. I wouldn't be a victim of circumstance. I chose my circumstances, and because that choice was deliberate, I could never be innocent."[43] McClure connects adventure with a fall from innocence for women: conscious choice means that a woman is judged for her actions in ways that women who follow men are exempt. And, as I discussed in the previous chapter, to the extent that adventure is gendered male, women must find different narrative routes or cease being "women."

However, women are not the only ones who use adventure as a form of spiritual therapy. Steven Callahan asserts that his "survival voyage" provided "insights into myself, but it also gave me the opportunity to embrace humanity despite its weaknesses and to forge new and meaningful relationships."[44] Peter Nichols embarks on a solo journey across the Atlantic in a wooden boat after the disintegration of his marriage: "I knew this would make me feel better about myself."[45] Nichols writes earlier, "but I am here at last. Not just sailing across the ocean to get to the other side, to Maine to sell the boat, as I originally set out to do; nor alone for lack of crew. I am sailing to meet my true self, and hoping to find an improved version."[46] Like the women cited above, Nichols views adventure as a means of personal transformation: the adventure "would make me feel better about myself" and provides a means "to find an improved version" of himself. The "true self" he seeks has been lost and adventure is a means to find it. Adjusting to sailing without his wife becomes an extended metaphor in *Sea Change* for learning to live without her.

However, unlike the women, who do not liken adventure to a test to prove their womanhood, Nichols also describes the adventure as a test of his manhood: "I must be a man about it."[47] Crouch, likewise, sees adventure as a test of his manhood. Crouch writes that if he "were more of a man," he would ask for "wild, insecure moments when fear has the bile up in my throat," but he does not "have the courage to ask for those moments": "But I know that I am the best man I can ever hope to be in precisely those moments of maximum fear and doubt." As a result, Crouch desires a continuous test. He confesses, "my secret desire is to be locked forever onto the cutting edge of an ascent."[48] In language that echoes the violent transformations found in the writings of Flannery O'Connor, Crouch attests to a goodness that might result when, as one of O'Connor's characters puts it, "if it had been [i.e., if there had been] somebody there to shoot her every minute of her life."[49] Only the constant threat of violence produces "the best man."[50]

Thus, the hero narrative often becomes an inextricable part of the spiritual narrative in men's adrenaline narratives. We see this in Alvah Simon's *North to the Night: A Spiritual Odyssey in the Arctic* as well. Simon must cope without his wife Diana when she leaves Tay Bay in the Arctic to care for her ailing father. While Simon does not want her to leave, the circumstances also mean the "hard adventure" he "had prayed for" was finally coming true. Isolation assures that the "hardness in its final degree could be granted...only by removing the comfort and support of Diana."[51] Cindy Ross emphasizes that the landscape barren of human inhabitation also taps into the "heaven...inside me and all of us," but she is able to come to this realization with her family in tow.[52] While both male and female authors construct their adventures in nature as the cure to their personal difficulties and as a means of personal transformation, male authors more often explicitly gender this transformation as becoming more of a man. This "hardness" is contrasted with the feminine, and, in Simon's case, specifically with the comforts of home that his wife provides and represents.

SECULAR SACRED EPIPHANIES

Ideally these adventures, like ritual or pilgrimage, initiate the participants into a better mental state, often marked by an epiphany. Nature, as we have begun to see, facilitates this spiritual work. Like Allison and Nichols, rafter Patricia McCairen seeks solace from her personal problems in nature: "The need to resolve the unresolvable questions of my life is what drives me into this vast canyon. And into my soul."[53] Throughout her book, McCairen articulates her desire for love and acceptance. Just as climbing Everest represents an internal journey for Allison, rafting the Colorado is a spiritual trip for McCairen: her "home of [the] soul" is on the river.[54] In fact, reborn on the river, she names her alter ego "Babe."[55] A shared notion of shattering the self as a means of cleansing also forms a key similarity with Jon Krakauer's spiritual discourse in *Into Thin Air*.

Danger is key to this particular iteration of spiritual transformation and the force that initiates epiphany. Jarid Manos, for example, describes such a journey and connects it to "ancient lore." Manos explains, "a plainsman or plainswoman is ultimately someone who embarks on a physical and/or spiritual journey marked by challenges, treachery, potential danger and uncertain outcome. At journey's end, one hopefully is wiser, strongerhearted, changed, different. This kind of journey has its roots in the most ancient lore of humankind."[56] Manos suggests that extreme adventure's roots lie deep in pilgrimage and its expected epiphany.

More closely appraising how the authors cope with fear further reveals how epiphany functions in these texts. As described above, emotional catharsis results from the adventure's painful physical and emotional demands. Barthes's use of *jouissance*—as a violent encounter that rips and shatters the ego—seems an especially accurate description of the extreme adventurer's spiritual catharsis.[57] The desire/fear element of *jouissance* often frames the adventurer's relationship with nature. Drunk and exhausted, bicycling adventurer Andrew Pham wonders "whether my journey is a pilgrimage or a farce."[58] Earlier in his narrative Pham explains, "touring solo on a bicycle, I discover, is an act of stupidity or an act of divine belief. It is intense stretches of isolation punctuated with flashes of pure terror and indelible moments of friendship. Mostly, it is dirty work particularly suitable for the stubborn masochist."[59] While Pham expresses doubt in this passage about his journey's larger significance, overcoming such moments of doubt and intense fear ultimately results in empowerment for the author.

McCairen, likewise, begins her account with a fearful encounter with nature as she scrambles up a canyon ledge. "A crippling fear" renders McCairen momentarily frozen on a small ledge. McCairen describes how she felt at the moment when she finally reaches safe ground: "Barely daring to breathe, I inch forward until I'm on flat, solid rock slabs twenty feet wide. Tears flood my eyes and for a moment I cry, each sob releasing the terror I had known only a moment before."[60] The theme of her willful rejection of security and the fear she must encounter to do so runs throughout McCairen's account. For example, she overcomes her anxieties about quitting her job to move west and become a raft guide. McCairen also confronts her fears about rafting solo. Her actions exact a certain amount of mental and physical pain in exchange for pleasure and self-actualization.

McCairen's frightening experiences, following Barthes's use of *jouis-*

sance, shatter her ego and eventually produce spiritual catharsis. For instance, McCairen says, "I questioned my sanity, my ability, my ego.... How much of my ego was tied up in doing this trip? Was even part of my decision based on wanting the approval of others?...I could lose my life."[61] Overcoming such moments of intense fear ultimately results in empowerment for McCairen. At the conclusion of *Canyon Solitude*, she remarks, "life is very much like a river trip. Some days I'll have perfect runs, and other days I'll eddy out and flounder around in murky water before continuing on downstream. But unlike in the past, now *I'm* the one at the oars."[62] The process of shattering and healing her ego creates a stronger person. Stacy Allison comes to a similar conclusion at the end of *Beyond the Limits*. Successfully climbing Everest serves as Allison's touchstone. She affirms, "It's a reminder, a challenge, from the highest spot on the world. *Look beyond the ordinary. There's always something more*. As long as I remember that, I know anything is possible."[63] Like McCairen, Allison feels empowered at her adventure's conclusion. Presumably, their readers share in this pleasure.

Jon Krakauer, notably, does not initially fear and agonize about his desire for dangerous adventure. Krakauer admits, "I knew that Everest had killed more than 130 people since the British first visited the mountain in 1921...But boyhood dreams die hard, I discovered, and good sense be damned....I said yes [to climbing Everest] without even pausing to catch my breath."[64] After the tragedy, and as he attempts to come to terms with his own role in the events, Krakauer describes the emotional toll: "The stain this has left on my psyche is not the sort of thing that washes off after a few months of grief and guilt-ridden self-reproach."[65] The 1996 Everest tragedy prevented the journey from fulfilling its ritual, cleansing goal. Unlike Allison, as a result, Krakauer leaves the mountain less secure than when he started. Despite its failure to fulfill conscious or unconscious positive ritual desires, *Into Thin Air* became a phenomenal best seller. In this instance, the armchair adventurers' reward may come from an affirmation of their superior intelligence for never actually attempting such a feat of excessive proportions. Or perhaps, just as writing ultimately proves cathartic for Krakauer, so does reading for the armchair adventurer.[66]

While danger is not necessarily part of the religious definition of pilgrimage or epiphany, pilgrimage's denotation of a long journey and its connotations of sacrifice imply a certain amount of physical discomfort. Joe Kane, for instance, emphasizes the role fear plays to focus attention and heighten spiritual awareness. Kane explains, "we were scared and tired, but those emotions concentrated our attention, told us that we were in a sacred place, a place untouched by humans and perhaps, until then, unseen."[67] Fear opens the adventurer to transformation and knowledge. The possibility that they are the first humans to visit this place also heightens the location's sacred nature. Implied here is that the location is unspoiled by humans. What is interesting about mountaineering narratives or any narrative that valorizes the equivalent of a "first ascent" is that those places often maintain their iconic status. Everest, as the highest point on earth, has this quality in spades. Thus, as Susan Birrell writes, "once 'conquered,' Everest took on an almost transcendent quality."[68] That is, the peak maintains "its iconic status as the ultimate symbol of aspiration and achievement."[69] Everest's status as the globe's tallest mountain above sea level guarantees at least a certain level of authenticity and prestige, despite the commercial climbing industry that has developed around it.

While not all adventurers insist on such extreme isolation, danger, and violence to achieve spiritual transformation, epiphany does come with a cost. Eddy Harris, for example, needed to confront his own mortality—be ready to die—in order to reap this benefit. Harris realizes, "and then I know what it is, what it has been, what it will be forever. If I want to live, if I want to live free and soar high in search of the glory, I have to be ready to die."[70] Without such risk or testing, there is no reward. As a result of his experiences, Harris undergoes spiritual transformation. He affirms, "the river has helped me to improve my soul, and that is everything to me."[71] In the words of Edward Abbey from *A Voice Crying in the Wilderness*, "the fear of death follows from the fear of life. A man who lives fully is prepared to die at any time."[72] Death attunes the adventurer to life, making him or her feel more alive than if s/he were following a less risky path.

Likewise, mountaineer Gregory Crouch emphasizes the active physical and spiritual work involved. Crouch describes a mountain in the Patagonian landscape as "ris[ing] dark and silver into the night, tall and proud like a god."[73] Notably, Crouch is also quick to point out, "but there is no great spiritual revelation that automatically goes along with the view."[74] Connection with god/nature requires more than simply enjoying a panoramic view. Cindy Ross explains why passive viewing is not enough: "I look down... and realize that heaven is under my feet as well as over my head. It's inside me and all of us. This is one of the reasons I have come to love the Great Divide Basin, with all its harshness and desolation. It has made me feel. A place this big and open and devoid of man-made things rips your heart wide open—for there is no place to hide—and then fills it back up with hope."[75] Experiencing "harshness and desolation" is what makes Ross "feel." Harris, Crouch, Callahan, and Ross, like other extreme adventurers who use spiritual rhetoric, emphasize that one must suffer in these "rip-your-heart-open, no-place-to-hide" landscapes to reap the full benefits of spiritual awakening and transformation. Thus, wilderness as the site for spiritual transformation must be coupled with a rite of passage to achieve successful spiritual transformation.

Once again, the adventurers emphasize that mindless risk or, in Alvah Simon's words, "a stunt" is not the goal. Rather, a studied risk produces the correct conditions. In this vein, Simon admits his "life was shaped by two distinct yet converging forces: a compulsive, even obsessive need to test myself, and a profound love of the natural world."[76] Simon clarifies that for this adventure in the Arctic he was "looking for a study, not a stunt.... The truth is that this was just a deeply personal adventure."[77] Lucy Jane Bledsoe similarly wonders if "climbing a mountain is nothing more than an act of worship" that results in "pure awe."[78] "Worship," in Simon's words, is a spiritual "study" rather than a "stunt." The "shocking tithe," as Lynn Schooler points out, often includes death.[79] These two features—studied risk and personal transformation—form spiritual nature's crux in adrenaline narratives. Risk initiates epiphany.

Calculation and control as well as awe all play a role in spiritual desire's epiphanies as well as their sublime settings, which I will discuss shortly. Where in English we refer to this feeling as the sublime, James Campbell explains that "the Inupiat, of Alaska's harsh Arctic coast, have a word to express the duality [of beauty and fear]: *uniari*, 'nervous awe.' The Tununirmiut of Baffin Bay call it *ilira*, and distinguish between it and the raw fear—*kappia*—that one might feel if he or she were thrown from a canoe into an icy Arctic river."[80] While some armchair adventurers may question extreme athletes' logic and mental sanity, as Berman and other extreme athletes underscore, "I'm not interested in killing myself, so for me it has to be a calculated risk" with equally calculated rewards.[81] While for some, epiphany is a secular feeling and experience, for others come realizations like "God rapidly was becoming more real" and "Nature is where I felt most connected to God."[82] Calculated risk brings such adventurers closer to God.

Ruth Anne Kocour describes how her acquaintance with danger produces liberation rather than constraint. Kocour emphasizes her own ability to control rather than a specific higher power. Kocour explains, "my experience on Denali bestowed on me a familiarity with death. I knew its face, its habits, its haunts. With that knowledge comes an incredible sense of freedom (though not recklessness) that now allows me to move through many aspects of life, including my continued pursuit of mountains, unencumbered. Living with death has taught me to stay in the moment, fully focused and aware, without fear of the future—to me, a far more enriching approach to life."[83] Like Berman and Simon, Kocour emphasizes calculated risk and its benefits for personal transformation. She states, "climbing a mountain is always a calculated risk, a puppeteer's dance between heaven and hell where one false step, one miscalculation, one simple turn of fate, can leave a mountaineer tangled in a broken lifeline and tumbling into an icy coffin."[84] Notably, Kocour's metaphor uses the image of a puppeteer— where an unknown puppeteer controls the adventurer's fate. Mountaineers in this sense are both the puppet and the puppeteer, where their reckoning of risk determines whether they live or die.

Rather than courting death, the athletes underscore balancing risk and its associated pleasures against the inevitability of accidents. This art demands the practitioners' fullest concentration and devotion, though adventurers also stress that their serious play is full of fun and humor. While Laurence Gonzales in *Deep Survival* points out humor's vital role in survival, he also stresses that arrogance and "reckless disregard for safety" lead to death.[85] Adventurers in these ways "play chess" (Gonzales's analogy, discussed in chapter 5) or, as I discuss in the next chapter, "dance" with nature, trusting in their experience and ability to read present conditions in order to adjust. Notably, these individual feelings bear no clear relation to sustainability and environmentalism. Further reflection is needed to translate an individual epiphany into environmental action.

Steven Callahan—despite his own gut-wrenching experience of being lost at sea for seventy-six days—downplays suffering in order to emphasize that being in wilderness and meeting the required tasks are what matter for individual transformation. Callahan believes that "the sea remains the world's greatest wilderness. To my mind, voyaging through wildernesses, be they full of woods or waves, is essential to the growth and maturity of the human spirit. It is in the wilderness that you really learn who you are. It is in facing the challenges of the wilderness that the thickness of your wallet becomes irrelevant and your capabilities become the truer measure of your value."[86] Callahan argues for a nonmaterialistic environmental ethic. Rather than economic wealth, Callahan seeks wilderness for a different kind of wealth or fame and a different measure of personal value. In wilderness one's net income is less important than the survival skills s/he possesses. As discussed previously, Callahan gestures toward the idea that one cannot buy his or her way into an "authentic" wilderness adventure; or, even if one does, nature, in the end, is a great equalizer.

For many adventurers, wilderness is not a place to shatter the self but a location to connect with something greater than the individual self. For

Cindy Ross and her family, which includes her husband and two small children, outdoor adventures are not about shattering identity to achieve spiritual awakening but rather (re)establishing a fundamental connection with nature. Ross sees "our greatest satisfaction—besides raising our wonderful children—is sharing the magic that we find out there in the big wild world."[87] Contrasting their experiences with a Disney vacation, Ross emphasizes that hiking constitutes more than "family 'vacations.' Our hike isn't a getaway. It's an extension of our life, our values—not a departure from life but an arrival. To us a Disney vacation is superficial, as thin as air. It blows by in an instant, a summer breeze. Our trek, however, is lasting—rock solid, like the mountains we walk on."[88] Ross echoes Jill Fredston's description that her adventures "are neither a vacation nor an escape, they are a way of life."[89] She also emphasizes their superior authenticity.

Ross's comparison with Disney is especially key. Her definition of nature in this passage depends on its contrast with Disney. Disney offers, as Jean Baudrillard argues in *Simulacra and Simulations*, the ultimate artificial place that assures us that what is outside Disney is real.[90] Disney is "superficial" and inauthentic, which makes the wilderness "real" by comparison. This fake-real binary hides wilderness/nature's artificial constructions. That is, Ross uses Disney's artificiality to heighten nature's reality and obscure the ways that nature, too, is a construction. Additionally, as Gabriela Nouzeilles points out, "living dangerously in the midst of nature is associated with the primitive as a marker of the real."[91] That is, wilderness adventure offers a tour of "the habitats associated with the vanishing Other, pushed to extinction or irreversibly transformed by modern civilization" and the opportunity to experience one's "own dormant, primal Other through physical exertion."[92] This is not to say that there are no meaningful differences between Disney and wilderness; however, their dependence on each other questions their value for long-term environmental sustainability. The issue is that both locations serve as fantastical, "magical" escapes rather than locations of sustainable lives. Ross, however, emphasizes that the wilderness is not a fantasy escape.

An important element in Ross's description is that, rather than placing wilderness in contrast to her family's everyday life, she places wilderness as an extension of their everyday life and values. That is, for Ross and her family, hiking represents an extension of a spiritual and physical path that they are already on. This idea contrasts with earlier descriptions in this chapter that emphasized extreme adventure as a pilgrimage to a specific extreme place or location—as separate from home and "regular life." This separation or lack of separation suggests different environmental ethics.

For some adventurers, a specific remote location becomes the focus of their pilgrimages: they inhabit other lives and places in order to return to these sacred places and recharge. Jon Krakauer points out in *Into the Wild*, for example, that Alaska is often the pilgrimage destination for such adventure seekers. He notes, "Alaska has long been a magnet for dreamers and misfits, people who think the unsullied enormity of the Last Frontier will patch all the holes in their lives. The bush is an unforgiving place, however, that cares nothing for hope or longing."[93] By contrast, Ross implies that, while more intense, their hiking trips are not radically different from their normal family life.

Alvah Simon makes a similar distinction between natural and unnatural and the spiritually damaging effects of society's disconnection from the natural environment. Simon asserts that "we are in no way soulfully tied to synthetic rubber and nylon. What we wear, what we eat, and, increasingly, what we do, no longer connect us to our origins or the land in which we live."[94] While iPhone marketers and users—among others—might disagree that people cannot be "soulfully" connected to the artificial or mechanical, Simon emphasizes what other extreme adventurers imply: their experience is more authentic, more real. Ross connects the loss of community and connection with nature with the increasing influence of technology on our lives: "The luxuries separate us from one another.... We've lost community."[95] As a result, wild, "natural" environments play a special role in (re)connecting individuals to each other as well as the earth.

By connecting to extreme nature, adventurers claim to access self-realizations and transformations not possible via other vehicles or settings. Significantly, this "naturalness" is often gendered. As Mark Stoddart asserts, "ski magazines articulate a discourse that positions male skiers as the 'natural' inhabitants of the mountainous sublime.... This conclusion is consistent with accounts of how mountainous wilderness areas have historically been defined as sites for men to embody adventurous forms of white masculinity through outdoor sport."[96] As I discussed in the previous chapter, gender and race impact the adventurers' access to the landscapes that conventionally elicit these spiritual connections and transformations. Ski resorts are described "as gender-neutral landscapes, where women and men are equally welcome. By contrast, skiers' interview talk suggests that the backcountry—which bears a greater resemblance to the mountainous sublime of ski magazines—is interpreted as a masculinized place."[97] If location inspires epiphany, these narratives underscore that access considerations demand attention by the contemporary environmental movement because remote, sublime vistas may not be available to everyone or serve as universal inspirations for spiritual transformation. The diction used to articulate this location and transformation for the adventurer and others constitutes another key element to understanding spiritual desire and its environmental implications.

APPROPRIATING THE LANGUAGE OF TRANSFORMATION

The predominately secular nature of these extreme pilgrimages is important to acknowledge. Liv Arnesen, for example, finds that skiing results in "splendor and a deep sense of connectedness that brings peace" and also admits "I am not a religious person, but the feeling is similar to the one I have heard some religious people describe: It's a reverence that makes everything else make sense."[98] Thus, religious language provides an analogy for secular experience. Steven Callahan, for example, admits his agnosticism in *Adrift*. Callahan acknowledges that "I wonder about God. Do I believe in Him? Somehow I cannot accept a vision of a super humanoid, but I believe in the miraculous and spiritual way of things—existence, nature, the universe. I do not know the true workings of that way. I can only guess and hope that it includes me."[99] Callahan disavows God, but believes in a "miraculous" world.

Graham Bowley describes a similar view in *No Way Down: Life and Death on K2* when he relates the following about climbers Hugues d'Aubarède and Philippe Vernay: "His friend Philippe Vernay in Lyon had tried to make d'Aubarède believe in God: If K2 was so beautiful it was because of God. But that was not the reason he was crazy about climbing. Yes, d'Aubarède fully appreciated the wonders of nature. But he didn't believe in God. Sorry, Philippe. He did, however, believe in something absolute, and that was probably what he was searching for."[100] As seen in these passages, the adrenaline narrative's evangelical thrust often emphasizes nature's mysteries and powers more than the existence of a Supreme Being or adherence to a specific religion.

In these representations, spirituality—as Bron Taylor defines it—focuses on "personal growth and gaining a proper understanding of one's place in the cosmos" and is "intertwined with environmentalist concern and action."[101] For example, Bowley describes a visit with Cecilie Skog, wife of Rolf Bae, who died on K2. In their conversation Skog describes her husband's love of the outdoors: "Despite her grief, Skog communicated something that I found infectious. It was a powerful joy for the outdoors—she called it a 'devotion to the outdoors'—a love of life in the open. I saw this same physical joy in the Spanish climber Alberto Zerain."[102] This "'devotion to the outdoors'" is, to apply Bron Taylor's definition, a "dark green religion" for the ways in which this devotion understands that "nature is sacred, has intrinsic value, and is therefore due reverent care," rather than a "green religion," "which posits that environmentally friendly behavior is a religious obligation."[103] Yet while adrenaline narratives do not represent environmentalism as a "religious obligation," some do incorporate specific religious practices and iconography.

Of course, not all extreme adventurers are atheists or agnostics. At the funeral of climber Gerard McDonnell, Father Noonan relates the significance of the mountain in Christianity and in McDonnell's life and death: "'It was on a mountain that Moses communicated with God,' Father Noonan went on. 'It was on a mountain where Jesus was transfigured. It was on a mountain that Gerard achieved one of his life's ambitions. It was such a spiritual experience that he even referred to it as being an honor to die on a mountain.'"[104] In the most extreme form, the entire adventure may be dedicated to God and/or viewed as an extension of religious teaching and practice. Glenn Frontin's *A River Calling: A Christian Father and His Sons* is an example of Christian adrenaline narrative. This canoe adventure narrative set in the American West connects the training required to be a Christian soldier with the author's military training. *Becoming Odyssa: Epic Adventures on the Appalachian Trail* by Jennifer Pharr Davis, who is a graduate of Samford University, also falls into the category of Christian adrenaline narratives. However, Davis, unlike Steam, whom she meets on the trail, is not "hiking the trail as a Christian missionary."[105] Davis explains, "I knew that I would share my beliefs if the subject came up in conversation on the trail, but purposely trying to start that conversation terrified me."[106] Other examples include David M. Barnes's *Faithful's Journey on the Appalachian Trail* and "Jack Mormon" Amy Irvine's *Trespass: Living at the Edge of the Promised Land*, which considers a loss of faith and wilderness, as well as Rob Schultheis, who connects shamanism and extreme sports in *Bone Games: Extreme Sports, Shamanism, Zen, and the Search for Transcendence*.[107] I discuss Eddy Harris's *Mississippi Solo* as another example shortly. These niche extended religious narratives are less common than those by author-adventurers who use spiritual language and religious references in their secular tales.

While adventurers do not usually claim to be members of any specified religion, adrenaline narratives frequently deploy spiritual rhetoric and symbols to describe the natural environment and its power. Sometimes these spiritual references are overt. Cindy Ross writes in *Scraping Heaven: A Family's Journey along the Continental Divide*, for example, "out here we are so close to heaven that we can reach up and scrape it with our fingernails."[108] K2 climber Alberto Zerain agrees: "Up here, on the summit slopes, you were close to the gods, or at least you felt you were."[109] In this sense, God can only be "found in nature," as Eustace Conway insists, and God is more accessible in the wilderness, especially on a mountaintop.[110] Conway's biographer Elizabeth Gilbert explains, "God is to be found only in nature. That, of course, is why they [Appalachian Trail hiking partners Eustace Conway and Frank Chambless] were out there on the trail, the better to find this godliness within themselves and the larger world. Nor were they embarrassed to talk about this godliness, night after night.... but Eustace and Frank weren't merely playing Indian—they were there on the brink of their manhood, living in the most earnest way they could, facing together every day's revelations and challenges."[111] Nature, in Thoreauvian fashion, provides the ideal setting for intense spiritual and philosophical introspection and debate. Such spiritual connection, as Gilbert also points out, is not the exclusive privilege of Indigenous peoples, and emphasizing this authenticity separates the serious spiritual seeker from those that merely "play" outdoors. I discuss white adventurers' use of Indigenous spiritualities later in the chapter.

For some, this serious play means discovering a heaven on earth. Climber Heidi Howkins explains, "realizing that there is a distance between what you know you have seen and what you know is possible inspires a humble, reverent sort of feeling. And so as the sea of blue peaks below emerged from the darkness and the atmosphere grew thinner, I prayed to the rocks."[112] Where Ross's description indicates one becomes closer to heaven (God) in nature, Howkins describes a heaven on earth. She prays directly "to the rocks." For Howkins, "prayer seemed like the natural, maybe even the necessary, mode for conversing with all the spirits in the air."[113] Howkins emphasizes that the natural environment inspires connection with the world larger than oneself. The multiple "spirits in the air" suggest a pantheistic view. This view, additionally, connects individual transformation to the outside—to forces beyond the mental or physical work required of extreme adventurers.

Simon in *North to the Night: A Spiritual Odyssey in the Arctic* describes one incident where he feels "a hidden hand had swept us from harm's way." For Simon, there is more than "coincidence" at work.[114] He sees a higher power—an invisible hand—at play in the events that shape his narrative.

> From the very start, our adventure seemed aligned with purposeful good fortune. Selling our wooden boat, changing dinghies, our preparation, re-

prieves, narrow escapes, even my apparent mistakes—all now appeared mere props meant to maneuver us toward specific lessons, some brutal, some gentle, some physical, some psychological or spiritual, but all timely and essential to our safety and growth. I looked up at Diana. Without words, I heard her asking herself the same questions as I. If we even began to accept the notion that our lives were not totally our own, then we had to wonder to where and for what purpose we were being led.[115]

Simon understands his successful adventure as due to forces not entirely of his own making. His description exploits a tension between the role of their individual human agency and fate or some "invisible hand" shaping the events. From the start, the adventure is blessed with "good fortune" and even apparent mistakes take on meaning in retrospect, leading them to "specific lessons."

While many adventurers reference a generic or secular sense of spirituality, others employ more specific religious references. For example, Mark Sundeen describes Daniel Suelo—"the man who quit money"—as "not a monk and [one who] does not claim to belong to the ranks of holy men," yet "he draws much of his inspiration from them."[116] In Suelo's words, the United States "'professes to be a Christian nation,'" but "'it's basically illegal to live according to the teachings of Jesus.'"[117] Suelo's extreme scavenging lifestyle is so free it is, ironically, viewed as both un-American and un-Christian. Explicit Catholic and Protestant Christian references are also peppered throughout Eddy Harris's narrative, *Mississippi Solo*. For example, he likens his experience on the Mississippi to "going to Mass, but no. No Mass could ever be as fulfilling as a day in this cathedral."[118] Similar to Howkins's experience in the thin air, Harris describes how, while on the river, barriers to God break down. God speaks through the breeze. Harris writes, "it was not a prayer, no more than the whole morning was a prayer. I did not pray. I was talking to God and He was talking to me and I heard Him and I felt Him in my heart and we communicated."[119] In Harris's case, nature facilitates a more direct mode of communication or connection with God. Kocour also uses the language of prayer, but in a more traditional sense. Prayers provide a means of assurance of safe passage: "With each step, a tiny prayer was offered to the mountain gods to help the crampon points gain solid purchase."[120] Kocour suggests that each step is a "tiny prayer" and that small petitions are also offered with each step to assure the team's safety.

These tiny prayers hint that not every adventurer feels a secure affinity to God while facing extreme conditions and danger. Simon, for example, rages at God: "'Leave me alone, damn it. I'm just an ordinary adventurer, not some fucking saint. Anyway, I don't even believe in you.'"[121] Even as adventurers employ religious language and pleas, they may not necessarily be religious or believe in a Western God. Fredston, for instance, confesses that her refusal to comment on good weather results in teasing from her partner. Fredston admits that "Doug mocks me for being superstitious; I am simply trying not to antagonize the spirits of the ocean, the powers behind the wind."[122] Her spiritual practices emphasize multiple spirits or forces at work instead of a singular God. Simon also confesses, "then, as now, I have no earthly idea who it is I am thanking. But I think I know what it is I am thankful for: the privilege of being a small, frail, faulted, but integral part of the magic and mystery of life on earth."[123] Simon emphasizes a more general, agnostic sense of "magic and mystery" rather than a specific religion.

While Callahan makes a similar observation to Harris, connecting sea travel with both a chapel and pilgrimage, he uses such language to connect with nature rather than God. Callahan declares that "from the first time I ventured from the shore in a boat, I felt that my spirit was touched. On my first offshore trip to Bermuda, I began to think of the sea as my chapel. It was my soul that called me to this pilgrimage."[124] The sea, like a chapel or church, is the vehicle through which Callahan worships and reconnects with nature and his spirit. Once stirred by nature, his "soul" desires repeated journeys across the sacred sea. Adventure is a spiritual practice, where the forest, summit, or body of water provides the house of worship and means of personal transcendence. Likewise, Manos's narrative worships the Earth rather than a specific God or gods: "I resigned myself to my fate.... The only thing that mattered now was Earth. I was in her service." His narrative flies between "immediate [physical] survival" and the "survival of the Earth. Everything was always immediate and to the extreme. I'd never learned how to adjust or balance myself within human life until it was too late."[125] Thus, both his adventure and worship style share the same defining characteristic: "extreme."

Manos clarifies his ecstatic spiritual vision in the following passage, which connects religious and social-justice language:

> This time of bloodshed, suffering and sorrow that had gripped this land for so long would be over. Not now, I understood, but within our lifetimes.... I knew I wouldn't bother breathing another day without the promise of a time 30 or 40 years from now when great cities and small hamlets alike are run entirely with energy from the Sun, when "minority" is a meaningless word, people can again kneel and drink di-

rectly from the lakes and streams, and there is equal opportunity, wellness, community and beauty for everyone, including the mighty buffalo survivors, whose brethren and grandchildren will again blacken the yellow grass plains, and smart-mouthed prairie dogs again stretch their million-year old civilization across hundreds of miles of freedom and vitality.[126]

The passage opens with a "time of bloodshed" and ends with an urban-pastoral description where racial and economic injustice disappears as solar energy increases and pollution decreases. Manos connects prairie dog civilization and success to human civilization and success.

Thus, for some adventurers nature connects them with an identifiable God (Conway, Ross, Harris) and for others it connects them with a godlike experience (Arnesen, Howkins, Callahan, Manos). Rob Schultheis claims "our wild playing, is making a kind of religion: an incoherent, catch-as-catch-can kind of religion, but a religion nonetheless."[127] Adventure in nature is its own religious-spiritual practice. Adventurers, furthermore, not only co-opt Western religious language for (secular) spiritual purposes, they also utilize Indigenous religions. Alvah Simon, for example, ultimately finds a spiritual connection as a result of his adventure in the Arctic. Rather than a Judeo-Christian God, Simon hopes he "found the Inuit way."[128] His journey, which required "isolation from humanity," results in the discovery of "the true essence of my humanness. I briefly and lightly touched the face of God. I cannot define it, I cannot defend it, but I can flatly state that I am here because my spirit protector was there. With that support and the help of history, nature, the Inuit, and my beloved Diana, I did something else, something of some importance, at least to me—I survived."[129] The "spirit protector" found in the Arctic extremes plays a fundamental role in Simon's personal transformation and his connection to the environment. As Bron Taylor points out, Indigenous, in this case Inuit, religious practices are often key to dark green religion, lending authenticity to Simon's spiritual encounter and ultimate transformation.[130] The question becomes whether or not such white adventurers are "merely playing Indian," and, thus, engaged in cultural appropriation rather than spiritual practice.[131]

Simon joins other white extreme adventurers in a turn to Indigenous spirituality. Simon's version involves animism, in which, as Bron Taylor explains, "animals come as oracles, providing wisdom, hope, or presaging an important event."[132] For example, Simon has a dream about a "mystical fox" trying to communicate with him: "suddenly a golden light washed over me, and I was filled with a peace I had never known. The message was somehow clear; I was just not yet ready for what the fox was trying to teach me. Everything unfolds perfectly and in its own time."[133] The fox as well as a raven and bear provide messages that Simon eventually learns to understand. Similarly, Jennifer Hahn appropriates a ritual learned from a "Native friend": "I tossed a stick wrapped with yarn, a grass blade, and a feather into Tongass Narrows.... A Native friend had suggested I do this. 'Tell the sea your dream. It will carry it outwards before you.' I liked that."[134] Adoption and appropriation of Indigenous spiritual practices provides white extreme pilgrims with additional language and symbolism to describe their spiritual connections with nature. Rather than relate a built environment—such as a church or chapel—with the natural environment, these scenes use organic elements as totems to frame their extreme pilgrimages. But even when done "right," as I discussed in the previous chapter in regard to ownership, the adrenaline narrative's patriarchal and colonial history makes such uses by white writers and adventurers questionable.

Significantly, the authors in these examples do not evangelize: an act that would clearly shift their interest in and adoption of Indigenous religion to cultural exploitation. In seeking "the Inuit way," Simon views Inuit culture as an environmental and spiritual model.[135] The "Inuit way" is not his only environmental and spiritual model. Simon focuses on synthesizing his available resources—"history, nature, the Inuit, and my beloved Diana"—to outline and understand his spiritual and environmental path.[136] Hahn hints she has permission to adopt the ritual blessing by stating, "a Native friend had suggested I do this."[137] Simon and Hahn tread carefully, attempting to avoid engaging in "white shamanism."

The reality television series *Dual Survival* provides a snapshot of why this careful negotiation is important and why such adoptions by whites are suspect. This television show presents two of the most powerful representations of nature: conquering and spiritual desires. As the show's title suggests, *Dual Survival* presents two experts with distinct approaches to achieve the same goal: survive and make it back to civilization. The challenge involves not only endurance and survival in a remote wilderness with limited resources, but also working with another person who has a dissimilar set of survival skills and ideologies. Dave Canterbury (replaced in season three by Joseph Teti) conquers nature. In the episode "Swamped," Canterbury succinctly characterizes his approach: "You come to the swamp, you'd better leave your skirt at the house."[138] Canterbury's approach does not allow for any performance of femininity. His appearance and approach are military. Nature is an enemy that must be respected even as the goal is to conquer and control it. Canterbury and Teti perform an extreme militarized masculinity, represented in their military backgrounds and camouflage clothing.

By contrast, Cody Lundin offers a spiritual and arguably more feminine or "skirted" alternative; he is a self-described minimalist and primitive skills survival expert. Lundin's performance on the show is best characterized as that of a "white shaman," a term I am borrowing from a documentary entitled *White Shamans, Plastic Medicine Men*.[139] That is, Lundin is a white man who culturally appropriates Indigenous culture and style for his own benefit. For example, Lundin never wears shoes, and his overall appearance—especially his braids— suggests an Indigenous approach and style. Lundin, who is the founder of the Aboriginal Living Skills School in Prescott, Arizona, notably does not claim to have native heritage or specific authorization from any Native American or Aboriginal nation. As emphasized in his dress and the carefully constructed visuals and photographs on his website, including a pen-and-ink drawing of Lundin building a fire with a bow drill, he plays Indian and appears to profit well from such performances.[140] This extreme version of "playing Indian," as Philip J. Deloria describes it, reminds us of consumable culture's mainstream popularity and role in solidifying individual and national identities, identities dependent, in this case, on violent cultural appropriations that erase more than they conserve and honor.

This is not to suggest that Indigenous peoples are automatically far superior environmentalists or that their practices are sacrosanct from critique. This "ecological Indian" stereotype demands impossibly high standards, setting up inevitable failure.[141] As Jill Fredston discovers, Indigenousness is not necessarily synonymous with environmentalism. Fredston notes the garbage near Kivalina, a "village of about 250 mostly Inupiat residents." Specifically, Kivalina "announced itself by increasing concentrations of floating or marooned Pampers, cans, and plastic."[142] The garbage both announces the village and the ways in which many contemporary Indigenous people live. Fredston's passage hints that Indigenous religious practices are not a simple cure for our environmental ills or for the ravages Indigenous people have disproportionately experienced as a result of colonialism. As a result, environmental racism as well as Indigenous environmentalism and religion play key roles in the contemporary landscape. Whether authors frame the environment in Western religious, Indigenous, agnostic, or atheist terms, location plays a key role in the spiritual authenticity of their experiences.

RAPTUROUS ENVIRONMENTS, ECSTATIC FEARS

While author-adventurers may depict nature as working for or against their expedition goals, the sensations themselves are not, theoretically, limited to natural environments. After all, one could participate in activities that produce risk's pleasures without having to be outdoors or fully engaging with the natural environment. Maria Coffey notes that "Margo Talbot insists that climbers are addicts—not to the activity itself, but to the mental state it enables them to reach."[143] Thus, is it merely incidental that these adrenaline athletes participate in mountain climbing, kayaking, and long-distance hiking rather than NASCAR or freestyle snowmobiling?

The adrenaline athletes' selected sports and descriptions of nature suggest the quality of their risky pleasures is enhanced by, if not always dependent upon, the extreme natural environments in which they are set. For the participants, their activities and locations have undeniable allure and are key to the risk aesthetic, which I outline in chapter 5, and their spiritual development. Maria Coffey shares a similar insight: "David Breashears lightheartedly founded Everest Anonymous, a self-help group for climbers unable to resist the lure of this mountain."[144] This allure is what keeps bringing Gregory Crouch as well as "a handful of climbers who find the opposing miseries of the Patagonian Andes irresistible...to this proving ground."[145] Descriptions of nature as sacred articulate the particular significance of place for the adrenaline narrative.

Extreme natural settings heighten the extraordinary or "miraculous" events described, raising the pitch of the transformative pilgrimage. Tom Hornbein notes, in his foreword to Maria Coffey's *Where the Mountain Casts its Shadow*, location's key role for extreme athletes. He reveals that "mountains are my spiritual home; more than anything else, they have shaped who I am and how I relate to the world and those who share it with me. These rationalizations are not mine alone, of course; most climbers voice similar beliefs to justify our pastime."[146] The idea that wilderness is a "spiritual home" or a place where adventurers can (re)discover their true selves and live authentically carries across adrenaline narratives.

For Robert Kull, who lived alone in the Patagonian wilderness as part of his interdisciplinary thesis, environmentalism has ignored this spiritual aspect at its own peril. Kull posits, "in some sense, environmentalism, with its focus on physical sustainability, is not asking the deeper questions. How can we live—and respectfully take other lives—in a way that allows us to honor the sacredness of all Life? How can we live so our activities don't rend us from the experience of belonging to the Earth and being part of the flow of Life? How can we sustain not only our own lives, but also the Life of the land and reestablish our sense of belonging and longing for the Sacred?"[147] Kull questions the environmental movement's lack of attention to spiritual desire. He argues that "to be fully human, we need relationship not only with other people but with the nonhuman world, with our own inner depths—and with Something Greater."[148] Both Hornbein and Kull emphasize extreme nature as the proper setting for this work. Kocour concurs: "If there is an explanation, it may be simply this: that the value of wild places lies in showing us the way back—that wilderness is but a path back to the center of our souls."[149] To experience nature is to experience the sacred, the magical.

Magical wild environments define the adrenaline narrative's sacred spaces. For Crouch, Patagonia and the drive to go there are connected with "childhood magic." Patagonia is a place where "every step was a discovery, charged with meaning, pregnant with possibility. That magic, that fascination, that discovery, that private world shared only with my picked companions—it's all here in Patagonia for me.... I will return as long as I am able to wrap that Patagonian magic around my heart."[150] Crouch emphasizes his personal ownership and control of this magical place: he selects his "companions" and is resolved to return "as long as I am able." Jill Fredston also uses magic in her description of Labrador. She understands that "the most special places are the ones that give texture to our dreams, that ground us, make us whole, remind us of what is real. When I think of Labrador, I not only see its landscape but feel a stirring within."[151] Certain places realize our dreams. Magic can be a part of the process as well as a quality of the place. "Magic," as Rob Schultheis describes, "becomes a kind of habit after we do the difficult, the near impossible, over and over and over again; a habit that operates down in those oldest and deepest levels of the brain and the mind. Where pain and fear can be alchemized into blissful, sublime confidence, and stumblebums wake up to find themselves dancing on the business end of pins."[152] These pointed, wild, and risky locations speak to and work their magic on the adventurer.

Simon also emphasizes that humans crave pilgrimage to special sacred and risky locations. Simon claims, "I am here because in the landscape of each and every human imagination lies one special place. Our inner compass keeps pointing us toward this spot, which is magnetic, mysterious, exotic, and alluring but, alas, always fringed by a frontier of our fears. Still, it is to this specific place that we are compelled to travel in order to know ourselves and, in so doing, call our lives complete."[153] Implicit in Simon's construction of sacred space are all the economic and social factors that may encourage or hinder individuals from embarking on a journey to such enigmatic sites. While our "inner compass" may direct us, "our fears" may hold us back. Fears, in this case, include not only the physical risk involved but also the cacophony of details required to leave our normal lives and set out on an epic adventure. Crouch agrees: "in our constant struggle to create security in a chaotic universe, most humans take root, set their feet in stone, and fight change. But change is a most implacable foe, one certain to sweep even his most conservative opponent into unknown seas."[154] As Simon suggests, if we do not embark on such a journey and embrace change, we cannot live full or truly fulfilling lives. Something will always be incomplete until we follow this inner compass. Moreover, as Crouch advises, resistance to change is futile. Change will come and "sweep" us into "unknown seas." Crouch argues we need to overcome our fears and jump in of our own accord.

The clear benefit of overcoming fear is that encounter with these sacred spaces produces transformation. The ability or inability to find meaning in tragedy or near-tragedy—a common plot point in the adrenaline narrative—offers further insight into these sacred-secular portrayals of nature. Gilbert explains Eustace Conway's views similarly, emphasizing that American culture especially needs such shocks to the system. She explains that "he is convinced that the only way modern America can begin to reverse its inherent corruption and greed and malaise is by feeling the rapture that comes from face-to-face encounters with what he calls 'the high art and godliness of nature.'"[155] Conway's "calling" is "nothing less than to save our nation's collective soul by reintroducing Americans to the concept of revelatory communion with the frontier. Which is to say that Eustace Conway believes that he is a Man of Destiny."[156] Significantly, this nature is not a benign, pastoral setting. Rather, nature is terrifying: a nature that can bewitch and beguile.

Gilbert also hints at the ways American exceptionalism, especially manifest destiny and frontier landscapes, amplify the spiritual journey and location in American adrenaline narratives. Such quests are fundamental to American (masculine) identity and spirituality. These "melodramas of beset manhood," as Nina Baym describes them, require a flight from domesticity to seek one's destiny on the road.[157] Huckleberry Finn, in this sense, offers a fictional, youthful version of the American adrenaline adventurer. The contemporary American adventurer's edgy "dirtbag" or vagabond lifestyles harken back to Huck's iconic American adventures. Nature often provides a terrifying beauty in such contemporary adventure tales.

Terrifying beauty sustains and entrances contemporary adventurers, playing a key role in their individual pilgrimages and transformations. For example, Bowley notes that why climbers climb is related to the mountain's terrible beauty: "K2 was terrifically beautiful—its beauty exceeding anything I had expected. Yet, still the questions remained. Why had they come? Why had I come? For me, their story possessed an archetypal force, specific to their time and location and the personalities involved, but also basic and timeless." Bowley goes on to say that the climbers were "attracted like flies to the light to some deeper meaning about themselves, human experience, and human achievement."[158] Here the location, notably not explicitly gendered feminine as we saw in chapter 2, nevertheless performs the same bewitching and beguiling vision that other authors describe in more clearly gendered terms. Bowley, for example, relates how Spanish mountaineer Alberto Zerain expresses the danger spiritual desire presents: its beauty and nearness "to the gods" were such that "you forgot there was work to be done to get up and down again."[159] Terrible beauty may mean adventurers lose sight of their exposure to danger.

Bowley stresses archetypal forces over specific national (American or otherwise) drives as leading adventurers down these dangerous paths. Reading adrenaline narratives for their pull on the American environmental imagination requires a negotiation between the broad, Western archetypal sublime and the specifically American context such representations invoke. Additionally, climbing culture in particular holds long-standing connections to Romanticism and the sublime: "This transference of mountaineering to the domain of the soul linked mountain climbing and mountains to Romantic ideas of the sublime."[160] Adrenaline narratives, especially those involving height, must address the sublime and its connection with spiritual desire.

Readers familiar with the sublime will recognize the traditional role beauty plays in facilitating a transcendent experience in the following passage, in which Bowley describes how the mountain views keep the climbers from worrying and from confronting the dangers of the late hour.

> Yet though they were hot and tired, they couldn't dwell on their problems for long. The view was just too beautiful. It made everything right. To their left were the heads of mountains, shining in the sun or wreathed in little trains of cloud. The world was on a gigantic scale. They could see the curving line of the earth's horizon.... This view, this feeling, this achieve-

ment is what they had come for. Despite the nagging anxiety about how long things were taking and the frustrations caused by the crowd, the climbers felt a sort of inner transcendence, an inner peace.[161]

The beautiful view is the reward and visual representation of their "inner transcendence" and "peace." As Dorceta E. Taylor writes, "sublime landscapes triggered strong emotions—fear, excitement, awe, and a sense of wonder. Sublime landscapes were described as sacred; one worshipped them but did not linger in their presence."[162] The adventurer seeks these sacred "triggers" and likewise does not "linger." Rather s/he seeks temporary respite in wilderness landscapes defined by man's absence: "where," as stated in the Wilderness Act of 1964, "man himself is a visitor who does not remain."[163] Taylor reminds us that the sublime is an important part of the American environmental imagination, seemingly shaping, in this instance, the definition of American wilderness itself.

The shock-and-awe characteristic of these extreme sacred spaces produces a secular-spiritual transformation for both the adventurer and the reader in an age that often sees scientific understanding as more legitimate than spiritual knowledge. As Douglas Anderson writes, "it is interesting that this soulful enhancement of life is widely experienced as a feature of extreme sports but is routinely downplayed as potential hocus pocus in our scientistic age."[164] The sublime experience and education that nature provides in the adrenaline narrative's largely secular-spiritual setting straddles this demarcation between ecology and spirituality.

POLLUTED SPIRITUALITY

Whether or not the adventurer presents a successful pilgrimage or epiphany, adventure readers as well as their authors seek spiritual solace in nature at the very moment nature most desperately needs "saving" from human abuses. Allison notes, for example, Everest's status as "the World's Highest Garbage Dump," and both Allison and Krakauer in *Into Thin Air* briefly discuss the clean-up efforts undertaken to alleviate this growing problem.[165] The most moving testimony of Everest's "environmental rape" appears in Krakauer's epilogue. In this section, Krakauer quotes at length a self-proclaimed "Sherpa orphan" who connects Everest's environmental and spiritual pollution. The author begins by providing background on how Sherpas came to the region: "My ancestors arrived in the Solo-Khumbu region fleeing from persecution.... There they found sanctuary in the shadow of 'Sagarmathaji,' 'mother goddess of the earth.' In return they were expected to protect that goddesses' [sic] sanctuary from outsiders." The "Sherpa orphan" goes on to lament the assistance provided to outsiders and failure to protect the "mother goddess": "But my people went the other way. They helped outsiders find their way into the sanctuary and violate every limb of her body by standing on top of her, crowing in victory, and dirtying and polluting her bosom."[166] The Sherpa orphan uses bodily violation and pollution to underscore the outsiders' lack of respect and the Sherpas' failure to care for and protect their mountain goddess.

Krakauer's sympathies for the Sherpas are illustrated in this passage where he cites the Sherpa orphan as an authority. However, even as Krakauer gives voice to Sherpa complaints and credence to a nonconquering relationship with nature, the narrative retreats to masculinist rhetoric. Krakauer's understated analysis that follows this passage misses the mark, further emphasizing the narrative's patriarchal bent. Displacing the blame back on nature, Krakauer states, "Everest seems to have poisoned many lives."[167] Krakauer's narrative structures nature as other and reverses the Sherpa's insistence that they—the Sherpas and foreign adventurers— have polluted the mountain. In essence, by making "herself" so tempting the mountain is held responsible for our ills. As the Sherpa orphan emphasizes, we have poisoned and failed nature. Our hubris, as Krakauer's introduction more clearly recognizes, is responsible for Everest's spiritual and environmental pollution.[168]

While most contemporary adrenaline narratives at least mention pollution in passing, complicated personal and business politics usually dominate the narratives. Susan Birrell notes, "it does not take a critical genius to uncover" that Everest narratives "produce and reproduce discourses on masculinity, class privilege, expansive nationalism and ethnocentrism."[169] The more engaging subplot, according to Birrell, when one turns to the events that transpired on Everest in 1996, lies in the ways the resulting narratives "bemoan the misuse and degradation of Everest thereby constructing Everest itself as endangered and in need of redemption."[170] She notes, in other words, what Jeffrey McCarthy identifies as a shift from conquering rhetoric to one of stewardship or caretaking.

McCarthy describes the "caretaking vision" in "Why Climbing Matters" as "about rescuing the sublime so that it may be experienced indefinitely." While McCarthy does not emphasize the spiritual nature of this desire, he does note that "this tension between being saved and being a savior is enacted in a setting that is itself at risk from development and use." McCarthy emphasizes that an inherent contradiction founds this representation: "the more North America's mountain landscape is threatened, the more mountaineering is deployed as caretaker of clean and powerful nature."[171] We must save nature so that we, in turn, may be saved by it. Nature, however, cannot be indefinitely sacrificed in the service of humans.

As discussed in the previous chapter, extreme adventure's lack of use value in contemporary society puts it at odds with the spiritual narratives it spins. That is, adventure is a selfish endeavor. Tom Hornbein, for example, notes that while the "mountaineer's pursuit" is not that different from others, "from the quest of Odysseus to that of soldiers in war," a "challenging difference is that the self-centered nature of the climber's game lacks an obvious value to society. The forces of adventure, risk, uncertainty must coexist for those who choose such paths in a state of irreconcilable tension with the rest of one's world."[172] Coffey concurs, noting "most mountaineers willingly admit that climbing is of no benefit to anyone but themselves."[173] As individual spiritual transformations have little impact on the larger world, adrenaline narratives may be seen to fail as environmental messengers.

This aspect of extreme adventure's selfishness is perhaps why Gregory Crouch wonders if climbing is a sin. Crouch considers, "one essential question remains: Does alpine ascent have value? Is it a noble endeavor honored by the gods, or a sin against the will of God? *I do not know.*"[174] Crouch ultimately decides he would rather risk hell than live a nonadventurous life. Crouch reveals, "I have made an intellectual choice for sin, for by climbing dangerous mountains, I do not honor the divine sanctity of life. I do violence against myself, against nature, and against God's will. If Dante is right, then, just past the bitter end, I will be condemned by snarling Minos to the Seventh Circle of Hell."[175] In the above passage Crouch considers himself a sinner because he acts dangerously, risking life and limb. In this sense, he sins because he does "not honor the divine sanctity of life."

Crouch does not elect to live a "safe" life, which he describes in the next paragraph as "gray" and "righteous." Crouch explains, "I cannot abide the thought of a gray righteous life lived among gray righteous souls. I will not live with only one horizon, spinning dull brown cloth and sowing a single plot of dirt. Do I choose wisely? *I do not know*, but I choose in full knowledge of the consequence of my sin. If that choice sends my soul into the eternal exile, then so be it. I will add my defiant voice to the cacophony of the damned."[176] This "gray righteous life" represents its own type of living hell for Crouch.

While Crouch decides he would rather be a sinner and climb, he simultaneously crafts an argument for his "righteousness." He would rather "add my defiant voice to the cacophony of the damned." While he expresses doubt about his decision—"Do I choose wisely? *I do not know*"—he emphasizes this is an "intellectual" rather than "emotional" choice: "I choose in full knowledge of the consequence of my sin." He is not simply acting out or rebelling mindlessly, but choosing a different way—one that does not condemn him to a "gray righteous life," even as it may result in an early death and eternal damnation.

Whether or not God or nature approves, the wilderness's harsh environment provides the transformative setting. Yet the environment is usually not the beneficiary of the adventurer's spiritual pilgrimage. In fact, wild environments produce what Cindy Ross's friend Nancy calls "the gift," which cannot be accessed from "climate-controlled cubicles": "The gift for her is the closeness of community and the connection to the earth."[177] Callahan also describes his personal transformation as a result of "two priceless gifts" the sea gave to him.[178] Harris likewise wonders what he gives the river in return for its bounty.[179] We have reached a point, however, where nature's gifts are no longer guaranteed to keep giving.

Examining representations of sacred nature within the contemporary context of extreme sports and a fundamentally bankrupt ecology reveals that nature as a vehicle of spiritual transformation dangerously objectifies nature: regulating nature to a human tool, however unpredictable, and an expected gift. In retrospect, for instance, McCairen recognizes that "the canyon's inhospitality, its exacting lessons...ultimately teach me more about myself than the natural world it contains."[180] Such statements suggest the extreme spiritual adventurer maintains an anthropocentric perspective. As a result, spiritual representations of nature become less about sustainability and more about individuality. Like the allegedly contrasting characters in *Dual Survival*, conquering and spiritual desires hold more in common than their different appearances may initially suggest. Both objectify nature for individual benefit.

Viewing nature as a transcendental object, as Krakauer does, dangerously mirrors a patriarchal elevation of feminine beauty that nonetheless denigrates women. As a result, we can begin to see why many ecofeminists prefer an erotic construction of desire because it locates agency within the "object" of desire. As I explore in greater detail in the next chapter, an erotic construction provides "a way to talk about qualitative dimensions of reality [of which nature is a part] without appealing to spiritual or purely intuitive explanations, a way to translate that which is conventionally called spiritual into that which is erotic."[181] In other words, a discourse describing humanity's relationship with nature does not necessarily need to couch felt connections in religious terms, an aspect of the spiritual rhetoric of desire that risks privileging individual over ecological salvation.

In these ways, the adventurers' narratives—specifically their search for personal cleansing and salvation—confirm how extreme adventure cures their ills but does little to cure environmental problems. While such anthropocentric representations and narrative structures are difficult to break, wilderness rower Jill Fredston in *Rowing to Latitude* and kayaker Jennifer Hahn in *Spirited Waters* indicate that adventurers can and are finding new routes to personal and environmental awareness via spiritual-erotic desire. I will conclude this chapter by briefly introducing these promising examples, which are explored in greater detail in the next chapter.

Fredston describes a blurring of self and landscape as key: "In the process of journeying, we seem to have become the journey, blurring the boundaries between the physical landscape outside of ourselves and the spiritual landscape within."[182] Fredston's description rejects an anthropocentric framing by blurring the boundaries between human and landscape, offering a spiritual rhetoric that seeks to combine individual and ecological salvation. Jennifer Hahn in *Spirited Waters* describes a similar spiritual-erotic interaction with nature that relies on the blurring of boundaries: "We must talk with many things. Seals and eagles. Water and wind. Columbine flowers and spruce trees. Land snails and lichens. By broadening our idea of companions, we discover we don't so much experience solitude, as multitude."[183] Nature in these passages is not landscape or setting for personal transformation, but character. Fredston and Hahn hint that reworking nature from an external setting for individual redemption to a character or agent that fosters permeable boundaries between self and other holds much ecological potential. I explore this potential further in the next chapter.

CHAPTER 4

EROTIC

NATURES

Responding to the Sherpa orphan's message quoted in Jon Krakauer's book about the 1996 Everest tragedy, *Into Thin Air*, climber Heidi Howkins questions in *K2: One Woman's Quest for the Summit* whether extreme adventure is doomed to repeat violent conquering and spiritual pollution. Recall from the previous chapter that the "Sherpa orphan" states that Sherpas "helped outsiders find their way into the sanctuary and violate every limb of her body by standing on top of her, crowing in victory, and dirtying and polluting her bosom."[1] As a result of reading the Sherpa's words, Howkins wonders, "Surely, I thought, there must be a way to climb on the mountain in a peaceful manner. Surely what matters is the way in which climbers climb, not our mere presence. Surely there is a way to show respect for the soul of the mountain."[2] In her remarks Howkins hopes to maintain access by adjusting methods. She also grants nature a soul, a term that evokes spiritual connotations and refers to the mountain's living "essence," or a moral and emotional quintessence separate from its physical "body."[3] Shifting the spiritual focus from the adventurer's soul to respecting the mountain's living essence, Howkins calls for a different way to engage nature. In doing so, Howkins hints that rather than discourage such work, extreme adventure may be uniquely, "surely" positioned to further environmental agendas in "the way in which climbers climb."

Research conducted by sociologists agrees. Some "nature-based sports can provide opportunities for females and males to challenge hegemonic masculinities and forms of femininity and so begin to understand their individual, collective and global responsibilities to nature."[4] The realization of this potential nevertheless proves difficult. Robert Kull, in *Solitude: Seeking Wisdom in Extremes*, writes about his struggle to craft a different kind of story, one not dependent on heroic masculinity. Kull notes that "stories of spiritual seekers or solitaries in the wilderness are often portrayals of heroic adventure. It's difficult to not slip into this mode, but I've tried. We already have enough of such writing, and in its most blatant form it's little better than checkout-counter publications flaunting the amazing lives of superhuman 'stars.'"[5] While difficult to accomplish, representing nature's active participation distinguishes erotic desire and avoids the pitfalls of spiritual and patriarchal objectification.

The readings that follow explore how erotic desire nurtures a different relationship with wilderness, whose difference could be summarized as follows: "Energetic movement prevents us from transforming nature's rocks into furniture."[6] Rather than conquering nature for human use as lifeless "furniture," erotic desire seeks to see, experience, and represent nature as a living essence—if not an actual living being. That is, adventure's erotic desire shifts the focus from an anthropocentric to a more ecologically nuanced understanding of the natural world and humanity's place and role within it, from objectification for personal gain to more mutually beneficial environmental relationships. Erotic desire, as a result, necessarily rewrites, if not jettisons, heroic masculinity, which means it also challenges conventional American myths that shape the environmental imagination. Erotic nature thus embodies the desires ecofeminist critic Greta Gaard expresses in "Ecofeminism and Wilderness" to address the androcentric, ethnocentric, and anthropocentric qualities embedded in the mainstream definition of wilderness and to "find a place in ecofeminism" for wilderness.[7]

This chapter explores examples of what ecofeminists refer to as erotic nature, where nature is presented in mutual and reciprocal rather than hierarchical and objectifying relationships, and highlights the ways in which erotic nature produces and fails to produce a different means to view and interact with nature, especially wilderness, in order to encourage environmentalism. Specifically, the sections that follow examine how representations of erotic nature self-consciously revise the American adrenaline narrative by countering heroic masculinity, seeking and listening to nature's voice, and engaging in a critical anthropomorphism that resists cultural appropriation, especially of Indigenous religions and practices. Before looking at each of these three aspects of erotic desire, I first outline how ecofeminists and others, including the authors of adrenaline narratives, rework theories related to our desire for and interaction with nature, especially wilderness, which provides the foundation for understanding erotic desire's mutuality and participatory nature.

NOTE ON THE USE OF THE TERM "EROTIC"

Before turning to erotic desire's theoretical framework, it is important to note that the erotic's popular connection within American culture to the pornographic presents a challenge to ecofeminist adoptions of the term. While not all feminists agree on an easy distinction between the pornographic and the erotic, this distinction, as expressed by Terry Tempest Williams, clarifies how conquering constructions of sexual desire differ from ecofeminist erotic desire and how "adventure porn" differs from what might be termed the adventurous erotic.[8] Williams argues that at present our pornographic notion of the erotic silences both women and nature. She explains, "the erotic world is silenced, reduced to a collection of objects we can curate and control, be it a vase, a woman, or a wilderness."[9] While Williams, an author known for writing about nature in spiritual terms, would probably disagree with the idea that her conception of the erotic can be separated from the spiritual/ecstatic, she makes a useful distinction between a *patriarchal pornographic* and an *ecofeminist erotic*. The pornographic objectifies and silences the erotic. Additionally, as Gaard points out, "both radical feminists and ecofeminists have been concerned with the liberation of wildness and the liberation of the erotic."[10] Ecofeminist erotic revision and resistance is especially key for reworking ideas about (virgin) American wilderness and its related transcendentalist and romantic sublime representations.

EROTIC DESIRE:
AN ECOFEMINIST EXPLORATION OF SELF/OTHER

Comparing recent theoretical work with representations from American adrenaline narratives for their environmental significance reveals their qualified success in revising or eliminating adventure's defining, objectifying, conquering (patriarchal, colonial), and spiritual anthropocentric frameworks. Erotic desire explores both "that which is biologically or even physiologically fixed" and that which is flexible in American representations of nature, especially where gender and animal behavior are concerned.[11] Annette Kolodny explains the work literature, and specifically metaphor, can do in this regard: "metaphor (and image-making, in general) may be our way of exploring, again and again, the potent and potential content of our archetypal structures, putting ourselves in touch with their changing contents or even changing those contents at will."[12] In other words, figurative language matters, both for what it can tell us about nature and American culture and for how it helps shape them both. Erotic desire, in short, enacts what climber Heidi Howkins, writer Robert Kull, and feminist Annette Kolodny call for: a different way to adventure and engage wilderness.

Annette Kolodny's *The Lay of the Land: Metaphor as Experience and History in American Life and Letters* (1975) and Susan Griffin's *Woman and Nature: The Roaring Inside Her* (1978) are among the first ecofeminist texts that rework the relationships between desire, men, women, and nature.[13] Not surprisingly, as the representations of nature and desire began to change in the early 1970s, so too did the theories that articulate their relationship. In terms of desire, feminist theorists began revising the concept of *jouissance*. French feminists, for example, built off Jacques Lacan's distinction between *jouissance* (feminine pleasure) and desire (masculine sexual force).[14] Luce Irigaray cites *parler-femme* (women's language) as the privileged site for unlimited *jouissance*.[15] More recently, feminists and other theorists have focused on the self/other relationship.

Recent scholarship on the self/other (human/nature) generally divides into two schools of thought. Scholars such as Chaia Heller, Linda Vance, and Greta Gaard prefer what Richie Nimmo refers to as "liminal intimacy, or intimacy at a distance, for which closeness lies not in possessing or bringing near, nor in knowing as such, but instead in a relational being-with-otherness that is comfortable with degrees of unknowing."[16] These scholars advocate for maintaining a clear boundary with or distance from the other. Chaia Heller, for example, identifies Nancy Chodorow and Jessica Benjamin as two theorists who reconceptualize desire in a manner harmonious with this strand of ecofeminism. Heller explains, "rejecting romantic notions of selfhood, notions predicated on a self that finds love and security only through a dialectic of predation and protection, these theorists offer the possibility of a kind of sociality marked by mutualism, a desire to see the other as part of, yet excitingly distinct from, the self."[17] Heller identifies the key characteristic that distinguishes this ecofeminist reconfiguration of desire, namely a shift from objectification to mutualism.

According to Linda Vance, maintaining some degree of distance between self and other additionally prevents "merely mov[ing] from an idealized Other to an idealized Self."[18] Vance cautions against defining nature as "rugged, independent, self-determining...[because] that sounds suspiciously like the idealized Western Man."[19] She specifically aims this critique against deep ecology.[20] Vance argues that "to assert that we know what those [nature's] interests are, on the basis of our own culturally bound values, seems hopelessly arrogant."[21] Erotic desire thus does not presume knowledge of the other and rejects both romantic and transcendentalist exploitative "notions of selfhood" in favor of "mutualism."

Other scholars, such as Stacy Alaimo and Timothy Morton, argue that collapsing and blurring rather than maintaining liminal dichotomies offers the best intervention and description. This is, as Morton argues, an "ecology without nature": "there is no such 'thing' as nature, if by nature we mean some thing that is single, independent, and lasting. But deluded ideas and ideological fixations do exist....Ideology resides in the attitude we assume toward this fascinating object [nature]. By dissolving the object, we render the ideological fixation inoperative."[22] Interconnected, fluid boundaries transform the rigid dualisms. Alaimo's concept of trans-corporeality similarly describes how humans are "always intermeshed" with their environment.[23] Thus, Alaimo also emphasizes blurred or "intermeshed" rather than defined liminal boundaries. Gaard agrees, while emphasizing the importance of "still preserving the distinct identities of each": "healing the culture/nature split requires replacing the master identity with a human identity capable of maintaining relationships in which the unique identities of Self and Other are preserved at the same time that connection is acknowledged."[24] Maintaining the "unique identities" while reconnecting fosters a "relational self" that does not require "the denial, erasure, or subsumption of Otherness."[25] Alaimo, in the ways her theory emphasizes porous bodies, agrees, while also emphasizing—following the tenets of posthumanism—"there can be no 'nature' outside the human."[26]

Donna Haraway's "significant otherness" perhaps maps a middle ground between these two camps. Notably, Alaimo critiques Haraway's conception of the cyborg: "Whereas ecofeminism seeks to strengthen the bonds between women and nature by critiquing their parallel oppressions...Haraway seeks to destabilize the nature/culture dualism that grounds the oppression of both women and nature."[27] However, Alaimo's conceptions of trans-corporeality and Haraway's cyborg/companion species function as complementary concepts that identify key aspects of how (non)human nature is represented. Haraway notes that her conception of the cyborg and companion species share important commonalities: "Cyborgs and companion species each bring together the human and non-human, the organic and technological, carbon and silicon, freedom and structure, history and myth, the rich and the poor, the state and the subject, diversity and depletion, modernity and postmodernity, and nature and culture in unexpected ways."[28] Haraway's "significant otherness" resembles liminality and the uncanny or familiar strangeness that some authors use to describe nature. Haraway's companion species and significant otherness, in this sense, both maintain and collapse the boundaries between binaries such as self/other and human/nonhuman.

Theorists and critics such as Diane Ackerman, Kevin Krein, Jeffrey McCarthy, and David Abram also address sensuous nature in relation to the self. While not couched in feminist terms, Ackerman describes mutual desire in *Deep Play*: "one becomes fascinated by an 'other,' in whose presence one feels exaltation."[29] Like Heller, Ackerman grants the other "separate but equal" ground. One feels fascination in the other's presence, as Ackerman notes, but one does not desire to conquer or oppress that other as the necessary means to exact pleasure, control, or transformation. Ackerman describes the intimate distance Gaard argues is key to self/other relations. Kevin Krein explains that nature provides the ideal other for adventurers' deep play: "It is my claim that the opportunity to play with such awesome partners [nature] is one of the principal sources of the attraction of adventure sports."[30] Positioning erotic desire as a mutual or—to use David Abram's term—a "participatory" form of interaction grants agency to the traditional "object of desire," be it nature or a woman.[31] Jeffrey McCarthy mentions Abram's "participatory perception" in "Why Climbing Matters."[32] McCarthy emphasizes in his discussion of mountaineering literature and representations of nature that "the life of the body pushes people beyond egocentrism."[33] Terri Field similarly argues that the body and embodiment are "essential" but not an essentialist part of ecofeminism.[34] That is, theorizations about and analysis of embodiment are not automatically essentialist. McCarthy's focus here remains on human benefits, but like Field he implies the embodied act of climbing reduces, if not eliminates, anthropocentric thinking.

Peter Stark describes a similar sense of distant-closeness or "a crystalline awareness of the world around one and at the same time a kind of obliteration of the separateness of the self" as emerging in "a difficult or risky situation in the wilderness" that requires "the total reliance on oneself and trust in one's teammates and the need for total focus."[35] Such extreme play offers a "liminal intimacy" that both maintains and blurs boundaries between self/other. In this view, according to Gaard, "it names our participation both in culture and in nature, thereby dismantling the human/nature dualism."[36] Whereas Alaimo's trans-corporeality and Morton's mesh describe more a deeply blended or mixed "natureculture," Haraway's "significant otherness" focuses on and describes "emergent practices" where "the players are neither wholes nor parts."[37] Rather than emphasizing how these theories are at odds, we can productively place them along a continuum that helps identify an equally multifaceted range of representations within American adrenaline narratives.

DANCING NATURES:
SELF/OTHER IN ADRENALINE NARRATIVES

As I will discuss in more detail in the section that addresses anthropomorphism, erotic desire embraces the full range of the self/other representations: blurred boundaries (Alaimo and Morton), "significant otherness" (Haraway), and liminal "distinct identities" (Gaard, Heller, and Vance). Where ecofeminists, among other theorists, disagree about the benefits of collapsing or maintaining self/other boundaries, erotic desire offers a continuum of separations and connections. While contradictory in theory, in practice erotic desire's messy, flexible embrace of both liminal/distinct and blurred/mixed boundaries allows for the greatest diversity in its representations of nature. In embracing the range represented in the theories, erotic desire shifts discussion from an unattainable perfection of representation to the work accomplished—and left to be done. Erotic desire, in this sense, is not strictly monogamous in theory or practice but polygamous or polyamorous. We see this polymorphous sensuality in Patricia McCairen's representation of the Colorado River.

Describing the Colorado River, McCairen in *Canyon Solitude: A Woman's Solo River Journey through the Grand Canyon* models a different way to pursue adventure by emphasizing the river's active role. McCairen says the river "dances with excitement, enjoying her display of potency, enticing me to join in her play."[38] The river *dances, entices*, and *invites* McCairen to *play*. A closer look at the passage further demonstrates the potential such active, participatory rhetoric contains. Rather than desiring nature as a primary means to exact salvation or as an entity to be conquered or controlled, McCairen personifies nature as an adventurous companion.

The river, embodied as a woman, and McCairen enter into an erotic relationship, or a relationship characterized by mutual and reciprocal rather than hierarchical and objectifying relations. The active river is characterized in sensuous terms: "Changing, changing, constantly changing, she casts a rhythmic, sensuous spell. A sleek, beautiful goddess, alluringly seductive, forgiving to those who love her, dispassionately indifferent to those who do not. Lovingly she folds herself around a rock, teasingly she laps at the shore, stroking and caressing it, forming and molding it to her desires.... Bedecked in a million diamonds, she dances a sunlit dream lost in ecstasy. In the flash of an instant she is capable of creating a bubbling, intoxicating happiness or a frustrating helplessness, the highest exhilaration or the deepest, darkest fear."[39] The litany of active verbs in the passage highlights nature's individual agency and desires. Rather than a blank slate onto which the adventurer writes the fulfillment of his or her desire, the river in the above passage defines and creates herself as well as shapes her landscape and those that observe her. More than landscape or backdrop, the river may withhold or give pleasure as well as feel ecstasy.

Furthermore, while McCairen genders the river female and the canyon male, calling them "Mother River and Father Canyon," rather than simply reifying gender stereotypes, the personifications emphasize nature's bigendered or androgynous qualities and underscore that the erotic encompasses more than (hetero)sexual desire.[40] Nature provides McCairen with nurturing, parental substitutes. The river also influences McCairen's emotions—"creating a bubbling, intoxicating happiness or a frustrating helplessness, the highest exhilaration or the deepest, darkest fear"—and exhibits an autoeroticism or a sensuous, ecstatic pleasure in her own creation. While connecting parental love and forms of shared and individual sexual desire may initially sound counterintuitive, this example highlights the erotic's dynamic and polymorphous sensuousness.

Christine Byl in *Dirt Work* describes a similar, exciting danger in relation to the other that results from resisting a romantic or transcendentalist anthropocentric point of view. Byl states, "part of what fascinates me about wild animals is the element of threat, not because they are bloodthirsty or even necessarily predators, but because their actions are not about me."[41] Byl echoes Aldo Leopold's recognition of the wolf's "fierce green fire."[42] Byl recognizes that she is not the center of the (animal) universe and goes on to explain, "the specter of danger mingled with curiosity results in an otherness that both beckons and warns."[43] This shift in perspective ideally results in ecological benefits so that we may avoid destructive actions that result in, as Leopold writes, "dustbowls, and rivers washing the future into the sea."⁴⁴ By reworking the relationship between self, other (nature/wilderness), and agency, McCairen, Leopold, and Byl together outline fundamental differences between conquering and spiritual desires and erotic desire. Rather than view the other through the controlling, objectifying gaze shared by conquering and spiritual desire, they focus on recognizing the other's agency and goals, which may be very different than their own.

Byl does not completely abandon the role wild animals play in her own self-discovery. She writes, "I want to make sense of creatures, at once exotic and kin, and as I try to interpret their presence against the backdrop of my own existence, it's a very short leap to the owl as talisman, elk a stately messenger from a wilder world. I am more eager to see what an animal means to me than what it means to itself."⁴⁵ By admitting she is "more eager to see what an animal means to me than what it means to itself," Byl recognizes she cannot completely decenter her existence.

McCairen and Byl thus demonstrate erotic desire's two hallmarks: egalitarianism or mutualism and active participation. Heller explains ecofeminist desire as "cooperative" and "revolutionary" because it resists patriarchal hierarchies.⁴⁶ The erotic understands nature as an autonomous subject or full participant rather than an object, divine agent, or intoxicating drug. Notably, Howkin's call for a different mode of climbing, Kull's wish for a different mode of writing, and McCairen's description of the active river also connect deeply with spiritual desire. As demonstrated in the passages above, connection may be expressed in both spiritual (transcendent) and sensuous (physical) terms. In erotic representations nature may be miraculous but not divine. McCairen, for example, describes the river as a "beautiful goddess" that casts a "sensuous spell."⁴⁷ The river's ability to allure and withhold pleasure from those that travel down and through it, furthermore, echoes conquering desire's feminized portrayals of a tempting, dangerous nature.

DANCING NATURES:
DISTINGUISHING BETWEEN CONQUERING, SPIRITUAL, AND EROTIC DESIRES

Such similarities raise questions about erotic nature's fundamental differences from conquering and spiritual attitudes. Richard L. Fern in *Nature, God, and Humanity* points out that viewing nature as itself describes a specific iteration of spiritual desire, religious naturalism: "religious naturalism detects inherent value in nature and natural processes: the wine is savored, the vine is valued for what it is, not as a means to some other, alien world; nature itself... is *the* place, the one and only place, where we encounter and live with sacred powers and persons."[48] Nature, according to religious naturalism, is a sacred place. If nature is sacred, then it cannot be secular.

Along these lines Michael P. Cohen questions, in his response to William Cronon's "The Trouble with Wilderness," "Is it possible, or desirable, to distinguish between the secular and sacred strains of environmentalism? Aside from the difficulty of making such distinctions, what will be the social or political effect of making them?"[49] While erotic nature does not, by definition, employ a religious framework or theological language, as I will discuss in more detail shortly in regard to Indigenous spirituality and critical anthropomorphism, erotic and spiritual desires often appear together because of their shared interest in nature's intrinsic, animated qualities. Key to distinguishing erotic from conquering and spiritual desires is how the passage portrays "the *essential* relationship between the natural world and the extreme athlete." Conquering desire presents a "*battle* against or attempt to *conquer* or *vanquish* part of the natural world" and spiritual desire offers "accounts of a quest for individual feelings of power." As Eric Brymer and Tonia Gray write in "Dancing with Nature: Rhythm and Harmony in Extreme Sport Participation," "in these accounts of extreme sports, the natural world has only anthropocentric worth, that is, it is recognized only for its use or value to humanity."[50] Nature is a resource.

Erotic desire, however, involves what Brymer and Gray identify as "dancing with nature": "The metaphor of 'dance' recognizes a dynamic, rhythmical, harmonious, fluid and responsive interplay between the extreme sport participant and nature."[51] "Planetwalker" John Francis agrees, while adding his own twist: "The wilderness I have come to experience is how they dance, the trees with long green needles."[52] Francis observes nature's dances, silently watching so that he may learn the steps, which are their own language. Later, Francis plays music and performs a dance that imitates a bird he observed.[53] His vow of silence, which lasted seventeen years, demands he use movement and music as a form of communication—with the people he meets as well as nature. Like dance, erotic desire stresses and values partnership, creativity, and improvisation.

Further, to explore these shared and distinct boundaries—between self/other and conquering/spiritual desire—requires assessing the degree to which such representations present environmental as well as human benefits. Is the primary benefit to the adventurer or to nature or to both the adventurer and nature? As initially discussed in chapter 2 in relation to consent and sexualized imagery, representing nature's agency may be seen to fall along a continuum, with pornographic (power over) at one end and erotic (power with) at the other. While sometimes collapsed, these terms may be usefully deployed to highlight key differences in the range of self/other relationships represented in adrenaline narratives and in the agency associated with the self/other, especially as it relates to erotic human-nature interactions.

As I will discuss in more detail in the next section, to realize erotic desire's revolutionary potential adventurers must revise if not jettison the narrative of heroic masculinity and its associated hierarchies related to self/other. In doing so, adventurers may first invoke and then reject or revise heroic masculinity. As I discussed in chapter 2, any narrative that does not reproduce or invoke heroic masculinity is hard-pressed to identify as adventure. As a result, adrenaline narratives must, by narrative design, address heroic masculinity. Eddy Harris, for example, describes nature in spiritual terms and as his "adversary" in *Mississippi Solo*.[54] However, he soon realizes "I am no match for this river or any piece of nature. No match at all. Whatever anger or aggression or spite that boiled in my soul and made me think I *was* such a match has departed. Nature is a super-heavyweight and I am but a flyweight. Don't for one second think you can enter into a competition with nature. The wind and the water and the earth will not lose. The river is telling me that."[55] Harris surrenders to nature, recognizing he can never match its power. Yet his surrender does not, at least at this point, fully transform conquering desire. The boxing metaphor maintains a competitive framework, while pointing out the opponents are severely mismatched. The ecological danger of this view is that nature will always win, no matter what we do or how we treat it.

However, rather than induce fear and aggression, this "revelation" "soothe[s]" Harris.[56] He admits, "to realize that I'm not big and brave and strong and handsome, not a know-it-all or a do-it-all, should spur me from this trip. But it doesn't. It urges me on."[57] In this passage, Harris most clearly revises the narrative of heroic masculinity, which does not result in failure. Rather, recognizing there is another way to interact with nature—a way that does not demand fighting or conquering—results in a "calm" merging with nature.

> My eyes are open now and I can see. Knowing I absolutely cannot win does a strange thing to me. I'm a trouble maker, a hard-head, yet suddenly I want to submit to a power greater than myself, to let the river lead me and take me where I need to go, to obey and accept its will as my own. To struggle against the river is to drain my strength. Then I shall surely

be powerless and lost. But to submit is to ride the wind like a leaf, to relax and become part of the river, part of the life around me. So I can be calm.[58]

Harris uses simile to compare himself to a leaf on the river. As such, he seems to embrace and take Aldo Leopold's call in *Sand County Almanac* to "think like a mountain" one step further: one must *become* like a leaf.[59] In *Rowing to Latitude*, Jill Fredston likewise shifts Leopold's rhetoric to fit the extreme circumstances: "When in the mountains, we have to think like an avalanche." She explains, "if we attempt to negotiate any wild place on our own terms, without heeding Nature's clues, we might as well be donning blinders and earplugs."[60] Both Harris and Fredston stress that one must observe carefully and follow "Nature's clues" in order to survive. Harris, moreover, merges with nature so he becomes "part of the life around me."

The adventurers thus demonstrate what Stacy Alaimo describes in *Bodily Natures* as "trans-corporeality," where "the human is always intermeshed with the more-than-human world."[61] Harris flips but initially maintains the nature/culture hierarchy when he places nature at the top by "[submitting] to a power greater than myself." This shift then results in trans-corporeality or "[becoming] part of the river, part of the life around me." For Timothy Morton, trans-corporeality is a "mesh" or "a nontotalizable, open-ended concatenation of interrelations that blur and confound boundaries at practically any level: between species, between the living and the nonliving, between organism and environment."[62] The mesh also forms the basis of queer ecology, or a set of interdisciplinary practices that, in Catriona Sandilands's words, aim "to disrupt prevailing heterosexist discursive and institutional articulations of sexuality and nature, and also to reimagine evolutionary processes, ecological interactions, and environmental politics in light of queer theory."[63] Harris also presents a "queer" submission to nature when he ceases to follow the conquering conventions demanded by heroic masculinity. Erotic desire, likewise, is a queer desire and ecology defined by the interconnected mesh, trans-corporeality, and rejection of heroic masculinity.

Like the mesh and trans-corporeality, erotic desire resists or destabilizes patriarchy's heteronormative hierarchies by emphasizing connections among plant and animal (human and nonhuman) species as well as inanimate environmental elements, such as water or mountains. Trans-corporeality shifts "the environment, which is too often imagined as inert, empty space or a resource for human use" to being "a world of fleshy beings with their own needs, claims, and actions."[64] This world is McCairen's river that dances, entices, and invites. As Alaimo points out in *Bodily Natures*, feminist theory should shift from "[disentangling] *woman* from *nature*" and gender as a social construct, which maintains and depends on the nature (sex) and culture (gender) binary, to "[undertaking] the transformation of gendered dualisms—nature/culture, body/mind, object/subject, resource/agency, and others."[65] In Jeffrey McCarthy's words, this distinct, nonobjectifying representation of and engagement with nature requires "connection," which "holds the promise of knowing nature another way."[66] McCarthy—like Howkins—insists on "another way."

Like Alaimo and Morton, McCarthy also defines connection as a view that "insists that human beings are fundamentally intertwined with their environment."[67] Jill Fredston, likewise, suggests that a combination of her selected sport and the environment she navigates predisposes such intimacy: "Our boats don't allow much insulation from the environment; they force us to be absorbed by it."[68] In this sense, nature is other or distinct from self, but it is not always a distant or clearly distinct presence. The human is "intertwined" with (McCarthy) or "absorbed by" (Fredston) the environment and vice versa. McCarthy's definition and Fredston's description, like Alaimo's trans-corporeality and Morton's mesh, stress "interconnection and intermingling."[69] The terminology, moreover, suggests a deep level of mixing—where human and environmental strands not only connect or touch, but also combine, producing "the 'unity' of self and environment."[70] How this "unity" comes about—whether presented as liminal or blurred—is key to ecofeminist reworkings of desire.

Gail D. Storey, for example, deconstructs the "resource/agency" and "nature/culture" dualisms during her unsuccessful bid to hike the entire Pacific Crest Trail with her husband. She describes her "entanglement" as a woman in nature, which, as Mara de Gennaro explains, "is to be unavoidably connected and interdependent with another, or with many others."[71] De Gennaro also emphasizes entanglement's "association...with states of captivity—with all the restricted freedom and potential terror that this implies."[72] Storey, a reluctant hiker and inexperienced camper, likewise collapses or entangles environment and self when she must leave the trail. At this point she experiences an epiphany that her husband, Porter, is no longer the only or perhaps even the primary reason she would like to stay on the trail.

> I wanted to be with Porter, yes, but even more, I felt inseparable now from the vast green and blue and white of the wilderness. I looked out on the lake, shimmering under the moon. I was as sturdy as the trees. I

flowed over obstacles like water over rocks. I was as solid as the mountains, as clear as the sky.

The wind blew through my heart. I was what knew the wind. What knew the world was here in me, pulsing in trees, water, rocks, mountains, moon.[73]

Storey compares herself with plants (trees) and inanimate nature (water, mountains, sky, moon) rather than personifies nature.[74] By blurring the boundaries between human and nature, she becomes "inseparable now from the vast green and blue and white of the wilderness." In blurring the boundaries, Storey does not erase or subsume the other, which Gaard cautions against.[75] Rather, Storey describes her healing of the nature/culture split, what Gaard argues produces "a different kind of perceptual orienteering, a different way of locating oneself in relation to one's environment."[76] The act of being in wilderness changes Storey's perspective. She primarily uses simile to mark this change: "sturdy as the trees," "solid as the mountains," "clear as the sky," "like water over rocks." Unlike McCairen's use of personification, which aesthetically or formally blurs or collapses (non)human boundaries, Storey's similes maintain a liminal distance between self and other, which Gaard also advocates as key. Where McCairen personifies nature, Storey compares herself to nature, applying nonhuman characteristics to herself. Both risk imagining the experience of the other (wilderness) in order to disrupt conventional hierarchies related to self/other and culture/nature.

DANCING NATURES:
WHO LEADS?

As we have seen in the examples above and the previous chapters, ecofeminists often valorize feminine characteristics associated with unity and critique masculine traits associated with conquering. As Humberstone explains in "Re-Creation and Connections in and with Nature," "cooperation with, and sensitivity to, the environment is valued instead of aggression and competition."[77] These gendered characteristics of the self relate to gendered understandings of nature. As a result, women may be uniquely socialized to work with rather than battle against nature. For example, drawing from Annette Kolodny's *The Land before Her* and Maureen Devine's *Woman and Nature*, Nancy Pagh explains why the female "marine tourists from the late eighteenth to mid-twentieth centuries" she studies tended to eschew confrontation or descriptions of "actively 'battling' the environment": "Because woman has been historically associated with nature (and, more specifically, with 'wild' nature),... woman does not conceive of herself as battling nature and emerging, reborn, from it."[78] One might expect, especially as a result of second- and third-wave feminist activism and scholarship, such noncombative representations in post-1970s adventure narratives would increase. However, as we have seen in the previous chapters, Pagh's findings for the late eighteenth to mid-twentieth centuries do not hold up for the range of post-1970s adrenaline narratives by women (and men).

Julie Rak's reading of Arlene Blum's *Annapurna: A Woman's Place* points out, for instance, the limitations of second-wave white feminism when it comes to these gendered politics: "Blum's belief in the universality of gender inequality means that she cannot think about the role that cultural differences played in the conflict."[79] In short, Blum exhibits the common fault of (white American) feminists who are not trained in intersectionality. That is, as Rak argues, "the struggles of these women—most of whom are American or who lived in the United States—in their attempt to apply feminist ideas of the 1970s to mountaineering clearly demonstrates [sic] the strengths and the limits of American feminisms in that period in the heady times before the final defeat of the Equal Rights Amendment in 1982."[80] A liberal feminism that relies solely on increased participation and inclusion is not enough.

Humberstone explains in "Re-Creation and Connections in and with Nature" how to move forward in ways that might avoid similar problems: "in order to appreciate the ways in which men and women engage in nature-based sports, we need to understand how both female and male bodies are constituted in such settings. This entails granting female and male bodies corporeal autonomy within material nature, while recognizing that particular cultures and ideologies shape individuals. It is particularly important to recognize how collective values influence decision-making processes. Nature-based activities may provide opportunities not only for instantaneous decision making in nature, but also for the development of greater environmental awareness."[81] Thus, while patriarchal culture often genders mutuality as feminine and competition as masculine, a key component of (eco)feminist revisions questions the benefit of maintaining gendered characteristics—as cultural or essentialist constructions—as a strategy to dismantle the patriarchy. Perhaps true change requires moving beyond or ending gender as well as nature.

Not everyone, furthermore, valorizes the feminist ethics that stress community and mutuality as key for environmental sustainability. Perhaps the most famous detractor is Slavoj Žižek. As demonstrated in a 2010 *New Scientist* interview with Liz Else, at the heart of Žižek's critique lies a skepticism about a (re)turn to feminine principles: "certain environmentalists delight in proving that every catastrophe—even natural ones—is man-made, that we are all guilty, we exploited too much, we weren't feminine enough. All this bullshit. Why? Because it makes the situation 'safer.' If it is us who are the bad guys, all we have to do is change our behavior. But in fact Mother Nature is not good—it's a crazy bitch."[82] In his response to the question "Does that mean the way that we think about such threats [ecological catastrophe] is wrong?," Žižek highlights the "bullshit" that results from an easy gender dichotomy, one that genders (bad) environmental destruction and exploitation masculine—the "bad guys"—and (good) changed behavior as feminine. Ecofeminists agree, in the sense that "it is important that ecofeminists do not hastily reject the masculine autonomous self and embrace the feminine relational self as the preferable foundation for an ecofeminist ecological conception of the self," because "both masculine and feminine gender roles are flawed conceptions of personhood and must be rejected, not combined, if women and men are to experience the full range of human abilities and emotions."[83] Patriarchal gender constructions enforce a rigid gender binary and gender roles that limit, if not fail, all genders.

Certainly, as we have seen in the previous chapters, both male and female adventurers engage conquering and spiritual desire. They are also equally capable of erotic desire. Yet what Žižek implies is not that males or females are "better" environmentalists, but rather that the call for changed gendered behavior does not deal with a fundamental reality that "Mother Nature is not good—it's a crazy bitch." In more exaggerated gendered terms, Žižek describes what Harris expressed in boxing terms, with nature as "superheavyweight" to our "flyweight."[84] Notably, Žižek's critique shifts between the gendered "Mother Nature" and "bitch" and the gender-neutral pronoun, "it." Žižek sees guilt about not being "feminine enough" or the desire to interact with nature in less "exploitative" ways as malarkey, because nature is fundamentally beyond our control—whatever our desires toward it. Where Harris relies on the predominately masculine metaphor of boxing to cast this realization about his changed understanding of heroic masculinity, Žižek contrasts and critiques the flip that values feminine over masculine traits. Thus, a key difference begins to emerge in how Žižek and Harris employ gender: Žižek maintains rather than transforms conventional gendered expectations.

Žižek's remarks and Gaard's emphasis on the work required to transform gender roles remind us why gender matters when discussing the environmental crisis and our representations of nature. Žižek cannot make his point without calling nature a "bitch." There is no rational way to deal with a crazy bitch. A dangerous feminine irrationality (nature) cannot be tempered by an implied rational masculinity (culture). Perhaps, though, what Žižek labels "crazy" suggests such desire toward nature retains an androcentric worldview. In other words, because nature's actions do not (always) place man's/humanity's interests as its center, it acts illogically—like a "crazy bitch." However, if we shift perspectives to see that women/nature do not (always) place the (hu)man at the center, then we begin to see, if not necessarily desire, women/nature in a different light. Erotic desire's focus on nature's agency challenges such anthropomorphic, if not androcentric, views. Both Harris and Žižek "relinquish mastery" in Alaimo's terms.[85] However, Harris reworks, if not deconstructs, heroic masculinity rather than maintaining conventional gendered tropes.

Harris is not the only adventurer engaged in reworking heroic masculinity to stress mutuality. Ruth Anne Kocour, for example, stresses that the mountaineer's approach to the mountain is key: one must "harness" rather than "fight." She explains, "I had figured out long ago that successful mountaineers learn to harness the mountain's energy, not fight it." Kocour continues, "it becomes an almost unconscious effort... a little magical."[86] While "harness" does not suggest that she gives up all control, she finds a "magical" way to work with rather than against nature. Joe Kane also understands nature as a living entity and something within which he can become absorbed. Kane understands that "a white-water river was so *alive*. If one were good enough—confident and skilled and strong—one became part of its spirit, absorbed its rhythms."[87] Kane describes the literal flow of the water and his kayak as well as the more spiritual connection—or the flow that comes when one is deeply engaged in an activity. This "deep play" results in a collapsing of boundaries between self and other, human and nature.

Steven Callahan also identifies a community and unity with nonhuman others in *Adrift*. Callahan notes that his forced exile results in a new understanding of his place within the larger world. He reveals that "drifting halfway across the Atlantic and learning to live like an aquatic caveman showed me time and again that I am less an individual than part of a continuum, joined to all things and driven by them more than I am in control of my own path."[88] Callahan's striped-down, "aquatic caveman" experience attunes him to his environment. He writes later, "it is just another irony with which my tale is filled—the heartfelt realization of one's insignificance yields a calming sense of being completely connected to the greater whole. As a tiny part of the world and humanity, I now feel more at peace and much larger than I ever felt as a man alone."[89] Like Harris in *Mississippi Solo*, Callahan finds connection when he embraces "insignificance" and abandons "control of my own path." Notably, Callahan also focuses on his individual transformation and change in perspective. His narrative, in this sense, remains structurally and thematically anthropocentric. Nature, however, is not objectified in order to produce this individual change. In this sense, as ecofeminist Val Plumwood argues, "here it is the visitor who is the taught and not the teacher, the transformed and not the transformer, visitors who must see themselves through the other's eyes, must bend themselves, as is appropriate for visitors, to the other's ways."[90] Callahan abandons a pornographic control or power over nature that produces his "peace" and bond with "the greater whole."

We see in these examples ecofeminism's fundamental goal to alleviate oppression in its various forms. The goal emerges in a commitment to disrupt conventional hierarchies of self/other and redefine the erotic as a mutually pleasurable/beneficial experience. Erotic desire seeks to listen and amplify rather than silence. Rather than understanding pleasure solely from the male gaze's perspective, which does not account for the desires of the observed object or only understands them via the "pleasures" of objectification, ecofeminists seek to construct a participatory gaze. In doing so, they also challenge the pleasure of being watched, a pleasure that the male gaze cultivates to maintain its power and control. Reworking erotic discourse thus revises the patriarchal discourses about woman/nature and desire. "The idea," as Krein puts it, "of 'conquering' some aspect of the natural environment has largely been replaced by the idea of interactively harmonizing with it."[91] Individuals must actively engage in this work, especially women, who have been largely defined by rather than the definers of wilderness experiences.

Suzanne Roberts in *Almost Somewhere*, for example, admits, "in truth most of my wilderness experiences had been defined for me by the men I dated or hoped to date. They chose the route, the goal, characterizing the way we would see the wilderness."[92] Roberts now seeks to find her own way into wilderness rather than follow the paths "defined for me." She needs to find her own narrative path and voice. The next three sections examine how the adventurer's journey must change in order to express erotic desire. Each section highlights important narrative "cairns" or markers that writers deploying erotic desire leave, with authors adding their own narrative rocks to mark the distinct path erotic desire forges. I then consider the two primary ways the erotic decolonizes desire before concluding with a discussion of erotic desire's environmental ethics.

EROTIC NARRATIVE CAIRNS: SELF-CONSCIOUSLY BREAKING HEROIC FORM TO CONNECT, NOT CONQUER

Perhaps the easiest way to identify erotic desire is when the author self-consciously breaks standard plot conventions in regard to heroic masculinity and the definition of wilderness, as in the Wilderness Act of 1964, as a place "untrammeled by man, where man himself is a visitor who does not remain."[93] This traditional definition understands wilderness as "retreat," or "a place to visit, a place for being refreshed and renewed."[94] As Linda Vance writes in "Ecofeminism and Wilderness," "until the basis for wilderness protection is radically reconceptualized, the task of stopping environmental degradation in nonwilderness areas will become increasingly Sisyphean."[95] While John Francis envisions wilderness as an "unspoiled landscape and solitude," he later says, "I can always experience the wilderness that is beside the road," suggesting that he also does not demand wilderness to be "untrammeled" or constitute large tracks of land.[96] Rather, wilderness is, as Roderick Frazier Nash describes, a "state of mind."[97] Reconceptualization requires the adventurer to provide a new impetus, one not bent on conquering or individual spiritual transformation, and one not dependent on virgin wilderness.

The adventurer's perspective is key: how s/he defines and approaches wilderness frames his/her interaction with it. As such, it may initially appear certain adventure sports and sportscapes are best suited for this work. The different desiring natures found in McCairen's rafting tale, Harris's canoe trip, and Krakauer's Everest narrative in part emerge from their different sports and sportscapes. Mark Sundeen suggests that "the desert draws a different type of person than the mountains, one whose place in American lore has been largely ignored because it doesn't fit the Manifest Destiny mythology of the industrious settler cutting a civilized swath in the savage forest."[98] However, the degree of difference in narrative form, representation of nature, and environmentalism due to distinct sports and sportscapes should not be overemphasized. Like the author's gender, the adventurer's sport and location does not automatically determine the narrative's representation of nature. Todd Balf's adrenaline narrative about rafting the Yarlung Tsangpo, a river the paddling community refers to as the "Everest of rivers," attests that the sport does not necessarily predict and determine an adventurer's relationship with nature.[99] Balf explains, "surviving days on end in big, pulsing whitewater, at the bottom of a bottomless canyon, was analogous to life at altitude, some said—each its own Death Zone."[100] All extreme adventures share grave danger in natural settings. All are pressured to fit their story into some version of heroic masculinity.

Revising adventure's goals eliminates heroic masculinity's conquering goals and plot. For Alvah Simon in *North to the Night*, this rejection of the standard measures of adventure meant that he did not embark on the expedition to set records.[101] They set none. As a result, success needed to be measured in a different way—in lessons learned, among them "that we all are born of this earth, that we are shaped both materially and mentally by its terrain, weather, flora, and fauna as surely as we now shape it."[102] Simon learns connection, defined in the way that Alaimo asserts, where "the human is always intermeshed with the more-than-human world."[103] Robert Kull makes a similar shift in how he frames his narrative, noting that his goal is not to conquer nature or experience spiritual transformation. Rather, Kull's "goal in the wilderness was not to conquer either the external world or my own inner nature, but to give up the illusion of ownership and control and to experience myself as part of the ebb and flow of something greater than individual ego. But the goal of attaining enlightenment was elusive—except when it was not."[104] Just as Eddy Harris eventually realizes he must surrender and "ride the wind like a leaf... relax and become part of the river," Kull seeks to immerse himself in the "ebb and flow of something greater."[105] His experience will still, hopefully, result in "enlightenment," but one less focused on "individual ego."

Sherry Simpson in *The Accidental Explorer: Wayfinding in Alaska* models both means of rewriting the narrative while still including the genre's recognizable landmarks. She revises both wilderness's definition and heroic masculinity's journey plot. In her introduction, for example, Simpson describes Alaska as "a place where the separation between nature and home seemed no more substantial than the faint rattle of a beaded curtain between doorways."[106] She goes on to complicate wilderness's definitional boundaries, stressing that "Alaska's Original Peoples have no comparable concept of wilderness because the word suggests a landscape untouched by humans, and such an untruth implies a lack of reciprocity between the natural, human, and spiritual worlds."[107] Simpson thus opens her story by challenging the blank "undiscovered" landscape upon which adrenaline narratives frequently depend. Simpson's nonlinear narrative, furthermore, resists "march[ing] across this page from camp to camp, from night to night, recounting the string of events."[108] Instead, Simpson's "wayfinding" renders "maps not of discovery, but of knowingness."[109] *The Accidental Explorer* self-consciously revises the adrenaline narrative's colonial setting and linear, goal-oriented journey plot.

While Simon, Kull, Simpson, and Fredston consciously design their adventures to resist heroic masculinity, other adventurers resist this narrative framework as the adventure and/or narrative progresses. Eric Brymer suggests in "Extreme Sports as a Facilitator of Ecocentricity and Positive Life Changes" that these narratives follow a process of transformation shared by many extreme sport participants: "the idea that participants battle against nature is transformed to one where nature takes a centric and meaningful position and the notions of 'no fear' and 'extreme Dude' are reframed as courage and humility."[110] Brymer explains, "being in nature as an extreme sport participant where death is a real potential might change the human tendency for anthropocentricity and replace it with ecocentricity and the realisation of true courage and humility."[111] The combination of extreme risk and a natural setting sets the stage for such transformations.

Tracking this transformation among extreme practitioners questions whether or not ecological epiphanies are available to or experienced by everyone. Brymer and Gray, for example, question whether or not their findings about extreme adventure are true only for "veteran practitioners": "We cannot tell from the research whether this ecocentric awakening is a typical outcome for extensive extreme sport experience or if an ecocentric perspective is characteristic of those participants who are more likely to continue participation to become veteran practitioners." Examples from adrenaline narratives such as Gail D. Storey's suggest rookie adventurers also experience "transformative," "heightened ecocentric awareness" as a result of "their extreme sports experiences."[112] Adrenaline narratives by rookies and experts map movement from and between a conquering, spiritual transformation and environmental awareness.

Suzanne Roberts, for example, states near the beginning of *Almost Somewhere* that she rejects "man's view of nature" and began her hike not to conquer but to discover her "own view of wildness." She knew she wanted a different narrative frame, but she did not know what it looked like when she embarked on her adventure. Roberts explains, "often people say they hike mountains because they are there. Even though some women have taken on this attitude, it seems to me that it is an internalization of man's view of nature. For Erika the idea of conquest made sense, but for me it didn't—and still doesn't—fit, yet I had no better way of looking at things, though in part maybe that's one of the reasons I was there: I was in search of my own view of wildness, my own connection to the natural landscape."[113] In searching for her own view of wildness, Roberts admits, "I had no language of my own for the landscape, no way to define myself within it."[114] While Roberts does not have a replacement for heroic masculinity, she hopes to discover it.

Roberts describes her struggle to find "a language of my own to describe the landscape in all its complexity," one not "relying upon the language of men, a language that doesn't take into account all the ways I felt about being in the mountains." She admits at this point that she "had not yet read Mary Austin, Isabella Bird, or Rachel Carson. I hadn't heard of Annie Dillard, Gretel Ehrlich, Linda Hogan, or Terry Tempest Williams. I wouldn't discover Lorraine Anderson's *Sisters of the Earth*, which was like a revelation to me, until that fall when I went on a search for women writing about the wilderness." For Roberts, literature provides the (imperfect) frame for her wilderness experience. Without these female models, Roberts makes do with what is available to her. She explains, "so, for the time being I continued to have imaginary conversations with John Muir."[115] In doing so, her ability to change the narrative is limited. She must find a way to break a different narrative trail.

Roberts describes the difference between what she seeks and those male writers that came before her. She realizes, "while these male writers [Charles Darwin, Henry David Thoreau, Edward Abbey, John Muir] sought autonomy, I craved community. Where they were out to conquer oceans and deserts, woods and mountains, I wanted only to connect."[116] Roberts stresses a connected community that can only be found in and with nature. Wilderness is the location and facilitator for community and connection. She later clarifies that both conquering and spiritual desires fail her. Roberts explains, "once on the trail, I began to see that neither construct worked—nature as threatening or nature as nurturing. John Muir may have found nature glorious, yet the glory was in Muir and in his response to the natural world. As far as I could tell, the mountains weren't going around trying to make me feel one way or the other."[117] Roberts is engaged in the process, in Brymer and Gray's words, of "moving beyond an internal-external duality ... [to] experience connectedness and reposition the natural world in their experience from 'Other' and 'Over-there' to merge with the 'Self' and 'Here.'"[118] Rejecting patriarchal (masculine "threatening") and spiritual (feminine "nurturing") constructions of nature, Roberts maps out a third possibility: unity and community.

Roberts eventually wrests control from a (heroic) masculine model and discovers something different—more true to her own experience and voice—by shifting the framing gaze. She now understands that "although

I had come to see the Sierra Nevada as *his* [Muir's] mountains, I hoped that I too might come to find that not only was I in the mountains but that the mountains were also in me."[119] Roberts moves from Muir's ownership and external framing to placing herself "in the mountains" and "the mountains...in me." Roberts shifts to trans-corporeality. In the end, Roberts "realized I had been relying on a male translation of nature rather than listening to my own voice. That night, of all the words I could have used to describe how I felt, the most accurate would have been *connected*."[120] While her focus shifts to "listening to my own voice" and not to nature's speech, Roberts attributes the trouble in achieving physical ease in the wilderness to the nature-culture split. As a result, she seeks to reconnect or blur the boundaries between nature and culture. For Roberts, "wildness can exist both outside and inside of us, whereas the very definition of wilderness seems to be the absence of humans, further separating us from our wild places and our very own wild natures."[121] Rather than see wilderness as "out there," Roberts shifts to see "wildness" as both "outside and inside." This suggestion of both/and instead of either/or is instructive, especially in regard to ecofeminist debates about self/other and how this debate informs the definition of wilderness.

EROTIC NARRATIVE CAIRNS:
REWORKING WILDERNESS

When Roberts blurs self/other, human/nature, and civilization/wilderness, she redefines wilderness and "connects." She also argues "wildness" is both self and other: "Wildness can exist both outside and inside of us."[122] Thus, while Vance prefers nature as *other* over nature as *self*—"Respect for nature as Other is, I think, preferable to a respect for nature as Self"[123]— Roberts suggests both are possible. Roberts enters the ecofeminist debate about self/other by suggesting both models have merit. Both are true in her experience. In this way, Roberts and erotic desire more generally embrace Val Plumwood's idea of "a theory of mutuality." This theory "acknowledges both continuity and difference." It also "provides an alternative way to view wilderness." Specifically, "in this framework, 'wilderness' does not designate an excluded place defined negatively, apart from self, alien and separate. Nor is wilderness assimilated to self."[124] If nature is not wholly self or other, "continuity and difference" emerge.

Reworking wilderness requires a reworking of the dominant figures of speech we use to describe nature. Catriona Sandilands suggests we move away from the two most common nature metaphors, "nature-as-female and nature-as-home," and replace them with "mystery."[125] This sense of mystery is distinct from the patriarchal "dark mystery" discussed in chapter 2. Nature as mystery refers to the "recognition of a moment in nature that overflows our ability to describe it. It is wild. It is not simply the diversity of nature, or our diversity *as* nature, but 'unspeakable' complexity."[126] As Sandilands states, this sense of mystery holds more in common with spiritual desire, and it also resembles the agnostic sense of "magic and mystery" I discussed in chapter 3.[127]

Christine Byl expresses a similar redefined understanding of wildness that seeks to describe what Sandilands terms nature's "'unspeakable' complexity." Byl focuses on voice and listening, explaining, "it sounds naïve to modern ears, tuned as they are to the realism of science and the pragmatism of [the] food chain, but the tenor of these old ways of being with animals indicates a critical understanding about interconnection: vulnerability need not always trigger fear."[128] Byl's definition stresses "interconnection" while retaining a sense of unbound freedom, which is key to American mythology and landscape.

A howl or cry rather than speech best articulates wildness. Byl suggests, "wild is head back hollering at the sky, a moment that contains the full world. Wild is not tame, not bound, not constrained, constricted, condensed. Wildness is big or it is small, but it is open—mouth, season, door, heart."[129] Wild's radical openness is freeing and frightening. It is an expression shared among many animals. Along these same lines Amy Irvine reminds her readers Henry David Thoreau calls for the preservation of "wildness": "He didn't say 'wilderness.' He knew that no piece of land— no matter how scenic or pristine—would restore what we have lost in ourselves."[130] Irvine also connects this wildness to a "howl" rather than a specific physical landscape.[131] This "primordial sound" or "chorus of those marvelously complex vocalizations would indeed be the world's salvation."[132] Wildness and freedom connect in ways mutually beneficial to humans and the environment.

The combination of wildness and freedom is characteristically American, too. Jonah Raskin explains, "the wild seems to have come already packaged in the American DNA, and American writers can't help but hear its call and walk on the wild side, too. In fact, the wilderness—as friend, foe, rough beast, and sacred place—has long provided American writers with a sense of place and distinguished them from their English literary cousins."[133] Irvine and Byl's descriptions of wildness, furthermore, enact the "wild democracy" Sandilands describes as "implicit in ecofeminist politics."[134] Wild or erotic democracy demands democratization, "a proliferation of discourses around nature, a validation of different experiences of nature."[135] Redefining wilderness, opening it beyond the virgin/whore dualism, is one means to practice wild democracy.

American adventurers question wilderness's quarantined status. Byl specifically redefines wilderness to challenge its pristine, "empty" status. She claims that "wilderness, the empty kind, is rare anywhere, and most of our places are not really untouched; we have always lived amid cultures on land. Old tin cans may undermine the claim of virgin wilderness, but they are relics that point us toward a candid way of seeing nature: not a distant diorama of a wilder place, but a home."[136] She cannot fully return to the "old ways" or promote nostalgia for a lost Eden.[137] Neither wilderness nor Byl are innocent. Byl's "old tin cans," moreover, allude to Mary Austin's "The Scavengers," which concludes, "there is no scavenger that eats tin cans, and no wild thing leaves a like disfigurement on the forest floor."[138] Where Austin condemns litter and humanity's wasteful inefficiency in comparison to "the economy of nature," Byl suggests old tin cans function to remind us wilderness is a landscape, or, in Byl's more intimate terms, "a home" shaped by human forces.[139] As Vance argues, such visible reminders are necessary, given that our definition of wilderness often relies on visible rather than invisible signs, such as "pollution, species extinction, fire and disease suppression": "as long as human actions are invisible, they can be ignored."[140] To see wilderness as "home" is—in both Byl's and Roberts's terms—to be connected with and understand humanity's impact on the landscape. We cannot bury this trash.

EROTIC NARRATIVE CAIRNS:
SILENCING HEROIC MASCULINITY

Other adventurers may resist the conventional demands of heroic masculinity and wilderness by simply refusing the adrenaline narrative altogether. African American climber and author James Edward Mills published a book-length account that documents his and other African Americans' experiences in the outdoors. *The Adventure Gap* includes a chapter devoted to Sophia Danenberg, the first African American woman to climb Everest. His account describes Danenberg as an athlete who does not actively seek the spotlight: "as an athlete with no sponsors to please, Sophia never felt compelled to boast about her 'first ascent.'" In fact, Mills says, "she was uncomfortable even discussing it."[141] Mills positions Danenberg as an unconventional adventurer—one who does not rely on sponsors or fame—and as a person who displays both stereotypically feminine (modesty) and stereotypically unfeminine (a penchant for risky behavior) characteristics.

Danenberg explains that her silence comes from being uncomfortable with the position in which the adrenaline narrative seems determined to place her: "I climb because I like to climb. And to have my birth bring more significance to it is tough for me.... I know that it has significance for other people, but I struggle with it in my head. It's almost embarrassing."[142] Danenberg suggests that there is not a story in her first assent of Everest, or at least one that she wants to frame in terms of her race and gender. Danenberg's discomfort may emerge from the limited narrative frame available to tell her story. While some may read her remarks as postracial, Danenberg, in fact, may be resisting the adrenaline narrative's rigid racial and gendered frames. Her silence, in this context, is a form of resistance rather than capitulation to the dominant narrative.

Identifying revisions and breaks in the heroic masculinity narrative is often difficult because erotic desire rarely appears by itself when the focus is adventure—especially in its more extreme forms. As we saw with Harris above, sometimes authors shift from conquering to connecting with nature. After declaring ownership of the river, Harris eventually realizes "what it was all about, what it was all for." Like Roberts, Kull, Kocour, and Kane, Harris collapses nature and life: "To drive the senses alive and then to calm them. To be able to see with the eye that is the heart's eye, to see life. To become one with the river, but more to become one with life."[143] Such moments suggest a suspension of the mind-body split as well as the nature/culture dichotomy. Mind and body are joined by "the heart's eye" and no longer separate in nature. "Heart's eye" collapses physicality and spirituality: to see with one's heart stresses an emotional, loving view.

Harris also embraces and collapses the good and bad, embodied in himself and "the river, the trees, the animals, the men and women, the wind. To feel it all rushing through my veins and to love it. To know that they are me and I am them. They and their generosity and goodness and beauty are what I want to be. They and their hate and shame and evil are what I am and what I try not to see." Here *Mississippi Solo* recalls Walt Whitman's *Leaves of Grass*, especially "Song of Myself," which similarly embraces contradictions and connections in its radically open characterization of America. "But it's all there, the many sides," Harris continues. Sounding a lot like Whitman, Harris writes, "and the faces of strangers are no longer strange. I recognize and know them all.... I have seen them, I have known them, I am them. There is no color that separates us, no race, no issue deeper than humanity to bind us."[144] Like Whitman, Harris emphasizes nature's transcendental aspects and defines America as an individual as well as an environment that "contain multitudes."[145]

The above examples from Harris demonstrate that the erotic is often a reworking of transcendentalism's conquering (patriarchal) and spiritual desires, more so than it is a complete jettisoning of these foundational desires: the erotic casts sex/gender and secular/spiritual in reconfigured terms. Not all examples complete a wholesale revision of both conquering and spiritual desires. As evident in the following passage from Harris's *Mississippi Solo*, an erotic representation of nature extends Leopold's "think like the mountain" to present nature thinking. The passage also emphasizes a "clean" spirituality by describing nature as "pristine and serene in its beauty": "But so pristine and serene in its beauty is this place, it can hardly be called majestic or imposing, overpowering or breathtaking. Instead, it whispers at you. It calls and sings sweetly, bathing you in melody that you finally notice and eventually feel and see, misting around you like a warm morning fog in spring, bathing you in delight and soothing you until you are at the same time both silent and on the edge of shouting with joy. It's not a Gothic cathedral, but a lovely little chapel whose absolute artistry you do not expect, and you're awestricken."[146] Harris describes nature in erotic and spiritual terms.

However, rather than present nature simply as an *object* of desire or emphasize nature as a means of personal transformation, in the above passage Harris describes nature as a sensate entity and highlights nature's mutual participation in the adventure. The environment whispers, calls, mists, and bathes. The result for the adventurer in this passage—"you're awestricken"—conforms to conventional spiritual desire, especially when paired with the chapel metaphor. The focus, moreover, remains on the adventurer's reaction and transformation within this environment. Harris's transformation emerges as he learns to recognize and listen to the subtle beauty of nature's "lovely little chapel."

William Cronon might suggest that Harris is engaged in revising our understanding of wilderness by shifting focus from the grand landscape traditionally associated with the sublime—"God was on the mountaintop, in the chasm, in the waterfall, in the thundercloud, in the rainbow, in the sunset"—to a smaller scale, a more quietly sublime landscape.[147] Nature is a "chapel," not a "Gothic cathedral." We see an emphasis on building an intimate relationship with nature earlier in Harris's narrative when he describes nature as a "relative" and a "friend" who he gradually gets to know, having "watched this river forever." When he embarks on his adventure, Harris describes the river being "as familiar to me as a relative." As he continues on his journey, Harris is eventually able to "see beyond the surface and river becomes friend."[148] The description of nature as a friend and relative retains self/other boundaries, but also describes nature as a close companion, who is both related by blood and a chosen relationship (friend).

This change from "relative" to "friend" comes about because the river reveals "more of what it truly is. It allows me an understanding that I could never have gotten without the risk of intimacy." Once again, Harris focuses on his transformation, changes made possible because of the nature of his extreme adventure that required him to get "intimate" with nature. Harris divulges that "as I strip the varnish off my own exterior and expose hidden layers, the river reciprocates and reveals to me what I otherwise would not have known." The word choice "reciprocates" also implies that the river matches the level of intimacy that Harris presents. The river offers unity as a means to facilitate Harris's transformation. Harris concludes, "that, then, is what I must be after, seeking an understanding of the river and through the mirror of friendship, an understanding of myself, and through the special unity offered by the river, a better way to see."[149] Harris's unity with nature changes his perspective; he now has a "better way to see." While anthropocentric, such individual transformation still holds potential, as individual change remains key to the environmental movement and the achievement of greater ecological health. In viewing nature differently, Harris offers hope that sound environmental treatment follows.

In contrast to Harris's erotic-spiritual presentation of participatory nature, conquering desire presents ecological descriptions that function primarily as "color" points in their texts. Rather than portraying nature as a polymorphous participant, patriarchal dramatic descriptions emphasize the fantastic elements the adventurers fight against. While climbing the Khumbu Icefall, for example, Krakauer in *Into Thin Air* describes the experience as both terrifying and beautiful; the ravishing icefall so intoxicates him that Krakauer's fear temporarily disappears. Nature appears transcendent and as a dangerously alluring beauty in fundamentally different ways than Harris describes.

Krakauer depicts the icefall's terrible beauty: "But if the Icefall was strenuous and terrifying, it had a surprising allure as well. As dawn washed the darkness from the sky, the shattered glacier was revealed to be a three-dimensional landscape of phantasmal beauty.... I meandered through a vertical maze of crystalline blue stalagmites. Sheer rock buttresses seamed with ice pressed in from both edges of the glacier, rising like the shoulders of a malevolent god.... For an hour or two [I] actually forgot to be afraid."[150] While the beauty is awe-inspiring, the dancing sunlight off the ice triggers a migraine-force headache. Krakauer questions that the headache "was due to the altitude, because it didn't strike until I'd returned to Base Camp. More likely it was a reaction to the fierce ultraviolet radiation that had burned my retinas and baked my brain."[151] Drinking in Everest's intoxicating beauty has its price. Furthermore, Krakauer is not transformed as a result. His vision, in fact, is worse: his "burned" retinas and "baked" brain produce pain without enlightenment. Krakauer's description thus holds more in common with Žižek's "crazy bitch" than with Harris's "friend." As I outlined in chapter 2, while Krakauer does not present a neat or successful narrative of heroic masculinity in *Into Thin Air*, he also does not fully revise or move away from its narrative structures and expectations. In the most tragic cases, the inability to revise heroic masculinity gets the adventurer killed.

Unconventional adventurer and eco-activist Timothy Treadwell, who was mauled and killed along with his companion by an Alaskan bear in 2003, is one such example. Colin Carman understands Treadwell as unable to escape "unfulfillable standards of masculinity," which, in turn, "drove Treadwell to swear off sociality altogether as he went into the wild to test his manhood."[152] The controversy about Treadwell primarily focuses on his unconventional methods in the wild, especially how he "lived with" the bears: "Over the years, Timothy is advised, warned, and urged to show restraint and take basic precautions, both for the bears' sake and his own—not just by the feds, but by biologists, photographers, pilots, and even similar-minded bear activists like Charlie Russell and Dr. Stephen Stringham. The latter two, despite a shared belief in intraspecies spirituality, can't convince him to use a bear fence or carry spray, and to be a bit more careful."[153] As a result, when Treadwell dies with his companion—even after "over thirteen seasons" of success (measured by not getting himself, a bear, or anyone else killed)—he experiences, like anyone who dies while engaging in risky behavior, special scrutiny. Treadwell inspired fierce defenders as well as critics. Jon Krakauer in *Into the Wild* discusses a similar debate about and a personal affinity to Chris McCandless. McCandless is also viewed as foolish and naïve by some and as a romantic idealist by others.

The inability to turn back from a summit or judge successfully risk's cost-benefit speaks to ways heroic masculinity may "blinker" adventurers. Treadwell, unlike Nick Jans—who admits he shares personality traits and life experiences with Treadwell—does not come to Alaska with a gun.[154] Jans explains, "while I wanted to become like the people I lived among, Timothy wanted them to become like him."[155] Jans goes on to explain that Alaskan culture, "rooted in killing," is one not shared by Treadwell.[156] Treadwell, as a result, is both inescapably defined by and resists heroic masculinity. His inability to escape heroic masculinity's grasp, combined with his simultaneous refusal to carry a gun or even pepper spray, results in divergent understandings of his life and death: Treadwell is simultaneously read as a failed hero, an alternative hero, or a mentally ill fool.

While they may differ in their interpretations, the adrenaline narratives by and about Timothy Treadwell seem determined to confine him within the narrative of heroic masculinity. Some cast Treadwell as a brave and sacrificing hero in line with traditional heroic masculinity: "One thing everyone seems to agree on: Timothy Treadwell, from start to finish, holds his own opinions and beliefs about bears, and keeps counsel largely with himself on the matter. And, right or wrong, he has major cojones."[157] In this passage Jans characterizes Treadwell as hypermasculine: opinionated, stubborn, and a man with "major cojones." His death, as a result, can also fit unsung or tragic hero models: "Treadwell's work registers a sacrificial and masochistic desire to ultimately die for his culture's fantasy of masculine nature (embodied in the totemic bear)."[158] Heroic masculinity kills Treadwell.

Others cast Treadwell as a fool, tragically mentally ill, or simply a dumb, failed actor who had no business in the Alaskan bush. This foolishness or, more severely, mental illness is what Ryan Hediger refers to as "the fatal madness of Treadwell's animal sympathy."[159] His questionable mental stability, affinity for animals, and overall performance feminizes Treadwell. June Dwyer notes Treadwell's failure at masculinity when she describes him as "particularly affecting and painful to watch because he assumes a childlike understanding between himself and the bears he spends time with."[160] Later in her essay she also discusses why he does not qualify as a "tragic hero."[161] Dwyer also describes Treadwell as an "unrestrained oddball."[162] As Hediger argues, labeling Treadwell a "freak" reaffirms "prevalent and reductive notions of the normal body by presenting extreme counterpoints."[163] Treadwell's baby talk combined with his cutesy animal names infantilizes him and the bears. Treadwell's childlike demeanor means he does not qualify for masculinity, let alone a heroic version.[164] By not carrying a gun, Treadwell abnegates phallic power: his feminized, childlike demeanor with wild nature, as a result, causes his death. Femininity, as Dave Canterbury reminds us, has no place in the wilderness: "You come to the swamp, you'd better leave your skirt at the house."[165] Hediger, writing about Herzog's film *Grizzly Man*, notes that "freakish Treadwell is killed because he will not acknowledge the apparently normal and sane notion that nature is dangerous, deadly, completely other."[166] Treadwell, in other words, proves Žižek's point that nature is a "crazy bitch."

Treadwell's death, as well as Krakauer's failure to break from heroic masculinity and engage erotic nature in *Into Thin Air*, may also be a product of their adventures' "inauthentic" design and tragic outcomes. Alan P. Dougherty argues in "Aesthetic and Ethical Issues Concerning Sport in Wilder Places" for an "authentic and appropriate" engagement with nature as the best means to encourage environmental benefits, proposing "that when sporting engagement with wilder places is both authentic and appropriate, the quality of sporting experience is both likely to be greater and that negative environmental impacts will be reduced."[167] Dougherty defines "authentic behavior" as follows: "Guided by Nature, such a model should engender behaviour appropriate to the well-being of the ecology and wildness of an area and... encourage and facilitate an enhanced sporting experience. Appropriate engagement should be sought because it is ethically and aesthetically sound with respect to location, while authenticity of engagement is to be found in that relationship to environment which is not overly mediated by technology. Under this description, practice would be guided by the principle of *adapting the activity to the environment*, rather than the environment to the activity."[168] Dougherty's description echoes the pure climbing and adventure ethos, discussed in chapter 2, that emphasizes little or no use of technology and eschews corporate influence. It also highlights erotic desire's emphasis on nature as a guide and facilitator of "appropriate engagement." While Treadwell eschews technology, especially equipment that might help keep him safe from bears, his inauthenticity stems from a failure to follow heroic masculinity's codes and—as I discuss shortly—scientific protocols. At stake is how Treadwell interacted with the bears and whether his methods have any merit. Did his extreme anthropomorphism kill him? Are his communications with bears delusional appropriations or an alternative science that recovers animal voice and subjectivity? The next two sections combine ecofeminism with postcolonial and animal studies in order to evaluate the adrenaline narrative's presentation of nonhuman voice and agency.

DECOLONIZING DESIRE: CRITICAL ANTHROPOMORPHISM

Feminist and postcolonial theory and writing has an established tradition of recovering voices. Just as Gayatri Chakravorty Spivak asked the question, "can the subaltern speak," ecocriticism increasingly asks the same question of a subaltern nature in the Anthropocene. Can nature speak? Will representations inevitably express the adventurers' desires instead of nature's? Exploring these questions requires going even further than Fayaz Chagani—who asks, in the title of his essay, "Can the Postcolonial Animal Speak?"—by extending Spivak's question to include "other sentient beings" as well as inanimate nature.[169] In doing so, ecocriticism, in the words of Mara de Gennaro, "must contend with enduring problems of voice and power that have long been matters of dispute in those discussions."[170] As Philip Armstrong points out, a critical reluctance to join animal and postcolonial studies emerges from the risk of "trivializing the suffering of human beings under colonialism."[171] However, merging environmental and postcolonial approaches "does not mean flattening the differences between humans and other animals" or inanimate nature, as pointed out by Chagani.[172] One means of addressing this issue, suggested by de Gennaro, is to "attend less to trying to speak for nonhumans, and more to examining what it means for humans to live with them."[173] This solution to the social and environmental justice problems raised by anthropomorphism, however, suggests there is no ethical way to anthropomorphize or represent nature's voice. Does anthropomorphism, even when self-conscious of its "humanising and colonising dynamic," do more environmental harm than good?[174] When we turn to adrenaline narratives, we encounter some who refuse to anthropomorphize and others who engage in a range of (critical) anthropomorphic representations.

Key is whether or not anthropomorphism is doomed to be, as Sowon S. Park puts it, "a mere fallacy—a conceptual prison-house into which we are inescapably locked, separating us from the non-humans."[175] Because survival often depends on the ability to listen to or read nature closely in order to determine risk, adrenaline narratives offer excellent test cases. Extreme adventurers often stress the importance of learning and understanding nature's language. They emphasize their close proximity and, as we saw above and in the previous chapters, immersion in their sport environments. This key skill mitigates physical risk to the adventurer and, arguably, represents their erotic desire or connection with nature. However, as Park points out, "the idea that we communicate with other creatures on the basis of shared objects, time and space is vehemently disputed by philosophers albeit along different philosophical paths."[176] New science increasingly challenges this viewpoint: "biology suggests otherwise. Neuroscientific discoveries in the last twenty years, building on evolutionary theory, have produced evidence which goes some way to supporting the idea that contrary to the idea of a radical abyss between species, there exists a continuum."[177] Additionally, perhaps literature and other arts should not be bound strictly by science, even in nonfiction writing.

The creative, if not perfectly scientific, tool of anthropomorphism may offer a nonphysical means to (re)connect with nature. As humans become more detached from physical nature, we may become more reliant on other means to foster connection: as Kim-Pong Tam, Sau-Lai Lee, and Melody Manchi Chao suggest, "environmentalists cannot rely solely on direct experience in nature as their promotion strategies. There is a strong need for other tactics. The present research hints at a potentially efficacious tactic: anthropomorphism."[178] Nevertheless, what anthropomorphic representations suggest regarding culture is still at issue. "Current environmental feminism argues," according to Barbara Humberstone, "that this revisioning [of Cartesian woman/nature, man/culture (sport) binaries and nonhuman exploitation] is premised on the significant connections between the oppression of women and other subalterns (oppressions as a consequence of race, class, sexuality and so forth) and the exploitation of nature."[179] At the heart of the debate about anthropomorphism is whether or not, as Richie Nimmo posits, "anthropomorphism ultimately manifests a humanising and colonising dynamic, asserting proximity and similarity at the cost of eradicating distance and alterity."[180] We see a range of engagements with anthropomorphism in American adrenaline narratives.

Adventurer Nancy Lord, for example, points out why writers are cautioned against anthropomorphic representations. Lord takes on the voice of these critics and admonishes, "writer to self: *Watch your language! You're sentimentalizing and anthropomorphizing. You're casting perfectly lovely animals into your pathetic soap opera. Bad, Bad!*"[181] In this passage, Lord identifies what Nimmo calls anthropomorphism's "deeply inscribed" connections "within modern and scientific ways of thinking." These ways of thinking connect anthropomorphism with "intellectual naivety, self-indulgence, superstition or infantilism, and thus as something to be scrupulously avoided by anyone who considered themselves rational and sensible."[182] Suzanne Roberts further explains in *Almost Somewhere*, "we were always attaching our ideas to natural objects, assigning some meaning that made us feel better or explained the unexplainable, when really, an albatross is a seabird, not a symbol."[183] Roberts similarly cautions against turning nature into a symbol. Doing so objectifies nature by imposing human desires upon it. Therefore, rather than expressing mutual intimacy, anthropomorphism offers another means to project human desires and objectify.

The injunction not to anthropomorphize nature perhaps helps explain why Peter Nichols in *Sea Change* refuses to personify the sea.

> In the worst of weathers, I've never felt the remotest ill will from the sea, or the least recognition. The ocean, like water in a glass, is absolutely impersonal. It makes no distinction between you and your little dreamboat, filled with your photo albums and all your hopes, and the windblown larva of a mayfly, or a barnacle, or a Styrofoam coffee cup. You're just there. The sea is doing its thing. You deal with it as well as you can, with your weather forecasts, your alarm clock, your sextant and chronometer and the rest of your bag of tricks.[184]

Nichols suggests a firm separation between the sea and humans. Steven Callahan also stresses nature's indifference, but he still assigns nature a female gender as he describes her motivations, or lack thereof. Callahan understands that "she has no wrath to vent. Nor does she have a hand of kindness to extend. She is merely there, immense, powerful, and indifferent. I do not resent her indifference, or my comparative insignificance. Indeed, it is one of the main reasons I like to sail: the sea makes the insignificance of my own small self and of all humanity so poignant."[185] Nature's indifference reminds Callahan of anthropocentricism's fictionality: humans are not the center of the universe.

The nonhuman world likely has distinct motivations and perspectives. Thus, while initial research suggests that authors that risk anthropomorphism foster environmental behavior in their readers—"Anthropomorphism fosters conservation behavior, and enhances connectedness to nature"[186]—we also need to examine the specific iterations of the range of ways to anthropomorphize. McCairen, for example, makes a different observation about mother nature's indifference as it relates to violence. McCairen states that "I can hardly blame Twenty-five Mile for exacting retribution on men who weren't wearing life jackets. It's well known Mother River doesn't like a smart aleck."[187] McCairen anthropomorphizes nature by giving it (personified as "Mother River") the power to observe, judge, and punish humans. She also finds that nature does not place humans in a privileged position and especially does not suffer fools.

While McCairen and Callahan personify nature's indifference differently, both authors advocate for a specific form of critical anthropomorphism: "liminal intimacy," to use Nimmo's term.[188] Liminal intimacy recognizes and uses the distance between self and other as a means to solve anthropomorphism's dilemmas. Nimmo explains liminal intimacy as "predicated upon the maintenance of a tension between knowing and unknowing, familiarity and strangeness, in which intimacy consists in respecting, living with and even cultivating distance and alterity, rather than seeking a closeness that would obliterate these; it implicitly recognises the fragility of authentic encounters with the other, and the colonising tendencies intrinsic to proximate intimacy."[189] Liminal intimacy is connection with a distance. Nimmo argues for a greater distance and separation than Morton's mesh and Alaimo's trans-corporeality imply.

Jennifer Pharr Davis suggests a shift to liminal intimacy by emphasizing the difference between "walking in" and "walking with" nature: "It took until the end of my journey, but I was no longer walking *in* nature, I was walking *with* it."[190] Rather than mix and blur boundaries, liminal intimacy—at least where anthropomorphism is concerned—maintains a critical distance and boundary between self and other. When we examine adrenaline narratives, we see adventurer-authors maintain this critical distance (e.g., Callahan, McCairen, Davis) as well as present a case for more intimate knowledge and relations with nature (e.g., Hahn, Treadwell). Both liminal and blurred representations offer ethical and representational advantages.

The potential for transformation and the nature of the transformation ultimately—whether liminal or blurred—determines the representation's erotic worth. This view argues for a case-by-case analysis rather than advocating for liminal/blurred as inherently good/bad modes of representing or otherwise engaging the other. Bart Welling argues in relation to wildlife films that human-animal encounters and affinities "provide viewers with heavily mediated but potentially transformative modes of access to the emotional lives of our non-human kin."[191] Welling emphasizes—"however close or distant, oppressive or respectful"—that "cinematic anthropomorphism" offers "a dynamic process based on affective, historical, ecological, economic, and other kinds of *relationships* between animals, filmmakers, and viewers."[192] Likewise, examples in adrenaline narratives of critical anthropomorphism—a term I use to encompass liminal and blurred representations—offers heightened insight as a result of the narrative's wilderness setting and the stress survival places on the narrative's human and nonhuman actors. Adrenaline narratives set the stage for this interaction: adventurers, often otherwise alone in the wilderness, are positioned to recognize nonhumans as part of their community.

The castaway Callahan's anthropomorphism of fish, for instance, results in community and connection, which are key to survival. As Tam, Lee, and Chao point out, "social connection enhances survival chance and mental health.... By anthropomorphizing nonhuman agents, individuals can establish the social connectedness they need."[193] Callahan, for example, personifies nature, specifically fish, and notes how they find fault with him and humanity more generally. Callahan imagines, "they have come for me. If I fall into the water, my doggies will devour me.... Perhaps the fish of the world have held council, have condemned man's insatiable appetite and exploitation of the sea. Man has justified it by calling it utilization of resources by a superior species. The fish have lost patience with his egotism."[194] Callahan imagines the fish exacting punishment for human crimes against nature. In this passage, Callahan refers to a third-person "man" and "his egotism" instead of "my" or "our" egotism. A distance remains between himself and other humans as well as the fish, even as he recognizes that the fish have met and justified his death due to our collective crimes against the sea. While he represents the fish finding fault with him, he also sees them as "friends" and "in many ways as my superiors." He reveals, "the dorados have become much more than food to me. They are even more than pets. I look upon them as equals—in many ways as my superiors."[195] Thus, this anthropomorphism has androcentric (individual survival) and biocentric (fish are superior) elements.

Callahan's biocentric view problematically maintains—as critics often point out in regard to biocentrism—the human/nature binary even as it flips center and periphery. Just as patriarchy cannot simply be replaced with matriarchy, the same holds true for anthropocentrism and biocentrism, especially if the nature/culture binary is maintained. Even ecocentrism may be framed as self-knowledge: according to Brymer and Gray, "from an ecocentric perspective, we can only really know our true selves if we experience and cross our civilized boundaries by re-turning to wildness, overcoming alienation and, ironically, confronting death."[196] Callahan, however, goes on to explain a more mutual relationship, suggesting this mutual give-and-take resembles an Indigenous worldview. Callahan explains, "their flesh keeps me alive. Their spirits keep me company. Their attacks and their resistance to the hunt make them worthy opponents, as well as friends. I am thankful for their meat and companionship and fearful of their power." Callahan must reckon with complex feelings about the fish that offer food and companionship. He concludes this thought with a claim to Indigeneity: "I wonder if my deep respect for them is related to my Indian ancestors' respect for all natural forces."[197] While the brief reference at the end of this passage lays claim to Indigenous ancestry, the connection remains tenuous, as Callahan does not describe a deep affinity to or include additional information about his Indigenous ancestors. Rather, he suggests the affinity is genetic, drawing upon ecological Indian stereotypes that place Indigenous people naturally closer to nature. Callahan's liminal intimacy, as a result, does not fully decolonize this thinking. I address anthropomorphism's connection to Indigenous spirituality more fully in the next section.

The ecological and cultural danger and potential of blurred (as opposed to liminal) anthropomorphizing can also be seen in the following passage from Alvah Simon's *North to the Night*. In this passage, Simon likens a bear mother to a human mother.

> The mother lumbered in a tight circle on a flat spot on the slope and plopped her thick buttocks down. She called to her club [sic] with a gruff cough. The happy cub bounded over full-steam, tumbling into her lap. The mother cradled her infant in those great arms and put its mouth to her teat. As the cub suckled hungrily, its mother looked out serenely on her home. She felt content. Here a scientist might say, "You cannot know that. There is no data." But I know it as certainly as when I look into the beaming face of a human mother. I saw tenderness, pride, and deep happiness.[198]

What Simon observes is not "data," and yet he makes a case that it is no less true.

As a result, Simon knows his description is bad science. At the same time, he carves out a space for the emotional world of animals. Maria Coffey in *Explorers of the Infinite* assesses that, when adventurers Karsten Heuer and Leanne Allison encounter "things science can't explain" while hiking with the Porcupine caribou herd, "they began to see nature as magical."[199] In this sense, what is not science is magic and what is not fact, fiction. A reappraisal of anthropomorphism suggests that the lack of "data" is not necessarily bad science: as Nimmo suggests, "to treat such phenomena as akin to data in a scientific experiment, with our own interpretations treated as hypotheses, would be to misapply skepticism in a manner that would profoundly blinker and inhibit us by excluding the interpretive competence that is intrinsic to our ability to participate in social life, and which has evolved in organic interconnection with our existence as social beings."[200] Nimmo makes the case for narrative as an acceptable form of environmental "data."

As we see above and in the previous chapters, successful extreme adventure (where the adventurer survives or otherwise achieves his/her goal) often depends on reading and listening to the environment. It is not enough to "think like a mountain," one must "think like an avalanche" and become "like a leaf" and read or otherwise intimately engage wilderness in order to survive. The quality of this intimacy also plays a key role in defining and identifying erotic desire. I mentioned at the end of chapter 3, for instance, that Jennifer Hahn writes, in *Spirited Waters*, "we must talk with many things. Seals and eagles. Water and wind. Columbine flowers and spruce trees. Land snails and lichens. By broadening our idea of companions, we discover we don't so much experience solitude, as multitude."[201] Hahn suggests that "by broadening our idea of companions," we will "discover" nature's language and—as Howkins called for—a path to a "surely" new way to experience wilderness adventure. Hahn's language and sentiment shares an affinity with Donna Haraway's understanding of nonhuman companions as well as Alaimo's trans-corporeality. She maintains liminal intimacy and experiences trans-corporeality's "multitude."

DECOLONIZING DESIRE:
LISTENING TO AND BECOMING SUBALTERN NATURE

Erotic desire presents a range of models: rather than argue for one "right" engagement, the liminal, blurred, and significant otherness representations suggest we embrace a confounding diversity. Liminal intimacy or blurred boundaries, adopted for the specific self/other relationship, require greater flexibility but perhaps best embody nature's and American culture's own radical contradictions and experimentations. As Haraway writes about this challenging work, "the permanent search for knowledge of the intimate other, and the inevitable comic and tragic mistakes in that quest, commands my respect, whether the other is animal or human, or indeed, inanimate."[202] Whether experienced as liminal, significant, or blurred intimacy, nature is not landscape in these erotic examples, but character. Such representations, says Chagani, "remind us, as do the 'songs' of whales and the 'chatter' of dolphins, of the vulnerability that we share with other living beings."[203] These disparate injunctions to think like, become, and converse with nature help create the community and mutuality that define erotic desire. Nature's voice or silencing plays a key role in understanding nature's agency and representation. Representing nature as having its own distinctive voice is one way authors stress mutualism and "a desire to see the other as part of, yet excitingly distinct from, the self."[204] The idea of engaging in a conversation with nature or representing nature as having a distinctive voice appears in many adrenaline narratives.

For Jill Fredston, sharing nature's voice is paramount to her environmental aims. Fredston explains that she has "felt increasing urgency to give voice to the caribou that graze without fear along the Labrador shore, to the wide-shouldered brown bears of the Alaska Peninsula who depend upon the annual migration of salmon, to fjords uncut by roads or power lines.... What finally galvanized me into writing... was the even more tangible reminder of the fragility of all that surrounds us."[205] Fredston "give[s] voice" to nature in order to further environmental awareness and emphasize connection and community. Her writing enacts what de Gennaro identifies as narrative's "redemptive functions" by telling, in Thom van Dooren and Deborah Bird Rose's formulation, "the embodied, situated, kinetic and narratival nature of place" as "enacted and expressed by multiple species."[206] I examine these "redemptive functions" in greater detail in chapter 6.

In learning and listening to nature's story, Fredston feels compelled to tell it. Harris's story similarly concludes with a rejoinder: "the voice of the river" tells him "'you're all right. You've done a good thing and come a long way. But don't forget that it was me who brought you here, me who helped you, me who allowed you to do this thing. I'm stopping you here so you'll always know that.'" Harris promises he "won't forget" and shares a brandy with the river.[207] As with Fredston, the act of listening results in engagement. Where Fredston writes to share her knowledge with others, Harris must remember. He cannot tell his story without remembering his indebtedness to the river. How adventurers translate the quality of nature's voice in their narratives provides an effective way to judge the story's desiring natures.

Cindy Ross describes ecological community and connection when she explains how her children talk to nature. Ross describes how "the kids yell across the lake to the granite cirque we sit in and it echoes their voices. The land is talking back to them, and it tells them of the largeness of their world."[208] The passage also exposes the potential danger of listening to nature as an echo of human speech. Such cases would seem to support extending Spivak's argument about the subaltern to nature: humans will inevitably impose themselves on and silence nature. Fredston, on the other hand, describes the river's "rich" language. The land "talking back," in this case, is not an echo of human speech but direct, active speech from the river itself: "The river speaks a language rich in verbs—it is constantly rippling, sliding, eddying, burbling, and bending. Perhaps for that reason it made me feel very much alive, conscious of myself within an ever-changing mosaic of time and space."[209] Listening to the river's language makes Fredston feel more alive and conscious of her trans-corporeality—"conscious of myself within an ever-changing mosaic of time and space."

Jennifer Hahn goes even further by placing herself in the physical position of a caddis midgeon and salmon in order to experience what they hear, see, and feel. She moves from passive listening and seeks to "become": "Naked, I thrust myself beneath the shallow rapids and grabbed tight to one large stone. I held firmly, bearing the icy drumroll of current, just as I imaged a caddis midgeon gripped a pebble to keep from washing away. I had come to experience, for one glorious, throbbing minute, what a salmon might hear in its river of birth—water falling in a hundred places at once, singing like a thousand choirs of river angels. I had come to hear the river sing."[210] Where Fredston listens to nature and feels more alive as a human being, Hahn literally jumps in with both feet to "become" a fly larva and a salmon: in doing so, she seeks to hear, see, taste, smell, and feel from their perspective, not her own. Hahn attempts, if only briefly, to leave human culture and enter the consciousness inhabited by insects and fish. In becoming fish, she hopes to hear "the river sing."

Timothy Treadwell represents one of the most controversial figures in regard to extreme wilderness adventure and anthropomorphism. Like Hahn, Treadwell imitates animal behavior, that of bears especially; however, Treadwell sustains his conversations with and imitations of the bears for more than thirteen Alaskan summers before he and his companion are mauled and killed by a bear. Nick Jans describes Treadwell's sustained, "increasingly feral" behavior as "a conscious and an unavoidable process" of being alone in the wild: "More and more, Timothy imitates his ursine companions—their body movements, postures, and habits, their vocalizations. Even as he casts the bears in human form, he strives to become one of them. He tells himself, 'I am grizzly.' He plunges across ice-water glacial torrents, walks on all fours, and thinks in grunts or growls."[211] For some, as Jans writes in his introduction, Treadwell is "the man who wanted to become a bear, and died trying."[212] As mentioned previously, people view Treadwell variously as "a martyr," "a fool," "a cynical, self-serving narcissist," and "a menace to wildlife."[213] Jans concludes, though, "if nothing else, the death of Timothy Treadwell reflects the extent to which we project our own beliefs upon the universe."[214] In this assessment, which emphasizes Treadwell's projection onto nature, Jans eliminates reading Treadwell as an advocate of erotic desire and critical anthropomorphism, chremamorphism, or zoomorphism.

Treadwell offers a compelling test of blurred intimacy or transcorporeality because the lack of distance appears to have contributed to, if not acted as the sole cause, of his and his companion's death. While Jans does not use the term "liminal intimacy," he similarly explains that "most bear biologists agree that attempting to prove that grizzlies and humans can make nicey-nice is less about species survival than ideology and personal agenda. The point is moot to the bears, who couldn't care less about human trust or physical affection. They're too busy being themselves, and are at best indifferent to our existence unless we insinuate ourselves into their lives."[215] The biologists stress that Treadwell did not maintain critical distance. Ryan Hediger, writing about the controversial "ecowarrior" Treadwell, also notes that "Treadwell is then faulted for his scientific weaknesses, obscuring the existence and importance of narrative genres about animals."[216] Hediger invokes both an older model that condemns Treadwell's science, one where extreme adventure was pursued, as Bart Vanreusel points out, "in the interests of natural science," and an alternative model that values animal narrative for its ecological impact.[217]

Treadwell's book, Among Grizzlies, is described by Jans as "decidedly unscientific" and "riddled with anthropomorphic interpretations and informed by emotion rather than logic, completely lacking any systematic approach or data."[218] Hediger points out that while Treadwell's book and observations do not follow scientific methods, they arguably still have narrative worth. Treadwell was an aspiring actor. As such, we might consider the performative worth of his literal and figurative body of work. Hediger explains, "literary scholars might shift the terms here to note the resistance in these critiques to the problematic but crucial form of knowledge that is narrative."[219] Narrative offers—to borrow science's term—its own form of data.

Perhaps we might even find a space to join narrative and scientific data. Queer ecology opens a space for Treadwell's grizzly identity and identification. Colin Carman makes a case for Treadwell's queer ecology: "It is not Treadwell's identity that I read as queer but his attempts both to theorize and to embody human/animal subjectivity."[220] Carman explains, "Treadwell's relentless personification of other species is the clearest expression of his queer anthropomorphism, the belief not only that animals are humanlike but that humans are irrepressibly animal-like because of their shared sexual nature."[221] Carman suggests that Treadwell reminds us that the characteristics we reserve for humanity actually are not exclusive: nonhumans, especially animals, are more close than distant. While not presented or explained in these terms, this view bears (pun intended) a resemblance to animism, a characteristic often shared among a range of Indigenous religions. This blurring of human-animal is also seen in Ursula K. Le Guin's novella, *Buffalo Gals, Won't You Come Out Tonight*. Understanding human-animal connections is key to the protagonist's transformation in the story. How adventurers and other authors incorporate animism becomes key. Treadwell's extreme case fuses damaging, patriarchal, heroic masculinity and an alternative, queer, or critical anthropomorphism.

Returning to the passage from Simon helps clarify this queer ecology's potential. The reader should not misread Simon's description of the mother bear as mere personification. Rather, Simon emphasizes the "fact" of the bear's emotional intelligence via observation. Emotion, Simon suggests, is not humans' exclusive terrain: animals feel, too. Thus, Simon's critical anthropomorphism does not assume that certain characteristics, such as emotion, can only be exhibited by humans. As Nimmo puts it, "strictly speaking, the term 'anthropomorphism' presumes that certain human characteristics are exclusively human, and the central point of this work is to challenge precisely that, to show that mindedness, intentionality, subjectivity and self-hood, social communication, culture and complex cognition, are not exclusively human but distributed throughout multiple species."[222] Likewise, Simon contends that emotions, specifically contentment, love, and happiness, are not exclusive to humanity. Liminal intimacy's danger lies in its investment in distinct, unique human characteristics. It fails to realize that "despite perceptions that human beings are unique amongst animals and superior to the rest of nature, we are part of nature in the same way that other animals are part of nature."[223] On the other hand, unmediated intimacy—where the boundaries are blurred—risks appropriating the other.

As David Abram points out in his definition of participation, theories of mutuality also often connect with Indigenous views of nature. As a result, any form of anthropomorphism risks cultural appropriation—especially when the adventurer is white. Building from the work of French anthropologist Lucien Lévy-Bruhl, Abram defines "participation" as characterizing "the animistic logic of indigenous, oral peoples—for whom ostensibly 'inanimate' objects like stones or mountains are often thought to be alive, for whom certain names, spoken aloud, may be felt to influence at a distance the things or beings that they name, for whom particular plants, particular animals, particular places and persons and powers may all be felt to *participate* in one another's existence, influencing each other and being influenced in turn."[224] We see this connection to animism in adrenaline narratives. Nancy Lord explicitly negotiates and highlights the boundary between appropriation and appreciation: "Hardheaded and unsentimental, I'm not one to go around burning sage or sprinkling corn in imitation of someone else's sacred ceremonies. I know what I am not. But I also remember something that Barry Lopez once said: that we don't need to be a people to learn from them."[225] In other words, Lord suggests that one does not have to be Indigenous or adopt the spiritual practices and ceremonies of Indigenous peoples in order to learn respect for the land or how nature communicates. Jill Fredston's use of Indigenous views of nature and animism in her adrenaline narratives provides a case in point.

Fredston in *Rowing to Latitude* builds on Koyukon knowledge, sharing the view of never feeling alone in nature. Fredston explains, "to Koyukons, the natural world was a source not only of life but of spiritual power; the natural and the supernatural were entwined. A person in nature was never alone; he moved through a world that was aware, endowed with signs, and easily offended. Birds and spruce trees and hills were all part of his community."[226] A community comprised of humans and nonhumans is key to erotic desire and many Indigenous environmental ethics. The diverse people that Fredston encounters—"Natives, homesteaders, miners, trappers, dog mushers, and others who live along the river"[227]—also live an integrated life with their environment: "Their hopes and needs and cultures are as integral a part of the landscape as the surrounding green hills and spindly black spruce trees swaying in the breeze."[228] Fredston suggests we all depend on natural resources in an intimate way. "Natives, homesteaders, miners, trappers, dog mushers, and others who live along the river" as well as the "green hills and spindly black spruce trees" all share an integrated relationship with the environment that blurs the boundary between self and other. What separates these individuals and groups is what they do with this "integrated" knowledge.

While not attributed as Indigenous knowledge, Hahn, likewise, writes in *Spirited Waters*, "it struck me then what indifferent, if not odious, boundaries we strike between the living and the dead. Stones are lifeless. Trees are verdant.... When it comes to having souls, we get even more persnickety. Humans have them, trees don't." Hahn questions the boundaries between living and dead and what has a soul and what does not. She talks to all the elements in nature, including the "ocean, moon, otters, sea urchins, and *Yemaya* [her kayak]." She recognizes rocks as animate, living elements: "That very night on Gabriola Island I decided that rocks, even if they aren't furred, horned, or leafy, are as alive as anything else."[229] While Rob Schultheis describes rocks as cruel, he clarifies, "they weren't really cruel, of course—if they had any thoughts at all, they were the slow, gentle ones I imagine rock must have—but they looked cruel to me."[230] Cruel or gentle, to use John Atherton's word, wilderness has not been transformed into "furniture."[231] Hahn and Schultheis push their reader to see even rocks as living entities. Their descriptions reflect their experiences: the data they have observed.

Narrative's—and specifically critical anthropomorphism's—promise lies in its ability to animate the landscape for its readers. Erotic desire seeks to do this in such a way that the reader will come to the same conclusion as Hahn: one's environment is alive, including the rocks, and that life demands respect. Sowon S. Park, in this vein, argues that anthropomorphism's ethical benefits far outweigh the potential costs in the form of scientific or cultural misuses: "one could develop the argument that if othering dehumanizes the human by transforming differences into ideological hierarchies and diminish [sic] other species with whom we share life, anthropomorphism humanizes the non-human with no less transformative implications. Even while we acknowledge ultimate unknowability, the process of reasoning and inferring has deep political and ethical implications. For treating agents as human or non-human has a powerful impact on whether those agents are going to be treated as moral agents."[232] For Park, the environmental and social justice benefits are clear: "humaniz[ing] the non-human" offers the clearest path for ethical, moral agency. Reworking the patriarchal valorization of "virgin wilderness," heroic masculinity, and anthropomorphism requires a new environmental ethic—just as revaluing virginity, especially a female's, requires new sexual ethics.

AN EROTIC ENVIRONMENTAL ETHICS

As suggested in Byl's rejection of "virgin wilderness," erotic desire does not demand religious language in order to "purify" its sexual overtones, emphasizing the rhetorical and environmental advantages to selecting the erotic over the spiritual. As Vance argues, "idealized wilderness furthers dualistic thinking."[233] Where the spiritual—at least in some Western configurations—tends to disembody, the erotic sensuously embodies nature. The erotic embraces fecundity, dirt, and death, contrasting with a "clean" spirituality and its consequential emphasis on a virgin-whore dichotomy. Thus, the erotic's environmental ethic stresses mutuality and the advantages of recognizing one's trans-corporeality alongside its "significant otherness" and liminal intimacy.

As an environmental ethic, erotic desire relies upon a certain amount of deception: adventurers must "leave no trace" while recognizing that this invisibility and having no impact is a lie. Sean Ryan notes "minimum or low impact camping practices" constitute "one of the most significant manifestations" of outdoor recreation's environmental ethic and practice.[234] Jill Fredston explains that her adventuring ethics require an artistic combination of "leave no trace" with the understanding that environmental impact is an inevitable part of human existence. She explains that she along with her partner aim to teach her stepdaughter "what we knew about traveling through it [nature] without harming it or ourselves."[235] Fredston also recognizes that "part of the irony of loving the natural world is understanding that it would be better off without human presence."[236] Fredston and her partner stress that leaving no trace is an "art form": "we wanted her to know how to move through the country without leaving a sign that she had been there. This is not only a conservation imperative but an art form, the best hope for allowing whoever visits the same spot after us to experience the thrill of being in a place that feels wild and unspoiled."[237] As Fredston hints, the art lies in the deception: adventurers desire "untrammeled" wilderness, and those adventurers that come before are compelled to reproduce this fiction for those who come after them. This environmental ethic holds true for nonwilderness areas, too. We all must find ways to hold ourselves and others accountable for the impact we have on our environment.

This perspective also maintains a largely anthropocentric worldview: "wilderness is preserved from human 'development' and exploitation—not for its own sake, but rather for the experiences people have in it and for its moral worth as defined by humanity."[238] At the same time, Fredston recognizes "true wilderness may no longer exist in our bordered world, making the places where wildlife abounds and people are scarce, where the patterns and rhythms of nature are still dominant, all the more precious."[239] Virgin wilderness may be rare, not exist, or not be accessible to most people, but that does not mean we pollute at will. Additionally, if wilderness is, as Roderick Frazier Nash suggests, a "state of mind," even small patches of "trammeled" wilderness can possess the benefits generally reserved for pristine nature.[240] This lesson, along with listening to nature, form the environmental ethics supported by erotic desire.

Steven Callahan's stranded situation demanded he listen hard and learn quickly. It also granted him ample time to observe nature closely and consider his own ethical role within the environment. He observes, for example, that the dorados assist him in the hunt. The fish act "as if they are trying to help me, as if they do not mind mixing their flesh with mine."[241] Rather than martyrs, the fish as well as Callahan are represented as part of a greater, interconnected circle of life. Callahan sees his own predicted death at sea as part of this network. He imagines his body as fish food and the fish, in turn, becoming food for his ex-wife (who predicted he would die at sea). Callahan expects that "she will take the head, tail, and bones and heap them upon her compost pile, mix them with the soil so green life will sprout. Nature knows no waste."[242] McCairen learns a similar lesson on her chosen adventure: "She [the river] is a power that teaches those who open themselves to her.... She cares not if we learn: It is up to us to seek her out."[243] Callahan and McCairen seek knowledge and share how their lives are both insignificant and significant to the cycle.

The environmental ethic must also work beyond the adventure. Another key element to erotic nature is how its self/other representations connect or translate to life off the trail—in environments not conventionally understood as wilderness. After failing to hike the entire Pacific Crest Trail, Gail D. Storey still finds she is transformed by the experience and has new skills to cope with and understand her city life. Storey describes how "I'd thought I would find myself on the trail, but failure had brought me here [back home] to the fullness of what was left, beyond body, mind, persona."[244] While Storey was not able to complete the entire hike, the experience still prepares her for caring for her dying mother: "this was why I had hiked the trail. Here were the cycles of nature, sapling into tree into snag."[245] Storey transforms a key dualism. In this case she connects rather than separates human and tree mortality.

In her apartment complex's park, furthermore, she finds wilderness in the "small patch of nature reclaimed from the city's asphalt." She also sees wildness in the "clear eyes of the dogs" and a domestic cat with "the imperturbable gaze of the mountain lion in the high desert."[246] The wilderness Storey finds in the city and in domesticated animals demonstrates that while terms and terrain shift, boundaries between wild/domesticated, nature/culture, and animal/human remain blurred. She concludes, nevertheless, "I never much cared for nature, but nature cares for us."[247] Here Storey, like Harris, implies nature's caretaking knows no limit or at least does not demand mutual care in return. This view is not ecologically sustainable because it suggests an archetypal, all-powerful mother nature will always take care of us, no matter how we treat the environment. As a result, even in their transformation, (gendered) dualisms may seem fixed and, perhaps, even stacked against masculinity when judging their environmental value.

Erotic desire mirrors the same messy ambivalence at the adrenaline narrative's core. Erotic desire is not pure or perfect. It bears the traces of and interacts with the more dominant, objectifying desires. Todd Balf's *The Last River* demonstrates that the meshing of conquering, spiritual, and erotic rhetorics carries across different sports and may be found at varying degrees within one narrative. When the river communicates with the paddlers, for example, there is a subtle mix of bravado and respect. After one close call, Tom McEwan "is struck that the Tsangpo just delivered another message—and this one, well, it's somewhere between beware and a cross-this-line-if-you-dare ultimatum."[248] Here the river has a voice, which places the narrative in line with erotic desire, but its threatening message aligns it with a patriarchal tone. Furthermore, McEwan, who listens to the river, is described in spiritual and erotic terms: "more of a pilgrim than an explorer, the sort of person who doesn't come calling for the sake of the motherland or for scientific fame, but because his life is intertwined with all rivers, and this is the last one."[249] In this description, "pilgrim" invokes spiritual desire and an American myth of religious freedom, one that rejects "explorer" fame or conquering desire. The description "life...intertwined with all rivers" suggests erotic desire. These contradictory messages also emerge in the ways adrenaline narratives address colonialism. As erotic desire holds much in common with American Indigenous (spiritual) representations of nature, the predominately white American adventurers negotiate the boundary between appreciation and appropriation when they embrace Indigenous environmental ethics.

Erotic desire's naturecultures, a term that refers to the "synthesis of nature and culture that recognizes their inseparability in ecological relationships that are both biophysically and socially formed," cannot be boxed into one appropriate representation. This characteristic of erotic desire offers potential and danger.[250] Kevin Krein also emphasizes a fundamental ambivalence when one looks at adrenaline narratives as a whole. Krein argues, "interacting with powerful and unpredictable features of the natural world requires fluid responses that challenge human abilities. This is one of the deepest goals of athletic participation. But the features that challenge, and often bring out the best in adventure athletes, also contain dangers."[251] Fluidity and danger connect. Adrenaline narratives—even in their erotic modes—carry contradictory messages about the environment and humans' risky relationship to it. The relationship promises both greater rewards and costs. Thus, these representations of nature also provide roadmaps for engagements with nature as a risky entity to be conquered and controlled, as awesome tool for individual transformation, and as an erotic interlocutor. Risk races through them all. I will now turn to discussing what these engagements found in the American adrenaline narrative suggest about the relationship between risk, adventure, and environmental sustainability.

CHAPTER 5
RISKY
NATURES

Jon Krakauer, writing about Chris McCandless, makes a case for "risky behavior" in contemporary American culture. Krakauer posits that "it is hardly unusual for a young man to be drawn to a pursuit considered reckless by his elders; engaging in risky behavior is a rite of passage in our culture no less than in most others."[1] Krakauer in *Into the Wild* begins to map the place risky nature holds in contemporary American culture, highlighting its appeal as a testing ground and site for youthful self-discovery. Krakauer suggests a desire for risky nature is shared by nearly all cultures. James Edward Mills makes a similar observation about the "'kids'"—Rosemary and Tyrhee—on the Expedition Denali team, confirming this desire holds true for African American youth, too. Mills suggests that "Denali for them was more than just a mountain. It was a rite of passage."[2] Risk's contemporary appeal and function are not limited to a youthful rite of passage. Broadly speaking, risk shapes all contemporary culture. As Eric Brymer puts it, "risk is a culturally constructed phenomenon stemming from modern society's deep-seated aversion for, and obsessive desire to be 'liberated' from, uncertainty."[3] These seemingly universal cultural and individual values form risk's broad aesthetic and appeal. While not everyone may want to test themselves—personally or vicariously—against risky nature, adrenaline narratives tell the unique experiences of those that do.[4] Risk, as theme, plot, setting, and tone, and—increasingly—as a consequence of climate change, carries across all versions of adrenaline narratives. Risk forms the adrenaline narrative's pervasive desire. Without risk there is no adventure. Looking at the adrenaline narrative more closely deepens our understanding of risk's broad appeal as well as reveals risky nature's specifically American facets and its impact on how America understands climate change.

To understand the role and aesthetic of risk in American adrenaline narratives and its significance to our understanding of the American environmental movement, this chapter first outlines risk culture and its appeal, focusing on how adrenaline narratives generally address bodily and environmental risk. Risk's context (contemporary risk society) and appeal (adrenaline "madness") comprise two facets of the risk aesthetic. The third element is risk's embodiment in the adventurer (personal risk management). As risk is a gendered and raced concept, in this section I expand previous discussions from chapter 2 to evaluate how the adventurer's identity shapes and is shaped by risk. The fourth characteristic examined is the adrenaline narrative's risky setting (wilderness), including exploring the extent to which climate change has changed or is changing the adrenaline narrative. This is what I call a risk aesthetic, comprised of context, appeal, embodiment/management, and setting.

My definition of the risk aesthetic builds from similar scholarship that connects risk and narrative. In "High Risk Narratives: Textual Adventures," Peter K. Manning outlines "concepts borrowed from literary criticism such as narrative, voice, and perspective" in order to augment "qualitative sociology."[5] While "high risk narratives...are not ethnographies," their dramatic elements offer what Manning identifies as an important "complement" to other modes of cultural analysis.[6] Narrative puts the data into a comprehensible format. The adrenaline narrative, especially how it engages risk across multiple levels, is pedagogical. Ursula Heise explains, in *Sense of Place and Sense of Planet*, "the study of risk perception and their sociocultural framing must form an integral part of an ecocritical understanding of culture. At the same time, this cultural analysis can make a significant contribution to risk theory by foregrounding how new risk perceptions are shaped by already existing cultural tropes and narrative templates."[7] Risk teaches, in short, through narrative.

Adrenaline narratives provide models of failure and the successful management of environmental risks where human survival is at stake. What Heise calls the "slowly evolving risk scenarios [that] surround them on a daily basis" demonstrate to readers, according to Frederick Buell, "a way of dwelling actively within...environmental crisis."[8] As such, adrenaline narratives offer distillations of much larger risk and cultural processes, especially where the environment, race, and gender are concerned. Extreme athletes live in risky situations of their own making; likewise, contemporary culture has become "dangerized" by human choices.[9] We (un)consciously look to extreme adventure narratives for models related to modifying or otherwise engaging with nature where high-risk survival forms the stakes. Because we are all becoming more extreme risk takers when it comes to the environment, we may find the elite athlete's knowledge about risk instructive. Additionally, as adventure becomes more diverse, it offers a microcosm of cultural change and tests the ecofeminist assertion that forms of oppression are not distinct. Greater social (in)justice should correspond with environmental gains/losses and vice versa. Risk thus defines the American environmental imagination by offering a gauge to measure sustainability in the Anthropocene.

An examination of the adrenaline narrative's risky nature or narrative elements reaffirms America's "schizophrenic" environmental imagination.[10] Risky nature's significance continues the adrenaline narrative's paradoxical impulses to preserve and destroy. That is, risky adventure "in nature derives its added value precisely from the ecological quality of its surroundings. Yet at the same time, these activities themselves detract from that quality."[11] Risk's paradox in extreme sports—to risk death to feel alive—connects with the paradoxical environmental risks adventurers as well as the rest of us are willing to take. These risks have increasing significance as the effects of global climate change progress. Understanding the adrenaline narrative's risk aesthetic helps us understand our risky Anthropocene natures.

RISK AESTHETIC, CONTEXT: RISK SOCIETY

Cultures of the extreme reflect the contemporary zeitgeist. As I began to outline in chapter 1, contemporary culture is what Ulrich Beck describes as a "risk society," or "a *catastrophic society*. In it the *state of emergency* threatens *to become the normal state*."[12] Beck argues in his 1992 book *Risk Society*, "we do not *yet* live in a risk society, but we also no longer live *only* within the distribution conflicts of scarcity societies."[13] Signs increasingly point to risk society's global realization, especially where climate change and pollution are concerned. Using "highly developed nuclear and chemical productive forces" as an example, Beck explains that "in the risk society the unknown and unintended consequences come to be a dominant force in history and society."¹⁴ Global temperature changes, melting glaciers, and the great ocean garbage gyres are other specific examples of such "unknown and unintended consequences" of human activity.

Like the risks extreme athletes seek, the risk society is characterized by human-produced problems. These are environmental risks of our own making. Beck explains, "in contrast to all earlier epochs (including industrial society), the risk society is characterized essentially by a *lack*: the impossibility of an *external* attribution of hazards." These wicked problems stemming from global climate change are human-produced problems. According to Beck, "risks depend on *decisions*; they are industrially produced and in this sense *politically reflexive*." As a result, we have nobody to blame but ourselves for the pickle in which we find ourselves. As Beck argues, "while all earlier cultures and phases of social development confronted threats in various ways, society today is *confronted by itself* through its dealings with risks. Risks are the reflection of human actions and omissions, the expression of highly developed productive forces. That means that the sources of danger are no longer ignorance but *knowledge*; not a deficient but a perfected mastery over nature; not that which eludes the human grasp but the system of norms and objective constraints established with the industrial epoch."¹⁵ Beck could be describing the everyday decisions we all make related to global climate change as well as the individual decisions adrenaline adventurers make. In both cases we must confront ourselves and the consequences of critical decisions.

If we have, indeed, entered the Anthropocene, then we have also entered the risk society where human knowledge and action have become the dominant influence on the environment. As Molly Wallace writes in *Risk Criticism*, "Risk is...a useful watchword...not only because it references the dominant discourse of 'management,' but also because it highlights precisely what cannot be managed."¹⁶ Risk's paradoxical control and chaos has implications for our understanding of the global climate crisis: risk both provides the impetus to act and suggests its futility, or "what cannot be managed."

Jens Oliver Zinn echoes Beck and Wallace, emphasizing the results of this change in risk management. Zinn suggests that we have shifted from risking exploiting nature, where "protection, minimisation and avoidance of risk were emphasised," to risking modifying it, where nature is viewed "as something to be actively managed, designed, reinstated and changed": "Human impact on nature has become so intense and is ongoing, and nature is so complex that humanity is required to accept its significant role in shaping and producing nature as well as the need for active decision-making under conditions of uncertainty that such developments produce."[17] The adrenaline athlete, similarly, may use technology, past experience, and/or green practices to "manage" nature as well as continue to use the older, exploitative/protective model. We also see parallel changes in risk management in environmental activism.

The American environmental movement arguably becomes more radical as this risk management shift becomes more pronounced: Earth First! came on the scene in 1981 with the infamous "Cracking of Glen Canyon Damn [sic]," and "the fall of 1996 saw the first U.S. appearance of the Earth Liberation Front, which took property destruction to new heights."[18] Prior to these organizations, in the late 1970s the original ELF (Environmental Life Force) conducted campaigns in Northern California and Oregon. Direct-action environmentalism offers extreme, risky, "monkey-wrenching" wake-up calls and interventions in the form of civil disobedience and ecotage. Will Potter in *Green is the New Red* cites Edward Abbey's *The Monkey Wrench Gang* (1975) and Rachel Carson's *Silent Spring* (1962) as inspiring the radical American environmental movement.[19] As outlined in chapter 1, sports, along with the feminist and environmental movements, radicalized at about the same time. The same might be said of other so-called radical social justice movements, such as Black Power, which arguably reached its peak in the 1970s. Additionally, such activism continues today, through the Black Lives Matter and #MeToo movements as well as through the continued work of direct-action environmental groups. These radical social justice movements, as Kyle Kusz argues in "Extreme America: The Cultural Politics of Extreme Sports in 1990s America," also contribute to the crisis in white masculinity.

As American culture increasingly moves to a culture of extremes—environmentally, economically, politically—risk narratives have moved from counterculture to mainstream. Adrenaline narratives promote participation for all in extreme adventure and risk-taking lifestyles. The adrenaline narrative itself shifts, as Catherine Palmer points out, when partaking in environmental risk moves from highly trained athletes to the general public. The risks involved when popular media crafts a "conceptual collapse between risk and mainstream" results in "made-for-media versions of extreme sports," which "are short-lived *imitations* of risk, rather than serious sporting initiations."[20] Jill Fredston in *Snowstruck* agrees.

Fredston critiques contemporary culture's extreme mainstreaming: "To peruse the advertising in most major magazines is to embark on a journey of potential misadventure." Fredston asks, "When was the last time you leaped off a cliff after sipping a soft drink? Why is it that a picture of Mount Everest convinces us to buy an expensive watch or a skydiver's grin helps us choose a credit card? One automobile ad with a two-page color photograph of an SUV pulling a trailer full of glistening new snowmachines proclaims in oversize letters: THE MORE PEOPLE SCREAMING AT THE TOP OF THEIR LUNGS DOWN SNOW-COVERED SLOPES, THE MERRIER. Consequences are airbrushed from the ads as blithely as skin blemishes from the images of movie stars."[21] American consumers engage with risk as a fashionable lifestyle by purchasing extreme beverages and detergent as well as specialized equipment and clothing. As Fredston points out, "airbrushed" adventure porn sells. However, because the consequences are ignored, potential lessons are also obscured by these popular, risky lifestyle brands. The ads do not reflect reality.

In this sense, the adrenaline narrative promoted in such lifestyle advertising may actually do more to alienate us than connect us with nature. It may, in Linda Vance's words, "serve to reinforce the idea that humans are essentially alien to, and independent of, the natural world, and that human ingenuity can overcome all of nature's challenges."[22] While the mainstream commercialization of risky natures tends, as Palmer and Fredston argue, to downplay danger's negative consequences, other American adrenaline narratives—the majority selected for this study—focus on elite adventurers, the (potential) tragic consequences of white-knuckle risky behavior, and the extreme athlete's honed skills. Unlike the extreme representations in much mainstream media, the dangerous consequences are always nearby.

As I highlight in the final chapter, reading adrenaline narratives may result in more sustainable attitudes and practices, especially—as chapter 4 argued—if the narrative emphasizes erotic desire. However, increasing mainstream popularity also increases risk, and, in turn, heightened risks distract from fostering mutuality and sustainability. Esther Bott, for example, suggests climbing's increased popularity results in more extreme risk-taking: "Arguably, this popularisation has called the 'extremeness' of rock-climbing into question, leading to a potential dilution of its identity-giving qualities, inspiring some climbers to seek out niches in which to specialise in order to remain valued as 'extreme.'"[23] In other words, to maintain elite status, adrenaline athletes must continue to push the limits of their abilities and the sport into riskier territory. The same may be said for our quotidian approach to climate change. We increasingly become used to greater extremes. Extreme weather is the new normal: sunny-day flooding, increased ocean temperatures, and earlier spring leaf growth and flower bloom are all part of this new normal. As a result, understanding the risk aesthetic involves situating the protagonist's motivation to engage in risky behavior. Understanding why adrenaline athletes risk and how risks are mitigated offers possible insight into our collective willingness to risk climate change as well as the barriers that prevent more diverse participation in extreme sports.

RISK AESTHETIC, APPEAL: ADRENALINE "MADNESS"

While alpine climber Ruth Anne Kocour suggests that "the compulsion to climb mountains has no logical explanation," a variety of athletes and academic disciplines have tried.[24] For example, Ewert et al. summarize much of the scholarship that discusses motivation and outdoor adventure in the literature review section in their "Beyond 'Because It's There': Motivations for Pursuing Adventure Recreational Activities."[25] They also outline five challenges to studying motivation: its "fluid nature," the participants' "level of experience," and variability due to "activity type," "gender," and "experiential base."[26] Despite these research challenges, their study concludes, "what motivates an individual to participate in an adventure recreation activity can be linked to social, sensation-seeking, and self-image motives."[27] Environmental sustainability is notably absent from their list. Rather, "social-based factors" included "friends, image, escape, and competition with others or the environment."[28] Their research strongly links risk's motivations with conquering desire.

As the previous chapters demonstrate, an examination of the adrenaline narrative broadens our understanding of risk's appeal and representation, especially where nature is concerned. Richard Giulianotti in "Risk and Sport: An Analysis of Sociological Theories and Research Agendas" explains that studies of risk and sports fall into four categories of inquiry: "risk and calculation; risk themes of hedonism, voluntarism and transcendence; risk cultures and subcultures; and, risk and modernization."[29] These categories are helpful for narrative analysis as well. Adrenaline athletes regularly touch on these four areas, pointing out how risk shapes their voluntary and calculated activities, how risk defines their unique subculture, and how the risks they take are often misunderstood by the popular media, the general public, and their friends and families. Risk, as a result, forms an integral theme (a problem to be solved or managed) and a mode of producing suspense that threads throughout adrenaline narratives.

Risk's cultural range and appeal, moreover, entwines with the three primary desires toward nature: conquering, spiritual, and erotic. Giulianotti also outlines the three "aspects and discourses of risk-taking": "hedonism, voluntarism and transcendence."[30] Hedonistic risk correlates with conquering desire, transcendent with spiritual desire, and voluntaristic with erotic desire. Giulianotti explains that both hedonism and transcendence involve "the personal confrontation of specific ordeals or tests of endurance," whereas "voluntary risk-taking as an embodied experience is understood as a pleasuring process."[31] Hedonistic risk amplifies conquering desire, especially the narrative of heroic masculinity and its specific rites of passage to conquer and control. Transcendent risk also measures the individual sacrifices required for spiritual desire's transformation and self-discovery.

Risk amplifies both conquering and spiritual desire's objectification of nature. When "extreme sports are experienced primarily as 'risk,' with a motivation to prove oneself," as Brymer and Gray posit, then "nature is primarily an inert obstacle or antagonistic force."[32] Voluntaristic risk adds excitement to erotic desire, strengthening or collapsing the boundary between self and other. Voluntaristic risk, in this sense, facilitates the focus that initiates flow and deep play. Thus, we can begin to see how the stereotyped "adrenaline junkie" overemphasizes and oversimplifies risk's nuanced appeal and roles within adrenaline narratives and for individual adventurers.

The extreme athletes as well as many of the writers and scholars that write about them often work to overcome this stereotype. Brymer, for example, in "Risk Taking in Extreme Sports," "critique[s] the assumed relationship between extreme sports and risk taking through data emanating from a larger phenomenological study on extreme sports."[33] As Brymer goes on to point out, "while for some the initial motive to participate might be about the risk, thrills, glamour and excitement of these activities, there is evidence that suggests that motives change with continued participation."[34] Where simple thrill seeking may at times provide motivation, the more nuanced voluntaristic, hedonistic, and transcendent risk taking helps outline the finer contours.

Adrenaline authors frequently explicitly explore risk's place and meaning in their adventures. They nuance risk's alleged appeal for both audiences and athletes. In *Enduring Patagonia*, for example, Gregory Crouch freely admits the calculated trepidation involved in entering extreme environments. Crouch confesses that "to court these summits is to graft fear to your heart."[35] Yet most extreme athletes agree with Alvah Simon's summation about voluntary risk seeking: "Death is only one of many ways to lose your life."[36] The appeal, in this sense, is about living to the fullest rather than dying. Rather than "living a life of frustration," which "is a form of dying," William Pinkney decides to risk sailing solo around the world.[37] Pinkney describes the riskiest part of his journey—sailing around the Cape—as "My Everest of the Sea."[38] In doing so, Pinkney appraises his adventure's extreme risk level and further cements Everest as the standard by which extreme risk is measured. Risk, whether measured by Everest or some other means, offers more than hyperbole to boost the adventurers' accomplishments and narrative interest; it reveals a larger truth. Brymer in "Risk Taking in Extreme Sports: A Phenomenological Perspective" finds that participants feel "the real risk was ignoring this fact [death is a certainty] and as a result missing out on opportunities because of fear."[39] Thus, authors and athletes address death, but in doing so they often highlight the ways calculated risks define everyone's life.

Another aspect of the "adrenaline junkie" stereotype that extreme athletes must overcome is that they are addicted to danger and less capable, as a result, of calculating sustainable risk. Not all scholars and athletes, for example, connect deep play and flow, terms for the natural high and heightened concentration often experienced by adrenaline athletes, to fear and risk. Barbara Humberstone proposes that "this sense of oneness or numinousity is not necessarily fostered through fear, but mindful engagement may be constituted within physical practice in a natural environment. Each may have implications for environmental awareness and action."[40] Humberstone emphasizes nature's role as an optimal setting for deep play. Jennifer Woodlief likewise tweaks the stereotype by calling climbing "a drug of self-expression, of calmness, of centering" instead of adrenaline or fear.[41] Tori McClure in *A Pearl in the Storm* recounts how she deflected this stereotype when a reporter asked her, "'Are you an adrenaline junkie?'"[42] McClure responded, "'You try rowing twelve hours a day, every day, for three months and see how much adrenaline you get out of it.'"[43] McClure underscores the endurance required to sustain adventure's grueling, "Calvinistic" (to borrow Krakauer's phrasing) grind.[44]

However, not all athletes shun the "junkie" stereotype. While her "life [is] defined by risk and uncertainty," climber Steph Davis struggles when she loses two key "anchors": her marriage and career.[45] Skydiving jolts her out of her funk: "If this was what heroin felt like, I understood immediately how people dropped their lives into it."[46] Davis highlights the high and rush, where McClure stresses the tedium. The distinct sports, the relatively short and intense experience of skydiving versus long-distance rowing, in part contribute to the different "highs." While individual athletes may embrace or spurn the adrenaline junkie moniker, all extreme adventurers routinely discuss the role and careful management of risk and use it as a narrative tool to educate and engage readers.

In their discussions the adventurers uniformly agree that the associated, calculated risks are outweighed by their selected sport's benefits and their honed skills. In this vein, Kevin Krein argues against the "risk explanation," or that risk is *the* point of participating in" adventure sports.[47] Brymer agrees: "just because an extreme sport participant does not back away from the possibility of undesirable outcomes it does not mean that they are chasing risks."[48] The following conversation between Gail D. Storey and her husband Porter supports this view, emphasizing the benefits far outweigh the costs.

> "We keep risking our lives, but why?" I asked.
> "I ask myself that a lot," he said. "But I've never felt so alive."
> Life here came up close. Some wall between mountain and mind gave way, in the hidden rush of water under snow.[49]

Porter emphasizes the intense reality of their existence, which results in powerful, "up close" sensations. Storey expands on what this means in her exposition. She describes a "wall between mountain and mind" dissolving in the quick flow of water. Often, the intense concentration risk necessitates produces what Mihaly Csikszentmihalyi refers to as "flow." As Giulianotti points out, "Voluntary risk-taking as an embodied experience is understood as a pleasuring process, promoting optimal 'flow' sensations."[50] Athletes tend to describe these "valuable interactions" as pleasurable, which often gets linked to adrenaline.

The adventurers' comments suggest that risk's unique pleasures play a significant role in their sport cultures and are necessary for a fulfilling existence. For instance, Ruth Anne Kocour—while initially claiming that climbing defied logic—goes on to provide various reasons why she climbs and endures the associated risks. She explains that she climbs "because the high alpine world is a source of endless fascination that energizes and makes me feel more alive than at any other time in my life. I dream about mountaineering. It's in my blood and I dread the thought of a day when I might be physically unable to do it."[51] She also says, "as an artist, I climb for the visual feast," "because challenging situations thrill me," and "because I truly love being in the vertical environment—I'm at home there, totally at ease."[52] Likewise, for extreme kayaker Tao Berman risk is deeply connected to pleasure. Berman attests, "life would be boring without risk. Logically, it doesn't make sense that I'm risking my life just for the fun of it. But without fun, what is the purpose of life?"[53] Such characterizations of risk's pleasures are shared among male and female adventurers from a range of backgrounds and sports. Risk's shared appeal raises several questions: How does one connect risk with pleasure? What kind of aesthetic emerges? And, what might this connection-aesthetic reveal about the environmental imagination?

Laurence Gonzales's *Deep Survival: Who Lives, Who Dies, and Why* takes a scientific approach to why extreme athletes take "unnecessary" risks, examining risk's evolutionary, psycho-biological sources and implications. He compares wilderness sports with chess: "those of us who go into the wilderness and engage in dangerous sports are playing chess with Mother Nature."[54] That is, Gonzales's research suggests that risk's pleasure derives from this deeply nuanced, intense strategy game. Survival depends, like winning at chess, on a complex set of factors that involve both emotion and logic as well as the synthesis of past experiences combined with an ongoing analysis of the present. These complex actions form what Gonzales calls "mental models." Often, Gonzales points out, one's ability to navigate successfully a risky situation involves an ability to update consistently one's mental map.[55]

Berman succinctly illustrates Gonzales's theory of pleasurable risk and survival: "It's more than luck. It's setting goals that may look impossible to others and training so hard that I'm measuring risks from a different realm than those shaking their heads in dismay or disapproval. It's honing my instincts until they are trained reactions and surrounding myself with talented help."[56] Berman's remarks begin to reveal a different picture of the adventure athlete, in line with Kevin Krein's observation that "rather than characterizing adventure athletes as reckless thrill seekers (as the risk explanation does) those involved in adventure sports can be seen as athletes attempting to develop their skills so that they can take on more difficult challenges."[57] Berman's ability to not panic (key in Gonzales's analysis) helps him continually revise his mental models and "feel no fear or pressure."[58]

Berman thus agrees with the analysis that risk-seekers are not on a death mission: "But let's be perfectly clear: I do not have a death wish. It's risk I'm seeking, not death. And it's years of knowledge and practice, and years of honing my instincts, that I believe help me paddle the fine line between them."[59] Berman views risk as a crucial element in his adventure. It is the goal he "seeks." Extreme athletes' risk-seeking behaviors provide them with the pleasurable sensation of feeling fully alive and initiate flow or "deep play."[60] In this sense, risk is not the goal (as Berman claims), but rather a "by-product" of deep play: "Adventure sports are risky, but risk is best understood as a by-product, rather than the goal, of such sports."[61] What separates the extreme athlete is their skill and degree of (potential) risk in exchange for pleasure. While these differences are key, the everyday risks we take related to climate change are similarly but less intensely situated and experienced.

Risk is, in this sense, an aesthetic or element in both the adventure and nature's design that is key to the adventurer's life. Yet as Nick Jans points out when writing about Timothy Treadwell, "it's tough to pick the point at which acceptance of extreme danger slides into a submerged death wish."[62] Jans sees Treadwell's history of a "self-described flirtation with hard-core drugs and violence" as "an earlier manifestation of the same syndrome." Jans goes on to explain, "If Timothy Treadwell had an addictive personality, his drug of choice was never booze or cocaine. Like an extreme rock climber or big-wave surfer, he intensely loved what he was doing, where he was, and who he was with, but what hooked him was the danger."[63] Like the British rock climbers Victoria Robinson interviews, Jans suggests Treadwell must continually seek riskier experiences in order "to escape the mundane."[64] Defying consequences as the stakes become increasingly higher sounds a lot like climate change denial.

Assessing risk is difficult, moreover, because the line between normal and extreme keeps moving. Robinson makes this point in regard to the definition and perception of what is considered "extreme": "The concept of what is extreme, then, is not fixed and is rather a relational concept in regard to (shifting) subject positions and particular everyday practices when engaging in the sport."[65] This relational aspect connects risk in adrenaline narratives and risk perception in regard to climate change. While the science is clear, individual perceptions of acceptable risk, based on our perceptional models, make sustainable change—the equivalent of turning away from the immediate rewards offered by the summit in our sights—seem crazier than maintaining the current dangerous path. Moreover, what constitutes change—like what defines extreme—is relational, even as evidence of dramatic climate change stares us in the face.

Jans proposes our fascination with extreme sports and risk stems from the fact that we all have some attraction to risk. Jans points out that "a little of it resides in all of us; bungee jumping, three-hundred-horsepower sport sedans, and roller coasters wouldn't exist if we weren't a bit in love with the dark lady—all a matter of degree."[66] The "matter of degree," however, does not have universally clear and consistent gradations and may change based on other factors, like the type of activity or, as I discuss in chapter 2 and in more detail below, the gender and race of the adventurer. Assessing risk thus depends on multiple external (cultural) and internal (individual) factors. The multiple assessments of Treadwell illustrate risk's complex, intersecting layers to a tee.

Ultimately, Treadwell's crime, as Jans later points out, is not that he died, but that he did not die "in a socially more acceptable risky manner, such as in a NASCAR wreck or while climbing Everest."[67] Treadwell's friend Joel explains "that extreme skiers and other adventurers are often widely admired for routinely putting their lives on the line. He also argued that Treadwell not only understood and accepted the danger, but demonstrated, over thirteen years, both competence and an undeniable talent for coexisting with the Katmai bears."[68] Jans and Treadwell's friend Joel suggest that because Treadwell was not engaged in a recognizable recreation activity—such as an adrenaline sport like mountaineering or NASCAR—he was subject to more criticism than praise, despite his honed survival skills. The fact that he went to Alaska to live with grizzlies makes him a weirdo, not a hero.

The fact that Treadwell did not protect his female companion, Amie Huguenard, further compounds his crime and failure at heroic masculinity and an honorable death. While Craig Medred does not know Huguenard, he casts her as Treadwell's "innocent victim," a characterization based, at least in part, on the sentiments expressed in an email from Huguenard's "old boyfriend."[69] Her obituary, however, emphasizes her agency and knowledge of the risks. The obituary states Huguenard and Treadwell "knew their work came with the risk of consequences and accepted that challenge, because they believed and were successful in making a difference in the bears' lives."[70] Key for my analysis is the fact of the competing narratives about Huguenard's agency and Treadwell's responsibility and their mutual reliance on heroic masculinity.

The obituary follows a familiar tragic narrative by positing both Treadwell and Huguenard as fully aware of the risks. Their tragically heroic deaths offer catharsis in the form of knowing that they died doing what they loved. In Medred's scenario of an equally familiar failed and false heroic masculinity, the "new-age California talk[ing]" Treadwell "dupes" a woman who naively follows him into the Alaskan wilderness. As a female follower and victim, Huguenard assumes risk without responsibility. Treadwell, on the other hand, shoulders the brunt of the critique. The variations on Treadwell's narrative of failed heroic masculinity offer additional insight into understanding risk's appeal and function in adrenaline narratives.

Treadwell's inability to translate physical skill and knowledge to other forms of social capital especially results in critique. In sporting cultures such as big-wave surfing, "the most prestige [is reserved] for those who show excess courage in big waves."[71] Douglas Booth notes, "while most explanations of the contemporary surge in extreme sports focus on individual temperaments and the apparent psychological need for individuals to find meaning by risking their lives," there are "sociological factors" that also provide insight into the attraction to risk: "Big wave riders are surfing's warrior caste."[72] The "sociological factors" also offer insight into how adventurers' risk-taking is judged. Because Treadwell did not follow recognized scientific protocols and was not a scientist himself, his bear advocacy is usually not seen as legitimate. Treadwell ultimately fails according to this heroic model because his work/play do not successfully protect his female companion and further a sport or scientific knowledge. He assumes risks, as a result, that cannot be rewarded as artistic "pure play" or as socially redeemable. Treadwell, according to this logic, is understood as dangerous or foolish rather than admired for dying while doing something he loved.

RISK AESTHETIC, EMBODIMENT AND MANAGEMENT: ADRENALINE JUNKIES, CONTROL FREAKS

While Treadwell does not earn a place in the "warrior caste," his risk management skills were arguably more than sufficient—until they were not. Just as Joel explains in relation to Treadwell's long-term success living with the bears, Berman credits his own past experience and practice as key to helping him successfully manage, as opposed to "tolerate," the risks he "deliberately seek[s]...out. That's how one pushes the envelope of a sport."[73] Gonzales's research supports Berman's speculation that "perhaps a childhood of freedom to explore limits and perfect the art of calculating risks continues to stand me in good stead."[74] In fact, it is this history, according to Gonzales, that helps form one's mental model. However, the fact that, as for Berman, "in my line of work, there are so many close calls and near disasters that we don't take them too seriously," may work for or against the extreme athlete's survival.[75] Arrogance about risk and danger can lead to disaster.

Perhaps arrogance is what led to Treadwell's demise, or—perhaps—it was simply bad luck. Treadwell embodies what Gonzales describes as "positive mental attitude": "The true survivor isn't someone with nothing to lose. He has something precious to lose. But at the same time, he's willing to bet it all on himself."[76] We see a similar mentality in American attitudes toward the climate crisis. Susanne C. Moser, for example, lists the following challenges to communicating the realities of climate change: "invisibility of causes, distant impacts, lack of immediacy and direct experience of the impacts, lack of gratification for taking mitigative actions, disbelief in human's [sic] global influence, complexity and uncertainty, inadequate signals indicating the need for change, perceptual limits and self-interest."[77] Climate change's "slow violence" helps foster ignorance of its existance as well as confidence its effects will be mitigated by technology or some other type of human intervention.[78] Like heroic masculinity, humans pose both the problem and the solution. Moreover, because the consequences are felt so gradually, we continually adjust to a new normal and so have little incentive to change. How does one distinguish between confidence and arrogance when it comes to risk assessment? Where are such aesthetic lines drawn?

Berman sees his engagement with risks as purely logical. He claims that risk "forces me to make decisions based purely on calculation; no emotion is involved."[79] By contrast, Gonzales emphasizes the important role emotions play, especially fear, in risk taking and survival. Gonzales argues that "we think we believe what we know, but we only truly believe what we feel."[80] In other words, as Heise translates this passage from Beck's *Risk Society*, "in order to perceive risks as risks and to make them a reference point for one's own thought and action, one has to *believe* in fundamentally invisible causal connections."[81] The risk scenario described in this passage is slightly different than the risk assessments performed and described by extreme athletes. Beck's risk assessment is based on never having "consciously experienced" the risk, whereas the athletes stress that their mental and physical training prepares them, even when they encounter unfamiliar or new situations.[82] Adrenaline narratives suggest the ability to paddle between these streams of thought—emotion and logic/knowledge—may offer the best course for negotiating risk's treacherous waters.

Skill combined with passion or emotion may be a somewhat simplistic—but perhaps no less profound—definition of the individual risk aesthetic promoted by adrenaline narratives. Jill Fredston, for example, describes a reliance on "instincts" during "risky circumstances"; the key is "not thinking too much."[83] Emotion, according to Gonzales, is what confirms the truth of our experiences, which can work for or against an individual's survival as well as attitudes about climate change. Berman suggests that by controlling emotion he limits risk; however, like Fredston, Berman also relies on his instincts—honed through hours and hours of practice—to kick in once his boat hits the water. Research additionally shows "extreme sport participants are not inclined to search for uncertainty or uncontrollability."[84] Rather, these highly skilled practitioners "deliberately become very familiar with all the variables including the environment, their equipment, and the weather."[85] Thus, *control freak* may be a more accurate moniker than *adrenaline junkie*.

Significantly, while practice and experience reduce risk, they do not eliminate it. Gonzales explores the relationship between control and risk. Building on the work of Charles Perrow (*Normal Accidents* [1984]), Gonzales points out that risky situations such as extreme sports "self-organize" accidents: "The accidents are characteristic of the system itself."[86] In other words, accidents do not just happen. They are normal, and "efforts to prevent them always fail."[87] For some, climate change works the same way: it cannot be prevented and humans will adapt. Risk takers use their mental models to help determine their odds of success and failure, given that accidents will happen. As Gonzales explains, "we are human. Our attention is fragmentary. We get excited. We get tired. We get stupid. Of course, you can't make adventure safe, for then it's not adventure." Additionally, as the Mount Hood recreation officer tells Gonzales, "'if you made it so safe for everybody to get up there [Mount Hood], you'd have a lot more fatalities because people wouldn't recognize the risk.'"[88] Risk, thus, while acting as a deterrent for some, defines adventure's pleasures and acts as a reminder for participants to update and adjust their mental maps continually.

Risk facilitates deep play and connection with the natural environment. For armchair observers, furthermore, this risk aesthetic maintains a separation (foolish judgment) or encourages a connection (successful risk management) with the adventurer while building narrative tension. How the adventurer manages risk, moreover, may give us insight into the current environmental crisis, especially as the adventurers themselves increasingly address environmental and social justice causes. Looking more closely at the ways in which risks are gendered and raced reveals how risk both supports and undercuts environmental and social justice.

RISK AESTHETIC, EMBODIMENT AND MANAGEMENT: GENDER'S RISKY NATURES

As outlined in chapter 2, risk is not experienced in the same ways by all participants. As Heise explains in *Sense of Place and Sense of Planet*, Beck suggests in *World Risk Society* "that social status will not in the future function as a reliable indicator of risk exposure."[89] However, "sociologists have pointed out that little empirical evidence exists to support Beck's claim that social categorizations are indeed in the process of being rearticulated around issues of risk," and adrenaline narratives support this view.[90] As Heise clarifies and this chapter confirms, "technological and ecological risk scenarios superimpose themselves on and help to reinforce existing structures of social inequality, in that the world's poor and racial or ethnic minorities tend to be disproportionately exposed to risk, as well as, in quite a few cases, women."[91] Thus, while Susan Birrell and Nancy Theberge suggest nontraditional sports "hold greater promise for the realisation of alternative and resistant sport forms" by acting as a "springboard for the transformation of gender relations by dislodging the gender hierarchy that sport helps preserve," an examination of how adventurers experience risk suggests this is largely not the case—at least not yet—in extreme sports.[92]

Two themes emerge about the relationship between risk, gender, and race in post-1970 adrenaline narratives. First, physical risk or the fear of bodily harm in the form of injury or death polices female and minority adventurers in ways distinct from their white male counterparts. Second, the gendered and raced nature of extreme risk reveals white patriarchal privilege shapes adventure in profound ways. When looked at together, these themes of fear and containment suggest little has changed in the ways American adventurers are socialized in the twenty-first century to negotiate risk beyond home's borders. Nevertheless, women and racial and ethnic minorities persist in pushing against the physical and social boundaries that seek to control their risky business.

Motherhood especially highlights the double standards adventuring women must negotiate. The research that indicates motherhood impacts women's participation differently than fatherhood is confirmed by adrenaline narratives.[93] For example, a hiker on the trail asks Patricia Ellis Herr, who brings her five-year-old daughter with her, "Your husband doesn't mind? You taking her up here alone, I mean?" She responds by asking him if he puts the same question to the fathers he meets.[94] Herr believes people question her more—going so far as to suggest "taking a kid up a mountain is akin to child abuse"—because she is a mother of a daughter.[95] Melissa Balmain's *Just Us: Adventures and Travels of a Mother and Daughter* offers another take on mother-daughter adventure. This book chronicles the adult adventures undertaken by Balmain and her mother so that they may get to know each other better. Juxtaposing these narratives highlights how the child's age plays a key role in risk assessment. In fact, cultural expectations about responsibility may shift to the adult child, who is supposed to care for the parent in extreme situations. This comparison begins to highlight how critiques of motherhood and risk focus on women as potential and current mothers of young children.

The short video, "Carrie Cooper: 39 Weeks," succinctly illustrates risk's embodied nature.[96] Created for prAna (an activewear clothing company), the short documentary shows prAna ambassador Cooper rock climbing while thirty-nine weeks pregnant. The majority of comments about the video are positive—a fact perhaps reflecting the adventurous community that would access prAna's site and/or prAna's careful social media management. A couple of comments, though, question the risks Cooper takes. The comments reflect concerns similar to those expressed about the female climbers' deaths discussed in chapter 2.

For example, 305sFinestt writes the following about "Carrie Cooper: 39 Weeks": "I'm sorry, but I see this and can't help but [write] how wrong this is. I'm glad rock-climbing may be invigorating or something that's done to clear her mind. I'm glad that at the end of the day you can make a cute YouTube video about rock-climbing while pregnant. Yes, I see the safety harness [Cooper is top-rope climbing] but all it takes is one accident and two lives are changed forever. Even if that harness has less than a 1% chance of failing, why risk it? Careless in my opinion but people will say otherwise. Accidents do happen."[97] Another person (user name, apereiraytytyt) comments on Cooper's lack of a climbing helmet.[98] And user RuudJH compares Cooper's climbing while pregnant with "Michael Jackson dangling his kid over a balcony railing."[99] The handful of comments on YouTube and other sites where the video is posted are otherwise positive, describing the video as inspiring and beautiful. Via prAna's account, Cooper responded to the critiques and the support, noting, "accidents do happen and can happen anytime. Part of the reason to live life to its fullest while you can."[100] Cooper agrees with other adventurers that the benefits of a full life outweigh the potential risks.

When I show this video to my students or as part of a presentation, people—especially if they are not familiar with (top-rope) climbing or do not realize that Cooper is also wearing a custom harness—react similarly to 305sFinestt, questioning Cooper's wisdom at taking what appear to be unnecessary physical risks. The audience assumes control over Cooper's pregnant body, concerned her behavior would risk harm to the fetus like smoking, drinking alcohol, or consuming caffeinated beverages, which should also be avoided. They stress that she needs to suppress her individual desires in favor of her responsibilities as a pregnant woman. Because of the emphasis on risk, such caution is not usually rewarded in extreme sports.

While "caution in mountaineering is rarely celebrated or seen as heroic," "the responsible, family-minded mountaineer is but one of the new breed of climbing hero."[101] Although the "family-minded" participant has always been the rule for (potential) mothers, Coffey's remarks suggest one way in which (patriarchal) masculinity may be changing. Whether or not concern and public reward for being "family-minded" will be applied equitably to both fathers and mothers remains to be seen.

Mothers in adrenaline narratives are still policed and stereotyped in ways fathers do not experience. A 2018 article in *Outside* magazine points out mountaineering "hasn't allowed for much nuance in how moms are portrayed or accommodated." The article highlights how social media has played a role in changing the culture's and sponsors' minds. However, this, too, has potential drawbacks: "there's the danger that once an athlete has children, she'll fall into the default box of 'mom athlete' in the public perception, a phenomenon that doesn't happen nearly as often with men." Randall concludes, "simplifying their stories as 'having it all' or not being a 'good enough' mom doesn't do service to the gravity that motherhood deserves, whether or not a woman decides to have children."[102] Gender and race's "adventure gaps" further reveal the conservative side of risky natures.

RISK AESTHETIC, EMBODIMENT AND MANAGEMENT: GENDERED RISK REGIMES

Jason Laurendeau points out that edgework, a term used to describe risky physical activity, takes place in "gendered risk regimes," a phrase that refers to the "dominant understandings and practices that shape the gendered ways practitioners 'do risk,' and the particular ways they do gender from within a risk regime."[103] We see edgework's gendered characteristics in adrenaline classics such as Jon Krakauer's *Into Thin Air* as well as the more recent bestselling *Wild* by Cheryl Strayed. Strayed, for example, notes she has "done a lot of dumb and dangerous things in my life, but soliciting a ride with a stranger was not yet one of them. Horrible things happened... especially to women hitchhiking alone."[104] Yet hitchhiking is normal for Pacific Crest Trail hikers.

The narratives written by pioneering female adventurers such as Lynn Hill, Arlene Blume, and Stacy Allison, who were among the first to make space for female athletes in contemporary extreme outdoor adventure sports, self-consciously describe and navigate their sports' gendered risk regimes and risk's double standards. The acceptance of women often remains marginal: Christine Byl points out that "women in certain arenas are token, if welcome at all."[105] As Catherine Palmer confirms, "where women are involved in dangerous pursuits, all sorts of cultural definitions and limitations are placed upon their behaviour."[106] While America is defined in part by its adventuring spirit, women's thrilling adventures are often quickly critiqued and contained. "Gendered risk regimes" amplify when women leave home and enter spaces traditionally reserved for men; the same holds true for race.

Eritrean American writer and adventurer Rahawa Haile's discussion of the African American literature she read while thru-hiking offers a secular version of the "wilderness reading" as risky "spiritual practice" that Belden Lane discusses in "Backpacking with the Saints: The Risk-Taking Character of Wilderness Reading." While not focused on Christian texts, Haile's experience reading black literature while hiking similarly "indicate[s] the potentially revolutionary associations people make between explosive texts and the places where they read them."[107] Haile explains in her *BuzzFeed* article, "How Black Books Lit My Way along the Appalachian Trail," that she is never free from the threat of violence in America. She notes that "a thing I found myself repeatedly explaining to hikers who asked about my books and my experience wasn't that I feared them, but that there was no such thing as freedom from vulnerability for me anywhere in this land. That I might be tolerated in trail towns that didn't expect to see a black hiker, but I'd rarely if ever feel at ease."[108] Haile describes how she is not able to experience the same freedom as her white counterparts.

White privilege means the hikers she encounters try to convince her no such policing exists: she is free. Haile goes on to clarify, "few seemed to understand that simply because hikers had not targeted me did not mean I had ceased being a target. That I viewed every road crossing as a cue to raise shields, eyes open, ears alert.... Here, they [white hikers] were free, truly free, whereas I was only a little freer than before. That the difference between the two held centuries of slaughters in its maw. That we all carried fears. That some fears never slept."[109] Haile's survival depends on her reading the black literature she brings with her, the people she meets, and the environment. Those who meet her on the trail read her in a different way than they might in other environments. Her very presence on the trail, in fact, makes other hikers aware of their whiteness in ways, as one hiker put it, "'I never noticed... until I saw you.'"[110] Thus, Haile's black body acts as a filter for others' experiences. Her presence on the trail changes their experiences, even as she is not free from racial threats and attitudes that remind her there is no "escape" to the wilderness.

Female adventurers contend with this legacy that defines them as vulnerable objects rather than daring actors. Women's bodies map routes for conquest and survival. Suzanne Roberts in her narrative about hiking the John Muir Trail, for example, explains this normalized culture of sexualized violence (otherwise known as rape culture) as follows:

> Every woman who has ever been out camping alone knows that bears are nothing to fear compared to predatory men. Whether real or imagined, that fear is always there in the wilderness, riding on our backs like a heavy pack.... The fear is something to get past, an obstacle that is a nonissue for most men. Women don't enter the wilderness in the same way men do; we constantly return to our physical bodies and the ways in which they could be threatened, not by bears or bugs but by men. Our bodies become a filter between us and the landscape, preventing us from enjoying both.[111]

The risk and associated bodily fear Roberts and Haile describe are heightened by the outdoors but not unique to it. Additionally, Roberts explicitly identifies the female body as a "filter," which emerges as a common theme among women who discuss their experiences of navigating gendered risk regimes.

For women fear persists because, as Greta Gaard points out, "women are supposed to fear wilderness due to the possible threat of rape, or (if that doesn't work) the feebleness of their own survival skills, and many women do experience these fears and the resulting alienation from wilderness."[112] Writers and adventurers such as Krista Langlois write against this stereotype while not dismissing the very real fears and risks women face when adventuring alone. She claims, "the wild animals and crazy weather and existential doubts we experience in the backcountry are nothing compared to the dangers of the frontcountry." Langlois goes on to clarify, "a friend who thinks nothing of hurtling down mountainsides on a bike or skis doesn't even bother setting up a tent when she's alone at a campground anymore; after too many sleepless nights, she sleeps in her car with the doors locked instead."[113] Langlois differentiates between the physical risks her friend manages mountain biking or skiing and the physical risks of camping alone as a woman. While some find the outdoor community a "respite from the SHSA [sexual harassment and sexual assault] frequently experienced in the 'real' world," recent survey data indicates no difference between the risk of sexual harassment and sexual assault outdoors and "in the rest of society," which is to say it is "a public health crisis."[114]

Notably, Blair Braverman begins her adventure narrative *Welcome to the Goddamn Ice Cube* with a story of male intimidation. Braverman's memoir begins as she sits around a campfire and an older man declares that in his day, "'I sure could have fucked you.'" His remarks remind Braverman of an encounter "the day before" when "another man...had wrapped his arms around me from behind. *Treasure*, he'd whispered, *you're north of the moral circle now*."¹¹⁵ The men's harassment reminds Braverman that she has traveled into dangerous territory, beyond civilization's "moral circle." These aggressions not only shape the male-dominated environment through which Braverman travels, they also highlight the ways women's bodies, as Roberts describes, act as "filters."

While some women do, Braverman does not experience alienation from nature as a result of her sexual harassment and assault. Gaard explains, "women who have survived sexual abuse often experience a forced alienation from nature—from their own bodies, from their own sexual nature, as well as from wilderness; incest survivors often have a difficult time with extended wilderness travel since it does not afford them the opportunity to bathe frequently or to maintain their own standards of cleanliness, and others may find that coping with natural elements can trigger sensual flashbacks of the abuse."¹¹⁶ Braverman, instead, seeks bodily control in nature. She, for instance, contrasts the physical alertness required outside, in the bitter Arctic cold, versus inside the physically warm home of her host family, whose father made sexual advances. Braverman explains, "the thing about being outside, I realized, was that I had to be alert—to landmarks, to weather, to dusk—and yet that alertness on the mountain restored whatever it was that alertness at home had drained."¹¹⁷ Braverman finds solace in extreme nature in direct contrast to the physical dangers she fears at the hands of her host father.

When she later returns to Norway to attend a folk school focused on dogsledding and winter survival, Braverman remarks,

> I was often acutely frightened—of a sharp turn in the trail, of a tricky river crossing, during storms—and I lived, too, with a deeper fear: that the winter was only starting, that I had so many minutes and hours and days of cold and risk and potential injury. But it was refreshing to be afraid of something concrete. I was no longer scared of some unknown force, of confusion; no, I was afraid of hypothermia. I was afraid of being stranded in the wilderness. I was afraid of crashing the sled. I was as afraid as I'd been in Far's house [her host father], maybe even more, but suddenly that fear didn't make me crazy: it made me brave.¹¹⁸

Nature's extreme dangers are more manageable than her host father's confusing sexual advances. While she feels powerless at home, Braverman seeks and finds control in her ability to name nature's "concrete" dangers. Braverman later reflects, "if I'd accepted the word *rape*, maybe I would have discovered other words, ones that could have helped me make sense of my earlier experience."[119] Because she is unable to identify or name the sexual dangers she experiences, she must find other ways of coping. Her body filters these contrasting energies, becoming either "drained" or "restored."

Management of draining and sustaining risks becomes key for Braverman. She reflects, "I wanted to do anything that would make me feel like I was in charge of my own risks."[120] For Braverman, facing the Arctic's physical dangers offers potential control over the domestic risks she faces. She speculates, "if I could be safe in this land, maybe I could be safe in my own body. If I could protect my body, maybe I could live in this land."[121] Braverman emphasizes risk's embodied nature, dependent on location ("land") and her body, as well as risk's logical and emotional characteristics. She needs to feel safe in both her environment and body. Braverman directly relates the skills required to survive wilderness with the survival skills necessary to handle unwanted sexual advances.

Enduring sexual harassment often becomes a way for adventuring women to demonstrate their "toughness" rather than an opportunity to fight for change. While working as a guide in Alaska, for example, Braverman is constantly under a predatory male gaze until she begins a relationship with a male guide, Dan: "the men on the glacier dominated social life; their authority came with an edge of sexism that seemed at once inevitable and disconcerting." This behavior changed once she became Dan's girlfriend. Braverman explains, "the murmur of violence that had colored my first weeks on the ice dissolved instantly with Dan's arm around my waist. Suddenly I counted: mushers held tent flaps open for me, laughed at my jokes, took my feedback into account as they discussed problems with their dog teams or tourists. If I felt, privately, that Dan's approval proved I belonged on the ice, that sentiment was only reinforced by the ways in which others seemed to believe it, too."[122] Braverman will never become one of the boys, but she can be authorized and protected by them.

This "protection," however, comes at an extreme cost. Her relationship with Dan quickly sours. Braverman admits, "after a few weeks I accepted that Dan would fuck me regardless of what I said, so I turned my focus to getting it over fast."[123] She eventually ends the relationship; however, "choosing jurisdiction over my own body—felt like choosing exile from the very things in which his approval had granted me legitimacy."[124] Braverman exposes her complex complicity in the patriarchy and her struggle to give up the apparent privileges afforded her. While she does not immediately change the system, she does change herself. To be clear: it would be unrealistic to expect Braverman to change the system or her situation's institutionalized sexism single-handedly. In speaking out, furthermore, she is playing a key role in breaking the silence, a tactic that the #MeToo movement began to exploit in earnest in 2017. Additionally, Braverman's narrative includes the story of her current relationship with Quince, who is transgender.[125] Thus, by sharing their stories and holding individuals accountable for their sexual harassment and assault, women like Braverman are changing rape culture.

Significantly, the risk of sexual and racial violence exists in all environments, not just extreme ones. When Jennifer Pharr Davis is preparing to hike the Appalachian trail solo after graduating college, her father remarks, "'the main thing you have to worry about on the Appalachian Trail is people, and people are a threat everywhere.'"[126] While on the trail, Davis endures catcalls by drunk boys.[127] She experiences her most intense moments of anxiety when she is most likely to encounter others alone in a shelter: "I think most women have a fear of waking up next to a strange man and not knowing how he got there."[128] Braverman experiences a similar fear when camping alone as a young woman. She writes, "I remembered stories I'd heard from other women who camped alone: men who circled their tents, pressed the dark outlines of hands to the fabric, whispered threats like sweet nothings or else loudly considered other options. And those were the stories that ended well. There was no limit to the ways in which someone could hurt me."[129] Notably, the threat of physical violence is used to police women in the outdoors. Its psychic weight adds worry. Real or imagined, on or off the trail, such threats remind women of the costs of spurning male protection.

Despite the dangers and their fears, these women risk physical and emotional harm because the benefits for solo self-discovery outweigh the potential dangers and discomforts. Davis clarifies, for example, that she needed to hike solo because of the particular mode of personal development it fostered.[130] Haile similarly states, "I can confirm that one does not walk 2,000 miles across the face of this country as a black woman without building up an incredible sense of self. I have seen what I can be. I have heard the voices stop."[131] Additionally, as these female adventurers point out, the racialized and sexualized dangers faced in the wild are similar to what other women experience in less extreme environments. Braverman notes, "nothing that had happened to me...was beyond the normal scope of what happened to women all the time. Some harassment by an authority figure, a few sexual remarks, pressure from an insistent boyfriend? What woman *hadn't* experienced those things? It made me the same as everyone else, and luckier than many. It was just a natural result of being female and living in the world."[132] Suzanne Roberts goes so far as to suggest, "because of various fears of being in the outdoors alone, many women write from their own backyards."[133] These "tough girl" adventurers recognize rape culture and white supremacy exists in and beyond the wilderness.

Does, then, women's bodily presence in the wilderness make a difference? Jason Laurendeau and Nancy Sharara point out the difficulties associated with a liberal feminism that primarily addresses inclusion. They assert, "if women are making inroads into sport without challenging assumptions and structures that privilege men over women and particular kinds of men over others, then the transformative potential of their entrance is limited at best."[134] Should women not conquer the "assumptions and structures that privilege men over women," they are likely also not able to conquer their fears or the extreme natural environments in which they travel. For Roberts and her fellow female hikers, hiking without men made a difference: "Without them we had come to rely on each other and on ourselves. Luck and circumstances provided the chance to find our 'girl power.'" Roberts explains, "we learned to feel safe walking among them [mountains], to feel more at home in nature. And with each step we came closer to knowing ourselves."[135] Haile also notes how hiking helped others recognize their white privilege: her presence on the trail made a difference. Notably, women rather than men are doing the lion's share of the work to change the culture. As with racial inequality, the oppressed often bear a disproportionate burden to solve the problem. We cannot expect nature to likewise pick up the slack.

This potential for individual—if not cultural—transformation is what continues to motivate female extreme adventurers to risk beyond and against the odds. Erica Wilson and Donna E. Little in "Adventure and the Gender Gap" caution that adrenaline narratives "tend to promote the harshness, the difficulty, the foolhardiness, the discomfort, and the remoteness, not just in location, but in achievability," and that subsequently "there is an increasing tendency for adventure recreation to be solely perceived as skill, action, and conquest, rather than also incorporating dreams, learning, personal growth, and discovery."[136] While Wilson and Little maintain conventional "hard" and "soft" gender distinctions, their remarks highlight how broadening the narrative would attract a greater range of participants—whatever their sex/gender identities. Rachel Stein explains, "by analyzing how discourses of nature have been used to enforce heteronormativity, to police sexuality, and to punish and exclude those persons who have been deemed sexually transgressive, we can begin to understand the deep, underlying commonalities between struggles against sexual oppression and other struggles for environmental justice."[137] Greater institutional change is needed. Braverman reveals that she had "become acutely aware that adventure was a kind of violence, too. It was there in the mountains and the ice and the deep cold, the speed of the dogs and the changing weather.... [It] represented some hard masculinity that seemed to thrive in the north."[138] Braverman understands the narrative of heroic masculinity shapes her adventure. While she has trouble imagining adventure without it, she also does not want to embrace it.

Braverman ultimately does embrace a slightly revised version of heroic masculinity as key to overcoming her fears. Braverman does not "want to be shoved up against" "some hard masculinity" again: "I wasn't sure if I could handle it." However, she states that she must return north and face her demons in order to feel safe. She explains, "I wasn't sure I'd feel safe—anywhere, really—until I had proved to myself that I could."[139] However, rather than conquer nature, Braverman seeks to conquer or "prove" herself. She returns to feel better, to conquer her fears. Without changing adventure's heroic masculinity narrative, Wilson and Little suggest, the "progress [that] has been made" will not continue: "further acknowledgement and a reconfiguration of the experience of adventure are still required to help remove some of the ongoing constraints contemporary women face as adventure continues to be seen as unfeminine, a transgression of constructions of 'female' behavior, and a challenge beyond the skills of women participants."[140] As the above examples demonstrate, furthermore, for the narrative to change means also addressing the risks associated with rape culture.

RISK AESTHETIC, EMBODIMENT AND MANAGEMENT: RACE'S RISKY NATURES

Like rape culture, "a 'white wilderness' is socially constructed and grounded in race, class, gender and cultural ideologies."[141] As Carolyn Finney points out, America's environmental narrative is primarily white. As a result, "this narrative not only shapes the way the natural environment is represented, constructed, and perceived in our everyday lives, but informs our national identity as well."[142] Fear and risk for racial and ethnic minorities stem from a history of racial violence, especially lynching. For African Americans, "a tree became a painful symbol for many black people, reminding them that the color of their skin could mean death."[143] Being "out of place" risks death. Eddy L. Harris worries about the risks for "a black man alone and exposed and vulnerable" and wonders about the absence of blacks in the wild.[144] He observes, "you don't find many blacks canoeing solo down the Mississippi River and camping out every night. Why not? Are there evils out there to greet them if they do?"[145] Like the women's fears above, Harris's fears are grounded in truth and confirmed by his experience.

Harris is accosted by "two greasy rednecks" while cooking dinner one night.[146] The hunters demean him and implicitly question his right to be there with the greeting, "'Hey, boy! What you call yourself doing?'" Unable to defuse the situation, Harris flees when he sees "movement with one of the shotguns."[147] He dives into the water to escape and the hunters taunt him from the shore. Harris recounts, "then the danger returned. I heard them laughing and looking for me in the dark, calling out to me with hideous, taunting cries they might use for calling animals. I couldn't see them. I could only hear. They talked about the canoe and the tent and said I'd have to come out sooner or later." Fearing for his life, Harris aims and shoots his revolver in the direction of their voices. He explains his use of force: "My father taught me about guns and he told me never to use one to protect my belongings. They could be replaced. He told me to use a gun only if I were threatened and that if I wanted to scare someone, use something else. He told me to never aim a gun unless I planned to shoot, and to never shoot at a man unless I planned to kill him."[148] The men disperse after the shots, but Harris knows they will be back once they assume he is asleep and quickly seeks a safer place to camp.

Like the women, Harris finds one of the most dangerous elements on his trip is people, and white folks in particular. Harris responds with violence to survive. For William Pinkney, the first African American to solo-circumnavigate the globe, sailing—by contrast—offered a more level playing field and an "escape from the bonds of conformity, racism, and lack of respect because of one's background."[149] As Mills writes about mountaineering, "black or white, rich or poor, it's the mountain that decides whether or not you're going to stay."[150] Pinkney also mentions the racial politics in the seaports he visits. In South Africa, for example, he remarks, "it was a very interesting sight to the locals—a forty-seven-foot boat flying the American flag filled with colored people all gathered around a black man, enjoying ice cream in a place where there were no other people of color. I chuckled to myself as I watched the quizzical looks on the faces of the white people on the dock."[151] Pinkney is also "out of place," but finds himself more of an object of curiosity while in port rather than a target for violence.

Fears persist even as they are faced. At the end of her journey Suzanne Roberts notes, "I was still afraid of who might be out there with me, something I would no doubt have to navigate for the rest of my life. I supposed all women who want to go out into nature have to work through these fears, feelings that most men, and a few lucky women, never encounter." Roberts, nevertheless, eventually finds "the more time spent in wild places, the more the fear has receded, calmed perhaps by the natural world itself."[152] She states, "the John Muir Trail was more than a completed goal." She clarifies, "we didn't conquer the mountains; instead, we learned to feel safe walking among them, to feel more at home in nature. And with each step we came closer to knowing ourselves."[153] Roberts spurns the impetus to "conquer." Instead, she maps nature as a place to develop safety and security.

The threat of racial violence similarly haunts African Americans. Carolyn Finney points out that many African Americans do not enter wilderness environments, including national parks, because they often fear "two things: the unknown (primarily wildlife) and white people."[154] As a result, the national parks have employed a range of strategies, from "grassroots efforts to new hires and programs," including the African American National Parks Event.[155] While education can address the unknown, "living with the knowledge of slavery, lynching, and racial profiling has meant that African Americans have had to develop survival skills in order to confront potentially life-threatening situations. They do not need to turn to an expert in order to deal with any given situation; they *are* the experts."[156] These survival skills aim to defuse racism and its associated violence. Racism has taught African Americans to avoid isolation in the wilderness. As Haile emphasizes, American wilderness does not represent the same freedoms from cultural constraints for blacks. While hiking, she is "only a little freer than before."

When nature becomes home, as Roberts points out, fear retreats. However, not all have the luxury of escape. Finney notes that "for many of the African Americans that I have interviewed and spoken with, concern about one's safety from physical and or [sic] psychological harm was ever present in their environmental imaginary, regardless of where in the country they found themselves."[157] This is not to say "hush harbors"—historically wooded spaces where slaves would gather in secret—do not or no longer exist, but they are, as Harris's experiences in the wilderness and Finney's research demonstrate, contingent spaces. In contemporary culture, as Vorris L. Nunley examines, hush harbors are more likely to be the barber or beauty shop.[158] James Edwards Mills clarifies, "without the safety of numbers and locked doors, people of color may feel more vulnerable in the wilds of nature. They may opt to stay home, denying themselves and, potentially, future generations the opportunity to establish and enjoy a comfortable relationship with the outdoors."[159] These fears persist despite the fact the world outside extreme sports is likely even more dangerous. Sport climber Kai Lightner's mother, for example, explains, "'despite it being a predominantly white sport, he has never felt different or outcast despite the fact that he is usually the only black person at events. My fear is that outside of this community, his reality is very different.'"[160] This shifting, often paradoxical description of wilderness as both a safe, revitalizing haven and a dangerous, taxing minefield succinctly characterizes the adrenaline narrative's risky setting. The adventurer's racial and gender identity play key roles in how individuals map and navigate this risky terrain.

RISK AESTHETIC, SETTING: ADVENTURE IN THE ANTHROPOCENE

Risk as a characteristic of wilderness itself also helps form the adrenaline narrative's fourth element of the risk aesthetic. For the adrenaline narrative, risk's wilderness location plays a key role. Kevin Krein clarifies, in "Nature and Risk in Adventure Sports," "that adventure sports involve a kind of interaction with the natural world that is not found in other sporting activities, and that the experience of such interaction is valuable enough to justify the acceptance of the risks that accompany such activities."[161] Climate change increases and alters this risk. Molly Wallace in *Risk Criticism* emphasizes, "climate change requires new theoretical frames and approaches, not only to confront something wholly and radically unprecedented, but also, as Tom Cohen suggests, to 'reread...the archive in its entirety with different referentials.'"[162] As a result, does climate change demand a revised, if not new, adrenaline narrative?

Unlike the archive Wallace examines, adrenaline narratives are not characterized by irony.[163] Steven Callahan, for example, does not employ an ironic tone; however, he writes in *Adrift*, "it seems ironic that this pollution should serve as a signpost of my salvation."[164] Garbage as a welcome wagon is an ironic signal of his safety and survival. This is emblematic of the ironies, as Callahan says, "with which my tale is filled."[165] As a result, adrenaline narratives offer different insights into risk society in the Anthropocene. As I outline here and in the previous chapters, they largely demonstrate our collective denial and our confidence in the (eventual) management of environmental risk, even when faced with clear consequences and undefined remedies as well as the uneven distribution of risks among participants. Adrenaline narratives both suggest change and support the status quo.

Climate change, additionally, has increased environmental and physical risk. As Frederick Buell notes in "Global Warming as Literary Narrative," "risk is an inescapable facet of anthropogenic global warming, and also of the era of the Anthropocene it has helped produce."[166] Adventure traveler Daniel Glick also names human (in)action as the primary source of the current environment crisis. Glick argues, "at the source of nearly every environmental crisis, if you look deep enough, are the dual demons of poverty and overpopulation."[167] These "dual demons of poverty and overpopulation" also highlight the problems of the "capitalocene," which emphasizes the primary role capitalism has played and continues to play in the climate crisis.

Whether attributed broadly to human action or more specifically to capitalism, adventurers across sports and wilderness environments note climate change and pollution's impact. Alpinist Conrad Anker, for instance, emphasizes that "climate change and global warming are a very real threat to our passion for mountains."[168] Jennifer Jordan agrees and explains, "even the most climbable side of the mountain [Annapurna] is an avalanche trap, and like many mountains, it has suffered the ravaging effects of global warming, raining down on climbers an unpredictable flurry of rocks, ice seracs, and cornices that are melting out of the mountain at alarming rates."[169] Mountaineers are not the only ones concerned.

Water-based adrenaline narratives also address climate change. Miranda Weiss discusses the impact of climate change on fisheries and the declining population of red-throated loons.[170] Joe Kane laments the destruction of the Amazon.[171] Alvah Simon mentions how Chernobyl's nuclear fallout was felt in the North.[172] Simon also notes how the "vast but fragile ecosystem [of the North] could collapse in an epic disaster if we do not immediately curtail spreading our deadly toxins there. Our waterborne pollutants will infect the plankton to be absorbed by the fish and, in turn, the seal. Even the seal-eating bear will not fall the final victim, for all the scavengers—fox, raven, gull—will pass the poison, one to the other."[173] Jill Fredston likewise records global "'hot spots'" in *Rowing to Latitude*: "In the last hundred years, temperatures in these areas have risen by three times the global average."[174] Fredston, who wrote her master's thesis "on ice cores as indicators of environmental change," emphasizes the "indisputable" facts.[175] Fredston writes, "whatever its causes and long-term significance, it is indisputable that much of the Arctic and sub-Arctic has warmed by about 5°F in the last thirty years, compared to a global average of 1°F over the past century."[176] She also notes "pushing for increased energy efficiency could create more jobs than drilling" in Alaska.[177]

Everest provides an important case study for the ways climate change impacts extreme culture and the adrenaline narrative. Where Everest was once the sine qua non of extreme adventure, it has fallen from grace, at least in the eyes of some elite adventurers. For example, one of Kocour's climbing partners states, "'You don't want to go to Everest,'" because there is "'too much garbage, too many people, and it takes too damn long to climb.'"[178] Rob Schultheis refers to Everest as "the World's Tallest Tourist Trap."[179] Everest is overrun with climbers and is no longer as elite or pristine as a result.

As these remarks suggest, Everest's fall, moreover, is symptomatic of the larger field of extreme adventure sports. Schultheis explains, "adventuring as an extreme sport has fallen on hard times; everything really good, big, and authentic has already been done."[180] In order to get "climbers to respect it [Everest] again," climbers Cory Richards and Esteban Mena are attempting to establish a new route on Everest in 2019, "in the best style ['alpine style,' with no fixed ropes or supplemental oxygen] they can achieve." Richards wants people to understand, "'Everest is just such a cool place—it's so much more than the lines, the trash, and the dead bodies.'"[181] Their attempt emphasizes the difficulty in maintaining elite status when your sport or a specific location has gone mainstream and when making a name for yourself through unique accomplishments incurs greater risk: Everest's nonstandard routes have a death rate of thirty percent as compared to the two standard routes, which have a death rate of about three and one-half percent.[182] Increased risk also returns to an emphasis on conquering: the climbers will redeem Everest by blazing a new trail and making it elite again, effectively discovering and conquering Everest anew.

One of the key factors contributing to Everest's fall is pollution. While the degree of impact may be under debate, there is no doubt climbing Everest damages the fragile environment and garbage remains a perpetual problem at its extreme altitude.[183] *International Business Times*, for example, reports "an estimated 120 tons of trash is left behind each year by the Everest climbers."[184] Additionally, Byers's "Contemporary Human Impacts on Alpine Ecosystems in the Sagarmatha (Mt. Everest) National Park, Khumbu, Nepal" reports, "based on the results from five separate research expeditions conducted between 1984 and 2004," that "the Imja and Gokyo valleys have been significantly impacted during the past twenty to thirty years as a result of poorly controlled tourism."[185] Research, as reported in *Outside* magazine, also demonstrates that there is no doubt climate change has made climbing Everest more dangerous, especially through the Khumbu Icefall.[186]

Yet the allure of climbing the highest peak on earth remains—despite both increased commercialization and human and environmental dangers. As Greta Gaard observes, "denial seems to be the preferred response when there appears to be no possible alternative to the present functioning of Western culture."[187] While some elite "pure" climbers may spurn Everest in favor of less populated and polluted peaks, our continued willingness to climb and fascination with novel first and highest ascents speaks to our collective denial of climate change's impact. We apparently concur with Steve Olivier, who concludes "that...the actual benefits of participation in dangerous sports outweigh the potential negative costs, and that we have the right to engage in dangerous leisure activities that provide meaningful personal experiences."[188] We seem incapable of adding "refuse" to the reduce-reuse-recycle environmental ethic. Confidence in the management of risk prevails as long as personal benefits and short-term profits remain.

Americans maintain optimism despite the fact adventure clearly impacts the environment. As Brymer, Downey, and Gray point out, "Extreme sports, whether expeditions, competitions or solo events, have an effect on the natural world. Everest is famous not only for being the highest point on earth but also for the amount of rubbish that is left over each year. Even the 'death zone' is littered with discarded oxygen bottles."[189] When viewed "from a purely anthropocentric or materialistic perspective, the natural-world is *other* to humankind and valued only for its worth to humanity."[190] However, interviews with extreme sports participants suggest that "extreme sports facilitated an engagement with the natural world, which in turn triggered a change in behaviour" as it relates to sustainability and environmental justice.[191] When the adventurer's experience in nature produces a "sense of connection to the natural world and recognition of one's own place, and scale, within it," changed environmental attitudes may result.[192] These changed or heightened environmental actions do not necessarily push participants to stop adventuring. In fact, the connection may fuel desire for more adventures in extreme environments.

While authors and subjects of adrenaline narratives frequently express love of their sport's environment, they do not as frequently consider their impact on nature. This silence, if not blindness, follows the narrative of heroic masculinity: a journey's success or tragic failure remains focused on the individual rather than the environment or setting, which is there to provide the hero's challenge and serve as a scenic backdrop to the adventure. Like the global travel narratives Ursula Heise examines in "Journeys through the Offset World," adrenaline narratives and their associated protagonists and sports present the "unsustainable use of resources that [need] to be 'offset' in some way so as to remain ecologically justifiable."[193] As a result, according to Doug Christensen, "one might assume that extreme adventurers would use the stories they tell to make stronger cases for sustainable environmental practices. Unfortunately, so many adventure narratives (often called survival narratives) fail to communicate any noteworthy environmental ethic. Instead we typically get an age-old struggle of conquest, narcissism, and alienation from the land because of unconscious objectification."[194] They repeat, in other words, the conquering and spiritual desires described in chapters 2 and 3. The environment provides the challenge to be conquered or the backdrop against which the hero's story is told.

Even if they do not connect their adventure activities as part of the problem, many post-1970 adrenaline narratives at least mention pollution and/or climate change in passing. As Heywood and Montgomery note in regard to surfing, "most surfers have seen environmental problems along the coast, and have even been affected by water pollution, but invariably it clears up."[195] As a result, surfers' environmental awareness did not always lead to environmental activism.[196] In fact, "the most passionate responses to the environmental-activism question were those that spoke most directly toward one's own local ecosystem or 'playground,' rather than global trends."[197] Heywood and Montgomery imply that when adventure takes place in a remote wilderness—away from home—environmental connection and action are more difficult to sustain. We see this same ambivalence, especially toward foreign locations, alongside passionate denouncements of pollution—especially of those places adventurers consider home—in a range of adrenaline narratives.

Some adrenaline narratives offer detailed descriptions of polluted nature. These narratives engage in what Lawrence Buell describes in *Writing for an Endangered World* as "pastoral disruptions," or moments where the individual realizes their environment is not pristine but polluted.[198] Eddy Harris, for example, describes "foamy scum" that "looked like...a field of miniature icebergs." He "was surrounded by big puffs of soap-sudsy debris that were streaked with brown slime." Harris also speculates on the pollution's origin: "It could have been some kind of discharge from the barges or chemical fertilizer run-off from farms but I thought it must be sewage dumped into the river. I looked up the Arkansas River and the field of pollution extended for miles. I would have gotten sick if I hadn't been so angry. I didn't even want my canoe touching this muck, or my paddles and so I drifted through very slowly so I wouldn't have to paddle."[199] While Harris describes his anger and shares his disgust with his readers, his minimal environmental engagement is expressed in not wanting to touch the gunk.

Tania Aebi makes similar observations about water quality, reporting that she had been sailing in "the center of converging currents 100 miles off the coast of India and the filth was revolting": "Black oils covered the surface and garbage floated every 100 feet. Not only did we stop diving into the water, I didn't even want to wash my hands in it.... The filth that mired us—sludge, bags, plastics, styrofoam, dishwashing-liquid bottles, flip-flops and wrappers—coated the hulls of the boats with a thick black film. Olivier and I lamented how any sea life could survive such appalling pollution. Indeed, here the ocean seemed completely barren of life and the scene was sad enough to make one cry."[200] Like Harris, Aebi presents a vivid description of water pollution and her disgust, which results in physical revulsion and empathy for any life that survives and cannot escape these waters. Pollution is wholly other. Harris and Aebi do not recognize, in this sense, their own waste.

Both Harris and Aebi present versions of a NIMBY (Not in My Backyard) mentality, which poses a problem for the environmental movement. The poor and racial and ethnic minorities are the ones who most often have to deal with the brunt of environmental pollution. "Now, Native Americans, blacks, and Hispanics are experiencing yet another 'alienation from nature,' as their reservations, communities, and workplaces increasingly become the site of toxic waste deposits and pollution," Gaard reminds us.[201] They do not—as Harris and Aebi are able to do—drift through unaffected, with their anger and simple avoidance tactics serving as a sufficient prophylactic from illness. Such passages highlight how adventurers are tourists rather than residents who must deal with the pollution and its associated risks on a day-to-day basis. As tourists, they are also privileged Americans who do not need to make their home in polluted waters. The reader, likewise, may wish for the adventurer to hurry through polluted places.

Long-distance swimmer Lynne Cox in *Swimming to Antarctica* is not able to avoid physical contact with debris and pollution. She notes encounters with dead rats, "frothy brown scum," and a dead dog, for example, while swimming in the Nile.[202] Cox proclaims, "this river of life...was a river of death, and I wanted to run out of the water."[203] She describes the Nile as "not any shade of blue; it was dark brown, thick, and opaque, and it stank like something old and dying," and wonders "if I was going to get sick if I swam in that water. Never had I swum in any water as filthy."[204] Tolerating the extreme pollution becomes its own rite of passage and extreme risk. To accomplish her goals, Cox must swim through the filth. Like mountaineers walking by frozen dead bodies on Everest, the pollution serve as an extreme reminder of the risks Cox endures. In the words of Steven Callahan, garbage and pollution "serve as a signpost" for otherwise invisible environmental risks and consequences.[205]

Adventurers, even when traveling to remote, wild locations, sometimes cannot escape pollution and the effects of global warming. Recounting her travels in Greenland, rower Jill Fredston remarks in *Rowing to Latitude*, "in forty days, we had seen country as beautiful as any that exists. But for each fiery red slope, dark basalt cliff, and pure white ice tower, there was a shocking display of human waste. Garbage spilled out of the villages and drifted into almost every remote corner, breaking the magic of even the quietest cove. We came to dread landing because we knew it meant breaching the flotsam line of plastic containers, bottles, sanitary pads, diapers, and the bright yellow 'honey bucket' bags once containing human excrement that were so ubiquitous that they could double as Greenland's national flower."[206] Fredston draws a disturbing comparison between the landscape's striking natural beauty and its equally arresting pollution. At a distance the landscape displays rich natural reds, blacks, and whites. Up close, the shoreline reveals a maze filled with artificial yellow plastics. The description evokes for readers scenes of trash-filled beaches; often, for Americans, these scenes are associated with elsewhere. This is the waste most Americans place curbside or drop off at the dump and never see again.

Closer to home, Byl notes that the coastlines along the Gulf of Alaska are similarly "littered with junk. Empty orange juice jugs and busted electronics, the flotsam of a plastic-based culture." While there are "treasures" to be found—"hidden in the wreckage are glass fishing floats from Japanese nets, treasures that drift across the Gulf to end up on the Sound's beaches after big storms"—the trash spoils the view.[207] During long sailing days, Aebi also hopes to find treasures or exotic animal life, but she only discovers garbage. She recalls, "the incongruous sight of floating logs, plastic bags and barrels were the apex of my excitement. Always anticipating a treasure or strange ocean life, I would alter course and drift up to the blobs until it became obvious that each one was just another piece of garbage in the middle of the ocean."[208] Wilderness surprises by returning trash to consumers.

The American adventurers confront the consequences of "a plastic-based culture."

Both Aebi and Byl stress the lack of human presence—the vast wilderness in which they find themselves—yet, paradoxically, the constant reminders of humanity in the trash they see. "To us," Byl continues, "the beach felt close to untouched, and yet, up along the tide line, chocked beneath driftwood stumps and burnished logs, debris coiled around itself. Every trace of civilization, dumped, could end up here. Cracked plastic buoys, a raincoat, scraps of net, one flip-flop, Happy Meal toys. The junk surprised Chloe. No one pictures garbage on the Last Frontier."[209] The polluted reality, what Lawrence Buell calls a "mythography of betrayed Edens," does not match Alaska's frontier mythology.[210] Miranda Weiss similarly notes in *Tide, Feather, Snow*—a book that is also about Alaska—"we were ruining the very thing we'd all moved here for. We were bringing in so much stuff, our footprint was always spreading into places where no human development had existed before."[211] Byl and Weiss disrupt the American fiction of "untrammeled" wilderness and Alaska's place as the "last frontier."

Wilderness does not fit its "untrammeled" definition. Byl and Weiss point out how "the definition [of wilderness] is immediately inadequate, since it is now widely known that no area of the Earth is unaffected by white Western industrialized culture: toxins are carried in to 'wilderness' areas through the air and the rain, and 'wilderness' travelers leave trash in the most pristine areas."[212] Just as they cannot escape the trash and pollution, adventurers also increasingly cannot escape each other. Fredston laments, "as development shrinks the open spaces and technology makes the remaining spaces more accessible, this [not communicating with other adventurers met on the trail] may become the standard coping mechanism. We will have replaced the privilege of solitude with isolation."[213] From "traffic jams" on Everest to national parks overrun with cars and people, finding solitude in wilderness is increasingly difficult.

The prevalence of trash makes some adventurers more conscious of environmental issues and their own garbage. Solo sailor Tania Aebi says she did not realize the extent of the pollution in the Mediterranean until she saw it herself. She says, "I had read that the Mediterranean was a sea dying slowly of pollution, but had never dreamed that I would encounter a solid pavement of rubbish."[214] Suzanne Roberts explains how experiencing the "leave no trace" ethic changed her view of waste: "We carried all our own trash, which made me realize how much trash we produce in just one day, and that was after we had already taken everything out of the wrappers. It became clear to me that if we had to carry our own trash around all the time, we would not be so wasteful. We would think twice about buying things with so much plastic packaging."²¹⁵ Perhaps because others are questioning their environmental impact, extreme adventurers themselves are breaking the silence about the costs associated with their lifestyle sports.

The quickly disappearing glaciers of Glacier National Park spurs Christine Byl's ecological epiphany. Byl realizes that if she has children, they will not see the glaciers for which the park was named. She notes, "a new reality has emerged in the years since I first discovered Glacier."²¹⁶ The glaciers will all be gone. Byl records her surprise when she realizes, "like the grizzly bear on California's state flag, the story of Glacier's name will be a nod to something gone.... How startling, that a world I knew so well could vanish. And that despite my loving it, *in* my loving it, I helped it disappear."²¹⁷ Byl understands that her and others' love of wilderness may be its undoing, despite their good intentions.

The deep love extreme adventurers express for their sportscapes sometimes pushes them to engage in environmental advocacy. Stoddart reports, "outdoor sports participants may also draw upon their experience of and topophilia for particular sportscapes as motivations of environmental activism. This is illustrated, for example, by surfers whose embodied interactions with oceanic sportscapes [provoke] environmental awareness and activism."²¹⁸ Adventurers such as Alex Honnold have environmental foundations related to and supported by their reputations. The Honnold Foundation "reduces environmental impact and addresses inequality by supporting solar energy initiatives worldwide." Honnold's brief biography on the foundation's "About" page explains, "as a matter of principle and practicality, Alex lives as simply as possible. The Honnold Foundation is an extension of that ethic."²¹⁹ Their activism, nonetheless, may simply perpetuate environmental problems, encouraging more people to escape to wilderness while bringing the comforts of home with them.

Weiss describes a similar realization when she discusses Alaska's "culture of junk."²²⁰ Because "Alaska produces almost nothing," it imports almost everything.²²¹ Weiss observes an apparent assumption in Alaska that "almost nothing could be used up"—in the sense that resources (her examples are oil and gas) and natural features (wetlands, shoreline, trees) would never be depleted—while at the same time "this season of ice roads was getting shorter, threatening the slow-growing tundra beneath the heavy equipment."²²² Alaska, according to Weiss, depends on a fiction of self-reliance, while in reality, "despite the state's mythic character as fostering independence and rewarding the pioneering spirit, the Last Frontier relies more on federal assistance than any other state."²²³ Alaska, as the "last frontier," symbolizes America's paradoxical (in)dependence. Weiss observes, "everywhere I looked, I saw the homestead mentality of self-reliance and resourcefulness contrasting with depedence on modern conveniences."²²⁴ She concludes, "the search for the simple life could be incredibly complex."²²⁵ The desire for convenience and technical gear results in a larger ecological footprint, even for the "simple life."

Byl agrees, connecting these ideas about American self-reliance and authenticity to Thoreau and a lifestyle that extends beyond a defined adventure's timeline. Byl argues, "by these definitions [referring to Thoreau], which echo my own instinct, an authentic life will not be built on what we think ('I've escaped the city') or of what we buy (a pine bench for the entryway, the perfect work pants). Not of what we say ('buy local' and 'live in the moment') or even what we find (feathers, shells). An authentic life will be built, at least in part, of ordinary verbs: wake, plant, dig, mend, walk, lift, listen, season, note, bake, chop, store, stack, harvest, give, stretch, measure, wash, help, haul, sleep."²²⁶ Thus, "a key objective for adventure sports," according to Alan Dougherty, as well as for an authentically simple lifestyle broadly defined, "is the imaginative and aesthetically pleasing use of technology so that the possibility of a complex, multi-sensory and fulfilling engagement with Nature becomes more likely while keeping in check sports' negative environmental impact."²²⁷ Few adrenaline narrative authors, however, directly address their activity's "negative environmental impact." This suggests even erotic desire's collapsed or liminal boundaries may not foster sustainable adventure.

Adventure, rather, remains focused on getting closer to "authentic" (unpolluted) nature rather than accounting for activities that risk trampling fragile ecosystems or offering an escape for the privileged few to areas where "pure," unpolluted adventure may be experienced. Authenticity, in this sense, fosters patriarchal/spiritual adventure porn that maintains the status quo rather than risks a truly green adventure and environmental ethics.

RISK AESTHETIC IMPLICATIONS: PRAGMATIC ACTIVISM OR GREENWASHING?

Those author-adventurers that address environmental consequences and ethics narrate a struggle to determine the best course of action. Byl breaks down the environmental consequences as perceived from three different viewpoints: optimists, pessimists, and pragmatists. She explains, "the optimist in me hopes that people will always have the good sense to protect this place, and feels lucky for what I've received here. The pessimist in me knows that eventually, we kill what we love. The pragmatist in me hands the driver my ticket, takes a seat by the window, and watches, for new owlets in a nest above Igloo Creek, for bears on the braided Teklanika River bar, for the Toklat pack's wolf pups, chasing their own tails, not yet watching for me."[228] Byl's flexible environmental philosophy counters apocalyptic forecasting while not denying its possibility. She suggests we need to embody simultaneously the contradictory optimist and pessimist viewpoints while relying on an American pragmaticism, or the practical applications that both utopian and dystopian viewpoints may miss.

This turn to a pragmatic but nonetheless risky environmentalism, or one that follows the risk aesthetic to adapt and follow multiple models simultaneously, may offer the best of all worlds. Heywood and Montgomery also argue, "the 'pragmatic soul surfer'"—who is "resistant to and complicit with the dominant culture simultaneously"—offers untapped promise for the environmental movement.[229] They note, "the emergent demographic of pragmatic soul surfers—surfers 30 years of age and older who are gainfully employed but whose surfing gives them an alternative identity to that of their jobs, and for whom surfing creates a direct connection to and appreciation of the natural world—might be utilised as a resource by environmental organisations."[230] Notably, however, "only 35,000 American surfers, out of an estimated 2.5 million total nationwide, are members of Surfrider."[231] At stake is the degree to which the adrenaline narrative offers and inspires a pragmatic, risky environmentalism or is yet another form of radical greenwashing that maintains the status quo.

In addition to noting environmental conditions and their own measures to reduce environmental impact, adrenaline narratives may also incorporate an explicit environmental message or theme into their expeditions. Increasingly, as Gunnar Breivik predicted, we see the pursuit of extreme adventure connected to environmental causes.[232] Adventurer Gregg Treinish, in fact, "founded Adventurers and Scientists for Conservation in 2011 to pair adventure travelers with conservation scientists in need of data collection all over the world."[233] As Bart Vanreusel points out (drawing on the German sociologist and historian Henning Eichberg's scholarship), there have been a series of "green waves" that connect outdoor recreation and the environmental sciences and/or conservation.[234] Ebert and Robertson even conclude that "risks are sometimes worth taking" because the risks are "constitutively bound up with various other goods that everyone recognizes."[235] Education and awareness often serve as the adventure's communal good.

Daniel Glick and his children, for instance, travel around the world visiting ecologically fragile environments. Glick's narrative educates the reader about different fragile locations. Glick and his children visit, for example, the Orangutan Care Center, part of Orangutan Foundation International (OFI), in Indonesia. Glick describes OFI's sustainable conservation strategies, which—rather than emphasizing the orangutans—focus on an unpolluted area's long-term economic benefits over the short-term benefits of a timber harvest or gold mining. Glick explains, "as in so many international conservation efforts these days, OFI's central approach is to show local people that intact forests mean long-term economic activity—from tourism, environmental protection programs, and sustainable harvests from vibrant rivers and intact forests."[236] Rather than emphasize biocentric benefits or benefits for the tourists, the efforts focus on the local community. These tactics remain anthropocentric in order to convince people to adopt sustainable practices.

Maintaining and broadening anthropocentric benefits may be key to long- and short-term environmental change. It may also encourage an exhausting crisis mode. J. Calvin Giddings's goal in running the Apurímac River in Peru "'was to demonstrate, while it was still possible, that this river does have lasting values beyond those of hydropower and agriculture.'"[237] In *North to the Night*, Alvah Simon connects the simplicity required of his expedition to a broader environmental ethic that anyone could adopt: "our resources were so finite that we must not squander them. We had to use them with reverence. In less, we found more—more appreciation, more value. This truism is so simple, yet it evades us on a global scale. In our hearts we know it to be so, but we cannot help ourselves; we rip through our natural bounty with the reckless greed of unchecked children under a Christmas tree."[238] Risk requires adventurers to pare down life to its essentials. As a result, risk—a consciousness of it and an anticipation of it—fosters crisis environmental thinking. Such crisis thinking harnesses the stress to focus on what is most important and immediate when faced with finite resources. However, even as risk culture operates in a perpetual state of crisis, maintaining crisis environmental thinking risks exhaustion and/or the eventual failure to recognize crisis overall. Continuous crisis narratives in the media may deaden response. Everyday Americans, as a result, may not relate to adopting extreme environmental and risk models, and risking normalizing crisis thinking may also not be in our long-term best interest.

Adventurers and survivalists such as Eustace Conway make a case that their radical lifestyles nonetheless provide necessary and helpful models for others. Eustace Conway's philosophy, as described in Elizabeth Gilbert's *The Last American Man*, is "'Reconsider and Refuse. Before you even acquire the disposable good, ask yourself why you need this consumer product. And then turn it down. Refuse it.'"[239] Simon adheres to and models similar environmental ethics in his adventure. Simon explains that "we had come here to seek harmony with the land, the wildlife, and ourselves. We had adhered to the environmental adage: 'Take nothing but photographs; leave nothing but footprints.' We had carefully treated our waste, packaged our garbage. We had killed nothing."[240] Their care is rewarded in the knowledge they have inhabited wilderness in as minimally invasive ways as possible and in the new knowledge of and connection with nature that the experience provided. Paradoxically, according to Fredston, "the cultural need for a connection to land and sea may be even greater now than in centuries past": "subsistence is a line back through time, before cash-based economies and outside influences began to erode tradition."[241] Yet as noted above, the more people that embrace the "simple life" in Alaska or the suburbs, the harder it becomes to find solitude and maintain "untrammeled" wilderness.

The addition of environmental activism, moreover, offers new meaning to the hero's suffering and gives the adventurer something to save beyond him- or herself. A primary problem with the inclusion of environmentalism in adrenaline narratives is that the risks and benefits remain focused on the individual adventurer. In this sense, the increase in individuality and focus on "personal fulfilment" means "nature has thus moved into the background in the value hierarchy of outdoor sport enthusiasts."[242] Vanreusel notes that "whenever this recreational experience value gains greater emphasis, it is often at the cost of an ecologically responsible pursuit of outdoor sports."[243] In their paper "A Plea for Risk," Ebert and Robertson emphasize risk-taking's personal benefits, which include "engaging in adventurous activities, overcoming challenges, expressing one's agency, exhilaration, fulfilment, and so on. These are general goods that almost everyone agrees have value."[244] While "almost everyone agrees [they] have value," risk-taking's benefits for mountaineers, Ebert and Robertson's specific focus, are individual rather than community- or environmentally oriented. Risk's individuality encourages and maintains an anthropocentric focus.

The narrative and image of American environmentalism, moreover, share many of the same representational problems as the American adrenaline narrative. Aron Ralston's characterization in *Between a Rock and a Hard Place* of the "environmental sensibilities" shared by outdoor enthusiasts reveals the environmental movement's dominant narrative of white heroic masculinity. His description references Edward Abbey's iconic "combative conservationist; anti-development, anti-tourism, and anti-mining essayist; beer swiller; militant ecoterrorist; lover of the wilderness and women (preferably wilderness women, though those are unfortunately rare)."[245] These outdoorsy masculine models recall iconic American frontiersmen, following the environmental movement's paternalist line. Gilbert, after all, names Conway "the last American man." Ralston likewise cites Abbey, not Rachel Carson, not Winona LaDuke. The risky narrative of white heroic masculinity dominates the adrenaline narrative and narratives of iconic adventurous environmentalists. Do such adventurous environmentalists, as a result, inevitably tap colonial and misogynistic roots?

Byl remains optimistic that "contact with the land" will lead to stronger environmental conservation. She writes, "preservation efforts succeed because people come into contact with land, and begin to remember it, and want to protect it, the way we will protect children we know and love from harm faster than nameless children on the news. Trails in national parks and state forests and city preserves help people be 'in' nature in a way they don't dare, aren't able, or don't have time to on their own."[246] Byl's paternalist protection of nature—likening nature to "children we know and love"—risks simply inverting the Mother Nature model.

Not everyone, additionally, converts to environmentalism simply by spending time in nature. Simon tells the story of a pair of rare birds (gyrfalcons) whose location was shared with a visitor, after which the birds mysteriously disappeared. This leads Simon to question the significance of the disappearance of one pair of birds. Simon concludes it is the accumulation of small acts that have a huge impact: "person by person, decision by decision, year by year, we will either nurture and protect this natural treasure for future generations, or we will not and our world will be profoundly diminished."[247] Simon does not speculate on why some exploit nature and others seek "harmony" with it. Like the readers of Sarah Orne Jewett's "A White Heron," we are left to decide why someone would or would not choose to sacrifice the environment in favor of individual, immediate profit.

Fredston likewise is perplexed by the ways Settler Newfoundlander families handle their trash, which in her mind does not mesh with the love for their children and the landscape in which they live. She writes, "it seemed unfathomable that parents who displayed such obvious love toward their children could be so disrespectful of their surroundings."[248] Fredston's shock further reveals the failings of using children or our children's futures as motivation, even when they are not "nameless," to use Byl's word. This faulty logic derives from a paradigm Lee Edelman calls "reproductive futurism," which Margaret Hunt Gram characterizes as "a heteronormative cognitive pathology by which people and societies seek to suppress their own death drive and authenticate the existing social order by projecting themselves into an imagined future through the valorization of children and childbearing."[249] The reality is, however, that we are as willing to risk our children's future as we are our present. If our children's futures fail as a motivation, as Beck writes, the risk society requires new skills. Beck suggests that "in the risk society, additional skills become vitally necessary. Here *the ability to anticipate and endure dangers, to deal with them biographically and politically* acquires importance."[250] The adrenaline narrative rehearses old skills as well as requires additional ones.

RISKY ENDS TO JUSTIFY THE SUSTAINABLE MEANS

Gunnar Breivik predicted in his 2010 essay "Trends in Adventure Sports in a Post-modern Society" a merging of cultural trends: "With an increasing focus on contact with nature, global warming and environmental protection we could see a future development of 'green' versions of adventure sport."[251] Kyle Kusz, conversely, connects, in "Extreme America: The Cultural Politics of Extreme Sports in 1990s America," the rise of feminism with a "crisis of white masculinity" and the subsequent resurgent popularity of extreme sports.[252] Thus, extreme sports, especially those that take place in wilderness environments, offer a crucial connection and potential breaking point between environmental, social justice, and feminist politics, posing two questions: Are feminist, antiracist, and environmental ethics compatible with stereotypically hypermasculine wilderness sports or are these extreme movements inevitably and inescapably at odds with each other in American culture? And, is this turn to environmental awareness and environmentally themed adventures just another form of greenwashing?

My synthesis of adrenaline narratives and their risky cultural contexts suggests all of the above holds true. Risk pervades American adrenaline narratives and their sports: risk is embedded in the narrative's setting and tone, and risk—as a dangerous rite of passage or otherwise pervading characteristic of the action—structures the plot. Whatever the extreme sport, risk pervades the desiring natures presented. Palmer agrees, noting, "irrespective of whether one B.A.S.E. jumps, mountain bikes or snowboards, the specialised media of each sport promotes it in language that reflects the risky nature of the activity."[253] Part marketing hype and lifestyle brand, risk is a culture industry and a national trademark. Part of the emblematic American immigrant story is risking the journey to enjoy opportunities and freedom not available elsewhere. Like wilderness, America offers its own unique testing ground. Risk in contemporary American culture draws from archetypal testing grounds and specific national myths related to the frontier and freedom. Thematically, as a result, risky natures offer insight into American culture, including its "schizophrenic" environmental attitude leading to both the preservation and exploitation of nature.[254]

The environmental movement's connection to risky adventure and risky adventure's connection to environmentalism often perpetuate colonial and patriarchal practices—connections and practices that adrenaline narratives especially highlight. The American adrenaline narrative's cultural and literary contexts and resulting representations of risky nature suggest that as long as nature exists in the American imaginary as an exotic location, abstracted from or other from the everyday, it will continue to evoke contradictory and often destructive environmental impulses. Such findings highlight why it is difficult for American literature—to borrow from Joyce Carol Oates—to write "against nature." And, more specifically, why it is difficult to write adrenaline narratives, as Timothy Morton advocates, "without nature."

Adjusting narrative and behavioral paths is difficult, slow work, if it is possible at all, especially when the structures tap into archetypes and national myths. Adrenaline narratives, as Heise explains in relation to "environmental travelogues," "share with classical epic the endeavor to portray the world as a whole, and focus on struggles over the future at a heroic scale."[255] An examination of risk reveals partial rather than "whole" knowledge. Environmental causes implicitly or explicitly deflect or justify the adventure's otherwise unwarranted risks. The adventurer heroically risks to save the planet: "If travelers in ancient epics had to contend with the adversities imposed upon them by hostile gods, contemporary eco-travelers struggle with the adverse consequences of their own actions."[256] While there are notable exceptions, mostly the environmental consequences are met with silence in adrenaline narratives. Because they are not residents, adventurers often do little, if anything, to sustain the ecological health of the places they visit. Or, significantly, this environmental and social justice work is not the narrative's primary focus or message.

This pessimistic understanding follows Linda Vance. Ecofeminist critics

Greta Gaard and Linda Vance have distinct approaches to wilderness recreation and the risks and benefits it poses to advancing ecofeminism's goals. Vance argues, "wilderness recreation 're-creates' more than the self: it also re-creates the history of the conquest of nature, the subjugation of indigenous peoples, the glorification of individualism, the triumph of human will over material reality, and the Protestant ideal of one-on-one contact with God. And as for the elements of physical challenge and risk, I think it goes without saying that they appeal most to those for whom day-to-day mobility is a given, and for whom danger isn't always close at hand."[257] For Vance, the American adrenaline narrative is always already patriarchal and colonial. Wilderness, conceived as a place "free" from "relationships of domination," poses too great a risk to ecofeminism to be maintained. Social and environmental justice require the end of nature.

Gaard, however, makes a more optimistic case for wilderness recreation, suggesting it offers transformative possibilities not available in other environments. Gaard contends that "if we hope to offer a new paradigm to this industrialized culture of alienation from and domination of nature, stepping into wilderness for a time may allow us to do the reorienteering necessary to imagine that vision."[258] Gaard's view builds from research and from the testimony of the adrenaline athletes themselves that suggest time spent in the outdoors, especially wilderness, brings more benefits than risks. Adrenaline narratives realize this potential, too.

As I've begun to outline here and in the previous chapter, a few authors are breaking the heroic narrative form by recognizing their risky adventures may do more harm than good. There is potential in shifting the sole focus from the individual to include the larger community and environment. In doing so, for example, writers connect global warming's generalized risks to specific individuals and consequences. Hiker Gail D. Storey, for example, mentions climate change's impact on Pacific Crest Trail hiking. She specifically notes that "the PCT was maintained by the Pacific Crest Trail Association and other organizations. But it was still subject to detours and relocations because of wildfires, mudslides, and climate change."[259] Implicitly, readers may infer that their daily lives assume more inconvenience, if not risk, too, as a result of climate change. The question is whether or not such realizations will produce concrete change or if, like many of the extreme adventurers, we will continue on the same path, increasing plastic waste and CO_2 emissions. Rather than turning around, will we continue to seek the same individually defined summits despite the clear signs the weather has changed for the worse?

The risk aesthetic reveals that the challenge for both the contemporary American adrenaline narrative and environmental and feminist movements is to emphasize race and gender equality as two of the "various other goods that everyone recognizes." This would involve, in other words, the recognition of social justice achievements as something worth risking the more immediate comforts of home and the tests of wilderness. As a result, the challenge for contemporary American adrenaline narratives and the environmental movement entails redefining their heroic narratives. In doing so, new narratives emerge that break the silence, speaking truths to power that do not stifle women, minorities, or the environment. I discuss representative examples of restorative desires in the next chapter. When such narratives become the norm, as Gaard argues, adventure in nature will be worth the risks and reflective of a truly democratic American freedom.

For American culture at the beginning of the twentieth century, the end of the frontier arguably helped to facilitate the preservation of wilderness and, to the extent they are connected, democracy. The potential end of wilderness in the twenty-first century requires a radical rethinking of national identity—of what comes after wilderness or what we are willing to sacrifice in the service of nature and democracy. The risks described in adrenaline narratives remind us that how we seek to (re)connect with nature matters and that shifting hegemonic patterns require changing gendered and raced risk cultures along with a reevaluation of environmental risks. Applying the lessons learned from elite adventurers requires a shift from individual "adrenaline junkies" to community-oriented "control freaks," who ride an extreme edge of a hyperawareness that does not presume mastery—only the practiced knowledge of experience. The risks, nevertheless, remain substantial, even with such a shift. Until we address risk's intersectional influences on wilderness and American identity, we will likely continue to miss the mark in regard to climate change and social justice—wildly.

CHAPTER 6
RESTORATIVE
NATURES

Jon Krakauer in *Into the Wild* describes a youthful sense of entitlement or "God-given right" that he shared with Chris McCandless. He admits, "it is easy, when you are young, to believe that what you desire is no less than what you deserve, to assume that if you want something badly enough, it is your God-given right to have it."[1] Krakauer, like McCandless, went to Alaska as "a raw youth who mistook passion for insight and acted according to an obscure, gap-ridden logic. I thought climbing the Devils Thumb would fix all that was wrong with my life. In the end, of course, it changed almost nothing. But I came to appreciate that mountains make poor receptacles for dreams. And I lived to tell my tale."[2] Krakauer admits his youthful journey "changed almost nothing" about what "was wrong with [his] life." However, surviving the challenges he faced on Devils Thumb helped him realize "that mountains make poor receptacles for dreams." Yet I have spent much of the last five chapters discussing the desires or dreams we project onto mountains and other extreme wilderness landscapes. Krakauer himself discovers in *Into Thin Air* that at forty-one years old, when he receives the call to join an Everest expedition, "boyhood dreams die hard...and good sense be damned."[3] Like Krakauer, Americans seemingly need to learn the same lessons over and over again. Thus far, we also have "lived to tell [the] tale."

What draws us and Krakauer back—"good sense be damned"—is at least in part an American dream of rugged individualism that requires intense projection onto and objectification of wilderness. We envision wilderness as empty so that we may fill it with our desires. Whether one participates in them or not, extreme adventures may invoke a problematic nostalgia for the iconic American frontier as well as a transformative spirituality that (re)connects adventurers and readers to the natural world. As Roderick Frazier Nash writes, "take away wilderness and you take away the opportunity to be American."[4] Jedediah Purdy suggests, however, that "losing nature need not mean losing the value of the living world, but it will mean engaging it differently. It may mean learning to find beauty in ordinary places, not just wonder in wild ones. It may mean treasuring places that are irremediably damaged, learning to prize what is neither pure nor natural, but just is—the always imperfect joint product of human powers and the natural world."[5] Purdy suggests we can learn to love different natures.

This final chapter takes stock of what the American adrenaline narrative teaches us about nature, heroic masculinity, and the lasting power and potential of American wilderness. The next three sections address each of these topics individually. I then conclude by arguing in the final two sections that while the American adrenaline narrative teaches us that there is no faultless way to engage nature (and wilderness specifically), increasingly, adrenaline narratives are building from restorative ecology and restorative justice to not only represent nature in a different way but also to mend wrongs committed against the land and its inhabitants. Restorative desire offers a path forward for a future shaped by climate crisis. Key to restorative desire's potential is, as Purdy argues above, the ability to love different natures.

LEARNING TO LOVE DIFFERENT NATURES

Writing about John Burroughs's "small vision," Nancy Lord similarly points out the ways everyday nature has lost our attention. Lord explains that Burroughs's "nature wasn't bears but cows, not high-altitude peaks but wood roads, not wilderness but backyards. It's the kind of nature that gets little modern attention and is, for so many people today—despite its physical proximity—less appreciated than ever."[6] To the extent that the adrenaline narrative, however, depends on extreme environments, flora, fauna, and lifestyle, such a shift will be difficult. For American identity and the

American adrenaline narrative, "losing nature," especially its wildest extremes, requires a radical redefinition of the risky environments that foster the deep play and specific American identity participants seek. It may also demand revolutionary refusal.

To refuse, of course, means you already have access to privileges. Elizabeth Wheeler's essay and argument—"Don't Climb Every Mountain"—points out the extreme ableism at the root of nearly every adrenaline narrative: its body politics often assumes and valorizes what Rosemarie Garland Thomson refers to as "normates," or "the constructed identity of those who, by way of the bodily configurations and cultural capital they assume, can step into a position of authority and wield the power it grants them."[7] Wheeler specifically connects the concept of the normate to mountaineering and hiking, explaining, "people with disabilities generally do not have the physical and emotional reserves to throw ourselves into the abjection of the sublime—and we generally don't need to do so in order to get a keen sense of our bodily realities."[8] Wheeler points out the "unexamined ableism in ecocritical discourse" that "defines some people as closer to nature than others."[9] Adrenaline narratives largely rely on first-person narrative and, as a result, offer a "situated knowledge" with a "narrow focus [that] can eclipse the possibility of other body types and other landscapes."[10] Exceptions to the normate prove the rule instead of broadening the adrenaline narrative.

Wheeler explains how Supercrip stories further this stereotype rather than challenge it. She argues, "the Supercrip stereotype assumes that we can overcome our disabilities and do anything with our bodies if we have strong characters and we want it hard enough (which also assumes that if we can't overcome our disabilities it's because we are weak-willed and indifferent)."[11] According to Wilson and Little, this bootstrap, patriarchal conquering and spiritual transformation version of the adrenaline narrative demands "being more extreme than those who came before and that this should involve a degree of suffering to be truly adventurous. These images are often the hub of media presentations of adventure in action, but while eye catching, are also untouchable for the majority of people who do not match the written and visually recorded achievements and pursuits of others."[12] While the acceptance of limits goes against heroic masculinity, conquering desire, and the American "can do" spirit, recognition of what cannot and should not be done is a vital skill for living in our contemporary risk society.

Risk assessment in adrenaline narratives offers additional insight into the challenges reading the landscape poses and why sustainable choices are (not) made. In this regard, Wheeler does not suggest we need to stop climbing *all* mountains—nor do I. The danger of the currently dominant conquering and spiritual constructions of wilderness, as Wheeler implies and Barbara A. Barnes explicitly points out, is a dependence on and perpetuation of bootstrap neoliberalism. Barnes suggests that "because wilderness is imagined as a space utterly free of government interventions, and as a perfectly-level playing field, the 'wilderness experiences' produced in adventure sports narratives [are] perfectly suited to the production of the kinds of subjects imagined through neoliberal political formations, that is, subjects who are free, autonomous, flexible, and constantly seeking to reach their potential."[13] Wheeler implies a similar critique of neoliberalism and its purported freedoms for subjects who do not give up, which is also code for those who do not fail at heroic masculinity.

As the adrenaline narratives I examine have demonstrated, athletes must know when to push ahead and when to cut their losses and quit. This risk assessment is usually individual and anthropocentric: How much risk can be tolerated before the risk of human (one's own, most often) death becomes unacceptable? Increasingly, extreme adventurers may need to learn whether or not it is ethical to embark on the adventure for reasons beyond their own survival. John Oliver's 2019 *Last Week Tonight* segment about Everest makes just this point, breaking down how and why Everest is a problem and the resulting environmental and human costs.[14] "'Climbing Mount Everest was the biggest mistake I've ever made in my life,'" Krakauer admits. "'I wish I'd never gone.'"[15] Those who seek alternative paths, however, are often erased or excluded from the narrative. Such sacrifices often go unnoticed.

Quitting Everest, as professional guide Dave Morton discusses in a 2016 *Outside* magazine article, is not easy. While Morton does not cite environmental concerns, he mentions "wanting to spend more time with his family" as well as the disproportionate toll Everest climbing has on the local Sherpa population: "he also couldn't help but focus on one hard truth about the industry he loved—the fact that, over the past 15 years, nearly half the people who died on Everest were local hired help." Morton expresses uncertainty as to whether it is better to stop guiding and climbing or "'stick to it and try to improve it.'" Morton recognizes that his services will be replaced—perhaps with a guide who has less regard for sherpa safety. Yet as Luanne Freer, director of an emergency medical clinic at Everest, asks in this same article, "'How much louder does this mountain need to speak to tell us all it's not OK?'"[16] Freer suggests that we are refusing to listen to what nature conveys: climbing Everest is not sustainable. If one treats nature as setting, however, one will not be listening for it to speak. In Bart Vanreusel's terms, as long as Everest remains a "theatrical scene" or "backdrop" "in which individuals act out an industrial spectacle," its message will remain unheard.[17]

Profit complicates our notions of risk and sustainability in contemporary American culture. Denial and silence assure profit, especially for the more commercial areas of extreme sports. The adrenaline narrative suggests humans and the environment remain expendable. While working as a guide in Alaska for an excursion company that charged "tourists...$500 each—plus a fuel surcharge for those who weighed over 240 pounds," Blair Braverman recalls that "we were discouraged from acknowledging climate change, even as the glacier melted away beneath us."[18] To do so would hinder their goal "to provide a luxury experience, a taste of Real Alaska! with absolutely no discomfort, either physical or mental."[19] High- and low-octane adventurers need to think more critically about their sport, not simply because of individual risk but because of the risk posed to the very environments they love.

Maria Coffey in *Where the Mountain Casts Its Shadow* explains that the French sculptor Philippe Vouillamoz and British climber and artist Andy Parkin attempted to spur just this conversation by crafting "a massive work of art...from garbage left behind by climbers and skiers" on a glacier on the slope of Mont Blanc in order "to raise awareness of the impact of both sports [climbing and skiing] on such a fragile environment." She goes on to explain that "three years later" Parkin "collaborated with six sculptors and a number of other artists on a project...[that used] materials washed out of the glacier in the river."[20] In pushing participants to take responsibility for their actions, these examples invoke Beck's notion in *World Risk Society* of "risk-sharing," or an attempt to form a "'risk community' that shares the burden."[21]

As long as Everest remains profitable, however, environmental and social justice concerns will not tip the scales. As Elizabeth Mazzolini observes, "because of the capital it continues to be possible to raise, even in the face of retreating glaciers, as long as there are people willing and able to pay to go, climbing is indeed a sustainable business practice. In other words, sustainability seems to be more about sustainable capital than about sustainable environments."[22] Guide Dave Morton hints at these economic as well as psychological factors when he worries about how to craft a life after Everest: "'Things are simpler if you go to Everest,' he said. 'If you do this, it's very hard to have another life.'" Running a nonprofit that assists families of deceased sherpas offers Morton an alternative challenge, but one that involves "'constant sadness'" instead of the "'huge dopamine rush from being in the mountains.'" Whether or not Morton will find sufficient "closure" without revisiting Everest remains to be seen.[23] Much depends on whether he can redefine Everest's place within his environmental imagination, whether he—as well as the rest of us—can recognize that, as Jedediah Purdy suggests, "all simple ideas of nature are irretrievably gone."[24]

Elizabeth Wheeler and I share an interest in the gains possible if the American environmental imagination broadens and changes to view "nature as having bodies contiguous with human bodies."[25] This erotic view considers a wider, more diverse contingent of bodies and narrative frames. It rewrites heroic masculinity and conquering and spiritual desires' inspirational narratives. Wheeler frames erotic connection realistically and optimistically: "The human body and the bodies of nature can be stolen, but can also be reclaimed."[26] As this examination of the adrenaline narrative has demonstrated, when the body of wilderness moves beyond the virgin-whore dichotomy, such reclamation becomes possible. That is, as Purdy points out, "everyone living today is involved, intentionally or inadvertently, in deciding what to do with a complicated legacy of environmental imagination and practice, now that all simple ideas of nature are irretrievably gone."[27] The redeemed or restored nature that takes its place must contend with this "complicated legacy" while offering greater ambiguity than the certainty promised by "simple ideas."

In this sense, the environmental imagination must shift from thinking about nature, especially wilderness, as a static place to understanding nature as a shifting and dynamic process. Nature and our engagements in it are "like American democracy itself," which is to say the "American environmental imagination contains charismatic practices and ideas, but is also fraught with violence and exclusions. Both aspects deserve attention."[28] As a result, greater inclusion in the adrenaline narrative is something to be celebrated, while at the same time the tenor of the inclusion—its desires in and toward nature—should be examined closely.

BEYOND AMERICAN HEROIC MASCULINITY

The failed summit attempt by "Expedition Denali, a unique all African-American mountaineering team," provides a case in point. The expedition reworks heroic masculinity and the idea of what constitutes a "groundbreaking" feat. Rather than use the summit as the measure of success, their very presence breaks new ground and fulfills, at least in part, long-awaited American promises. Shelton Johnson explains, in the foreword to James

Edward Mills's *The Adventure Gap*, that "through their act we see that public lands and wilderness belong to *all* Americans. Their ascent of the highest peak in North America makes the statement that 'the pursuit of happiness,' for people brought to these shores in bondage, must of necessity lead to a mountaintop."[29] Johnson connects adventure with the civil rights movement, explaining that African American participants "extend the Civil Rights Movement vertically and horizontally to encompass all that's wild in America. And we claim our full inheritance as citizens of this country. We are saying that *we* are Americans."[30] Expedition Denali occupies the mountain as a means of claiming full American citizenship. While the team does not summit, they assert their collective agency nonetheless and, in Johnson's framing, conquer the barriers that would deny their "God-given" freedom.

James Edward Mills expands on this theme of freedom. Rather than view climbing's lack of "socially redeeming qualities" as a negative, Mills frames adventure's lack thereof as tapping into freedom. Mills recognizes that "climbing is a pastime available primarily to those with the disposable income and leisure time to squander on an activity that has virtually no socially redeeming qualities. That's probably why I, along with many other men and women around the world, enjoy it so much. Climbing is the very definition of freedom."[31] Mills goes on to explain, "I believe we experience genuine freedom when we make a conscious choice to set aside the comforts of warmth, family, and financial security just to climb to a high place and enjoy the view of a distant horizon. Though we live in a nation whose founding principle is freedom, far too many of us deprive ourselves of the opportunity to get beyond our daily urban routine to gaze upon the grandeur of the natural world. And too many of us depriving ourselves of nature are people of color."[32] Mills and Johnson adopt the adrenaline narrative in the service of racial justice.

Increased minority participation in the outdoors, moreover, advances environmental justice. If the environmental imagination fails to incorporate a wider, more diverse frame, then, as Mills asks, "what happens when a majority of the population has neither an affinity for nor a relationship with the natural world?"[33] In this scenario, blacks and other minorities are not only cut off from American identity, they also will be less likely to advocate for environmental justice. The gains in one area result in benefits to another.

Mills and Johnson share a confidence in the adrenaline narrative's access to freedom. As Barbara A. Barnes observes, "much of the value adventure sports hold for modern publics is shaped by the freedoms imagined to be associated with wilderness, along with the strengthening effects that wilderness experiences are imagined to have on national bodies."[34] Rather than "normalizing structures of history and society," Mills and Johnson explore and expose what Barnes points to as "the structural inequalities on which the very ideas of freedom and wilderness have themselves been constructed"[35]: "Indeed, 'natural' spaces constructed as sites of adventure are not, in fact, free. Their costs are found in the material and symbolic violences through which landscapes are emptied, in unjust exclusions that uphold the illusion of emptiness, and in the division of labor that 'underwrites [the adventurer's] economic freedom and the protection of his wilderness.'"[36] Just as climate change's impact on our environment grows by such gradual increments it is often difficult to grasp, especially if we do not live in a disproportionately affected area, so, too, is the cultural violence written on the landscape. While those who experience the violence remember, the privileged may enjoy the freedom to recreate there not knowing the full costs.

Other narratives that expose the barriers to American freedom are possible and actively written and shared. The short film *Sacred Strides*, for example, documents an intertribal, nearly eight-hundred-mile run to raise awareness about the Trump administration's drastic reduction of the Bears Ears National Monument. The event documented in the film, Sacred Strides for Healing, took place March 12–17, 2018. As a group they logged 1,240 miles.[37] Reporter Anna Callaghan explains, "prayer runs, which aren't protests or purely awareness-raising events, are a more personal way to honor and interact with these places. They've been organized for other reasons in recent years, like supporting the Standing Rock Sioux's fight against the Dakota Access oil pipeline in 2016."[38] The film emphasizes how running and prayer connect to heal tribal relations and as a tool for Native peoples to join together in a refusal to be erased from the landscape. Alicia Littlebear explains, "running back to our lands we feel that is healing that earth. That we are not gone. That we haven't left."[39] Littlebear highlights how prayer running is a means of "healing that earth" and of holding the United States accountable for agreements with Indigenous peoples. *Sacred Strides* records Indigenous culture's sacred, physical, and legal connections to the land. Where Johnson and Mills emphasize their rights as citizens of the United States, the participants in Sacred Strides for Healing emphasize their rights as federally recognized tribes within the United States.

Sacred Strides illustrates Barnes's point that adrenaline narratives hold potential beyond "individual self-improvement." Barnes explains that fulfillment of adventure's ecological and social justice potential requires historical understanding of the complex forces that shape the land. Barnes argues that "contemporary requirements for self-governing and fit citizen bodies, images, and narratives of wilderness adventure need not inevitably reiterate the arrogance of the nation's past in the West or its future ambitions. Rather, adventure narratives—and adventure sport—might imagine instead historical complexity and serve something beyond individual self-improvement."[40] Both Mills and Johnson, by reframing the American adrenaline narrative to include African Americans, are engaged in this work. Prayer running demonstrates how spiritual-physical connections to the land can build community rather than objectify the land for individual transformation. Author-adventurers—such as Jill Fredston, who writes to give voice to nature—increasingly join the work to extend the adrenaline narrative, opening it to flora and fauna as well as fjords and fuchsite.

While racially and ethnically diverse perspectives remain disproportionately absent from long-form narrative, other forms of outdoor adventure media are filling this gap. Companies such as NativesOutdoors, "a public benefit corporation (B-Corp) whose products serve to support indigenous people," connect "the outdoor industry, indigenous people, and conservation" in order "to foster cultural empowerment, not cultural appropriation."[41] Their website includes the blog *Temoa Journal*, which is "a platform for stories & perspectives on indigenous issues, those of indigenous people, and of our company NativesOutdoors. We will share stories that involve folks seeking adventure, culture, people, and a deeper look at our relationships to the natural world."[42] Along similar lines, the organization Native Women's Wilderness specifically "was created to bring Native women together to share our stories, support each other, and learn from one another as we endeavor to explore and celebrate the wilderness and our native lands."[43] Other similar outdoor networking and adventure promotional organizations include Outdoor Afro and Outdoor Asian.[44] Diversify Outdoors is "a coalition of social media influencers—bloggers, athletes, activists and entrepreneurs—who share the goal of promoting diversity in outdoor spaces where people of color, LGBTQIA, and other diverse identities have historically been underrepresented."[45] These sites mutually support and authorize bodies and body politics not stereotypically included as actors in the American adrenaline narrative or its frontier and wilderness myths.

AMERICAN WILDERNESS ADVENTURE'S LASTING POWER AND POTENTIAL

The divergent standpoints and views demonstrate how wilderness continues to inspire even as it also experiences constant threat. Wilderness continues to provide a vital setting for transformation. "One of the most valuable experiences that wilderness provides," according to Gaard, "is the opportunity for a different kind of perceptual orienteering, a different way of locating oneself in relation to one's environment."[46] The existence of new influencers, such as the adventurers featured by Diversify Outdoors, and of books like *Canyon Solitude* and *Mississippi Solo* indicates that paradigms may be shifting, changing the genre's objectifying hyper-adrenaline structures as well as the tenor of America's environmental imagination. The multiple constructions of desire toward nature found within these narratives hold the potential for future environmental changes. "Evidence suggests," as Humberstone points out, "that nature-based sports can not only reaffirm hegemonic masculinities (the 'Rambos') but also, in certain conditions, transform how both masculine bodies and the feminine are defined."[47] The transformation of nature depends on the transformation of the other, whether that other is constructed as nonhuman or the "wrong" adventuring body.

The convergence that begins in the 1970s of extreme sports, environmentalism, and social justice movements speaks to shared roots, realities, and futures. Changing heroic masculinity, as the previous chapters demonstrate, goes a long way in impacting the challenges that define them all. Even though heroic masculinity often provides the starting point, adrenaline narratives increasingly confirm that, as Eric Brymer and Tonia Gray put it, "rather than an egocentric focus [among participants in extreme sports] on personal achievement or triumph over nature, we find instead a deeper reflection on ecocentricity and connectedness with nature. Although they may first jump from cliffs or enter big waves or ride waterfalls for more shallow personal motives, they often find over time that they are, as John Muir too realized, 'hitched to everything else in the universe.'"[48] While the problems associated with, for example, climbing Everest question this research and associated environmental benefits, Everest may offer the exception that helps prove the more general rule—as long as the rest of wilderness adventure does not follow Everest's example. Whether or not our reading of adrenaline narratives focused on erotic desire likewise translates into positive environmental changes remains to be seen. However, evidence increasingly points to the ecological benefits of spending time with nature.

"Kinetic empathy" when applied to adrenaline sports refers to the concept of focused movement through wilderness that produces environmental feeling; it is a combination of risky edgework and flow.[49] As Humberstone reports, "evidence suggests that social and environmental justice movements, movements which build upon environmental awareness, are frequently spawned by people's involvement in nature-based adventure sport."[50] James Edward Mills similarly notes "there is a link between recreating in the outdoors and wanting to protect it."[51] As a result, these "'body pedagogics'" or "embodied adventurous practices in nature, whether they are perceived as high or low risk, are ambiguous and fluid and may challenge dominant sporting narratives of body/mind separation and potentially afford pedagogic processes or 'techniques of the body' fostering a form of shared 'kinetic empathy.'"[52] While there is growing evidence of this mind-body connection for the participants, the environmental benefits are less clear for the adrenaline narrative's armchair reader or viewer.

As a result, a paradox emerges when transformed adventurers share their experience through narrative or other arts, which raises the question whether the reader/viewer physically needs to be in nature in order for the environmental benefits to take effect. It follows that if reading produces greater empathy, it would also, like kinetic empathy, yield similar environmental action. Peter Stockwell argues, for example, "literary works—whether fictional or not—have an emotional and tangible effect on readers and on the real world in which we live with literature."[53] Engaging in and with adrenaline narratives may foster environmentalism. If one cannot picture oneself in the narrative, however, exclusion logically follows. Thus, representational politics remain important even as our imaginations may be able to occupy a range of (un)familiar bodies and experiences. Key here is the repetition of particular bodies and narratives rather than others—and the repetition's impact. For instance, as Wilson and Little point out, "the media often portrays men participating in risk-taking adventure in the outdoors and generally they are seen as heroic figures. Women, however, are less visible and their roles reflect more leisurely and feminine activities."[54] The contemporary American adrenaline narrative demonstrates that as gender roles shift, new models and paths are forged.

Christine Byl, for example, notes she "was not born to labor, not led to it by heritage or expectation.... In my case, despite a diverse family (teachers and tradesmen) and the climate of 1980s feminism, I inherited a common unspoken baseline. Boys took shop. Smart kids went to college."[55] She did not have female role models for the "dirt work" that becomes her life. Byl later remarks, "it was for me then, and remained for years, easier to take lessons from women.... I think what deeply unites us is the fact that most of us have so recently been beginners."[56] These new models, teachers, and alternative paths are needed as we are all beginners in the work required to address climate change. While mutuality holds promise, it is the emerging rather than the current dominant model.

As we have seen over the course of this book, for many adrenaline athletes nature remains a resource rather than another "body." Rob Schultheis, for example, implicitly argues for distinct, firm boundaries between wilderness and culture when he explains, "we must establish our own Outbacks and go out into them and bring the power there back into our everyday, 'civilized' lives as portable lodestars to keep us on track through the vast unnatural inanity of the modern world."[57] Nature's power is a resource that can be extracted and brought back to civilization as a means to keep our priorities straight. Whether framed as spiritual or conquering or some combination, nature remains a separate object—objectified for human use.

At the other extreme is an argument that we must become wild, rip ourselves free from civilization. This view calls not for the end of nature but for a return to nature via subsistence living. However, such a shift is not practical and turning to nature to model human life presents a host of problems as well. For instance, Daniel Suelo notes in "his observations of the natural world...[that] while there are a few industrious exceptions, like beavers and squirrels, most wild animals don't plan ahead. They take what is available—that is, plants and bodies of other animals—and when they die they give what they have: their own bodies."[58] As a result, Suelo concludes "the best-laid plans [are] folly" and so he relies on "chance" and "faith."[59] According to Suelo, "nature operates on a 'gift economy': animals freely take what is available and freely give what they have."[60] While even Suelo's family states "he's too extreme," he is, nevertheless, "fighting against greed" and "pride," which "are the two primary problems in America."[61] In advocating for such feral behavior, however, Suelo fails to account for the violence embedded in this "gift economy" and its place-specific relevance. In this light, Suelo still projects his views onto nature rather than understanding nature on its own terms and in context in order to negotiate his human engagement with it.

As William Cronon explains in *Changes in the Land*, it is likely more accurate to say that, like the early European settlers, many Americans today still do not recognize the ways wild animals plan. Cronon writes, "because animals, including people, feed on plants and other animals, the ways they obtain their food are largely determined by the cycles in which other species lead their lives."[62] While knowledge is not the same as planning, understanding the best ways to apply knowledge is a type of planning, as in Cronon's example of the Native Americans of New England: "Doing so required an intimate understanding of the habits and ecology of other species."[63] When our food cultures become distant from these seasonal cycles, as is true for much of America today, or when this seasonal knowledge is not obtained—true today and for the early European settlers new to the Americas—survival develops different strategies—the ones Suelo would like to change. Yet just as the early European settlers misread Native American land management, so, too, does Suelo seem to misunderstand nature's plan.[64] Recognizing the costs and consequences of taking nature's "gifts" brings us back in touch with the cycles of nature—whether we live off the grid, garden, or do our hunting and gathering at the supermarket. Negotiating both anthropocentric and biocentric points of view results in mutualism.

NO PERFECT DESIRING NATURE

An erotic construction of desire holds promise, but it is not the only available discourse. The erotics of nature, after all, are not about the policing of desire. No single *perfect* way exists to view nature and describe our desires toward it. "Nature always already defies its construction; it is always other, uncatchable," Catriona Sandilands reminds us. Sandilands explains, "it can never perfectly appear through politics because it embodies a moment that defies its constitution in discourse."[65] At the same time, we must recognize the limitations and dangers present in our contemporary desiring natures. As Jedediah Purdy explains, Americans approach nature with fear and love; the erotics of love, however, offer more promise: love "keeps the hand poised, extended in greeting or in an offer of peace. This gesture is the beginning of collaboration, among people but also beyond us."[66] This connection, key to erotic desire, holds sustainable promise.

Adrenaline narratives encourage us to examine nature and adventure from all angles. While objectifying forms dominate, Wilson and Little note that adventure's process offers multiple entry points for change.

> Adventure is challenge, newness, and learning. It can be physical, but it can also be an emotional, cognitive and/or social risk. If we acknowledge multiple levels and aspects of adventure and allow individuals to value them, an opportunity and desire for continued participation may also evolve. At the very least, as professions that strive to inspire and promote learning or encourage growth, challenge, and newness, we need to recognize that people's lived experiences with adventure recreation are not uni-dimensional. Adventure can be dynamic in people's lives. If leaders

and participants understand the essence of its benefit and enjoyment, we can construct adventure in a variety of ways, thus negotiating a plethora of potential constraints that serve to limit accessibility.⁶⁷

Adventure that accommodates "a variety of ways" should not only increase individual "accessibility" but also involve nature as a mutual actor. While not all adrenaline narratives agree on the role nature plays—a force to be conquered, a location for inspiration and transformation, or the ultimate playmate—they do agree that nature sets the defining qualities for their sports.

This paradoxical relationship—to preserve, play with and in, and exploit—continues to define the American environmental imagination's boundary disputes. Perhaps a focus on negotiating these extremes is what is needed now and for the near future. Purdy explains, "paradox, partiality, and the mixed-up character of everything have come after the grasp at wholeness that began the ecological age."⁶⁸ In recognizing our exploitation and understanding the problems in preserving virgin wilderness, we may begin to shift our environmental imagination from rigid objectification to a more fluid erotic mutuality. The American environmental imagination—like nature itself—is not "whole" but rather partial or always in process: likewise, nature becomes living when we recognize we cannot capture it "whole" without killing it.

The adrenaline narrative's simultaneously confused, contradictory, and (un)changing desiring natures can be seen in the video "The North Face: Your Land," set to My Morning Jacket's cover of Woody Guthrie's "This Land is Your Land." The ad crystalizes the contemporary American adrenaline narrative into its key component desires, offering a mash-up of racially diverse extreme athletes, iconic American wilderness and urban landscapes—matched to the song's lyrics—and a full range of adventure sports, including backcountry skiing, mountain biking, sailing, kayaking in extreme whitewater, urban and desert running, rafting, slacklining, and climbing. The opening sets the ad's tone and highlights the adrenaline narrative's shifting dynamics. As the brief instrumental opening plays, a vast "adventure porn" mountain vista appears, and then a close-up of an African American male adventurer drinking in the view. Like Johnson and Mills, the ad claims adventure and the American landscape for an increasingly diverse American population: the lyrics "this land is your land" are sung as we see his face.⁶⁹

The music's tempo increases and in the rapid-fire shots that follow we see beautiful people having fun—primarily in the wild outdoors. They laugh while running through a "golden valley" and even American buffalo are depicted as roaming free.[70] The advertisement includes cameos by famous extreme athletes from The North Face's global athlete team, including climber Alex Honnold, "filmmaker and alpinist Renan Ozturk rowing a raft, endurance runner Dean Karnazes running on what looks like the moon, and mountaineer Hilaree O'Neill smiling."[71] But even if you do not recognize their faces, you will recognize the American freedom that the song, the American landscapes, and the extreme sports connect to The North Face's "Never Stop Exploring" slogan. In the advertisement we see people connecting with the outdoors: they conquer mountains, experience awe in nature, and engage in deep play in and with nature—all set to Guthrie's radical lyrics.

As the *New York Times* points out, Guthrie's most radical verse ("As I went walking I saw a sign there / And on the sign it said 'No Trespassing.' / But on the other side it didn't say nothing, / That side was made for you and me.") is softened by the ad's imagery.[72] The article notes that "while the lyrics seem to advocate defying authority, the commercial takes a softer approach, showing a kindly rancher happily opening a gate to let some climbers onto his property, and Mr. Carpenter [vice president for global marketing at The North Face] said the perspective aligned with the philosophy of the brand."[73] While these radical politics are softened to fit brand philosophy, The North Face partnered with the 21st Century Conservation Service Corps, which benefits from sales of the song. The corps (established "within the United States Interior Department") "hires veterans and at-risk young people to restore and preserve public land," and, as part of its campaign, The North Face "is contributing $250,000 to the corps."[74] Thus, the advertisement combines key facets of the contemporary American adrenaline narrative in order to sell the North Face brand and an inclusive, environmentally and socially conscious version of rugged American identity: it links extreme adventure, American freedom accessible to a racially diverse population, and environmental justice.

Its focus on a racially and gendered mix of extreme normate athletic bodies speaks to ways the contemporary American adrenaline narrative has and has not changed. Notably in this regard, no recognizably Indigenous peoples are included. In this sense, the American landscapes presented in the advertisement continue their active disappearance and a refusal to recognize land claims. This land is not their land. The contemporary American adrenaline narrative presented in the video remains focused on a narrow version and vision of heroic masculinity, even as "diverse" bodies participate. In other words, the video's fit, elite athletes and models have more in common than their seeming gender and ethnic diversity belies.

Despite its deep flaws, when I view advertisements like the one described above I maintain a delicate hope for erotic rhetoric's potential and for the adrenaline narrative's benefits to outweigh its negatives—because, like David Abram, I see stories bound to the landscape, as adrenaline narratives are, holding the vital potential to alleviate our ecologically destructive separation from nature.[75] I remain more optimistic than Doug Christensen, who argues that "adventurers [inescapably] buy into a system of materialism and cultural alienation instead of a culture of communion and reverence for the earth."[76] While I agree environmentalism, as Crouch says of "spiritual revelation," does not "automatically [go] along with the view," there is also evidence that even so-called impure or inauthentic, commercialized adventure may lead to greater ecological thinking and action.[77] Christensen and I agree that the "hero frame" shapes adrenaline narratives in ways that make alternative routes difficult.[78] Narratives that jettison or revise the hero frame hold the most potential.

While writing also represents an ecological danger for Abram, because "writing down oral stories renders them separable, for the first time, from the actual places where the events in those stories occurred," Abram's analysis implies that the key to judging ecologically sound adrenaline writing is the degree to which it accomplishes the former—a connection to the land—as opposed to the latter—alienation.[79] Additionally, sharing stories—whether they are written down or visually told—contributes to the work of repopulating and reanimating wilderness. Recently, for example, Indigenous Women Hike and Project 562 released a video and blog post to share the story of hiking the Nüümü Poyo, or "what the world knows as the John Muir Trail" (JMT). The video and blog post about this event use a range of strategies to (re)claim the American adrenaline narrative and Native Americans' place in the land's story and history. Thus, an emerging desire materializes: restorative.

RESTORATIVE DESIRES

Building from the tenets of restoration ecology and restorative justice, this emergent restorative desire seeks to fill the silences created by colonialism, racism, and patriarchy. Where restoration ecology aims to return the land as closely as possible to its previous state, restorative desire does not seek origins or a past utopian Eden. Rather, it moves forward without forgetting the past. The video and blog about hiking the Nüümü Poyo offer, for example, an often silenced or "erased" view: "Although this area and the JMT are well known, the history of the land and its original people have been systemically erased and continue to be overlooked."[80] Restorative desire strives to address disturbances and foster a healthy, sustainable ecosystem attentive to historical and ongoing erasures.[81] In healing the land, as we saw with prayer running, we also find community. The women who participated in the hike also did so without permits, citing the American Indian Religious Freedom Act of 1978, because "'we're not going to ask for a permit to access our own land.'"[82] They participate, in other words, in restoring and rebuilding "a sense of justice."[83]

In sharing their story, the Nüümü Poyo hikers reclaim their place while invoking the adrenaline narrative's characteristic desires. For instance, the video's stunning landscapes and blog post's descriptions of the physical challenges the women face resemble the adventure porn and spiritual suffering often depicted in conquering and spiritual desires. The emphasis on Indigenous people as "masters of a thriving environment in which all beings lived in harmony" invokes the ecological Indian stereotype as a means to counter views of the Ahwahnechee people as "dirty" (a word Tazbah Chavez, in reporting about the hike on the Project 562 blog, specifically notes John Muir used to describe the Ahwahnechee).[84] The women's radical politics—symbolized in the video's closing silhouette still of the women, who all have one arm raised in a fist—also adds to the "extreme" nature of their hike.[85] Their politics, in other words, are as risky as the environment through which they moved. They demand justice. They demand recognition.

Notably, rather than objectifying nature, the protagonists, narrative frame, and content focus on (re)claiming: to remind those using the trail "that these are still our ancestral territories and that we're still here."[86] In this sense, they are engaged in, to quote Wenzel et al., "reaffirming a shared value-consensus" and opening a bilateral conversation to achieve this goal: "Justice is restored when the relevant principles and values that have been violated by the offense are re-established and re-validated through social consensus."[87] Much of this bridge building is accomplished by the hike's focus on education as well as adventure. The women taught other hikers their culture and language. For example, "along the [JMT] trail these women were often teachers to hikers. They said the interactions were surprisingly and overwhelmingly positive. They would bring up the Nüümü place names and used every opportunity as a learning opportunity when meeting someone." At least one park ranger supported the women's non-permit hike.⁸⁸ The encounters along the trail led to greater and mutual understanding and to the reaffirmation of shared values.

Such restorative narratives fulfill the promise Doug Christensen points to at the end of his essay: "the possibility that future adventure narratives might explore survival and sustainability in their largest sense—that future hero frames might celebrate symbiotic reverence for the natural world as much as they celebrate individual triumph."⁸⁹ As armchair and/or actual adventurers, our responsibility also includes seeking out and amplifying such narratives, to give them the audience to (re)claim adventurous bodies and join the work of reimagining America's environmental imagination.

The present state of the environment gives us little reason to hope our collective desiring natures are changing to a degree that would ensure significant material changes will result in the near future. However, there is hope in their ability to be reclaimed and rewritten in ways that do not perpetuate erasure and exploitation, but rather focus on education and the mutual reaffirmation of shared values. Indigenous Women Hike demonstrates this restorative desire in how it participates in the formation of Sandilands's "ecological democracy."⁹⁰ Founder Jolie Varela stood "with her relatives against the Dakota Access Pipeline. Upon returning home she wanted to figure out how to keep the sacred fire burning in her own community. Indigenous Women Hike is her sacred fire."⁹¹ Indigenous Women Hike fosters ecological democracy, or "a diversity of voices, a variety of perceptions, a proliferation of values and experiences of nature," by empowering Indigenous women through connection with the land.⁹² The adrenaline narrative's increasing popularity, especially in its reclaimed and erotic forms, hints at a fragile but powerful potential—a delicate hope that, if not nurtured and shared, will, along with nature, become extinct.

❖ ❖ ❖

I might never have traveled to Tibet had I never read *Into Thin Air*, which in turn led me to reading more books, blogs, and other media about extreme adventure. I traveled in part to see for myself the places I read about, deepening my appreciation and commitment to environmental and social justice while simultaneously increasing my own carbon footprint. This book faults Krakauer's patriarchal construction of desire, but his writing also started me on my physical journey to Tibet and my mental journey through the adrenaline narrative. *Into Thin Air*'s struggles with the rhetorics of desire produce a fascinating read. Thus, I agree with Katherine Ericson, who argues that Krakauer's metaphors ultimately "can be read as a pointed call for environmental reform."⁹³ For these reasons and more, I continue to enjoy and recommend Krakauer's books. And this, in truth, is this book's message: adrenaline narratives that lead to eco-action contain great potential and influence.

As this final chapter brings the book to its conclusion, I hope that rather than leaving you lost, you will see that I have taken you to a crossroads. American crossroads, as Eric Blehm notes about the "wide cement platform" that constitutes the Four Corners Monument, do not always spark optimism: "we have poured upon it concrete and asphalt. That says more than I could ever write about America. Destroy it to celebrate it."⁹⁴ Our past and present decisions to "pave paradise" do not inspire hope. However, these narrative crossroads locate the borders of the adrenaline narrative's ecotonal generic structures and map territory ripe for ecocritical exploration. What relationships with wilderness will you forge? What kind of adventure do you desire?

APPENDIX

LIST OF CONTEMPORARY AMERICAN ADRENALINE NARRATIVES

This list is not meant to be exhaustive. Rather, it aims to inspire deeper reading and discovery beyond the analysis presented in this book. Specific titles discussed in the previous chapters are noted by an asterisk. My public Zotero library, American Adrenaline Narrative, provides a more extensive list of primary and secondary sources related to the genre: https://www.zotero.org/groups/25094/american_adrenaline_narrative. Know of an American adrenaline narrative that should make my list? Please tweet the title or link to @drkj. Follow the hashtag #adrenalinenarrative for updates.

NONFICTION BOOKS
(BY YEAR AND ALPHABETICAL BY AUTHOR)

Roberts, David: *Deborah: A Wilderness Narrative* (1970)
Keith, Sam, and Richard Proenneke: *One Man's Wilderness: An Alaskan Odyssey* (1973)
Zwinger, Ann H.: *Run, River, Run: A Naturalist's Journey down One of the Great Rivers of the West* (1975)
Blum, Arlene: *Annapurna: A Woman's Place* (1980)*
McGinniss, Joe: *Going to Extremes* (1980)
Leamer, Laurence: *Ascent: The Spiritual and Physical Quest of Legendary Mountaineer Willi Unsoeld* (1982)
Klein, Clayton: *Cold Summer Wind* (1983)
Schultheis, Rob: *Bone Games: Extreme Sports, Shamanism, Zen, and the Search for Transcendence* (1984)*
Callahan, Steven: *Adrift: Seventy-Six Days Lost at Sea* (1986)*
Fons, Valerie: *Keep it Moving: Baja by Canoe* (1986)
Lopez, Barry Holstun: *Arctic Dreams: Imagination and Desire in a Northern Landscape* (1986)*
Roberts, David: *Moments of Doubt and Other Mountaineering Writings* (1986)
Steger, Will, with Paul Schurke: *North to the Pole* (1987)
Harris, Eddy L.: *Mississippi Solo: A River Quest* (1988)*
Aebi, Tania, with Bernadette Brennan: *Maiden Voyage* (1989)*
Kane, Joe: *Running the Amazon* (1989)*
Kesselheim, Alan: *Water and Sky: Challenging the Northern Wilderness* (1989)
Morgan, Dodge: *The Voyage of American Promise* (1989)

Nelson, Richard: *The Island Within* (1989)
Anderson, Scott: *Distant Fires: Duluth to Hudson Bay* (1990)
Krakauer, Jon: *Eiger Dreams: Ventures among Men and Mountains* (1990)
Harris, Eddy L.: *Native Stranger: A Black American's Journey into the Heart of Africa* (1992)
Theroux, Paul: *The Happy Isles of Oceania: Paddling the Pacific* (1992)
Allison, Stacy, with Peter Carlin: *Beyond the Limits: A Woman's Triumph on Everest* (1993)*
Fromm, Pete: *Indian Creek Chronicles* (1993)*
Huntington, Sidney, and Jim Rearden: *Shadows on the Koyukuk: An Alaskan Native's Life along the River* (1993)
Holtel, Bob: *Soul, Sweat, and Survival on the Pacific Crest Trail* (1994)
Giddings, J. Calvin: *Demon River Apurímac: The First Navigation of the Upper Amazon Canyons* (1996)
Krakauer, Jon: *Into the Wild* (1996)*
Waterman, Jonathan: *Kayaking the Vermilion Sea: Eight Hundred Miles down the Baja* (1996)
Fletcher, Colin: *River: One Man's Journey down the Colorado, Source to Sea* (1997)
Krakauer, Jon: *Into Thin Air: A Personal Account of the Mt. Everest Disaster* (1997)*
Nichols, Peter: *Sea Change: Alone across the Atlantic in a Wooden Boat* (1997)*
Bryson, Bill: *A Walk in the Woods* (1998)*
Deming, Alison Hawthorne: *The Edges of the Civilized World: A Journey in Nature and Culture* (1998)
Kocour, Ruth Anne, with Michael Hodgson: *Facing the Extreme: One Woman's Tale of True Courage, Death-Defying Survival and Her Quest for the Summit* (1998)*
McCairen, Patricia: *Canyon Solitude: A Woman's Solo River Journey through the Grand Canyon* (1998)*
Simon, Alvah: *North to the Night: A Spiritual Odyssey in the Arctic* (1998)*
Wickwire, Jim, and Dorothy Bullitt: *Addicted to Danger: A Memoir about Affirming Life in the Face of Death* (1998)
Bangs, Richard: *The Lost River: A Memoir of Life, Death, and Transformation on Wild Water* (1999)
Clare, Eli: *Exile and Pride: Disability, Queerness, and Liberation* (1999)*
Least Heat-Moon, William. *River-Horse: The Logbook of a Boat across America* (1999)*
Pham, Andrew X.: *Catfish and Mandala: A Two-Wheeled Voyage through the Landscape and Memory of Vietnam* (1999)*
Balf, Todd: *The Last River: The Tragic Race for Shangri-La* (2000)*
McKibben, Bill: *Long Distance: Testing the Limits of Body and Spirit in a Year of Living Strenuously* (2000)*
Crouch, Gregory: *Enduring Patagonia* (2001)*
Fredston, Jill: *Rowing to Latitude: Journeys along the Arctic's Edge* (2001)*
Hahn, Jennifer: *Spirited Waters: Soloing South through the Inside Passage* (2001)*
Howkins, Heidi: *K2: One Woman's Quest for the Summit* (2001)*
Twight, Mark: *Kiss or Kill: Confessions of a Serial Climber* (2001)*
Weihenmayer, Erik: *Touch the Top of the World* (2001)*
Whittaker, Tom, and Johnny Dodd: *Higher Purpose: The Heroic Story of the First Disabled Man to Conquer Everest* (2001)*
Gilbert, Elizabeth: *The Last American Man* (2002)*
Hill, Lynn, with Greg Child: *Climbing Free: My Life in the Vertical World* (2002)*

LIST OF CONTEMPORARY ADRENALINE NARRATIVES 235

Ross, Cindy: *Scraping Heaven: A Family's Journey along the Continental Divide* (2002)*
Schooler, Lynn: *The Blue Bear: A True Story of Friendship and Discovery in the Alaskan Wild* (2002)
Arnesen, Liv, and Ann Bancroft, with Cheryl Dahle: *No Horizon Is So Far: Two Women and Their Historic Journey across Antarctica* (2003)*
Brown, Chip: *Good Morning Midnight: Life and Death in the Wild* (2003)
Glick, Daniel: *Monkey Dancing: A Father, Two Kids, and a Journey to the Ends of the Earth* (2003)*
Campbell, James: *The Final Frontiersman: Heimo Korth and His Family, Alone in Alaska's Arctic Wilderness* (2004)
Cox, Lynne: *Swimming to Antarctica: Tales of a Long-Distance Swimmer* (2004)*
Ralston, Aron: *Between a Rock and a Hard Place* (2004)*
Blum, Arlene: *Breaking Trail: A Climbing Life* (2005)*
Francis, John: *Planetwalker: 22 Years of Walking, 17 Years of Silence* (2005)*
Fredston, Jill: *Snowstruck: In the Grip of Avalanches* (2005)*
Hancock, Bill: *Riding with the Blue Moth* (2005)
Jans, Nick: *The Grizzly Maze: Timothy Treadwell's Fatal Obsession with Alaskan Bears* (2005)*
Jordan, Jennifer: *Savage Summit: The Life and Death of the First Women of K2* (2005)*
Madgic, Bob: *Shattered Air: A True Account of Catastrophe and Courage on Yosemite's Half Dome* (2005)
McKibben, Bill: *Wandering Home* (2005)
Petersen, David: *On the Wild Edge: In Search of a Natural Life* (2005)
Pinder, Eric: *North to Katahdin* (2005)
Roberts, David: *On the Ridge Between Life and Death: A Climbing Life Reexamined* (2005)
Bledsoe, Lucy Jane: *The Ice Cave: A Woman's Adventures from the Mojave to the Antarctic* (2006)*
Blehm, Eric: *The Last Season* (2006)*
O'Neill, Dan: *A Land Gone Lonesome: An Inland Voyage along the Yukon River* (2006)
Pinkney, William: *As Long As It Takes: Meeting the Challenge* (2006)*
Viesturs, Ed, with David Roberts: *No Shortcuts to the Top: Climbing the World's 14 Highest Peaks* (2006)
Butler, Elias, and Tom Myers: *Grand Obsession: Harvey Butchart and the Exploration of Grand Canyon* (2007)
Davis, Steph: *High Infatuation: A Climber's Guide to Love and Gravity* (2007)
Frontin, Glenn: *A River Calling: A Christian Father and His Sons, a Canoe Adventure, a Spiritual Journey That Would Last a Lifetime* (2007)*
Johnson, Wayne: *White Heat: The Extreme Skiing Life* (2007)
Manos, Jarid: *Ghetto Plainsman* (2007)*
Tabor, James M.: *Forever on the Mountain* (2007)
Berman, Tao, with Pam Withers: *Going Vertical: The Life of an Extreme Kayaker* (2008)*
Homer, Jill: *Ghost Trails: Journeys through a Lifetime* (2008)
Irvine, Amy: *Trespass: Living at the Edge of the Promised Land* (2008)*
Kantner, Seth: *Shopping for Porcupine: A Life in Arctic Alaska* (2008)
Kull, Robert: *Solitude: Seeking Wisdom in Extremes: A Year Alone in the Patagonia Wilderness* (2008)*

Malusa, Jim: *Into Thick Air: Biking to the Bellybutton of Six Continents* (2008)*
Silverwood, John, and Jean Silverwood: *Black Wave: A Family's Adventure at Sea and the Disaster That Saved Them* (2008)
Simpson, Sherry: *The Accidental Explorer: Wayfinding in Alaska* (2008)*
Hanc, John: *The Coolest Race on Earth: Mud, Madmen, Glaciers, and Grannies at the Antarctica Marathon* (2009)
Lord, Nancy. *Rock, Water, Wild: An Alaskan Life* (2009)*
McClure, Tori Murden: *A Pearl in the Storm: How I Found My Heart in the Middle of the Ocean* (2009)*
McDougall, Christopher: *Born to Run: A Hidden Tribe, Superathletes, and the Greatest Race the World Has Never Seen* (2009)*
McKittrick, Erin: *A Long Trek Home: 4,000 Miles by Boot, Raft and Ski* (2009)
Obmascik, Mark: *Halfway to Heaven: My White-knuckled—and Knuckleheaded—Quest for the Rocky Mountain High* (2009)
Ollestad, Norman: *Crazy for the Storm: A Memoir of Survival* (2009)
Parfet, Bo, with Richard Buskin: *Die Trying: One Man's Quest to Conquer the Seven Summits* (2009)
Weiss, Miranda: *Tide, Feather, Snow: A Life in Alaska* (2009)*
Barnes, David M.: *Faithful's Journey on the Appalachian Trail* (2010)*
Bowley, Graham: *No Way Down: Life and Death on K2* (2010)*
Davis, Jennifer Pharr: *Becoming Odyssa: Epic Adventures on the Appalachian Trail* (2010)*
Jordan, Jennifer: *The Last Man on the Mountain: The Death of an American Adventurer on K2* (2010)
Lankford, Andrea: *Ranger Confidential: Living, Working, and Dying in the National Parks* (2010)
Lawrence, Sarahlee: *River House: A Memoir* (2010)
Lynn, Schooler: *Walking Home: A Journey in the Alaskan Wilderness* (2010)*
Morrison, Dan: *The Black Nile: One Man's Amazing Journey through Peace and War on the World's Longest River* (2010)
Ostman, Cami: *Second Wind: One Woman's Midlife Quest to Run Seven Marathons on Seven Continents* (2010)*
Richey, Warren: *Without a Paddle: Racing Twelve Hundred Miles around Florida by Sea Kayak* (2010)
Davidson, Jim, and Kevin Vaughan: *The Ledge: An Adventure Story of Friendship and Survival on Mount Rainier* (2011)
Gessner, David. *My Green Manifesto: Down the Charles River in Pursuit of a New Environmentalism* (2011)*
Grange, Kevin: *Beneath Blossom Rain: Discovering Bhutan on the Toughest Trek in the World* (2011)
Lane, John: *My Paddle to the Sea: Eleven Days on the River of the Carolinas* (2011)
Sundeen, Mark: *The Man Who Quit Money* (2011)*
Sunderland, Abby, and Lynn Vincent: *Unsinkable: A Young Woman's Courageous Battle on the High Seas* (2011)
Herr, Patricia Ellis: *Up: A Mother and Daughter's Peakbagging Adventure* (2012)*
Roberts, Suzanne: *Almost Somewhere: Twenty-Eight Days on the John Muir Trail* (2012)*
Slakey, Francis: *To the Last Breath: A Memoir of Going to Extremes* (2012)

Strayed, Cheryl: *Wild: From Lost to Found on the Pacific Crest Trail* (2012)*
Woodlief, Jennifer: *A Bolt from the Blue: The Epic True Story of Danger, Daring, and Heroism at 13,000 Feet* (2012)*
Zuckerman, Peter, and Amanda Padoan: *Buried in the Sky: The Extraordinary Story of the Sherpa Climbers on K2's Deadliest Day* (2012)
Buckles, Julie: *Paddling to Winter* (2013)
Byl, Christine: *Dirt Work: An Education in the Woods* (2013)*
Davis, Steph: *Learning to Fly* (2013)*
Ilgunas, Ken: *Walden on Wheels: On the Open Road from Debt to Freedom* (2013)
Samet, Matt: *Death Grip: A Climber's Escape from Benzo Madness* (2013)
Storey, Gail D.: *I Promise Not to Suffer: A Fool for Love Hikes the Pacific Crest Trail* (2013)*
Carpenter, Novella: *Gone Feral: Tracking My Dad through the Wild* (2014)
Finnegan, William: *Barbarian Days: A Surfing Life* (2015)
Greenfield, Rob: *Dude Making a Difference: Bamboo Bikes, Dumpster Dives and Other Extreme Adventures across America* (2015)*
Honnold, Alex, with David Roberts: *Alone on the Wall* (2015)
Quinn, Carrot: *Thru-Hiking Will Break Your Heart: An Adventure on the Pacific Coast Trail* (2015)
Branch, Michael P.: *Raising Wild: Dispatches from a Home in the Wilderness* (2016)
Braverman, Blair: *Welcome to the Goddamn Ice Cube: Chasing Fear and Finding Home in the Great White North* (2016)*
Campbell, James: *Braving It: A Father, a Daughter, and an Unforgettable Journey into the Alaskan Wild* (2016)*
Ilgunas, Ken: *Trespassing across America: One Man's Epic, Never-Done-Before (and Sort of Illegal) Hike across the Heartland* (2016)*
Branch, Michael P.: *Rants from the Hill: On Packrats, Bobcats, Curmudgeons, a Drunken Mary Kay Lady & Other Encounters with the Wild in the High Desert* (2017)
Caldwell, Tommy: *The Push: A Climber's Journey of Endurance, Risk, and Going beyond Limits* (2017)
Finkel, Michael: *The Stranger in the Woods: The Extraordinary Story of the Last True Hermit* (2017)
Fitzgerald, Holly: *Ruthless River: Love and Survival by Raft on the Amazon's Relentless Madre de Dios* (2017)*
Synnott, Mark: *The Impossible Climb: Alex Honnold, El Capitan, and the Climbing Life* (2018)
Anderson, Heather: *Thirst: 2600 Miles to Home* (2019)
Oliver-Tierney, Lori K.: *Trudge: A Midlife Crisis on the John Muir Trail* (2019)
Van Hemert, Caroline: *The Sun is a Compass: A 4,000-Mile Journey into the Alaskan Wilds* (2019)

DOCUMENTARY FILMS
(BY YEAR AND ALPHABETICAL BY TITLE)

Everest (1998)
Vertical Frontier (2002)
Touching the Void (2003)
Riding Giants (2004)
First Descent (2005)
Grizzly Man (2005)
The Runner: Extreme UltraRunner David Horton (2006)

Bicycle Dreams (2009)
Race across the Sky (2009)
Running America (2009)
180° South: Conquerors of the Useless (2010)*
Alone on the Wall: Alex Honnold (2010)*
Into the Cold: A Journey of the Soul (2010)*
Ride the Divide (2010)
The Art of Flight (2011)
Chasing Ice (2012)
The Summit (2012)
High and Hallowed: Everest 1963 (2013)*
Mile… Mile and a Half (2013)
An American Ascent (2014)*
The Barkley Marathons: The Race That Eats Its Young (2014)
K2: Siren of the Himalayas (2014)
Only the Essential: A Hike from Mexico to Canada on the Pacific Crest Trail (2014)
Sunshine Superman (2014)
Valley Uprising (2014)
The Great Alone (2015)
The Long Start to the Journey (2015)
Meru (2015)
Sherpa (2015)*
America Wild: National Parks Adventure (2016)
The Fourth Phase (2016)
Given (2016)
Karl Meltzer: Made to Be Broken (2016)
Elevation Change (2017)
Fishpeople (2017)
Under an Arctic Sky (2017)
All Who Dare (2018)
Dawn Wall (2018)
Free Solo (2018)*
Project Y (2018)
Sacred Strides (2018)*
Figure It Out: On the Hayduke Trail (2019)

SOCIAL MEDIA AND WEBSITES

Adrenaline Beast: http://www.adrenalinebeast.com
Adventure Journal: https://www.adventure-journal.com
Base Camp Magazine: https://basecampmagazine.com
Diversify Outdoors: https://www.diversifyoutdoors.com
Indigenous Women Hike: https://www.indigenouswomenhike.com
Joy Trip Project: https://joytripproject.com
Latino Outdoors: http://latinooutdoors.org
Melanin Base Camp: https://www.melaninbasecamp.com
National Geographic, Exploration and Adventure: https://www.nationalgeographic.com/adventure
Native Women's Wilderness: https://www.nativewomenswilderness.org
Outdoor Afro: https://outdoorafro.com
Outdoor Asian: https://www.outdoorasian.com
Outdoor Project: https://www.outdoorproject.com
Outdoor Women's Alliance: https://www.outdoorwomensalliance.com
Outside Online: https://www.outsideonline.com
Planet Mountain: https://www.planetmountain.com/english/home.html
Queer Nature: https://www.queernature.org
Roam TV, Raw Adventure: https://www.youtube.com/channel/UCr6p75S0xW4Oxg1Y_oFULIw
She Explores: https://she-explores.com
Sustainable Play: https://sustainableplay.com
Temoa Journal (blog of NativesOutdoors): https://natives-outdoors.org/blog
Terra Incognita: https://www.terraincognitamedia.com

NOTES

CHAPTER 1. DESIRING NATURES

1. The Tibetan name is also spelled Qomolangma. The official Chinese name is Zhumulangma. Hereafter I will use the name most Americans recognize, Everest.
2. The pass is the highest point along the Friendship Highway.
3. "Adventure Ready Styles." "The Sundance Story" can be found on their website's "About Us" page: https://www.sundancecatalog.com/category/customer+service/about+us.do.
4. Ryman, "Wausau to Highlight Extreme Sports Potential to Attract Young Professionals."
5. Everest is still growing, or maybe not: although disputed, 29,029 feet is the current official elevation. A 1999 study led the U.S. National Geographic Society to state Everest's elevation as 29,035 feet, and China disputes the official elevation, claiming it is thirteen feet lower. Additionally, there is debate as to whether or not the 2015 earthquake in Nepal reduced its elevation. A team is remeasuring Everest in 2019 (Leung, "Nepalese Climbers").
6. The appendix includes a list of contemporary American adrenaline narratives referenced in the book as well as additional selected examples.
7. While an in-depth exploration of how this term applies (or not) to pre-1970s adventure/travel nonfiction and non-U.S. subjects is beyond the scope of my research, I welcome other scholars' discussion of its suitability and usefulness for the earlier epochs briefly summarized here.
8. Anne C. McCarthy, "Reading the Red Bull Sublime," 545.
9. Bardenwerper, "Steal the Thunder."
10. Domosh and Seager, *Putting Women in Place*, 155.
11. Domosh and Seager, 155–56.
12. Macfarlane, *Mountains of the Mind*, 15.
13. Peedom, *Mountain*, 00:16:13–00:16:16, 00:21:40–00:21:48.
14. Macfarlane, *Mountains of the Mind*, 177.
15. Macfarlane, 177.
16. Hester Blum, *News at the Ends*, 155. See also Blum's *View from the Masthead*.
17. Stowe, *Going Abroad*, 55.
18. American West Photographs.

19. Peary, *Discovery of the North Pole*, 245.
20. Counter, *North Pole Legacy*, 67.
21. Mills, *Adventure Gap*, 181, 184.
22. See Sherry B. Ortner's *Life and Death on Mt. Everest: Sherpas and Himalayan Mountaineering* (1999), Jamling Tenzing Norgay's *Touching My Father's Soul: A Sherpa's Journey to the Top of Everest* (2001), Peter Zuckerman and Amanda Padoan's *Buried in the Sky: The Extraordinary Story of the Sherpa Climbers on K2's Deadliest Day* (2012), and the film directed by Jennifer Peedom, *Sherpa* (2015).
23. Macfarlane, *Mountains of the Mind*, 17.
24. "Climbing Mount Everest Is Work for Supermen."
25. Macfarlane, *Mountains of the Mind*, 14, 18.
26. *Surfing Magazine*'s online (1964–2017) archive: https://www.surfer.com/surfing-magazine-archive. Information about the Cape Fear Surfing Archive: https://library.uncw.edu/surf/about.htm. Information about Appalachian Mountain Club Library and Archives: https://www.outdoors.org/about/amc-library. The Canebrake Archive: http://www.canebrakes.com/archive.html.
27. National Parks, Exploration and Adventure: https://www.archives.gov/research/exploration-expansion/research/exploration-expansion/index.
28. Ryan, *Theorizing Outdoor Recreation and Ecology*, 2.
29. *Oxford English Dictionary Online*, "Extreme, Draft editions July 2002," accessed September 6, 2018, https://www.oed.com/view/Entry/67168.
30. McKibben, *Long Distance*, 100.
31. Humberstone, "'Outdoor Industry,'" 22.
32. Brymer, "Risk Taking," 218.
33. Kusz, "Extreme America," 197.
34. Oliver, "Extreme Explained," 109. As the article notes, extreme skiing is first associated with Chris Landry's 1978 descent of Pyramid Peak near Aspen, Colorado.
35. Balf, *Last River*, 275.
36. *National Geographic*'s weekly extreme or adventure photos can be accessed online: https://adventure.nationalgeographic.com/adventure/extreme-photo-of-the-week. The last post was in October 2016. The *60 Minutes Presents* episode "Going to Extremes" first aired 26 February 2012 (https://www.cbspressexpress.com/cbs-news/releases/view?id=30834). A transcript of the episode broadcast on 29 December 2013 is also available online (https://www.cbsnews.com/news/60-minutes-going-to-extremes).
37. Belinda Wheaton offers a similar history of extreme sports in "Introduction: Mapping the Lifestyle Sport-Scape" (2–4). She also emphasizes extreme sports' "roots in the counter-cultural social movement of the 1960s and 1970s" and how many of the new extreme sports had origins in North America and "were then imported to Europe by American entrepreneurs" (3).
38. This list of terms is selected from the *Oxford English Dictionary*'s "eco- (comb. form)" entry, which lists over eighty such "eco" terms. *Oxford English Dictionary Online*, s.v. "eco- (comb. form)," accessed September 6, 2018, https://www.oed.com/view/Entry/59377.
39. Gessner, *My Green Manifesto*, 25.
40. Vivanco, "Work of Environmentalism," 11.
41. Nash, *Wilderness and the American Mind*, 341.
42. Vivanco, "Work of Environmentalism," 10.
43. Glick, *Monkey Dancing*, xviii.

44. Schrepfer, *Nature's Altars*, 241.
45. Glick, *Monkey Dancing*, xxv.
46. Glick, xvii.
47. Glick, 64.
48. Glick, 65.
49. Glick, 276; emphasis in original.
50. Garrard points outs the wilderness trope is "the most potent construction of nature available to New World environmentalism" and "came to cultural prominence in the eighteenth century" (*Ecocriticism*, 66).
51. Cater, "Playing with Risk?," 318.
52. Kusz, "Extreme America," 199. Kusz cites several studies that outline this crisis in white masculinity in the United States, including Susan Faludi's *Stiffed: The Betrayal of the American Man* (1999), Michael Kimmel's *Manhood in America: A Cultural History* (1996), Fred Pfeil's *White Guys: Studies in Postmodern Domination and Difference* (1995), and David Savran's *Taking it Like a Man: White Masculinity, Masochism, and Contemporary American Culture* (1998). Kusz also examines the "re-centering of white masculinity in post-9/11" America in "Remasculinizing American White Guys" (209).
53. James, *Storyworld Accord*, 3, 29.
54. Lawrence Buell, *Environmental Imagination*, 2.
55. Lopez, *Arctic Dreams*, 228.
56. Macfarlane, *Mountains of the Mind*, 19.
57. Lawrence Buell, *Environmental Imagination*, 2; emphasis added. See endnote 2 from the introduction for discussion of works by environmental philosophers who advance this claim (426). Among those not included in Buell's list I would add Paul Shepard's *Nature and Madness*, Joseph W. Meeker's *Comedy of Survival*, and David Abram's *Spell of the Sensuous*.
58. Love, "Revaluing Nature," 213.
59. Lawrence Buell, *Environmental Imagination*, 2.
60. Lawrence Buell, 2.
61. Simon, *North to the Night*, 5.
62. Simon, 137; emphasis in original.
63. Nouzeilles, "Touching the Real," 196.
64. Nouzeilles, 197.
65. See Jorgenson, "Consumption and Environmental Degradation," 374–75, 378–81.
66. Cuomo, *Feminism and Ecological Communities*, 1.
67. Gonzales, *Deep Survival*, 64.
68. Graham Huggan considers a similar range of contemporary texts in "Going to Extremes: Reflections on Travel Writing, Death and the Contemporary Survival Industry." Graham labels these texts as a subgenre of travel writing, which he calls extreme travel writing (296).
69. Bruce Barcott, for example, characterizes mountaineering as "the most literary of all sports" in his 1996 *Harper's Magazine* article "Cliffhangers: The Fatal Descent of the Mountain-Climbing Memoir" (65).
70. Katheryn Hume in the English Department at Penn State University was also instrumental in the coining of this term and genre. While I was a graduate student in a summer class she suggested that I frame my argument about these texts in generic terms.
71. Sample titles under the Adrenaline Classics series include the "survival sto-

ries" anthology series edited by Clint Willis. Titles especially appropriate to this essay include *Ice: Stories of Survival from Polar Exploration, High: Stories of Survival from Everest and K2, Epic: Stories of Survival from the World's Highest Peaks, Climb: Stories of Survival from Rock Snow and Ice* (edited with David Roberts), and *Rough Water: Stories of Survival from the Sea*.

72. Extreme Sports Channel: http://extreme.com. X Games: http://xgames.espn.com. See also *Mob: Stories of Death and Betrayal from Organized Crime* and *Kennedys: Stories of Life and Death in an American Family*. This broader definition of the "action-adventure" genre is also used in Gina Marchetti's chapter about film and television, "Action-Adventure as Ideology."

73. Krein, "Nature and Risk in Adventure Sports," 81.
74. Krein, 88.
75. "About Primal Quest."
76. Harman, *Guerrilla Metaphysics*, 251; emphasis in original.
77. Morton, *Ecology without Nature*, 5.
78. Wilderness Act of 1964, § 1131(c).
79. Cohen, "Comment," 34.
80. Cohen, 34.
81. Strayed, *Wild*, 233.
82. Strayed, 234.
83. Gaard, "Ecofeminism and Wilderness," 6.
84. Baldick, "Travelogue."
85. Birrell, "Approaching Mt. Everest," 13.
86. Laing and Crouch, "Myth, Adventure and Fantasy at the Frontier," 131, 132, 133. I discuss the third and fourth elements in greater detail in chapter 3, "Spiritual Natures." For a discussion of "footsteps travel writing" see Christopher M. Keirstead's "Convoluted Paths."
87. Laing and Crouch, "Myth, Adventure and Fantasy at the Frontier," 135.
88. Laing and Crouch, 135.
89. Laing and Crouch, 135, 136.
90. Laing and Crouch, 135–36.
91. Laing and Crouch, 136; emphasis in original.
92. Morton and Norton, *High and Hallowed*.
93. Malloy, *180° South*.
94. Copeland, *Into the Cold: A Journey of the Soul*.
95. Arnesen and Bancroft, *No Horizon Is So Far*, 104.
96. Manos, *Ghetto Plainsman*, 237.
97. Peedom, *Sherpa*.
98. See Dorceta E. Taylor's *Rise of the American Conservation Movement* for a more inclusive environmental history.
99. Adhikari, "The Everest Brawl."
100. Jeffrey Mathes McCarthy, "Why Climbing Matters," 158. McCarthy also makes this argument in the introduction to his edited collection, *Contact: Mountain Climbing and Environmental Thinking* (2).
101. Jeffrey Mathes McCarthy, "Why Climbing Matters," 161.
102. I first outlined three of these "desiring natures" (patriarchal, spiritual, and erotic) in my 2002 *Genre* article, "Desiring Natures: The American Adrenaline Narrative." At about the same time my article appeared, Jeffrey Mathes McCarthy similarly identified three representations of nature in a 2002 *Philosophy & Geog-*

raphy article about mountaineering literature, "A Theory of Place in North American Mountaineering." He returns to this topic in a 2008 *ISLE* article, "Why Climbing Matters," and similarly identifies "conquest, caretaking, and connection" as the three representations of nature (160). While we characterize these representations of nature in slightly different terms, which reflect important differences in how we understand these desires, our arguments share an identification of two objectifying representations of nature (conquering/patriarchal, caretaking/spiritual) and one representation that emphasizes mutuality (connecting/erotic). As we are discussing the same desire, in this book I have adopted McCarthy's "conquering" term for what I labeled patriarchal desire in my *Genre* article. McCarthy explains the objectifying natures of the conquest and caretaking categories as follows: "In the move from conquest to caretaking, the objectifying category has shifted from viewing nature as a commercial or imperial resource to viewing nature as what Odell calls 'a shrine' and what others cast in the reverent terms people reserve for museums" ("A Theory of Place," 185).

Additionally, while not outlined in exactly the same terms, Chaia Heller's *Ecology of Everyday Life: Rethinking the Desire for Nature* also inspires these desires. She outlines "five fingers of social desire," which include "sensuality, association, differentiation, development, and political opposition" (96). Other texts that map one or more versions of these desires include Carolyn Merchant's *Radical Ecology: The Search for a Livable World*, Susan Griffin's *The Eros of Everyday Life: Essays on Ecology, Gender and Society*, and Catrin Gersdorf's "Ecocritical Uses of the Erotic."

103. Purdy, *After Nature*, 7.
104. Barcott, "Cliffhangers," 65. For an overview of American mountaineering's cultural history, see the epilogue to Susan R. Schrepfer's *Nature's Altars* (231–42).
105. Twight, *Kiss or Kill*, 35.
106. Birrell, "Approaching Mt. Everest," 13.
107. Howkins, *K2: One Woman's Quest for the Summit*, 133.
108. Crouch, *Enduring Patagonia*, 51, 53.
109. Malusa, *Into Thick Air*, 269.
110. Malusa, 3.
111. Malusa, 4.
112. Anne C. McCarthy, "Reading the Red Bull Sublime," 547.
113. Malusa, *Into Thick Air*, 232.
114. Weiss, *Tide, Feather, Snow*, 55.
115. Nelson, *The Island Within*, 7.
116. Weiss, *Tide, Feather, Snow*, 163–64.
117. Fredston, *Rowing to Latitude*, 45.
118. Weiss, *Tide, Feather, Snow*, 108.
119. Ross, *Scraping Heaven*, 120.
120. Ross, 135.
121. Kocour, *Facing the Extreme*, 5.
122. Weiss, *Tide, Feather, Snow*, 163. See Lynn Hill's *Climbing Free* for a description of her climb.
123. Vivanco, "Work of Environmentalism," 8.
124. Vivanco, 9.
125. Lianos and Douglas, "Dangerization and the End of Deviance," 262.
126. Vivanco, "Work of Environmentalism," 9.
127. Else, "Slavoj Žižek: Wake up and Smell the Apocalypse," 28.

128. Dorceta E. Taylor, "Highlights: The State of Diversity," 1.

129. Ker Than reports that Philip Henderson, who is a member of the Pioneer Climbing Expedition team, was part of a National Geographic/The North Face 2012 Everest expedition, but illness prevented his summit attempt. Elliot Boston has had the Seven Summits in his sights since at least 2001. According to a 2001 *Los Angeles Times* article by Joe Mozingo, Boston was originally scheduled to climb Everest in March 2003. Renne Gardner's "High Goals" and Bruce Barcott's "Go Tell It on the Mountain" also covered Boston's Everest goal. (Gardner's article is no longer available. *OC Metro* closed in 2014, and the associated website where her article appeared has been discontinued.) Boston is also a member of the Pioneer Climbing Expedition team. The expedition's website (http://www.pioneerclimbing.com) was last updated in 2009 and is now no longer available. Their Facebook page, however, is still active (https://www.facebook.com/Pioneer-Climbing-Expedition-Inc-194065770623395). Stephen Shobe is the director of Pioneer Climbing Expedition and was also a member of the Expedition Denali team.

130. Potter and Adkins, *American Ascent*.

131. These include books by Tom Whittaker (with Johnny Dodd), who was the first disabled man to climb Everest, and Erik Weihenmayer, who was the first blind man to summit. Interestingly, Weihenmayer's book jacket classifies his book under "Inspiration/Adventure." New Zealander Mark Inglis, who lost both legs below the knee to frostbite, has published four books about his adventures, including one about his experience climbing Everest, *Legs on Everest* (2006).

132. Wheeler, "Don't Climb Every Mountain," 556, 554. I return to Wheeler's argument in the final chapter.

133. Mills, *Adventure Gap*, 57.

134. Mat Johnson, *Pym*, 39.

135. Mat Johnson, 115.

136. Schulz, *Black Hiker with Blair Underwood*.

137. For a discussion of how outdoor marketing and advertising promotes the "adventure gap," see Derek Christopher Martin's "Apartheid in the Great Outdoors: American Advertising and the Reproduction of a Racialized Outdoor Leisure Identity." In this article, Martin argues "the position that there exists a stereotyped leisure identity that is associated with wildland leisure activities that results in fewer Black Americans participating in outdoor recreation" (514). Several critics explore mountaineering's colonial and postcolonial implications. See, for example, Peter L. Bayers's *Imperial Ascent: Mountaineering, Masculinity, and Empire* and Reuben Ellis's *Vertical Margins: Mountaineering and the Landscapes of Neoimperialism*. Dianne D. Glave's *Rooted in the Earth: Reclaiming the African American Environmental Heritage* also recovers black participation in the outdoors.

138. Mills's *Adventure Gap* includes a chapter devoted to Danenberg. For a fuller discussion of Danenberg, see chapter 4 herein, "Erotic Natures."

139. Haile (@RahawaHaile), "And then you sell a book about it."

140. Crane, "Adventurer & Activist Cason Crane."

141. Wheeler, "Don't Climb Every Mountain," 555.

142. Lynn Hill, *Climbing Free*, 125.

143. Howkins, *K2: One Woman's Quest for the Summit*, ii–iii.

144. Berman, *Going Vertical*, 193.

145. LaGrone, "Slogans That Sell the Service."

146. Gilbert, *Last American Man*, 125.

147. Trombold, "High and Low in the Himalayas," 90.
148. Trombold, 91.
149. Trombold, 100.
150. Dufresne, "On the Road to Trincomalee," 120.
151. Dufresne, 115.
152. Jeffrey Mathes McCarthy, "A Theory of Place," 179.
153. Krakauer, *Into the Wild*, 182.
154. Shepard, *Nature and Madness*, 11.
155. Shepard, 119; ellipsis in original.
156. Jacobs, *Death and Life of Great American Cities*, 445.
157. Ackerman, *Deep Play*, 104, 107.
158. Beck, *Risk Society*, 183; emphasis in original.
159. Greshko, "Amphibian 'Apocalypse.'"
160. Williams, "The Erotic Landscape," 30.
161. *Oxford English Dictionary Online*, s.v. "Anthropocene (*n.* and *adj.*)," accessed December 20, 2015, https://www.oed.com.ezproxy.stockton.edu/view/Entry/398463.
162. Purdy, *After Nature*, 237.

CHAPTER 2. CONQUERING NATURES

1. Krakauer, *Into Thin Air*, 3. Stephen Slemon also notes Krakauer's imperial gesture in this passage from *Into Thin Air* in "Climbing Mount Everest," 17.
2. Krakauer, *Into Thin Air*, 4.
3. Krakauer, xv–xviii.
4. Bayers, *Imperial Ascent*, 129.
5. Bayers, 128.
6. Krakauer, *Into Thin Air*, 4.
7. For a discussion of Krakauer's cognitive dissonance, see Burke and Sparkes, "Cognitive Dissonance."
8. Connell, *Masculinities*, 37.
9. Wheaton, "'New Lads,'" 135.
10. Humberstone, "'Outdoor Industry,'" 29. For additional discussion of the concept of hegemonic masculinity, see Connell and Messerschmidt's "Hegemonic Masculinity: Rethinking the Concept," which offers a "comprehensive reexamination of the ['contested'] concept" (830).
11. Connell, "An Iron Man," 93.
12. Ford and Brown, *Surfing and Social Theory*, 107.
13. Frohlick, "'That Playfulness,'" 180.
14. Kusz, "Extreme America," 199.
15. Kusz, 203.
16. Kusz, 204.
17. Coffey, *Where the Mountain*, 81.
18. Gurian, "When Feminism Goes Too Far."
19. Chisholm, "Climbing Like a Girl," 20.
20. Chisholm, 33, 35.
21. Gurian, "When Feminism Goes Too Far."
22. Laing and Crouch, "Myth, Adventure and Fantasy at the Frontier," 137.
23. Roberts, *Almost Somewhere*, 63, 68, 140.

24. I pick up this discussion about the connection between authenticity or pure "realness" as contrasted against commercial fakery in chapter 3 where I discuss how Cindy Ross contrasts her family adventures with a Disney vacation.

25. Kollin, "Survival, Alaska Style," 149.

26. Krakauer, *Into Thin Air*, 193. To his credit, Krakauer lists the Sherpas included in each expedition on Everest in 1996 and addresses various class issues pertaining to Sherpa guides at several points throughout *Into Thin Air*. See especially the following pages: 55–58, which explain the financial impact the climbing community has had on the Sherpa economy; 68–69, which address expeditions' exploitation of Sherpa labor; and 96, 114, and 122, which give insight into the vital and often invisible labor provided by Sherpas.

For a more detailed, anthropological account of the evolving relationship between Sherpas and mountaineers, see Sherry B. Ortner's *Life and Death on Mount Everest*. An earlier version of Ortner's research, "Thick Resistance," appeared in *Representations*. For a critique of Ortner's argument, see Susan Frohlick's "The 'Hypermasculine' Landscape of High-Altitude Mountaineering." The essay identifies two problems with Ortner's analysis and argues that, "for Ortner, masculinity becomes an unproblematic site for theorizing the power differences between sahibs and Sherpas" (85). Recently, HBO's *Real Sports with Bryant Gumbel* did a segment about the high price Sherpas pay so the (wealthy) elite have a chance to climb Everest ("Everest INC").

27. Krakauer, *Into Thin Air*, 150–56. Trombold analyzes Krakauer's description of Pittman in "High and Low in the Himalayas," 93–95. Jennifer Jordan, as I discuss later, does as well in *Savage Summit*.

28. Krakauer, *Into Thin Air*, 44.

29. Bowley, *No Way Down*, xx.

30. Bowley, 146.

31. Ten thousand dollars was the 1992 Nepalese price according to Krakauer in *Into Thin Air* (26). He also notes an additional $1,200 was also required by each individual climber (26).

32. Balf, *Last River*, 202. See the chapter "Sera Monastery, near Lhasa, November, 3, 1998" in *Last River*, especially pages 249–56, for Balf's critique of the increasingly corporate National Geographic Society and its "rapidly expanded for-profit division" (250).

33. Lynn Hill, *Climbing Free*, 67.

34. Krakauer, *Into Thin Air*, 23.

35. Monahan, "Ambient Dominion."

36. Mortimer, Kemple, and Rosen, *Alone on the Wall*, 02:09–02:52. Honnold, with David Roberts, wrote a book with the same title, *Alone on the Wall*.

37. Mortimer, Kemple, and Rosen, 03:05.

38. Mortimer, Kemple, and Rosen, 20:43–21:05.

39. Mortimer, Kemple, and Rosen, 09:51–10:23.

40. Chin and Vasarhelyi, *Free Solo*, 24:53–25:40.

41. Chin and Vasarhelyi, 27:50–29:39.

42. "Naked and Afraid" (web page), Discovery Channel.

43. Trombold, "High and Low in the Himalayas," 92. For a discussion of "the agonistic relation between discourses of purity and discourses of technology in…mountaineering texts," see Jon Gordon's "Means and Motives" (2).

44. Crouch, *Enduring Patagonia*, 209.
45. Crouch, 46.
46. For a more sustained, systematic reading of Crouch's *Enduring Patagonia*, see Nouzeilles's "Touching the Real," 203–8.
47. Jordan, *Savage Summit*, xi–xii.
48. Lynn Hill, *Climbing Free*, 136.
49. Lynn Hill, 138.
50. Arnesen and Bancroft, *No Horizon Is So Far*, 41.
51. Arnesen and Bancroft, 42.
52. Arnesen and Bancroft, 42.
53. Arnesen and Bancroft, 44.
54. Arnesen and Bancroft, 50.
55. Barry, Sharma and Najar, "Sherpas Move to Shut Everest in Labor Fight." For an account of the 2013 "Everest brawl" from a Sherpa perspective, see *Outside* magazine's article "The Everest Brawl: A Sherpa's Tale" (Adhikari).
56. Mozingo, "Proving He Can Climb the Highest Mountain."
57. Hornbein, "Foreword," xii.
58. Martin, "Apartheid in the Great Outdoors," 514.
59. McNiel, Harris, and Fondren, "Women and the Wild," 40.
60. McNiel, Harris, and Fondren, 40.
61. McNiel, Harris, and Fondren, 41.
62. Grothjan, "Backpacking Is My Respite."
63. Kwak-Hefferan, "Why Women Shouldn't Worry about Hiking Alone."
64. Lieu and Rennison, *Sexual Harassment and Sexual Assault*, 11.
65. Joyce, "Out Here, No One Can Hear You Scream."
66. McDougall, *Born to Run*, 54.
67. Jennifer Pharr Davis, *Becoming Odyssa*, 229.
68. Jennifer Pharr Davis, 61.
69. Saatchi, "Stop Making Movies about White Guys Doing Cool Shit."
70. Harris, *Mississippi Solo*, 14.
71. Harris, 14.
72. Harris, 7, 13.
73. Pham, *Catfish and Mandala*, 11.
74. Pham, 29.
75. Pham, 77.
76. Manos, *Ghetto Plainsman*, 230.
77. Least Heat-Moon, *River-Horse*, 439.
78. Least Heat-Moon, 130.
79. Least Heat-Moon, 15.
80. Least Heat-Moon, 42.
81. Least Heat-Moon, 28.
82. Least Heat-Moon, 462.
83. Birrell, "Approaching Mt. Everest," 5.
84. Bott, "New Heights in Climbing and Tourism," 23.
85. I should note that one of the "dudes" on Discovery's *Dude, You're Screwed* reality TV show is African American. There are also survivalists of color as part of the ensemble cast of *The Colony*, a simulated postapocalyptic show on Discovery. Survival programing with ensemble casts is sometimes more diverse in terms of both

race and gender. Nevertheless, risky adventure's protocols police the presence of others, just as they do white men, steering all bodies to conform to hegemonic masculine codes.

86. While Walker is American and his company, Matt Walker Full Engagement Living (http://mattwalkeradventure.com) is based in Mazama, Washington, the participants featured in the film *The Five Elements of Adventure* are all European males. The other four elements named in the film are: "uncertain outcome," "passion," "mindfulness," and "companionship."

87. Diana Ellis Hill, *Five Elements of Adventure*, 2:12–2:30.

88. Diana Ellis Hill, 5:02. On the touristic gaze, see Franklin and Crang, "Trouble with Tourism," 10.

89. Bott, "New Heights in Climbing and Tourism," 31.

90. Kane, *Running the Amazon*, 129; emphasis in original.

91. Birrell, "Approaching Mt. Everest," 7.

92. Krakauer, *Into the Wild*, 155–56.

93. Krakauer, 156.

94. Quoted in Ralston, *Between a Rock and a Hard Place*, 299.

95. Sandilands, "Wild Democracy," 138.

96. Griffin, *Woman and Nature*, 47–48.

97. Griffin, 49.

98. Rak, "Social Climbing on Annapurna," 114.

99. Rak, 114.

100. See Ortner, *Life and Death*, 185–216.

101. Rak, "Social Climbing on Annapurna," 127.

102. Rak, 127.

103. Krein refers to Bridgers as "her" ("Nature and Risk in Adventure Sports," 90) in his discussion of the passage. However, Bridgers's brief biography in *To the Extreme*, in which his "Out of the Gene Pool and into the Food Chain" appears, refers to people "half his age" (179) and reviews of his book also identify him as male.

104. Bridgers, "Out of the Gene Pool," 186.

105. Purdy, *After Nature*, 38.

106. Purdy, 40.

107. Krein, "Nature and Risk in Adventure Sports," 90.

108. Bridgers, "Out of the Gene Pool," 187.

109. Krein, "Nature and Risk in Adventure Sports," 90.

110. Krein, 90.

111. Wagner, "A Lesson to Be Learned," 499.

112. Crouch, *Enduring Patagonia*, 133.

113. Crouch, 159.

114. Crouch, 213.

115. Crouch, 20.

116. Crouch, 80.

117. Kane, *Running the Amazon*, 114; emphasis in original.

118. Fredston, *Rowing to Latitude*, 250.

119. Segal, *Theorizing about Myth*, 145.

120. Crouch, *Enduring Patagonia*, 6.

121. Kocour, *Facing the Extreme*, 109.

122. Howkins, *K2: One Woman's Quest for the Summit*, 69–70.

123. For a representative reading of Griffin's essentialism, see, for example, Carol Stabile's essay, "'A Garden Inclosed Is My Sister': Ecofeminism and Eco-Valences."
124. Griffin, *Woman and Nature*, 49.
125. Cuomo, *Feminism and Ecological Communities*, 120.
126. Manos, *Ghetto Plainsman*, 238.
127. Kocour, *Facing the Extreme*, 31.
128. Kocour, 110–11.
129. Quoted in Stoddart, "Constructing Masculinized Sportscapes," 114.
130. Increasingly, expeditions are engaging in efforts to offset or lower their ecological footprint and increase awareness about the climate crisis. Protect our Winters, for example, is a nonprofit organization "founded by professional snowboarder Jeremy Jones in 2007" that aims to transform "passionate outdoor people into effective climate advocates" ("About POW"). A 2011 white paper written by Kristine Schindler and Jennifer Kraus, *Estimating the Carbon Footprint of Mountaineering Expeditions*, addressed the topic of mountaineering's carbon footprint, but it has since been removed from the hosting website, Source Intelligence: http://www.sourceintelligence.com.
131. Anker, "Climate and Climbers."
132. Crouch, *Enduring Patagonia*, 200.
133. Arnesen and Bancroft, *No Horizon Is So Far*, 4.
134. Kocour, *Facing the Extreme*, 128.
135. Kocour, 137.
136. Beedie, "Legislators and Interpreters," 25.
137. Jeffrey Mathes McCarthy, "Why Climbing Matters," 162.
138. Kane, *Running the Amazon*, 77.
139. Harris, *Mississippi Solo*, 217.
140. Ralston, *Between a Rock and a Hard Place*, 95.
141. Kocour, *Facing the Extreme*, 123.
142. Kocour, 127.
143. Crouch, *Enduring Patagonia*, 134.
144. Rak, "Social Climbing on Annapurna," 112.
145. Weiss, *Tide, Feather, Snow*, 233.
146. Weiss, 270.
147. Weiss, 247.
148. Kocour, *Facing the Extreme*, 202.
149. Kocour, 238.
150. Kocour, 242.
151. Kocour, 234.
152. Kocour, 230.
153. Frohlick, "Negotiating the 'Global,'" 526.
154. Frohlick, 535.
155. Frohlick, 540.
156. Rak, "Social Climbing on Annapurna," 110.
157. Stoddart, "Constructing Masculinized Sportscapes," 108.
158. Rak, "Social Climbing on Annapurna," 111.
159. Simon, *North to the Night*, 311.
160. Kocour, *Facing the Extreme*, 264.
161. McCairen, *Canyon Solitude*, 199.

162. Coffey, *Where the Mountain*, 147.
163. Phillips, "Spaces of Adventure," 591.
164. Phillips, 591.
165. Hooks, *Feminism Is for Everybody*, 4.
166. *TV Guide* published an account of the dispute between Lundin and the Discovery Channel, "Special Report: The Dangerous Side of Survival TV" (Peisner). Dave Canterbury, the other original cast member, was replaced in season 3 by Joseph Teti. I discuss this television show in greater detail in chapter 3.
167. Pagh, "An Indescribable Sea," 1.
168. Ford and Brown, *Surfing and Social Theory*, 88.
169. Arlene Blum, *Breaking Trail*, 230.
170. Roberts, *Almost Somewhere*, 9.
171. Gregory, "Epilogue," 292.
172. Stoddart, "Constructing Masculinized Sportscapes," 111.
173. Stoddart, 120.
174. McCairen, *Canyon Solitude*, 116.
175. Arnesen and Bancroft, *No Horizon Is So Far*, 135.
176. Arnesen and Bancroft, 102.
177. McClure, *Pearl in the Storm*, 28.
178. Jordan, *Savage Summit*, 1.
179. Arlene Blum, *Breaking Trail*, 51.
180. Kocour, *Facing the Extreme*, 122.
181. Jordan, *Savage Summit*, 261.
182. Jordan, 286.
183. Arlene Blum, *Breaking Trail*, 258–59.
184. Arlene Blum, 259.
185. Howkins, *K2: One Woman's Quest for the Summit*, 185.
186. Quoted in Coffey, *Where the Mountain*, 11.
187. Coffey, 11.
188. Arnesen and Bancroft, *No Horizon Is So Far*, 170.
189. Arlene Blum, *Breaking Trail*, 38.
190. Fredston, *Rowing to Latitude*, 134.
191. McClure, *Pearl in the Storm*, 199.
192. Jordan, *Savage Summit*, 207; emphasis in original.
193. Howkins, *K2: One Woman's Quest for the Summit*, 208.
194. Arlene Blum, *Breaking Trail*, 46.
195. Arlene Blum, 47.
196. Arnesen and Bancroft, *No Horizon Is So Far*, 35.
197. Jordan, *Savage Summit*, 3.
198. Arnesen and Bancroft, *No Horizon Is So Far*, 14.
199. Arnesen and Bancroft, 35.
200. Arlene Blum, *Breaking Trail*, 240.
201. Nichols, *Sea Change*, 183.
202. Nichols, 183.
203. Kocour, *Facing the Extreme*, 230.
204. Allison, *Beyond the Limits*, 7.
205. Krakauer, *Into Thin Air*, 23.
206. Ultra-endurance sports, especially in running and swimming, have similar hang-ups about assistance.

207. Bowley, *No Way Down*, 44.
208. Crouch, *Enduring Patagonia*, 176.
209. Coffey, *Where the Mountain*, 70.
210. Lynn Hill, *Climbing Free*, 269.
211. Howkins, *K2: One Woman's Quest for the Summit*, 239.
212. Arnesen and Bancroft, *No Horizon Is So Far*, 17.
213. Arnesen and Bancroft, 20.
214. Greenfield, *Dude Making a Difference*, 15.
215. Greenfield, 23, 271.
216. Ilgunas, *Trespassing across America*, 261.
217. Coffey, *Where the Mountain*, 77.
218. Aebi, *Maiden Voyage*, 138.
219. Greenfield, *Dude Making a Difference*, 11–14.
220. Greenfield, 12.
221. Gilbert, *Last American Man*, 58.
222. Coffey, *Where the Mountain*, 83–84.
223. Gilbert, *Last American Man*, 124.
224. Crouch, *Enduring Patagonia*, 210.
225. Weiss, *Tide, Feather, Snow*, 270.
226. Weiss, 270.

CHAPTER 3. SPIRITUAL NATURES

1. Krakauer, *Into Thin Air*, 174.
2. Krakauer, xvii.
3. Coffey, *Explorers of the Infinite*, xiv.
4. Bron Taylor, *Dark Green Religion*, ix.
5. Bron Taylor, ix.
6. Dorceta E. Taylor, *Rise of the American Conservation Movement*, 24.
7. Bron Taylor, *Dark Green Religion*, 9.
8. Costigan, Rose, and Tinney, "The Role of Spirituality," 41.
9. Jacobs, *Death and Life of Great American Cities*, 445.
10. Crouch, *Enduring Patagonia*, 6.
11. Allison, *Beyond the Limits*, 6.
12. Allison, 7. Allison is not the only elite female athlete to discuss an abusive relationship. Heidi Howkins, for example, also mentions her abusive marriage (*K2: One Woman's Quest for the Summit*, 27). I discuss Blair Braverman's abusive boyfriend in chapter 4.
13. Lynn Hill, *Climbing Free*, 269–70.
14. Hahn, *Spirited Waters*, 13.
15. Hahn, 13.
16. Hahn, 59; ellipsis in original.
17. Hahn, 59.
18. Arnesen and Bancroft, *No Horizon Is So Far*, 3.
19. In "Backpacking with the Saints: The Risk-Taking Character of Wilderness Reading," Belden C. Lane offers a different approach to wilderness and spirituality, focusing on how wild locations impact the understanding of Christian literature. Lane explores "wilderness reading," or the "spiritual practice" that is "generally undertaken in solitude in a place that puts the reader on edge, cut off from the

safe assurances of the familiar" (24). Lane "use[s] wilderness reading as a way of talking about the risk and relinquishment to which we expose ourselves in reading classic texts anywhere" (23). He explains, "Spiritual reading is always a dangerous exercise, threatening to overthrow our previous ways of looking at the world. Sometimes the *place* of the reading adds even more to the vulnerability we encounter through the text itself" (23; emphasis in original).

20. Kocour, *Facing the Extreme*, 8.
21. Kocour, 205.
22. Kocour, 228.
23. Kocour, 4.
24. Ralston, *Between a Rock and a Hard Place*, 150; emphasis in original.
25. Howkins, *K2: One Woman's Quest for the Summit*, 135.
26. Fredston, *Rowing to Latitude*, 28.
27. Arnesen and Bancroft, *No Horizon Is So Far*, 24.
28. Ostman, *Second Wind*, 62.
29. Ostman, 66.
30. Ostman, 246.
31. Ostman, 285.
32. Kocour, *Facing the Extreme*, 269.
33. Kocour, 235.
34. Kocour, 269.
35. McClure, *Pearl in the Storm*, 286.
36. McCairen, *Canyon Solitude*, 116.
37. McClure, *Pearl in the Storm*, 286.
38. Rak, "Social Climbing on Annapurna," 120.
39. Simon, *North to the Night*, 9.
40. Fredston, *Rowing to Latitude*, xi.
41. "Woman's Solo Hiking Trip."
42. McClure, *Pearl in the Storm*, 265.
43. McClure, 265–66.
44. Callahan, *Adrift*, 236.
45. Nichols, *Sea Change*, 201.
46. Nichols, 183.
47. Nichols, 183.
48. Crouch, *Enduring Patagonia*, 50.
49. O'Connor, "A Good Man Is Hard to Find," 23.
50. Crouch, *Enduring Patagonia*, 50.
51. Simon, *North to the Night*, 125.
52. Ross, *Scraping Heaven*, 242.
53. McCairen, *Canyon Solitude*, 9–10.
54. McCairen, 56.
55. McCairen, 12, 22–23.
56. Manos, *Ghetto Plainsman*, 442.
57. See Stephen Heath's "Translator's Note" in Barthes's *Image, Music, Text*, 9. Heath explains that Barthes's use of the term has no direct translation in English. He specifically notes that *jouissance* refers to "a radically violent pleasure…which shatters-dissipates-loses…[the] ego" (9).
58. Pham, *Catfish and Mandala*, 110.
59. Pham, 33.

60. McCairen, *Canyon Solitude*, 5, 6.
61. McCairen, 33–34.
62. McCairen, 246.
63. Allison, *Beyond the Limits*, 282; emphasis in original.
64. Krakauer, *Into Thin Air*, 30–31.
65. Krakauer, 352–53.
66. In "'No Anthems Playing in My Head,'" Gene McQuillan understands *Into Thin Air* as both a "tragedy" and as a "lampooning of the modern climbing scene" (63).
67. Kane, *Running the Amazon*, 111.
68. Birrell, "Approaching Mt. Everest," 15.
69. Birrell, 15.
70. Harris, *Mississippi Solo*, 248.
71. Harris, 243.
72. Abbey, *Voice Crying in the Wilderness*, 36.
73. Crouch, *Enduring Patagonia*, 158.
74. Crouch, 49–50.
75. Ross, *Scraping Heaven*, 242.
76. Simon, *North to the Night*, 10.
77. Simon, 20.
78. Bledsoe, *Ice Cave*, 102.
79. Schooler, *Walking Home*, 8.
80. Campbell, *Braving It*, xv.
81. Berman, *Going Vertical*, 9.
82. FitzGerald, *Ruthless River*, 154, 218.
83. Kocour, *Facing the Extreme*, 7.
84. Kocour, 1–2.
85. Gonzales, *Deep Survival*, 258.
86. Callahan, *Adrift*, 234.
87. Ross, *Scraping Heaven*, 323. Ross, an advocate for children's wilderness exploration, claims the outdoor classroom trumps the virtual one (73). Nevertheless, Ross admits adventure may be more spiritual without children (143).
88. Ross, 17.
89. Fredston, *Rowing to Latitude*, xi.
90. Baudrillard, *Simulacra and Simulation*, 12–14.
91. Nouzeilles, "Touching the Real," 198.
92. Nouzeilles, 198.
93. Krakauer, *Into the Wild*, 4.
94. Simon, *North to the Night*, 249.
95. Ross, *Scraping Heaven*, 150.
96. Stoddart, "Constructing Masculinized Sportscapes," 116.
97. Stoddart, 117.
98. Arnesen and Bancroft, *No Horizon Is So Far*, 20.
99. Callahan, *Adrift*, 54.
100. Bowley, *No Way Down*, 116.
101. Bron Taylor, *Dark Green Religion*, 3.
102. Bowley, *No Way Down*, 218.
103. Bron Taylor, *Dark Green Religion*, 10.
104. Bowley, *No Way Down*, 214.
105. Jennifer Pharr Davis, *Becoming Odyssa*, 68.

106. Jennifer Pharr Davis, 68.
107. Schultheis, *Bone Games*, 50–72.
108. Ross, *Scraping Heaven*, 242.
109. Bowley, *No Way Down*, 65.
110. Gilbert, *Last American Man*, 56.
111. Gilbert, 56.
112. Howkins, *K2: One Woman's Quest for the Summit*, 21.
113. Howkins, 21.
114. Simon, *North to the Night*, 318.
115. Simon, 318.
116. Sundeen, *Man Who Quit Money*, 49.
117. Sundeen, 27.
118. Harris, *Mississippi Solo*, 101.
119. Harris, 101.
120. Kocour, *Facing the Extreme*, 215.
121. Simon, *North to the Night*, 183.
122. Fredston, *Rowing to Latitude*, 93.
123. Simon, *North to the Night*, 184.
124. Callahan, *Adrift*, xvii.
125. Manos, *Ghetto Plainsman*, 410.
126. Manos, 419.
127. Schultheis, *Bone Games*, 178.
128. Simon, *North to the Night*, 324.
129. Simon, 324–25.
130. Bron Taylor, *Dark Green Religion*, 9.
131. Gilbert, *Last American Man*, 56.
132. Bron Taylor, 30.
133. Simon, *North to the Night*, 180.
134. Hahn, *Spirited Waters*, 26.
135. Simon, *North to the Night*, 324.
136. Simon, 324.
137. Hahn, *Spirited Waters*, 26.
138. Soholt, "Swamped," 39:28–32.
139. Terry and Hart, *White Shamans, Plastic Medicine Men*.
140. "About Cody Lundin."
141. See Krech, *Ecological Indian*.
142. Fredston, *Rowing to Latitude*, 113.
143. Coffey, *Explorers of the Infinite*, 5.
144. Coffey, *Where the Mountain*, 6–7.
145. Crouch, *Enduring Patagonia*, 6.
146. Hornbein, "Foreword," xiii.
147. Kull, *Solitude*, 276.
148. Kull, xii.
149. Kocour, *Facing the Extreme*, 234.
150. Crouch, *Enduring Patagonia*, 148.
151. Fredston, *Rowing to Latitude*, 171.
152. Schultheis, *Bone Games*, 144.
153. Simon, *North to the Night*, 6.
154. Crouch, *Enduring Patagonia*, 115.

155. Gilbert, *Last American Man*, 13.
156. Gilbert, 13.
157. Baym, "Melodramas of Beset Manhood," 130.
158. Bowley, *No Way Down*, 225.
159. Bowley, 65.
160. Rak, "Social Climbing on Annapurna," 113.
161. Bowley, *No Way Down*, 43.
162. Dorceta E. Taylor, *Rise of the American Conservation Movement*, 26.
163. Wilderness Act of 1964, § 1131(c).
164. Anderson, "Reading Water," 77.
165. Allison, *Beyond the Limits*, 140. See Allison, 140–41; and Krakauer, *Into Thin Air*, 77–78.
166. Quoted in Krakauer, *Into Thin Air*, 372.
167. Krakauer, 373.
168. Krakauer, xviii.
169. Birrell, "Approaching Mt. Everest," 13.
170. Birrell, 14.
171. Jeffrey Mathes McCarthy, "Why Climbing Matters," 163.
172. Hornbein, "Foreword," xiv.
173. Coffey, *Where the Mountain*, 69.
174. Crouch, *Enduring Patagonia*, 213; emphasis in original.
175. Crouch, 214.
176. Crouch, 214; emphasis in original.
177. Ross, *Scraping Heaven*, 150.
178. Callahan, *Adrift*, 235.
179. Harris, *Mississippi Solo*, 178.
180. McCairen, *Canyon Solitude*, 5–6.
181. Heller, *Ecology of Everyday Life*, 115.
182. Fredston, *Rowing to Latitude*, xii.
183. Hahn, *Spirited Waters*, 209.

CHAPTER 4. EROTIC NATURES

1. Krakauer, *Into Thin Air*, 372.
2. Howkins, *K2: One Woman's Quest for the Summit*, 195–96.
3. *Oxford English Dictionary Online*, s.v. "soul (n.)," accessed April 20, 2019, https://www.oed.com/view/Entry/185083.
4. Humberstone, "Re-Creation and Connections," 388. Humberstone does not claim *all* adventure sports automatically fall into this category: "This article has proposed that particular forms of *ethical* nature-based sports may sow the seeds of environmental awareness which can reap a groundswell informing and constituting 'mass social movements', which as [Ulrich] Beck... argues, are the leading edge of a new politics in a new type of society" (389; emphasis in original).
5. Kull, *Solitude*, 47.
6. Atherton, "Philosophy Outdoors: First Person Physical," 44.
7. Gaard, "Ecofeminism and Wilderness," 6–7.
8. See also Laura Kipnis's essay, "(Male) Desire and (Female) Disgust: Reading *Hustler*," for a representative critique.
9. Williams, "The Erotic Landscape," 29.

NOTES TO CHAPTER FOUR

10. Gaard, "Ecofeminism and Wilderness," 13.
11. Kolodny, *Lay of the Land*, 160.
12. Kolodny, 160.
13. Much could be written on the relevance of French and Indigenous feminisms to ecofeminist revisions of desire. I only begin to highlight the rich connections between ecofeminist erotic desire, French feminism, and Indigenous cosmologies. See Barbara T. Gates's "A Root of Ecofeminism: *Ecoféminisme*" for a discussion of the indebtedness of U.S. ecofeminism to Françoise d'Eaubonne's work. Chris Cuomo's first chapter in *Feminism and Ecological Communities*, "The Ecofeminist Project," outlines more broadly the "collection of efforts and positions" that has helped form ecofeminism (22). See also the collection *Reweaving the World: The Emergence of Ecofeminism* edited by Irene Diamond and Gloria Feman Orenstein; and Catriona Sandilands's "Wild Democracy: Ecofeminism, Politics, and the Desire Beyond."
14. Gelfand, "Feminist Criticism, French," 46.
15. Gelfand, 48.
16. Nimmo, "From Over the Horizon," 26.
17. Heller, *Ecology of Everyday Life*, 83.
18. Vance, "Ecofeminism and Wilderness," 66.
19. Vance, 66.
20. Vance, 66–68.
21. Vance, 67.
22. Morton, *Ecology without Nature*, 19–20.
23. Alaimo, *Bodily Natures*, 2.
24. Gaard, "Ecofeminism and Wilderness," 13.
25. Gaard, 14.
26. Alaimo, "Trans-Corporeality," 437.
27. Alaimo, "Cyborg," 133.
28. Haraway, *Companion Species Manifesto*, 4. For a discussion of "the *non-reciprocal* emotional attachment that humans feel for many animals," see June Dwyer's "A Non-companion Species Manifesto: Humans, Wild Animals, and 'The Pain of Anthropomorphism'" (74; emphasis in original).
29. Ackerman, *Deep Play*, 87.
30. Krein, "Nature and Risk in Adventure Sports," 91.
31. Abram, *Spell of the Sensuous*, 57.
32. Jeffrey Mathes McCarthy, "Why Climbing Matters," 172.
33. Jeffrey Mathes McCarthy, 170.
34. Field, "Is the Body Essential for Ecofeminism?," 39. See also Colleen MackCanty's "Third-Wave Feminism and the Need to Reweave the Nature/Culture Duality," which examines embodiment in third-wave feminism.
35. Stark, *Last Breath*, 8.
36. Gaard, "Ecofeminism and Wilderness," 24.
37. Haraway, *Companion Species Manifesto*, 7, 8. For an overview of the term "natureculture," see Nicholas Malone and Kathryn Ovenden's "Natureculture."
38. McCairen, *Canyon Solitude*, 52.
39. McCairen, 51–52.
40. McCairen, 244.
41. Byl, *Dirt Work*, 12.
42. Leopold, *Sand County Almanac*, 130.

43. Byl, *Dirt Work*, 13.
44. Leopold, *Sand County Almanac*, 132.
45. Byl, *Dirt Work*, 12.
46. Heller, *Ecology of Everyday Life*, 95. See Connie Bullis's essay "Retalking Environmental Discourses from a Feminist Perspective: The Radical Potential of Ecofeminism" for a discussion of ecofeminism's revolutionary potential. This essay explains how ecofeminism offers an alternative reimagining, rather than reproducing the Western "modernist, patriarchal paradigm" (123). Gaard also addresses ecofeminism's radical potential in how it redefines "Western culture's relationship with wilderness": "The radical potential for initiating a transformation of Western culture's relationship with wilderness lies in the master identity embracing its animal nature as well. Such a recognition would reclaim a crucial part of the Self, which has been projected onto the Other, a necessary step toward eliminating the oppression of all Others" ("Ecofeminisim and Wilderness" 24).
47. McCairen, *Canyon Solitude*, 51.
48. Fern, *Nature, God and Humanity*, 109; emphasis in original.
49. Cohen, "Comment," 33.
50. Brymer and Gray, "Dancing with Nature," 138; emphasis in original.
51. Brymer and Gray, 138.
52. Francis, *Planetwalker*, 79.
53. Francis, 81–82.
54. Harris, *Mississippi Solo*, 26.
55. Harris, 36; emphasis in original.
56. Harris, 36.
57. Harris, 36–37.
58. Harris, 37.
59. Leopold, *Sand County Almanac*, 132.
60. Fredston, *Rowing to Latitude*, 242.
61. Alaimo, *Bodily Natures*, 2.
62. Morton, "Guest Column," 275–76.
63. Sandilands, "Queer Ecology," 169.
64. Alaimo, *Bodily Natures*, 2.
65. Alaimo, 5.
66. Jeffrey Mathes McCarthy, "Why Climbing Matters," 163.
67. Jeffrey Mathes McCarthy, 163.
68. Fredston, *Rowing to Latitude*, 21.
69. Jeffrey Mathes McCarthy, "A Theory of Place," 186.
70. Jeffrey Mathes McCarthy, 187.
71. De Gennaro, "Multispecies Stories, Subaltern Futures," 319. For a discussion of entanglement in recent ecocriticism, see 318–21.
72. De Gennaro, 319.
73. Storey, *I Promise Not to Suffer*, 166.
74. As far as I know, no specific term designates assigning plant qualities to a human, as Storey does in this passage by comparing herself to trees. "Chremamorphism" refers to assigning humans the characteristics of inanimate objects, as Storey does by comparing herself to mountains, water, and the sky.
75. See Gaard, "Ecofeminism and Wilderness," 14–15.
76. Gaard, 17.

77. Humberstone, "Re-Creation and Connections," 387.
78. Pagh, "An Indescribable Sea," 1, 11.
79. Rak, "Social Climbing on Annapurna," 136.
80. Rak, 133.
81. Humberstone, "Re-Creation and Connections," 387–88.
82. Else, "Slavoj Žižek," 28.
83. Gaard, "Ecofeminism and Wilderness," 14.
84. Harris, *Mississippi Solo*, 36.
85. Alaimo, *Bodily Natures*, 17.
86. Kocour, *Facing the Extreme*, 55; ellipsis in original.
87. Kane, *Running the Amazon*, 70; emphasis in original.
88. Callahan, *Adrift*, xii.
89. Callahan, 236–37.
90. Plumwood, *Feminism and the Mastery of Nature*, 164.
91. Krein, "Nature and Risk in Adventure Sports," 89.
92. Roberts, *Almost Somewhere*, 18.
93. Wilderness Act of 1964, § 1131(c).
94. Francis, *Planetwalker*, 87.
95. Vance, "Ecofeminism and Wilderness," 61.
96. Francis, *Planetwalker*, 75, 87.
97. Nash, *Wilderness and the American Mind*, 5.
98. Sundeen, *Man Who Quit Money*, 128.
99. The phrase "known in paddling circles as the 'Everest of rivers'" appears on the 2000 hardcover edition's inside left flap.
100. Balf, *Last River*, 90.
101. Simon, *North to the Night*, 323.
102. Simon, 324.
103. Alaimo, *Bodily Natures*, 2.
104. Kull, *Solitude*, 47.
105. Harris, *Mississippi Solo*, 37; Kull, *Solitude*, 47.
106. Simpson, *Accidental Explorer*, 5.
107. Simpson, 11–12.
108. Simpson, 34.
109. Simpson, 208.
110. Brymer, "Extreme Sports as a Facilitator," 47.
111. Brymer, 48.
112. Brymer and Gray, "Developing an Intimate 'Relationship,'" 371.
113. Roberts, *Almost Somewhere*, 16.
114. Roberts, 20.
115. Roberts, 161.
116. Roberts, viii.
117. Roberts, 149.
118. Brymer and Gray, "Developing an Intimate 'Relationship,'" 371.
119. Roberts, *Almost Somewhere*, 161.
120. Roberts, 251; emphasis in original.
121. Roberts, 64.
122. Roberts, 64.
123. Vance, "Ecofeminism and Wilderness," 68.

124. Plumwood, *Feminism and the Mastery of Nature*, 163.
125. Sandilands, "Wild Democracy," 147.
126. Sandilands, 148; emphasis in original.
127. Sandilands, 147.
128. Byl, *Dirt Work*, 131–32.
129. Byl, 66.
130. Irvine, *Trespass*, 342–43.
131. Irvine, 343.
132. Irvine, 345.
133. Raskin, "Calls of the Wild on the Page and Screen," 198.
134. Sandilands, "Wild Democracy," 135.
135. Sandilands, 145.
136. Byl, *Dirt Work*, 92.
137. Byl, 132.
138. Austin, *Stories from the Country of Lost Borders*, 40.
139. Austin, 40.
140. Vance, "Ecofeminism and Wilderness," 64.
141. Mills, *Adventure Gap*, 119.
142. Quoted in Mills, 119–20.
143. Harris, *Mississippi Solo*, 221.
144. Harris, 221.
145. Whitman, *Leaves of Grass*, line 1326.
146. Harris, *Mississippi Solo*, 15.
147. Cronon, "Trouble with Wilderness," 10.
148. Harris, *Mississippi Solo*, 67.
149. Harris, 67.
150. Krakauer, *Into Thin Air*, 103–4.
151. Krakauer, 107.
152. Carman, "Grizzly Love," 518.
153. Jans, *Grizzly Maze*, 41.
154. Jans, 176.
155. Jans, 177.
156. Jans's *The Grizzly Maze* largely refutes Werner Herzog's portrayal of Treadwell in the film *Grizzly Man* (2005), which Jans claims is "a product of artful editing and selection" (xiii). Stefan Mattessich argues that Treadwell's story devolves into a "farce" ("Anguished Self-Subjection," 53).
157. Jans, *Grizzly Maze*, 42.
158. Carman, "Grizzly Love," 510.
159. Hediger, "Timothy Treadwell's Grizzly Love," 83.
160. Dwyer, "Non-Companion Species Manifesto," 75.
161. Dwyer, 83.
162. Dwyer, 82.
163. Hediger, "Timothy Treadwell's Grizzly Love," 84.
164. See Stefan Mattessich's "Anguished Self-Subjection."
165. Soholt, "Swamped," 39:28–32.
166. Hediger, "Timothy Treadwell's Grizzly Love," 87.
167. Dougherty, "Aesthetic and Ethical Issues," 94.
168. Dougherty, 96; emphasis in original.

169. See Chagani, "Can the Postcolonial Animal Speak?," 620. Walter Putnam similarly asks, "Can the Subaltern Growl?" (see 124), and Timothy Mitchell questions, "Can the Mosquito Speak?"
170. De Gennaro, "Multispecies Stories, Subaltern Futures," 316. See also Kirksey, Schuetze, and Helmreich, "Introduction: Tactics of Multispecies Ethnography."
171. Armstrong, "Postcolonial Animal," 413.
172. Chagani, "Can the Postcolonial Animal Speak?," 634.
173. De Gennaro, "Multispecies Stories, Subaltern Futures," 316.
174. Nimmo, "From Over the Horizon," 25.
175. Park, "Who Are These People?," 4.
176. Park, 7.
177. Park, 8.
178. Tam, Lee, and Chao, "Saving Mr. Nature," 519.
179. Humberstone, "Re-Creation and Connections," 384.
180. Nimmo, "From Over the Horizon," 25.
181. Lord, *Rock, Water, Wild*, 129; emphasis in original.
182. Nimmo, "From Over the Horizon," 15.
183. Roberts, *Almost Somewhere*, 214.
184. Nichols, *Sea Change*, 40.
185. Callahan, *Adrift*, 20.
186. Tam, Lee, and Chao, "Saving Mr. Nature," 514.
187. McCairen, *Canyon Solitude*, 85.
188. Nimmo, "From Over the Horizon," 26.
189. Nimmo, 33.
190. Jennifer Pharr Davis, *Becoming Odyssa*, 286; emphasis in original.
191. Welling, "On the 'Inexplicable Magic of Cinema,'" 82.
192. Welling, 82, 91; emphasis in original.
193. Tam, Lee, and Chao, "Saving Mr. Nature," 515.
194. Callahan, *Adrift*, 70.
195. Callahan, 126.
196. Brymer and Gray, "Developing an Intimate 'Relationship,'" 363.
197. Callahan, *Adrift*, 126.
198. Simon, *North to the Night*, 282.
199. Coffey, *Explorers of the Infinite*, 130.
200. Nimmo, "From Over the Horizon," 18.
201. Hahn, *Spirited Waters*, 209.
202. Haraway, *Companion Species Manifesto*, 35–36.
203. Chagani, "Can the Postcolonial Animal Speak?," 631.
204. Heller, *Ecology of Everyday Life*, 83.
205. Fredston, *Rowing to Latitude*, xii.
206. De Gennaro, "Multispecies Stories, Subaltern Futures," 315; van Dooren and Rose, "Storied-Places in a Multispecies City," 2.
207. Harris, *Mississippi Solo*, 250.
208. Ross, *Scraping Heaven*, 204.
209. Fredston, *Rowing to Latitude*, 104.
210. Hahn, *Spirited Waters*, 207.
211. Jans, *Grizzly Maze*, 22.
212. Jans, xii.
213. Jans, 153.

214. Jans, 153.
215. Jans, 201.
216. Hediger, "Timothy Treadwell's Grizzly Love," 94.
217. Vanreusel, "From Bambi to Rambo," 273.
218. Jans, *Grizzly Maze*, 57.
219. Hediger, "Timothy Treadwell's Grizzly Love," 96.
220. Carman, "Grizzly Love," 510.
221. Carman, 511.
222. Nimmo, "From Over the Horizon," 22.
223. Brymer and Gray, "Developing an Intimate 'Relationship,'" 363.
224. Abram, *Spell of the Sensuous*, 57; emphasis in original.
225. Lord, *Rock, Water, Wild*, 162.
226. Fredston, *Rowing to Latitude*, 92.
227. Fredston, 86.
228. Fredston, 87.
229. Hahn, *Spirited Waters*, 196.
230. Schultheis, *Bone Games*, 9–10.
231. Atherton, "Philosophy Outdoors: First Person Physical," 44.
232. Park, "Who Are These People?," 11.
233. Vance, "Ecofeminism and Wilderness," 63.
234. Ryan, *Theorizing Outdoor Recreation and Ecology*, 2.
235. Fredston, *Rowing to Latitude*, 175.
236. Fredston, 182.
237. Fredston, 186.
238. Humberstone, "Re-Creation and Connections," 385.
239. Fredston, *Rowing to Latitude*, 186.
240. Nash, *Wilderness and the American Mind*, 5.
241. Callahan, *Adrift*, 146.
242. Callahan, 193.
243. McCairen, *Canyon Solitude*, 51.
244. Storey, *I Promise Not to Suffer*, 179.
245. Storey, 200.
246. Storey, 179.
247. Storey, 210.
248. Balf, *Last River*, 196.
249. Balf, 52.
250. Malone and Ovenden, "Natureculture," 848.
251. Krein, "Nature and Risk in Adventure Sports," 91.

CHAPTER 5. RISKY NATURES

1. Krakauer, *Into the Wild*, 182.
2. Mills, *Adventure Gap*, 50.
3. Brymer, "Risk Taking," 220.
4. See Steve Olivier's "Moral Dilemmas of Participation" for a discussion of the ethics of risk in contemporary culture.
5. Manning, "High Risk Narratives," 285.
6. Manning, 297.
7. Heise, *Sense of Place*, 13.

NOTES TO CHAPTER FIVE

8. Heise, 142; Frederick Buell, *From Apocalypse to Way of Life*, 190.
9. Lianos and Douglas, "Dangerization and the End of Deviance," 262.
10. Jacobs, *Death and Life of Great American Cities*, 445.
11. Vanreusel, "From Bambi to Rambo," 274.
12. Beck, *Risk Society*, 78-79; emphasis in original.
13. Beck, 20; emphasis in original.
14. Beck, 22.
15. Beck, 183; emphasis in original.
16. Wallace, *Risk Criticism*, 11.
17. Zinn, "Living in the Anthropocene," 388.
18. Kuipers, *Operation Bite Back*, 27, 262.
19. Potter, *Green Is the New Red*, 53.
20. Palmer, "Death, Danger and the Selling of Risk," 58; emphasis in original.
21. Fredston, *Snowstruck*, 165.
22. Vance, "Ecofeminism and Wilderness," 63.
23. Bott, "New Heights in Climbing and Tourism," 22.
24. Kocour, *Facing the Extreme*, 3. See also John H. Kerr and Susan Houge Mackenzie's "Multiple Motives for Participating in Adventure Sports."
25. Ewert et al., "Beyond 'Because It's There,'" 92-93.
26. Ewert et al., 93-94.
27. Ewert et al., 107.
28. Ewert et al., 92.
29. Giulianotti, "Risk and Sport," 541.
30. Giulianotti, 545.
31. Giulianotti, 544.
32. Brymer and Gray, "Developing an Intimate 'Relationship,'" 366.
33. Brymer, "Risk Taking," 219.
34. Brymer, 222.
35. Crouch, *Enduring Patagonia*, 3.
36. Simon, *North to the Night*, 27.
37. Pinkney, *As Long As It Takes*, 59.
38. Pinkney, 125.
39. Brymer, "Risk Taking," 229.
40. Humberstone, "Adventurous Activities," 566.
41. Woodlief, *Bolt from the Blue*, 125.
42. McClure, *Pearl in the Storm*, 27.
43. McClure, 27.
44. Krakauer, *Into Thin Air*, 174.
45. Steph Davis, *Learning to Fly*, 13.
46. Steph Davis, 29.
47. Krein, "Nature and Risk in Adventure Sports," 80; emphasis in original.
48. Brymer, "Risk Taking," 233.
49. Storey, *I Promise Not to Suffer*, 164.
50. Giulianotti, "Risk and Sport," 544.
51. Kocour, *Facing the Extreme*, 5.
52. Kocour, 4, 5.
53. Berman, *Going Vertical*, 134.
54. Gonzales, *Deep Survival*, 49.
55. Gonzales, 82.

56. Berman, *Going Vertical*, 2–3.
57. Krein, "Nature and Risk in Adventure Sports," 87.
58. Berman, *Going Vertical*, 6.
59. Berman, 127.
60. See Diane Ackerman's 1999 book *Deep Play*.
61. Krein, "Nature and Risk in Adventure Sports," 91.
62. Jans, *Grizzly Maze*, 63.
63. Jans, 63.
64. Robinson, "Taking Risks," 121.
65. Robinson, 122.
66. Jans, *Grizzly Maze*, 63.
67. Jans, 152.
68. Jans, 168.
69. Medred, "Woman Who Died with 'Bear Guru' Was Duped."
70. "Amie Lynn Huguenard."
71. Booth, "Surfing," 104.
72. Booth, 104.
73. Berman, *Going Vertical*, 127.
74. Berman, 20.
75. Berman, 107.
76. Gonzales, *Deep Survival*, 225–26. On positive mental attitude, see 177–92.
77. Moser, "Communicating Climate Change," 31.
78. Nixon, *Slow Violence*, 2.
79. Berman, *Going Vertical*, 128.
80. Gonzales, *Deep Survival*, 64.
81. Heise, *Sense of Place*, 151. Heise translates the passage from Ulrich Beck, *Risikogesellschaft* (Frankfurt: Suhrkamp, 1986), 96.
82. Heise, 151. Heise translates the passage from Ulrich Beck, *Risikogesellschaft* (Frankfurt: Suhrkamp, 1986), 96.
83. Fredston, *Rowing to Latitude*, 115.
84. Brymer, "Risk Taking," 223.
85. Brymer, 223.
86. Gonzales, *Deep Survival*, 107.
87. Gonzales, 113.
88. Gonzales, 144.
89. Heise, *Sense of Place*, 148.
90. Heise, 148.
91. Heise, 149.
92. Birrell and Theberge, "Feminist Resistance," 371, 366.
93. Humberstone, "'Outdoor Industry,'" 25.
94. Herr, *Up*, 75–76.
95. Herr, 226.
96. "Carrie Cooper: 39 Weeks."
97. 305sFinestt, "I'm sorry, but." The comment by 305sFinestt has been deleted. Responses to the comment, however, are still available as of 2019.
98. Apereiraytytyt, "Did you eat the helmet?"
99. RuudJH, "39 weeks pregnant and climbing."
100. prAna, "Accidents do happen and can happen anytime."
101. Coffey, *Where the Mountain*, 74, 75.

102. Randall, "Kids and an Exciting Mountain Career?"
103. Laurendeau, "Gendered Risk Regimes," 301.
104. Strayed, *Wild*, 47.
105. Byl, *Dirt Work*, xiv.
106. Palmer, "Death, Danger and the Selling of Risk," 65.
107. Lane, "Backpacking with the Saints," 23.
108. Haile, "How Black Books Lit My Way."
109. Haile.
110. Haile.
111. Roberts, *Almost Somewhere*, 52.
112. Gaard, "Ecofeminism and Wilderness," 10.
113. Langlois, "Stop Telling Women."
114. Lieu and Rennison, *Sexual Harassment and Sexual Assault*, 11, 4.
115. Braverman, *Welcome to the Goddamn Ice Cube*, 2.
116. Gaard, "Ecofeminism and Wilderness," 10.
117. Braverman, *Welcome to the Goddamn Ice Cube*, 30.
118. Braverman, 66–67.
119. Braverman, 221; italics in original.
120. Braverman, 49.
121. Braverman, 3.
122. Braverman, 114.
123. Braverman, 121.
124. Braverman, 176.
125. Braverman, 182–83.
126. Jennifer Pharr Davis, *Becoming Odyssa*, 33.
127. Jennifer Pharr Davis, 93–94.
128. Jennifer Pharr Davis, 61.
129. Braverman, *Welcome to the Goddamn Ice Cube*, 190.
130. Jennifer Pharr Davis, *Becoming Odyssa*, 72.
131. Haile, "How Black Books Lit My Way."
132. Braverman, *Welcome to the Goddamn Ice Cube*, 221; emphasis in original.
133. Roberts, *Almost Somewhere*, ix.
134. Laurendeau and Sharara, "'Women Could Be,'" 27–28.
135. Roberts, *Almost Somewhere*, 247.
136. Wilson and Little, "Adventure and the Gender Gap," 190.
137. Stein, "Introduction," 7.
138. Braverman, *Welcome to the Goddamn Ice Cube*, 184.
139. Braverman, 184.
140. Wilson and Little, "Adventure and the Gender Gap," 200.
141. Finney, *Black Faces, White Spaces*, 3.
142. Finney, 3.
143. Finney, 60.
144. Harris, *Mississippi Solo*, 7.
145. Harris, 14.
146. Harris, 206.
147. Harris, 207.
148. Harris, 208.
149. Pinkney, *As Long As It Takes*, 13.
150. Mills, *Adventure Gap*, 110.

151. Pinkney, *As Long As It Takes*, 110.
152. Roberts, *Almost Somewhere*, 251.
153. Roberts, 247.
154. Finney, *Black Faces, White Spaces*, 106.
155. Root, "Changing the Face of National Parks."
156. Finney, *Black Faces, White Spaces*, 106; emphasis in original.
157. Finney, 117.
158. For a discussion of hush harbors and hush harbor rhetoric, see Nunley, *Keepin' It Hushed*. Nunley describes these rural and urban spaces as both "counterpublics" and "internally directed" spaces in the sense that they are not "anchored in a concern with countering White or mainstream surveillance" (34).
159. Mills, *Adventure Gap*, 61.
160. Mills, 161.
161. Krein, "Nature and Risk in Adventure Sports," 80.
162. Wallace, *Risk Criticism*, 161. In this passage Wallace quotes from Tom Cohen's essay "Anecographics," 45.
163. Wallace, 31–32.
164. Callahan, *Adrift*, 183.
165. Callahan, 236.
166. Frederick Buell, "Global Warming as Literary Narrative," 274. See part two of Ursula K. Heise's *Sense of Place and Sense of Planet* for a discussion of theories of risk in relation to the local and global.
167. Glick, *Monkey Dancing*, 282.
168. Anker, "Climate and Climbers."
169. Jordan, *Savage Summit*, 159.
170. Weiss, *Tide, Feather, Snow*, 103–5, 201–24.
171. Kane, *Running the Amazon*, 250–51.
172. Simon, *North to the Night*, 291.
173. Simon, 264.
174. Fredston, *Rowing to Latitude*, 144.
175. Fredston, 272.
176. Fredston, 273.
177. Fredston, 160.
178. Kocour, *Facing the Extreme*, 86. Elizabeth Mazzolini summarizes Everest's contemporary "fall from grace" in her introduction to *The Everest Effect* (2). For additional information on Everest's fall from grace, see Michael Kodas's *High Crimes*.
179. Schultheis, *Bone Games*, 84.
180. Schultheis, 86.
181. Bisharat, "What's Harder than Summiting Everest?"
182. Bisharat.
183. Mazzolini, *Everest Effect*, 3–5. See also McConnell, "Solving Environmental Problems," which concludes with three recommendations for "minimiz[ing] the impact of our journey through life, particularly when that journey involves adventure travel in developing countries" (366).
184. Sinha, "8 Tons of Trash."
185. Byers, "Contemporary Human Impacts," 112.
186. Callaghan, "Climate Change Is Melting Everest."
187. Gaard, "Ecofeminism and Wilderness," 19.

NOTES TO CHAPTER FIVE

188. Olivier, "Moral Dilemmas of Participation," 106.
189. Brymer, Downey, and Gray, "Extreme Sports as a Precursor," 195.
190. Brymer, Downey, and Gray, 196; emphasis in original.
191. Brymer, Downey, and Gray, 199.
192. Brymer, Downey, and Gray, 202.
193. Heise, "Journeys through the Offset World," 63.
194. Christensen, "Adventure Narratives," 164.
195. Heywood and Montgomery, "'Ambassadors'" 167.
196. Heywood and Montgomery, 168.
197. Heywood and Montgomery, 169.
198. Lawrence Buell, *Writing for an Endangered World*, 37.
199. Harris, *Mississippi Solo*, 212-13.
200. Aebi, *Maiden Voyage*, 216.
201. Gaard, "Ecofeminism and Wilderness," 9.
202. Cox, *Swimming to Antarctica*, 108, 116.
203. Cox, 108.
204. Cox, 107.
205. Callahan, *Adrift*, 183.
206. Fredston, *Rowing to Latitude*, 275.
207. Byl, *Dirt Work*, 135.
208. Aebi, *Maiden Voyage*, 193.
209. Byl, *Dirt Work*, 141.
210. Lawrence Buell, *Writing for an Endangered World*, 37.
211. Weiss, *Tide, Feather, Snow*, 194.
212. Gaard, "Ecofeminism and Wilderness," 6.
213. Fredston, *Rowing to Latitude*, 220.
214. Aebi, *Maiden Voyage*, 257.
215. Roberts, *Almost Somewhere*, 140-41.
216. Byl, *Dirt Work*, 23.
217. Byl, 23; emphasis in original.
218. Stoddart, "Constructing Masculinized Sportscapes," 110.
219. "About," Honnold Foundation.
220. Weiss, *Tide, Feather, Snow*, 188. See especially 187-99 in Weiss for a description and analysis of Alaska's junk culture.
221. Weiss, 192.
222. Weiss, 104, 178.
223. Weiss, 73.
224. Weiss, 144.
225. Weiss, 151.
226. Byl, *Dirt Work*, xvii-xviii.
227. Dougherty, "Aesthetic and Ethical Issues," 103.
228. Byl, *Dirt Work*, 167.
229. Heywood and Montgomery, "'Ambassadors,'" 169.
230. Heywood and Montgomery, 170.
231. Warshaw, "Environmentalism and Surfing," 187.
232. Breivik, "Trends in Adventure Sports," 270.
233. Moye, "Weird Science with Adventurer Gregg Treinish."
234. Vanreusel, "From Bambi to Rambo," 273-74.
235. Ebert and Robertson, "A Plea for Risk," 64.

236. Glick, *Monkey Dancing*, 154.
237. Quoted in Kane, *Running the Amazon*, 82.
238. Simon, *North to the Night*, 112.
239. Gilbert, *Last American Man*, 75.
240. Simon, *North to the Night*, 285.
241. Fredston, *Rowing to Latitude*, 150.
242. Vanreusel, "From Bambi to Rambo," 277.
243. Vanreusel, 278.
244. Ebert and Robertson, "A Plea for Risk," 62.
245. Ralston, *Between a Rock and a Hard Place*, 11.
246. Byl, *Dirt Work*, 183.
247. Simon, *North to the Night*, 285.
248. Fredston, *Rowing to Latitude*, 186.
249. Gram, "Freedom's Limits," 301. Edelman himself defines reproductive futurism in *No Future* as "terms that impose an ideological limit on political discourse as such, preserving in the process the absolute privilege of heteronormativity by rendering unthinkable, by casting outside the political domain, the possibility of a queer resistance to this organizing principle of communal relations" (2).
250. Beck, *Risk Society*, 76; emphasis in original.
251. Breivik, "Trends in Adventure Sports," 270.
252. Kusz, "Extreme America," 199.
253. Palmer, "Death, Danger and the Selling of Risk," 56–57.
254. Jacobs, *Death and Life of Great American Cities*, 445.
255. Heise, "Journeys through the Offset World," 64.
256. Heise, 67.
257. Vance, "Ecofeminism and Wilderness," 71.
258. Gaard, "Ecofeminism and Wilderness," 24.
259. Storey, *I Promise Not to Suffer*, 29.

CHAPTER 6. RESTORATIVE NATURES

1. Krakauer, *Into the Wild*, 155.
2. Krakauer, 155.
3. Krakauer, *Into Thin Air*, 31.
4. Nash, *Wilderness and the American Mind*, 262.
5. Purdy, *After Nature*, 9–10.
6. Lord, *Rock, Water, Wild*, 178.
7. Thomson, *Extraordinary Bodies*, 8.
8. Wheeler, "Don't Climb Every Mountain," 566.
9. Wheeler, 553.
10. Wheeler, 554.
11. Wheeler, 556–57.
12. Wilson and Little, "Adventure and the Gender Gap," 189.
13. Barbara A. Barnes, "'Everybody Wants to Pioneer,'" 233.
14. Pennolino, "Everest." In order to fulfil the desire to climb Everest ethically and safely, *Last Week Tonight* created a humorous solution in the form of a website, TheTopofMtEverest.com. The site allows you to "climb" Everest by putting your face into an image of a climber at the summit.
15. Buxton, "Jon Krakauer Says."

16. Streep, "Dave Morton Is Quitting Everest."
17. Vanreusel, "From Bambi to Rambo," 278.
18. Braverman, *Welcome to the Goddamn Ice Cube*, 111, 112.
19. Braverman, 111.
20. Coffey, *Where the Mountain*, 220. The first work, *Récuper'Art*, and the second work, *Alerte Éléphant: "Espèce-espace en danger,"* can be viewed at Andy Parkin's website, http://www.andyparkin.com/fr/installations.html.
21. Beck, *World Risk Society*, 16.
22. Mazzolini, *Everest Effect*, 133.
23. Streep, "Dave Morton Is Quitting Everest."
24. Purdy, *After Nature*, 9.
25. Wheeler, "Don't Climb Every Mountain," 572.
26. Wheeler, 572.
27. Purdy, *After Nature*, 9.
28. Purdy, 27.
29. Shelton Johnson, "Foreword," 17.
30. Shelton Johnson, 17; emphasis in original.
31. Mills, *Adventure Gap*, 25.
32. Mills, 26.
33. Mills, 38.
34. Barbara A. Barnes, "'Everybody Wants to Pioneer,'" 233.
35. Barbara A. Barnes, 233.
36. Barbara A. Barnes, 233. Barnes quotes here from Charis Thompson, "Back to Nature? Resurrecting Ecofeminism after Poststructuralist and Third-Wave Feminisms," *Isis* 97, no. 3 (September 2006): 510.
37. Callaghan, "800 Miles with Bears Ears Prayer Runners."
38. Callaghan.
39. Woodward, Callaghan, and Sullivan, *Sacred Strides*, 03:16–03:22.
40. Barbara A. Barnes, "'Everybody Wants to Pioneer,'" 253.
41. DiGiulian, "Sasha DiGiulian x Tommy Caldwell." This description appeared on the NativesOutdoors website in the past. The information is still accurate; however, the NativesOutdoors website now states, "Our mission is simple: We are in business to empower indigenous communities through our products and storytelling for a sustainable world" ("NativesOutdoors"). Additional information is also available on their 1% for the Planet member page, https://directories.onepercentfortheplanet.org/business-members/nativesoutdoors.
42. "Temoa Adventures."
43. "Home: Mission," Native Women's Wilderness.
44. Outdoor Afro: https://outdoorafro.com/about. Outdoor Asian: https://www.outdoorasian.com/about.
45. "Get Connected," Diversify Outdoors.
46. Gaard, "Ecofeminism and Wilderness," 17.
47. Humberstone, "Re-Creation and Connections," 387.
48. Brymer and Gray, "Dancing with Nature," 136.
49. Humberstone, "Adventurous Activities," 568.
50. Humberstone, 569.
51. Mills, *Adventure Gap*, 58.
52. Humberstone, "Adventurous Activities," 569.
53. Stockwell, *Cognitive Poetics*, 152. Much of the research on empathy and read-

ing focuses on fiction. See Suzanne Keen, *Empathy and the Novel*, which "presents a comprehensive account of the relationships among novel reading, empathy, and altruism, exploring the implications for literary studies of the widely promulgated 'empathy-altruism' hypothesis" (vii).

54. Wilson and Little, "Adventure and the Gender Gap," 189.
55. Byl, *Dirt Work*, xiv.
56. Byl, 17.
57. Schultheis, *Bone Games*, 171.
58. Sundeen, *Man Who Quit Money*, 160.
59. Sundeen, 161.
60. Sundeen, 198.
61. Sundeen, 248.
62. Cronon, *Changes in the Land*, 37.
63. Cronon, 37.
64. For a discussion of how early European settlers misread Native American land management, see Cronon, 53.
65. Sandilands, "Wild Democracy," 150.
66. Purdy, *After Nature*, 288.
67. Wilson and Little, "Adventure and the Gender Gap," 199.
68. Purdy, *After Nature*, 227.
69. Burkard, "North Face," 0:00–0:08.
70. Burkard, 0:49–0:51, 0:53–0:54.
71. Moulton, "North Face and My Morning Jacket."
72. The "no trespassing" sequence is found at Burkard, *North Face*, 1:00–1:13. Full lyrics to the song are available on the Woody Guthrie Archives website: http://www.woodyguthrie.org/Lyrics/This_Land.htm. Additionally, the lyric was originally written by Guthrie as follows: "There was a big high wall there that tried to stop me. / The sign was painted, said 'Private Property.' / But on the backside, it didn't say nothing. / This land was made for you and me." For an overview of the song's origin and history, see Nick Spitzer's "The Story of Woody Guthrie's 'This Land Is Your Land.'"
73. Newman, "Telling Urbanites to Flee the Cities."
74. Newman.
75. Abram, *Spell of the Sensuous*, 176–79.
76. Christensen, "Adventure Narratives," 174.
77. Crouch, *Enduring Patagonia*, 49–50.
78. Christensen, "Adventure Narratives," 174.
79. Abram, *Spell of the Sensuous*, 183.
80. Chavez, "Hiking the Nüümü Poyo."
81. See Cairns, Muhr, and Bundy, "Restoration Ecology."
82. Chavez, "Hiking the Nüümü Poyo."
83. See Wenzel et al., "Retributive and Restorative Justice.," 376.
84. Chavez, "Hiking the Nüümü Poyo."
85. "Indigenous Women Hike," 3:06–3:15. The raised fist as an image of solidarity and resistance has a history dating back to the early twentieth-century labor movement and has been used by a range of social justice organizations, including, perhaps most famously in an American context, the Black Power movement.
86. "Indigenous Women Hike," 3:06.
87. Wenzel et al., "Retributive and Restorative Justice," 375, 378.

88. Chavez, "Hiking the Nüümü Poyo."
89. Christensen, "Adventure Narratives," 178.
90. Sandilands, "Wild Democracy," 135.
91. "Meet Jolie," Indigenous Women Hike.
92. Sandilands, "Wild Democracy," 135.
93. Ericson, "Into Thick Air: Metaphors That Matter," 92.
94. Blehm, *Last Season*, 97.

BIBLIOGRAPHY

305sFinestt. "I'm sorry, but," 2012 [deleted] comment posted on "Carrie Cooper: 39 Weeks." prAna YouTube Channel, YouTube. https://www.youtube.com/watch?v=lV5fRqgCBOw.

Abbey, Edward. *A Voice Crying in the Wilderness (Vox Clamantis in Deserto): Notes from a Secret Journal.* New York: St. Martin's Griffin, 1989.

"About." Honnold Foundation. https://www.honnoldfoundation.org/about. Accessed April 30, 2019.

"About Cody Lundin." Cody Lundin. http://www.codylundin.com/bio.html. Accessed June 1, 2015.

"About POW." Protect Our Winters. https://protectourwinters.org/about-us. Accessed August 1, 2019.

"About Primal Quest." Primal Quest Expedition. http://primalquest.co.nz/edition_8/about-primal-quest. Accessed September 6, 2018.

Abram, David. *The Spell of the Sensuous: Perception and Language in a More-Than-Human World.* New York: Vintage, 1997.

Ackerman, Diane. *Deep Play.* New York: Vintage, 2000.

Adhikari, Deepak. "The Everest Brawl: A Sherpa's Tale." *Outside Online*, August 13, 2013. https://www.outsideonline.com/outdoor-adventure/climbing/mountaineering/everest-2013/Tashi-Sherpa-Interview.html.

"Adventure Ready Styles." Sundance email, August 31, 2012. Mill Archive. https://www.milled.com/Sundance/adventure-ready-styles-new-for-fall-f9u9hGN7Qt4DVRgX.

Aebi, Tania, with Bernadette Brennan. *Maiden Voyage.* New York: Ballantine Books, 1996.

Alaimo, Stacy. *Bodily Natures: Science, Environment, and the Material Self.* Bloomington: Indiana University Press, 2010.

———. "Cyborg and Ecofeminist Interventions: Challenges for an Environmental Feminism." *Feminist Studies* 20, no. 1 (Spring 1994): 133–52. https://doi.org/10.2307/3178438.

———. "Trans-Corporeality." In *Posthuman Glossary*, edited by Rosi Braidotti and Maria Hlavajova, 435–38. London: Bloomsbury Academic, 2018.

Allison, Stacy, with Peter Carlin. *Beyond the Limits: A Woman's Triumph on Everest.* Boston: Little, Brown, 1993.

American West Photographs. National Archives, August 15, 2016. https://www.archives.gov/research/american-west.

"Amie Lynn Huguenard." *Indianapolis Star*, October 13, 2003. https://www.legacy.com/obituaries/indystar/obituary.aspx?n=amie-lynn-huguenard&pid=143476359.

Anderson, Douglas. "Reading Water: Risk, Intuition, and Insight." In *Philosophy, Risk and Adventure Sports*, edited by Mike McNamee, 71–79. New York: Routledge, 2007.

Anker, Conrad. "Climate and Climbers." *Rock and Ice*, July 2018. https://rockandice.com/snowball/climate-and-climbers.

apereiraytytyt. "Did you eat the helmet?" 2012 comment posted on "Carrie Cooper: 39 Weeks." prAna YouTube Channel, YouTube. https://www.youtube.com/watch?v=lV5fRqgCBOw.

Armstrong, Philip. "The Postcolonial Animal." *Society & Animals* 10, no. 4 (December 2002): 413–19. https://doi.org/10.1163/156853002320936890.

Arnesen, Liv, and Ann Bancroft, with Cheryl Dahle. *No Horizon Is So Far: Two Women and Their Historic Journey across Antarctica*. New York: Penguin Books, 2004.

Atherton, John (Michael). "Philosophy Outdoors: First Person Physical." In *Philosophy, Risk and Adventure Sports*, edited by Mike McNamee, 43–55. New York: Routledge, 2007.

Austin, Mary. *Stories from the Country of Lost Borders*. Edited by Marjorie Pryse. New Brunswick, N.J.: Rutgers University Press, 1987.

Baldick, Chris. "Travelogue." *Oxford Dictionary of Literary Terms*. Oxford Reference Online. https://www.oxfordreference.com/view/10.1093/acref/9780198715443.001.0001/acref-9780198715443-e-1162.

Balf, Todd. *The Last River: The Tragic Race for Shangri-La*. New York: Three Rivers, 2000.

Balmain, Melissa. *Just Us: Adventures and Travels of a Mother and Daughter*. Boston: Faber & Faber, 1998.

Barcott, Bruce. "Cliffhangers: The Fatal Descent of the Mountain-Climbing Memoir." *Harper's*, August 1996, 64–69.

———. "Go Tell It on the Mountain." *Outside Online*, February 2001. https://www.outsideonline.com/1889246/12-step-cliff-program.

Bardenwerper, Will. "Steal the Thunder." *Outside Online*, March 14, 2019. https://www.outsideonline.com/2391820/indian-relay-horse-racing.

Barnes, Barbara A. "'Everybody Wants to Pioneer Something Out Here': Landscape, Adventure, and Biopolitics in the American Southwest." *Journal of Sport and Social Issues* 33, no. 3 (August 2009): 230–56. https://doi.org/10.1177/0193723509338860.

Barnes, David M. *Faithful's Journey on the Appalachian Trail*. Self-published, CreateSpace, 2010.

Barry, Ellen, Bhadra Sharma, and Nida Najar. "Sherpas Move to Shut Everest in Labor Fight." *New York Times*, April 22, 2014. https://www.nytimes.com/2014/04/23/world/asia/sherpas-delay-everest-climbs-in-labor-fight.html.

Barthes, Roland. *Image, Music, Text*. Translated by Stephen Heath. New York: Hill and Wang, 1977.

Baudrillard, Jean. *Simulacra and Simulation*. Translated by Sheila Faria Glaser. Ann Arbor: University of Michigan Press, 1994.

Bayers, Peter L. *Imperial Ascent: Mountaineering, Masculinity, and Empire*. Boulder: University Press of Colorado, 2003.

Baym, Nina. "Melodramas of Beset Manhood: How Theories of American Fiction Exclude Women Authors." *American Quarterly* 33, no. 2 (Summer 1981): 123-39. https://doi.org/10.2307/2712312.

Beck, Ulrich. *Risk Society: Towards a New Modernity*. Translated by Mark Ritter. London: Sage, 1992.

——. *World Risk Society*. Malden, Mass.: Polity Press, 1999.

Beedie, Paul. "Legislators and Interpreters: An Examination of Changes in Philosophical Interpretations of 'Being a Mountaineer.'" In *Philosophy, Risk and Adventure Sports*, edited by Mike McNamee, 25-42. New York: Routledge, 2007.

Berman, Tao, with Pam Withers. *Going Vertical: The Life of an Extreme Kayaker*. Birmingham, Ala.: Menasha Ridge Press, 2008.

Birrell, Susan. "Approaching Mt. Everest: On Intertextuality and the Past as Narrative." *Journal of Sport History* 34, no. 1 (Spring 2007): 1-22.

Birrell, Susan, and Nancy Theberge. "Feminist Resistance and Transformation in Sport." In *Women and Sport: Interdisciplinary Perspectives*, edited by D. Margaret Costa and Sharon R. Guthrie, 361-76. Champaign, Ill.: Human Kinetics, 1994.

Bisharat, Andrew. "What's Harder than Summiting Everest? Getting Climbers to Respect It Again." *National Geographic*, April 5, 2019. https://www.nationalgeographic.com/adventure/2019/04/cory-richards-attempts-everest.

Bledsoe, Lucy Jane. *The Ice Cave: A Woman's Adventures from the Mojave to the Antarctic*. Madison, Wis.: Terrace Books, 2006.

Blehm, Eric. *The Last Season*. New York: Harper Perennial, 2007.

Blum, Arlene. *Annapurna: A Woman's Place*. Berkeley, Calif.: Counterpoint, 2015.

——. *Breaking Trail: A Climbing Life*. New York: Scribner, 2005.

Blum, Hester. *The News at the Ends of the Earth: The Print Culture of Polar Exploration*. Durham, N.C.: Duke University Press, 2019.

——. *The View from the Masthead: Maritime Imagination and Antebellum American Sea Narratives*. Chapel Hill: University of North Carolina Press, 2008.

Booth, Douglas. "Surfing: From One (Cultural) Extreme to Another." In *Understanding Lifestyle Sports: Consumption, Identity and Difference*, edited by Belinda Wheaton, 94-109. New York: Routledge, 2004.

Bott, Esther. "New Heights in Climbing and Tourism: Jordan's Wadi Rum." *Journal of Tourism and Cultural Change* 11, no. 1-2 (June 2013): 21-34. https://doi.org/10.1080/14766825.2013.768253.

Bowley, Graham. *No Way Down: Life and Death on K2*. New York: Harper, 2010.

Braverman, Blair. *Welcome to the Goddamn Ice Cube: Chasing Fear and Finding Home in the Great White North*. New York: Ecco, 2016.

Breivik, Gunnar. "Trends in Adventure Sports in a Post-Modern Society." *Sport in Society* 13, no. 2 (March 2010): 260-73. https://doi.org/10.1080/17430430903522970.

Bridgers, Lee. "Out of the Gene Pool and into the Food Chain." In *To the Extreme: Alternative Sports, Inside and Out*, edited by Robert E. Rinehart and Synthia Sydnor, 179-89. Albany: State University of New York Press, 2003.

Brymer, Eric. "Extreme Sports as a Facilitator of Ecocentricity and Positive Life Changes." *World Leisure Journal* 51, no. 1 (January 2009): 47-53. https://doi.org/10.1080/04419057.2009.9674581.

———. "Risk Taking in Extreme Sports: A Phenomenological Perspective." *Annals of Leisure Research* 13, no. 1–2 (January 2010): 218–38. https://doi.org/10.1080/11745398.2010.9686845.

Brymer, Eric, Greg Downey, and Tonia Gray. "Extreme Sports as a Precursor to Environmental Sustainability." *Journal of Sport & Tourism* 14, no. 2–3 (August 2009): 193–204. https://doi.org/10.1080/14775080902965223.

Brymer, Eric, and Tonia Gray. "Dancing with Nature: Rhythm and Harmony in Extreme Sport Participation." *Journal of Adventure Education and Outdoor Learning* 9, no. 2 (December 2009): 135–49. https://doi.org/10.1080/14729670903116912.

———. "Developing an Intimate 'Relationship' with Nature through Extreme Sports Participation." *Leisure/Loisir* 34, no. 4 (December 2010): 361–74. https://doi.org/10.1080/14927713.2010.542888.

Buell, Frederick. *From Apocalypse to Way of Life: Environmental Crisis in the American Century*. New York: Routledge, 2003.

———. "Global Warming as Literary Narrative." *Philological Quarterly* 93, no. 3 (Summer 2014): 261–94.

Buell, Lawrence. *The Environmental Imagination: Thoreau, Nature Writing, and the Formation of American Culture*. Cambridge, Mass.: Belknap Press of Harvard University Press, 1995.

———. *Writing for an Endangered World: Literature, Culture, and Environment in the U.S. and Beyond*. Cambridge, Mass.: Belknap Press of Harvard University Press, 2003.

Bullis, Connie. "Retalking Environmental Discourses from a Feminist Perspective: The Radical Potential of Ecofeminism." In *The Symbolic Earth: Discourse and Our Creation of the Environment*, edited by James G. Cantrill and Christine L. Oravec, 123–48. Lexington: University Press of Kentucky, 1996.

Burkard, Chris, dir. "The North Face: Your Land." The North Face YouTube Channel, YouTube, October 26, 2014. https://www.youtube.com/watch?v=tll-4WONtgo.

Burke, Shaunna M., and Andrew C. Sparkes. "Cognitive Dissonance and the Role of Self in High Altitude Mountaineering: An Analysis of Six Published Autobiographies." *Life Writing* 6, no. 3 (December 2009): 329–47. https://doi.org/10.1080/14484520903082942.

Buxton, Ryan. "Jon Krakauer Says Climbing Mount Everest Was The 'Biggest Mistake' Of His Life." *Huffington Post*, August 14, 2015. https://www.huffpost.com/entry/jon-krakauer-climbing-mt-everest-was-the-biggest-mistake-of-my-life_n_55ce124ce4b055a6dab0273c.

Byers, Alton. "Contemporary Human Impacts on Alpine Ecosystems in the Sagarmatha (Mt. Everest) National Park, Khumbu, Nepal." *Annals of the Association of American Geographers* 95, no. 1 (March 2005): 112–40. https://doi.org/10.1111/j.1467-8306.2005.00452.x.

Byl, Christine. *Dirt Work: An Education in the Woods*. Boston: Beacon Press, 2013.

Cairns, John, Jr., Jeffrey Muhr, and Marie H. Bundy. "Restoration Ecology." In *Environmental Encyclopedia*, 4th ed., 2:1416–18. Detroit: Gale, 2011.

Callaghan, Anna. "800 Miles with Bears Ears Prayer Runners." *Outside Online*, August 8, 2018. https://www.outsideonline.com/2325341/bears-ears-run-prayer-run-native-american-youth-activists.

———. "Climate Change Is Melting Everest." *Outside Online*, April 12, 2016. https://www.outsideonline.com/2067651/climate-change-melting-everest.

Callahan, Steven. *Adrift: Seventy-Six Days Lost at Sea*. Boston: Mariner Books, 2002.

Campbell, James. *Braving It: A Father, a Daughter, and an Unforgettable Journey into the Alaskan Wild.* New York: Crown, 2016.
Carman, Colin. "Grizzly Love: The Queer Ecology of Timothy Treadwell." *GLQ: A Journal of Lesbian and Gay Studies* 18, no. 4 (October 2012): 507-28. https://doi.org/10.1215/10642684-1600716.
"Carrie Cooper: 39 Weeks." prAna YouTube Channel, YouTube, October 4, 2011. https://www.youtube.com/watch?v=lV5fRqgCBOw.
Cater, Carl I. "Playing with Risk? Participant Perceptions of Risk and Management Implications in Adventure Tourism." *Tourism Management* 27, no. 2 (April 2006): 317-25. https://doi.org/10.1016/j.tourman.2004.10.005.
Chagani, Fayaz. "Can the Postcolonial Animal Speak?" *Society & Animals* 24, no. 6 (November 2016): 619-37. https://doi.org/10.1163/15685306-12341421.
Chavez, Tazbah. "Hiking the Nüümü Poyo: An Act of Love by Indigenous Women." *From the Road: 562 Blog.* Project 562. http://www.project562.com/blog/hiking-the-nueuemue-poyo-an-act-of-love-by-indigenous-women. Accessed September 12, 2018.
Chin, Jimmy, and Elizabeth Chai Vasarhelyi, dir. *Free Solo.* 2018; New York: National Geographic Documentary Films, 2018.
Chisholm, Dianne. "Climbing Like a Girl: An Exemplary Adventure in Feminist Phenomenology." *Hypatia: A Journal of Feminist Philosophy* 23, no. 1 (January-March 2008): 9-40.
Christensen, Doug. "Adventure Narratives and the Ethos of Survival." In *Rhetorics, Literacies, and Narratives of Sustainability,* edited by Peter N. Goggin, 164-79. New York: Routledge, 2009.
Clare, Eli. *Exile and Pride: Disability, Queerness, and Liberation.* Reissue edition. Durham, N.C.: Duke University Press, 2015.
"Climbing Mount Everest Is Work for Supermen: A Member of Former Expeditions Tells of the Difficulties Involved in Reaching the Top." *New York Times,* March 18, 1923, X11.
Coffey, Maria. *Explorers of the Infinite: The Secret Spiritual Lives of Extreme Athletes— and What They Reveal about Near-Death Experiences, Psychic Communication, and Touching the Beyond.* New York: Penguin, 2008.
———. *Where the Mountain Casts Its Shadow: The Dark Side of Extreme Adventure.* New York: St. Martin's Griffin, 2005.
Cohen, Michael P. "Comment: Resistance to Wilderness." *Environmental History* 1, no. 1 (January 1996): 33-42. https://doi.org/10.2307/3985061.
Cohen, Tom. "Anecographics: Climate Change and 'Late' Deconstruction." In *Impasses of the Post-global: Theory in an Age of Climate Change,* vol. 2, edited by Henry Sussman, 32-57. Ann Arbor, Mich.: Open Humanities Press, 2012.
Connell, R. W. "An Iron Man: The Body and Some Contradictions of Hegemonic Masculinity." In *Sport, Men, and the Gender Order: Critical Feminist Perspectives,* edited by Michael A. Messner and Donald F. Sabo, 83-95. Champaign, Ill.: Human Kinetics, 1990.
———. *Masculinities.* Berkeley: University of California Press, 1995.
Connell, R. W., and James W. Messerschmidt. "Hegemonic Masculinity: Rethinking the Concept." *Gender & Society* 19, no. 6 (December 2005): 829-59. https://doi.org/10.1177/0891243205278639.
Copeland, Sebastian, dir. *Into the Cold: A Journey of the Soul.* 2010; Marina Del Rey, Calif.: Vision Films, 2010. http://www.intothecold.org.

Costigan, Philip, Patricia Rose, and Mary Tinney. "The Role of Spirituality in the Development of an Eco-Centric Culture." *Social Alternatives* 26, no. 3 (Third Quarter 2007): 41–44.

Counter, S. Allen. *North Pole Legacy: Black, White, and Eskimo*. Amherst: University of Massachusetts Press, 1991.

Cox, Lynne. *Swimming to Antarctica: Tales of a Long-Distance Swimmer*. New York: Mariner Books, 2005.

Crane, Cason. "Adventurer & Activist Cason Crane." Cason Crane. https://www.casoncrane.com. Accessed May 23, 2019.

Cronon, William. *Changes in the Land: Indians, Colonists, and the Ecology of New England*. New York: Hill and Wang, 1983.

———. "The Trouble with Wilderness: Or, Getting Back to the Wrong Nature." *Environmental History* 1, no. 1 (January 1996): 7–28. https://doi.org/10.2307/3985059.

Crouch, Gregory. *Enduring Patagonia*. New York: Random House Trade Paperbacks, 2002.

Csikszentmihalyi, Mihaly. *Flow: The Psychology of Optimal Experience*. New York: Harper Perennial Modern Classics, 2008.

Cuomo, Chris J. *Feminism and Ecological Communities: An Ethic of Flourishing*. New York: Routledge, 1998.

Davis, Jennifer Pharr. *Becoming Odyssa: Epic Adventures on the Appalachian Trail*. New York: Beaufort Books, 2010.

Davis, Steph. *Learning to Fly*. New York: Simon & Schuster, 2013.

de Gennaro, Mara. "Multispecies Stories, Subaltern Futures." In *Futures of Comparative Literature: ACLA State of the Discipline Report*, edited by Ursula K. Heise, 314–23. London: Routledge, 2017.

Deloria, Philip J. *Playing Indian*. Rev. ed. New Haven, Conn.: Yale University Press, 1999.

Diamond, Irene, and Gloria Feman Orenstein, eds. *Reweaving the World: The Emergence of Ecofeminism*. San Francisco: Sierra Club Books, 1990.

DiGiulian, Sasha. "Sasha DiGiulian x Tommy Caldwell: Native Lands and Conservation w. Access Fund." *Sasha DiGiulian* (blog), July 1, 2019. http://sashadigiulian.com/sasha-digiulian-x-tommy-caldwell-native-lands-and-conservation-w-access-fund-10am-on-a-tuesday.

Domosh, Mona, and Joni Seager. *Putting Women in Place: Feminist Geographers Make Sense of the World*. New York: Guilford, 2001.

Dougherty, Alan P. "Aesthetic and Ethical Issues Concerning Sport in Wilder Places." In *Philosophy, Risk and Adventure Sports*, edited by Mike McNamee, 94–105. New York: Routledge, 2007.

Dufresne, John. "On the Road to Trincomalee: The Renaissance of Travel/Adventure Literature in the United States." *North Stone Review* 10 (1991): 111–23.

Dwyer, June. "A Non-companion Species Manifesto: Humans, Wild Animals, and 'The Pain of Anthropomorphism.'" *South Atlantic Review* 72, no. 3 (Summer 2007): 73–89.

Ebert, Philip A., and Simon Robertson. "A Plea for Risk." *Royal Institute of Philosophy Supplements* 73 (October 2013): 45–64. https://doi.org/10.1017/S1358246113000271.

Edelman, Lee. *No Future: Queer Theory and the Death Drive*. Durham, N.C.: Duke University Press, 2004.

Ellis, Reuben J. *Vertical Margins: Mountaineering and the Landscapes of Neoimperialism*. Madison: University of Wisconsin Press, 2001.

Else, Liz. "Slavoj Žižek: Wake up and Smell the Apocalypse." *New Scientist* 207, no. 2775 (August 28, 2010): 28–29.

Ericson, Katherine. "Into Thick Air: Metaphors That Matter." In *A Wilderness of Signs: Ethics, Beauty, and Environment after Postmodernism*, edited by Joe Jordan, 85–93. Newcastle: Cambridge Scholars, 2006.

"Everest INC.: The Exploitation and Death of the Sherpas." *Real Sports with Bryant Gumbel*. HBO, August 21, 2018. https://www.hbo.com/real-sports-with-bryant-gumbel/all-episodes/august-2018.

Ewert, Alan, Ken Gilbertson, Yuan-Chun Luo, and Alison Voight. "Beyond 'Because It's There': Motivations for Pursuing Adventure Recreational Activities." *Journal of Leisure Research* 45, no. 1 (2013): 91–111. https://doi.org/10.18666/jlr-2013-v45-i1-2944.

Fern, Richard L. *Nature, God and Humanity: Envisioning an Ethics of Nature*. Cambridge: Cambridge University Press, 2002.

Field, Terri. "Is the Body Essential for Ecofeminism?" *Organization & Environment* 13, no. 1 (March 2000): 39–60.

Finney, Carolyn. *Black Faces, White Spaces: Reimagining the Relationship of African Americans to the Great Outdoors*. Chapel Hill: University of North Carolina Press, 2014.

FitzGerald, Holly Conklin. *Ruthless River: Love and Survival by Raft on the Amazon's Relentless Madre de Dios*. New York: Vintage, 2017.

Ford, Nick, and David Brown. *Surfing and Social Theory: Experience, Embodiment and Narrative of the Dream Glide*. New York: Routledge, 2006.

Francis, John. *Planetwalker: 22 Years of Walking. 17 Years of Silence*. Washington, D.C.: National Geographic Books, 2009.

Franklin, Adrian, and Mike Crang. "The Trouble with Tourism and Travel Theory?" *Tourist Studies* 1, no. 1 (June 2001): 5–22. https://doi.org/10.1177/146879760100100101.

Fredston, Jill. *Rowing to Latitude: Journeys along the Arctic's Edge*. New York: North Point, 2001.

———. *Snowstruck: In the Grip of Avalanches*. Orlando, Fla.: Harcourt, 2005.

Frohlick, Susan. "The 'Hypermasculine' Landscape of High-Altitude Mountaineering." *Michigan Feminist Studies* 14 (1999–2000): 83–106.

———. "Negotiating the 'Global' within the Global Playscapes of Mount Everest." *Canadian Review of Sociology* 40, no. 5 (December 2003): 525–42. https://doi.org/10.1111/j.1755-618X.2003.tb00003.x.

———. "'That Playfulness of White Masculinity': Mediating Masculinities and Adventure at Mountain Film Festivals." *Tourist Studies* 5, no. 2 (August 2005): 175–93. https://doi.org/10.1177/1468797605066926.

Fromm, Pete. *Indian Creek Chronicles: A Winter Alone in the Wilderness*. New York: Picador, 2003.

Frontin, Glenn. *A River Calling: A Christian Father and His Sons, a Canoe Adventure, a Spiritual Journey That Would Last a Lifetime*. Mustang, Okla.: Tate, 2008.

Gaard, Greta. "Ecofeminism and Wilderness." *Environmental Ethics* 19, no. 1 (Spring 1997): 5–24. https://doi.org/10.5840/enviroethics199719136.

Gardner, Renne. "High Goals." *OC Metro*, October 18, 2001, http://www.ocmetro.com/metro1801/sportslo1801.html.

Garrard, Greg. *Ecocriticism*. New York: Routledge, 2004.

Gates, Barbara T. "A Root of Ecofeminism: Ecoféminisme." *ISLE: Interdisciplinary*

Studies in Literature and Environment 3, no. 1 (Summer 1996): 7–16. https://doi.org/10.1093/isle/3.1.7.

Gelfand, Elissa. "Feminist Criticism, French." In *Encyclopedia of Contemporary Literary Theory: Approaches, Scholars, Terms*, edited by Irena R. Makaryk, 44–50. Toronto: University of Toronto Press, 1993.

Gersdorf, Catrin. "Ecocritical Uses of the Erotic." *Bucknell Review: A Scholarly Journal of Letters, Arts and Sciences* 44, no. 1 (2000): 175–91.

Gessner, David. *My Green Manifesto: Down the Charles River in Pursuit of a New Environmentalism*. Minneapolis: Milkweed Editions, 2011.

"Get Connected." Diversify Outdoors, accessed August 30, 2018. https://www.diversifyoutdoors.com/get-connected.

Gilbert, Elizabeth. *The Last American Man*. New York: Penguin, 2003.

Giulianotti, Richard. "Risk and Sport: An Analysis of Sociological Theories and Research Agendas." *Sociology of Sport Journal* 26, no. 4 (December 2009): 540–56. https://doi.org/10.1123/ssj.26.4.540.

Glave, Dianne D. *Rooted in the Earth: Reclaiming the African American Environmental Heritage*. Chicago: Lawrence Hill Books, 2010.

Glick, Daniel. *Monkey Dancing: A Father, Two Kids, and a Journey to the Ends of the Earth*. New York: PublicAffairs, 2004.

Gonzales, Laurence. *Deep Survival: Who Lives, Who Dies, and Why: True Stories of Miraculous Endurance and Sudden Death*. New York: W. W. Norton, 2003.

Gordon, Jon F. "Means and Motives: The Mystification of Mountaineering Discourse." *Postcolonial Text* 2, no. 4 (2006): 1–14.

Gram, Margaret Hunt. "Freedom's Limits: Jonathan Franzen, the Realist Novel, and the Problem of Growth." *American Literary History* 26, no. 2 (Summer 2014): 295–316. https://doi.org/10.1093/alh/aju020.

Greenfield, Rob. *Dude Making a Difference: Bamboo Bikes, Dumpster Dives and Other Extreme Adventures across America*. Gabriola Island, B.C.: New Society, 2016.

Gregory, Derek. "Epilogue." In *Vancouver and Its Region*, edited by Graeme Wynn and Timothy R. Oke, 291–97. Vancouver: University of British Columbia Press, 1992.

Greshko, Michael. "Amphibian 'Apocalypse' Caused by Most Destructive Pathogen Ever." *National Geographic*, March 28, 2019. https://www.nationalgeographic.com/animals/2019/03/amphibian-apocalypse-frogs-salamanders-worst-chytrid-fungus.

Griffin, Susan. *The Eros of Everyday Life: Essays on Ecology, Gender and Society*. New York: Anchor Books, 1996.

———. *Woman and Nature: The Roaring Inside Her*. New York: Harper & Row, 1978.

Grothjan, Sarah. "Backpacking Is My Respite from Sexual Harassment." *Outside Online*, August 27, 2018. https://www.outsideonline.com/2320816/backpacking-my-respite-sexual-harassment.

Gurian, Davita. "When Feminism Goes Too Far." *Evening Sends* (blog), January 17, 2017. http://www.eveningsends.com/when-feminism-goes-too-far.

Hahn, Jennifer. *Spirited Waters: Soloing South through the Inside Passage*. Seattle: Mountaineers Books, 2001.

Haile, Rahawa. "And then you sell a book about it." Twitter, @RahawaHaile, February 8, 2018, 10:49 a.m., https://twitter.com/rahawahaile/status/961628019587559430.

———. "How Black Books Lit My Way along the Appalachian Trail." *BuzzFeed News*,

February 2, 2017. https://www.buzzfeednews.com/article/rahawahaile/how-black-books-lit-my-way-along-the-appalachian-trail.

Haraway, Donna J. *The Companion Species Manifesto: Dogs, People, and Significant Otherness*. Chicago: Prickly Paradigm Press, 2003.

Harman, Graham. *Guerrilla Metaphysics: Phenomenology and the Carpentry of Things*. Chicago: Open Court, 2005.

Harris, Eddy L. *Mississippi Solo: A River Quest*. New York: Holt Paperbacks, 1998.

Hawk, Tony. *Between Boardslides and Burnout: My Notes from the Road*. New York: It Books, 2002.

Hawk, Tony, and Sean Mortimer. *Hawk: Occupation: Skateboarder*. New York: It Books, 2001.

Heath, Stephen. "Translator's Note." In *Image, Music, Text*, by Roland Barthes, 7-11. New York: Hill and Wang, 1977.

Hediger, Ryan. "Timothy Treadwell's Grizzly Love as Freak Show: The Uses of Animals, Science, and Film." *ISLE: Interdisciplinary Studies in Literature and Environment* 19, no. 1 (Winter 2012): 82-100. https://doi.org/10.1093/isle/iss025.

Heise, Ursula K. "Journeys through the Offset World: Global Travel Narratives and Environmental Crisis." *SubStance: A Review of Theory and Literary Criticism* 41, no. 1, issue 127 (2012): 61-76.

———. *Sense of Place and Sense of Planet: The Environmental Imagination of the Global*. New York: Oxford University Press, 2008.

Heller, Chaia. *Ecology of Everyday Life: Rethinking the Desire for Nature*. Montreal: Black Rose Books, 1999.

Henson, Matthew A. *A Negro Explorer at the North Pole*. New York: Frederick A. Stokes, 1912.

Herr, Patricia Ellis. *Up: A Mother and Daughter's Peakbagging Adventure*. New York: Broadway Paperbacks, 2012.

Heywood, Leslie, and Mark Montgomery. "'Ambassadors of the Last Wilderness'? Surfers, Environmental Ethics, and Activism in America." In *Tribal Play: Subcultural Journeys Through Sport*, edited by Kevin Young and Michael Atkinson, 153-72. Bingley, UK: Emerald JAI, 2008.

Hill, Diana Ellis, dir. *The Five Elements of Adventure*. 2015; Biarritz, France: Xtreme Video, 2015.

Hill, Lynn, with Greg Child. *Climbing Free: My Life in the Vertical World*. New York: W. W. Norton, 2002.

"Home: Mission." Native Women's Wilderness. https://www.nativewomenswilderness.org. Accessed August 30, 2018.

Honnold, Alex, with David Roberts. *Alone on the Wall*. New York: W. W. Norton, 2016.

hooks, bell. *Feminism Is for Everybody: Passionate Politics*. New York: Routledge, 2014.

Hornbein, Tom. "Foreword." In *Where the Mountain Casts Its Shadow: The Dark Side of Extreme Adventure*, by Maria Coffey, xi-xv. New York: St. Martin's Griffin, 2005.

Howkins, Heidi. *K2: One Woman's Quest for the Summit*. Washington, D.C.: National Geographic Books, 2001.

Huggan, Graham. "Going to Extremes: Reflections on Travel Writing, Death and the Contemporary Survival Industry." In *Seuils et traverses: Enjeux de l'écriture du voyage*, vol. 2, edited by Jan Borm, 295-302. Brest, France: Centre de Recherche Bretonne et Celtique, 2002.

Humberstone, Barbara. "Adventurous Activities, Embodiment and Nature: Spiritual, Sensual and Sustainable? Embodying Environmental Justice." *Motriz: Revista de educação física* 19, no. 3 (July/September 2013): 565–71. http://dx.doi.org/10.1590/S1980-65742013000300006.

———. "The 'Outdoor Industry' as Social and Educational Phenomena: Gender and Outdoor Adventure/Education." *Journal of Adventure Education and Outdoor Learning* 1, no. 1 (2000): 21–35. https://doi.org/10.1080/14729670085200041.

———. "Re-Creation and Connections in and with Nature: Synthesizing Ecological and Feminist Discourses and Praxis?" *International Review for the Sociology of Sport* 33, no. 4 (December 1998): 381–92. https://doi.org/10.1177/101269098033004005.

Ilgunas, Ken. *Trespassing across America: One Man's Epic, Never-Done-Before (and Sort of Illegal) Hike across the Heartland.* New York: Blue Rider Press, 2016.

"Indigenous Women Hike." Matika Wilbur YouTube Channel, YouTube, September 9, 2018. https://www.youtube.com/watch?v=r9JJr8ETo2U.

Inglis, Mark. *Legs on Everest.* Auckland, N.Z.: Random House New Zealand, 2006.

Irvine, Amy. *Trespass: Living at the Edge of the Promised Land.* New York: North Point, 2008.

Jacobs, Jane. *The Death and Life of Great American Cities.* New York: Vintage Books, 1992.

Jacobson, Kristin J. "Desiring Natures: The American Adrenaline Narrative." *Genre* 35, no. 2 (Summer 2002): 355–82. http://doi.org/10.1215/00166928-35-2-355.

James, Erin. *The Storyworld Accord: Econarratology and Postcolonial Narratives.* Lincoln: University of Nebraska Press, 2015.

Jans, Nick. *The Grizzly Maze: Timothy Treadwell's Fatal Obsession with Alaskan Bears.* New York: Plume, 2006.

Johnson, Mat. *Pym: A Novel.* New York: Spiegel & Grau, 2011.

Johnson, Shelton. "Foreword." In *The Adventure Gap: Changing the Face of the Outdoors* by James Edward Mills, 15–17. Seattle: Mountaineers Books, 2014.

Jordan, Jennifer. *Savage Summit: The Life and Death of the First Women of K2.* New York: It Books, 2006.

Jorgenson, Andrew K. "Consumption and Environmental Degradation: A Cross-National Analysis of the Ecological Footprint." *Social Problems* 50, no. 3 (August 2003): 374–94. https://doi.org/10.1525/sp.2003.50.3.374.

Joyce, Kathryn. "Out Here, No One Can Hear You Scream." *HuffPost Highline*, March 16, 2016. https://highline.huffingtonpost.com/articles/en/park-rangers.

Kane, Joe. *Running the Amazon.* New York: Vintage, 1990.

Keen, Suzanne. *Empathy and the Novel.* New York: Oxford University Press, 2007.

Keirstead, Christopher M. "Convoluted Paths: Mapping Genre in Contemporary Footsteps Travel Writing." *Genre: Forms of Discourse and Culture* 46, no. 3 (Fall 2013): 285–315. https://doi.org/10.1215/00166928-2345524.

Kerr, John H., and Susan Houge Mackenzie. "Multiple Motives for Participating in Adventure Sports." *Psychology of Sport and Exercise* 13, no. 5 (September 2012): 649–57. https://doi.org/10.1016/j.psychsport.2012.04.002.

Kipnis, Laura. "(Male) Desire and (Female) Disgust: Reading *Hustler*." In *Ecstasy Unlimited: On Sex, Capital, Gender, and Aesthetics*, 119–41. Minneapolis: University of Minnesota Press, 1993.

Kirksey, Eben, Craig Schuetze, and Stefan Helmreich. "Introduction: Tactics of Multispecies Ethnography." In *The Multispecies Salon*, edited by Eben Kirksey, 1–24. Durham, N.C.: Duke University Press, 2014.

Kocour, Ruth Anne, with Michael Hodgson. *Facing the Extreme: One Woman's Tale of True Courage, Death-Defying Survival and Her Quest for the Summit*. New York: St. Martin's Press, 1999.

Kodas, Michael. *High Crimes: The Fate of Everest in an Age of Greed*. New York: Hyperion, 2008.

Kollin, Susan. "Survival, Alaska Style." In *Postwestern Cultures: Literature, Theory, Space*, edited by Susan Kollin, 143-55. Lincoln: University of Nebraska Press, 2007.

Kolodny, Annette. *The Lay of the Land: Metaphor as Experience and History in American Life and Letters*. Chapel Hill: University of North Carolina Press, 1975.

Krakauer, Jon. *Into the Wild*. New York: Anchor Books, 2007.

———. *Into Thin Air: A Personal Account of the Mt. Everest Disaster*. New York: Anchor Books, 1998.

Krech, Shepard, III. *The Ecological Indian: Myth and History*. New York: W. W. Norton, 1999.

Krein, Kevin. "Nature and Risk in Adventure Sports." In *Philosophy, Risk and Adventure Sports*, edited by Mike McNamee, 80-93. New York: Routledge, 2007.

Kuipers, Dean. *Operation Bite Back: Rod Coronado's War to Save American Wilderness*. New York: Bloomsbury, 2009.

Kull, Robert. *Solitude: Seeking Wisdom in Extremes: A Year Alone in the Patagonia Wilderness*. Novato, Calif.: New World Library, 2009.

Kusz, Kyle. "Extreme America: The Cultural Politics of Extreme Sports in 1990s America." In *Understanding Lifestyle Sports: Consumption, Identity and Difference*, edited by Belinda Wheaton, 197-213. New York: Routledge, 2004.

———. "Remasculinizing American White Guys in/through New Millennium American Sport Films." *Sport in Society* 11, no. 2-3 (March 2008): 209-26. https://doi.org/10.1080/17430430701823448.

Kwak-Hefferan, Elisabeth. "Why Women Shouldn't Worry about Hiking Alone." *Backpacker*, September 14, 2015. https://www.backpacker.com/skills/beginner/wilderness-threats/why-women-shouldnt-worry-about-hiking-alone.

LaGrone, Sam. "Slogans That Sell the Service: A Brief History of U.S. Navy Television Ads after the End of the Draft." *USNI News*, May 29, 2015. https://news.usni.org/2015/05/29/slogans-that-sell-the-service-a-brief-history-of-u-s-navy-television-ads-after-the-end-of-the-draft.

Laing, Jennifer H., and Geoffrey I. Crouch. "Myth, Adventure and Fantasy at the Frontier: Metaphors and Imagery behind an Extraordinary Travel Experience." *International Journal of Tourism Research* 11, no. 2 (March/April 2009): 127-41. https://doi.org/10.1002/jtr.716.

Lane, Belden C. "Backpacking with the Saints: The Risk-Taking Character of Wilderness Reading." *Spiritus: A Journal of Christian Spirituality* 8, no. 1 (Spring 2008): 23-43. https://doi.org/10.1353/scs.0.0009.

Langlois, Krista. "Stop Telling Women Not to Go into the Backcountry Alone." *Adventure Journal*, March 21, 2017. https://www.adventure-journal.com/2017/03/stop-telling-women-not-to-go-into-the-backcountry-alone.

Laurendeau, Jason. "'Gendered Risk Regimes': A Theoretical Consideration of Edgework and Gender." *Sociology of Sport Journal* 25, no. 3 (September 2008): 293-309. https://doi.org/10.1123/ssj.25.3.293.

Laurendeau, Jason, and Nancy Sharara. "'Women Could Be Every Bit As Good As Guys': Reproductive and Resistant Agency in Two 'Action' Sports." *Journal of*

Sport and Social Issues 32, no. 1 (February 2008): 24–47. https://doi.org/10.1177/0193723507307819.

Least Heat-Moon, William. *River-Horse: The Logbook of a Boat across America*. New York: Penguin Books, 2001.

Leopold, Aldo. *A Sand County Almanac: And Sketches Here and There*. Oxford: Oxford University Press, 1949.

Leung, Hillary. "Nepalese Climbers to Remeasure Mount Everest." *Time*, April 9, 2019. http://time.com/5566400/nepalese-climbers-remeasuring-everest.

Lianos, Michaelis, and Mary Douglas. "Dangerization and the End of Deviance: The Institutional Environment." *British Journal of Criminology* 40, no. 2 (March 2000): 261–78. https://doi.org/10.1093/bjc/40.2.261.

Lieu, Charlie, and Callie Marie Rennison. *Sexual Harassment and Sexual Assault in the Climbing Community*. N.p.: SafeOutside, 2018. Available at static1.squarespace.com/static/55830fd9e4b0ec758c892f81/t/5b8413600ebbe8b9b8e35787/1535382377824/SafeOutside-SHSA-Report.pdf.

Lopez, Barry Holstun. *Arctic Dreams: Imagination and Desire in a Northern Landscape*. New York: Bantam Books, 1989.

Lord, Nancy. *Rock, Water, Wild: An Alaskan Life*. Lincoln: University of Nebraska Press, 2009.

Love, Glen A. "Revaluing Nature: Toward an Ecological Criticism." *Western American Literature* 25, no. 3 (Fall 1990): 201–15. https://doi.org/10.1353/wal.1990.0079.

Macfarlane, Robert. *Mountains of the Mind: Adventures in Reaching the Summit*. New York: Knopf, 2004.

Mack-Canty, Colleen. "Third-Wave Feminism and the Need to Reweave the Nature/Culture Duality." *NWSA Journal* 16, no. 3 (Autumn 2004): 154–79.

Malloy, Chris, dir. *180° South: Conquerors of the Useless*. 2010; New York: Magnolia Pictures, 2010. http://www.180south.com.

Malone, Nicholas, and Kathryn Ovenden. "Natureculture." In *The International Encyclopedia of Primatology*, edited by Agustín Fuentes et al., 848–49. Hoboken, N.J.: John Wiley & Sons, 2016. http://doi.org/10.1002/9781119179313.wbprimo135.

Malusa, Jim. *Into Thick Air: Biking to the Bellybutton of Six Continents*. San Francisco: Sierra Club Books, 2008.

Manning, Peter K. "High Risk Narratives: Textual Adventures." *Qualitative Sociology* 22, no. 4 (December 1999): 285–99. https://doi.org/10.1023/A:1022003520356.

Manos, Jarid. *Ghetto Plainsman*. Fort Worth, Tex.: Temba House, 2007.

Marchetti, Gina. "Action-Adventure as Ideology." In *Cultural Politics in Contemporary America*, edited by Ian Henderson Angus and Sut Jhally, 182–97. New York: Routledge, 1989.

Martin, Derek Christopher. "Apartheid in the Great Outdoors: American Advertising and the Reproduction of a Racialized Outdoor Leisure Identity." *Journal of Leisure Research* 36, no. 4 (2004): 513–35. https://doi.org/10.1080/00222216.2004.11950034.

Mattessich, Stefan. "An Anguished Self-Subjection: Man and Animal in Werner Herzog's *Grizzly Man*." *English Studies in Canada* 39, no. 1 (March 3, 2013): 51–70. https://doi.org/10.1353/esc.2013.0016.

Mazzolini, Elizabeth. *The Everest Effect: Nature, Culture, Ideology*. Tuscaloosa: University of Alabama Press, 2016.

McCairen, Patricia C. *Canyon Solitude: A Woman's Solo River Journey through the Grand Canyon*. Berkeley, Calif.: Seal Press, 1998.

McCarthy, Anne C. "Reading the Red Bull Sublime." *PMLA* 132, no. 3 (May 2017): 543–57. https://doi.org/10.1632/pmla.2017.132.3.543.

McCarthy, Jeffrey Mathes. *Contact: Mountain Climbing and Environmental Thinking.* Reno: University of Nevada Press, 2008.

———. "A Theory of Place in North American Mountaineering." *Philosophy & Geography* 5, no. 2 (2002): 179–94. https://doi.org/10.1080/10903770220152407.

———. "Why Climbing Matters." *ISLE: Interdisciplinary Studies in Literature and Environment* 15, no. 2 (Summer 2008): 157–74. https://doi.org/10.1093/isle/15.2.157.

McCauley, Lucy, ed. *Women in the Wild: True Stories of Adventure and Connection.* 2nd ed. San Francisco: Travelers' Tales, 2004.

McClure, Tori Murden. *A Pearl in the Storm: How I Found My Heart in the Middle of the Ocean.* New York: Harper, 2009.

McConnell, Robert M. "Solving Environmental Problems Caused by Adventure Travel in Developing Countries: The Everest Environmental Expedition." *Mountain Research and Development* 11, no. 4 (November 1991): 359–66. https://doi.org/10.2307/3673719.

McDougall, Christopher. *Born to Run: A Hidden Tribe, Superathletes, and the Greatest Race the World Has Never Seen.* New York: Alfred A. Knopf, 2009.

McKibben, Bill. *Long Distance: Testing the Limits of Body and Spirit in a Year of Living Strenuously.* New York: Rodale, 2010.

McNiel, Jamie N., Deborah A. Harris, and Kristi M. Fondren. "Women and the Wild: Gender Socialization in Wilderness Recreation Advertising." *Gender Issues* 29, no. 1–4 (December 2012): 39–55. https://doi.org/10.1007/s12147-012-9111-1.

McQuillan, Gene. "'No Anthems Playing in My Head': Epiphany and Irony in Contemporary Mountaineering Writing." *Aethlon: The Journal of Sport Literature* 16, no. 1 (Fall 1998): 49–65.

Medred, Craig. "Woman Who Died with 'Bear Guru' Was Duped." ESPN.com, May 31, 2006. http://www.espn.com/outdoors/general/news/story?page=c_fea_AK_bear-guru_duped_woman.

Meeker, Joseph W. *The Comedy of Survival: Literary Ecology and a Play Ethic.* Tucson: University of Arizona Press, 1997.

"Meet Jolie." Indigenous Women Hike. https://www.indigenouswomenhike.com/meet-jolie. Accessed April 22, 2019.

Men's Journal Editors. *Wild Stories: The Best of* Men's Journal: *Ten Years of Great Writing.* New York: Crown, 2002.

Merchant, Carolyn. *Radical Ecology: The Search for a Livable World.* New York: Routledge, 1992.

Mills, James Edward. *The Adventure Gap: Changing the Face of the Outdoors.* Seattle: Mountaineers Books, 2014.

Mitchell, Timothy. "Can the Mosquito Speak?" In *Rule of Experts: Egypt, Techno-Politics, Modernity*, 19–53. Berkeley: University of California Press, 2002.

Monahan, Erin. "Ambient Dominion: How *Free Solo* Points to An Epidemic of Toxic Masculinity." *Terra Incognita* (blog), December 7, 2018. https://www.terraincognitamedia.com/features/ambient-dominion-how-free-solo-points-to-an-epidemic-of-toxic-masculinity2018.

Mortimer, Peter, Nick Kemple, and Nick Rosen, dirs. *Alone on the Wall: Alex Honnold.* 2010; Boulder, Colo.: Sender Films, 2010. https://vimeo.com/ondemand/aloneonthewall/149308596.

Morton, David, and Jake Norton, dirs. *High and Hallowed: Everest 1963*. 2013; Biarritz, France: Xtreme Video, 2013. http://highandhallowed.com.

Morton, Timothy. *Ecology without Nature: Rethinking Environmental Aesthetics*. Cambridge, Mass.: Harvard University Press, 2009.

———. "Guest Column: Queer Ecology." *PMLA* 125, no. 2 (March 2010): 273–82. https://doi.org/10.1632/pmla.2010.125.2.273.

Moser, Susanne C. "Communicating Climate Change: History, Challenges, Process and Future Directions." *Wiley Interdisciplinary Reviews: Climate Change* 1, no. 1 (January/February 2010): 31–53. https://doi.org/10.1002/wcc.11.

Moulton, Sam. "The North Face and My Morning Jacket Collaborate on 'This Land is Your Land.'" *Outside Online*, November 11, 2014. https://www.outsideonline.com/1927176/north-face-and-my-morning-jacket-collaborate-land-your-land.

Moye, Jayme. "Weird Science with Adventurer Gregg Treinish." *Elevation Outdoors Magazine*, September 20, 2013. https://www.elevationoutdoors.com/exclude/weird-science-with-adventurer-gregg-treinish.

Mozingo, Joe. "Proving He Can Climb the Highest Mountain." *Los Angeles Times*, June 16, 2001. https://www.latimes.com/archives/la-xpm-2001-jun-16-me-11140-story.html.

"Naked and Afraid." Discovery Channel. https://www.discovery.com/tv-shows/naked-and-afraid. Accessed April 19, 2019.

Nash, Roderick Frazier. *Wilderness and the American Mind*. 5th ed. New Haven, Conn.: Yale University Press, 2014.

"NativesOutdoors." NativesOutdoors. https://www.natives-outdoors.org. Accessed August 30, 2018.

Nelson, Richard. *The Island Within*. New York: Vintage, 1991.

Newman, Andrew Adam. "Telling Urbanites to Flee the Cities." *New York Times*, October 26, 2014. https://www.nytimes.com/2014/10/27/business/media/telling-urbanites-to-flee-the-cities-.html.

Nichols, Peter. *Sea Change: Alone across the Atlantic in a Wooden Boat*. New York: Penguin, 1998.

Nimmo, Richie. "From Over the Horizon: Animal Alterity and Liminal Intimacy beyond the Anthropomorphic Embrace." *Otherness: Essays and Studies* 5, no. 2 (September 2016): 13–45.

Nixon, Rob. *Slow Violence and the Environmentalism of the Poor*. Cambridge, Mass.: Harvard University Press, 2011.

Norgay, Jamling Tenzing, with Broughton Coburn. *Touching My Father's Soul: A Sherpa's Journey to the Top of Everest*. San Francisco: HarperCollins, 2001.

Nouzeilles, Gabriela. "Touching the Real: Alternative Travel and Landscapes of Fear." In *Writing Travel: The Poetics and Politics of the Modern Journey*, edited by John Zilcosky, 195–210. Toronto: University of Toronto Press, 2008.

Nunley, Vorris L. *Keepin' It Hushed: The Barbershop and African American Hush Harbor Rhetoric*. Detroit: Wayne State University Press, 2011.

Oates, Joyce Carol. "Against Nature." In *(Woman) Writer: Occasions and Opportunities*, 66–76. New York: Dutton, 1988.

O'Connor, Flannery. "A Good Man is Hard to Find." In *A Good Man Is Hard to Find, and Other Stories*, 1–23. New York: Harcourt Brace Jovanovich, 1977.

Oliver, Peter. "Extreme Explained: An Inside Look at Extreme Skiing: Its Roots, Its Meaning, Its Devotees." *Skiing*, November 1990, 109–16.

Olivier, Steve. "Moral Dilemmas of Participation in Dangerous Leisure Activities."

Leisure Studies 25, no. 1 (January 2006): 95–109. https://doi.org/10.1080
/02614360500284692.

Ortner, Sherry B. *Life and Death on Mt. Everest: Sherpas and Himalayan Mountaineering*. Princeton: Princeton University Press, 2001.

———. "Thick Resistance: Death and the Cultural Construction of Agency in Himalayan Mountaineering." *Representations* 59 (Summer 1997): 135–62. https://doi.org/10.2307/2928818.

Ostman, Cami. *Second Wind: One Woman's Midlife Quest to Run Seven Marathons on Seven Continents*. Berkeley, Calif.: Seal Press, 2010.

Pagh, Nancy. "An Indescribable Sea: Discourse of Women Traveling the Northwest Coast by Boat." *Frontiers: A Journal of Women Studies* 20, no. 3 (January 1999): 1–26. https://doi.org/10.2307/3347216.

Palmer, Catherine. "Death, Danger and the Selling of Risk in Adventure Sports." In *Understanding Lifestyle Sports: Consumption, Identity and Difference*, edited by Belinda Wheaton, 55–69. New York: Routledge, 2004.

Park, Sowon S. "'Who Are These People?': Anthropomorphism, Dehumanization and the Question of the Other." *Arcadia: Internationale Zeitschrift für Literaturwissenschaft* 48, no. 1 (2013): 150–63. https://doi.org/10.1515/arcadia-2013-0007.

Peary, Robert Edwin. *The Discovery of the North Pole*. London: Hodder and Stoughton, 1910.

Peedom, Jennifer, dir. *Mountain*. 2017; New York: Greenwich Entertainment, 2017.

———. dir. *Sherpa*. 2015; Universal City, Calif.: Universal, 2015.

Peisner, David. "Special Report: The Dangerous Side of Survival TV." TVGuide.com, October 29, 2014. https://www.tvguide.com/news/survival-tv-special-report-1088519.

Pennolino, Paul, dir. "Everest." Season 6, episode 16, *Last Week Tonight*. Aired June 23, 2019, on HBO. Segment available at http://www.youtube.com/watch?v=BchxomS7XOY.

Pham, Andrew X. *Catfish and Mandala: A Two-Wheeled Voyage through the Landscape and Memory of Vietnam*. New York: Picador, 2000.

Phillips, Richard S. "Spaces of Adventure and Cultural Politics of Masculinity: R. M. Ballantyne and *The Young Fur Traders*." *Environment & Planning D: Society & Space* 13, no. 5 (October 1995): 591–608. https://doi.org/10.1068/d130591.

Pinkney, William. *As Long As It Takes: Meeting the Challenge*. Piermont, N.H.: Bunker Hill, 2006.

Plumwood, Val. *Feminism and the Mastery of Nature*. New York: Routledge, 1993.

Potter, George, and Andrew Adkins, dirs. *An American Ascent*. 2014; Silver Spring, Md.: RLJ Entertainment, 2014. http://www.anamericanascent.com.

Potter, Will. *Green Is the New Red: An Insider's Account of a Social Movement under Siege*. San Francisco: City Lights Books, 2011.

prAna. "Accidents do happen and can happen anytime," 2012 Comment on "Carrie Cooper: 39 Weeks," prAna YouTube Channel, YouTube. https://www.youtube.com/watch?v=lV5fRqgCBOw.

Purdy, Jedediah. *After Nature: A Politics for the Anthropocene*. Cambridge, Mass.: Harvard University Press, 2015.

Putnam, Walter. "African Animals in the West: Can the Subaltern Growl?" In *Remembering Africa*, edited by Elisabeth Mudimbe-Boyi, 124–49. Portsmouth, N.H.: Heinemann, 2002.

Rak, Julie. "Social Climbing on Annapurna: Gender in High-Altitude Mountaineering Narratives." *English Studies in Canada* 33, no. 1–2 (March/June 2007): 109–46. https://doi.org/10.1353/esc.0.0030.

Ralston, Aron. *Between a Rock and a Hard Place*. New York: Atria Books, 2004.

Randall, Cassidy. "Kids and an Exciting Mountain Career? It's Complicated." *Outside Online*, July 26, 2018. https://www.outsideonline.com/2320326/motherhood-career-guides-mountain-athletes-complicated.

Raskin, Jonah. "Calls of the Wild on the Page and Screen: From Jack London and Gary Snyder to Jon Krakauer and Sean Penn." *American Literary Realism* 43, no. 3 (Spring 2011): 198–203. https://doi.org/10.5406/amerlitereal.43.3.0198.

Roberts, Suzanne. *Almost Somewhere: Twenty-Eight Days on the John Muir Trail*. Lincoln: University of Nebraska Press, 2012.

Robinson, Victoria. "Taking Risks: Identity, Masculinities and Rock Climbing." In *Understanding Lifestyle Sports: Consumption, Identity and Difference*, edited by Belinda Wheaton, 113–30. New York: Routledge, 2004.

Root, Tik. "Changing the Face of National Parks." *National Geographic News*, February 1, 2017. https://news.nationalgeographic.com/2017/02/diversity-in-national-parks.

Ross, Cindy. *Scraping Heaven: A Family's Journey along the Continental Divide*. Camden, Maine: Ragged Mountain Press, 2002.

RuudJH. "39 weeks pregnant and climbing," 2014 YouTube comment on "Carrie Cooper: 39 Weeks," prAna YouTube Channel, YouTube. https://www.youtube.com/watch?v=lV5fRqgCBOw.

Ryan, Sean. *Theorizing Outdoor Recreation and Ecology: Managing to Enjoy "Nature"?* New York: Palgrave MacMillan, 2015.

Ryman, Dale. "Wausau to Highlight Extreme Sports Potential to Attract Young Professionals." Fox WZAW, March 14, 2019. https://www.wsaw.com/fox/content/news/Wausau-to-highlight-extreme-sports-potentional-to-attract-young-professional-507157951.html.

Saatchi, Anaheed. "Stop Making Movies about White Guys Doing Cool Shit." *Melanin Base Camp* (blog), April 2, 2019. https://www.melaninbasecamp.com/around-the-bonfire/2019/4/2/stop-making-movies-about-white-guys-doing-cool-shit.

Sandilands, Catriona. "Queer Ecology." In *Keywords for Environmental Studies*, edited by Joni Adamson, William A. Gleason, and David N. Pellow, 169–71. New York: New York University Press, 2015. Available at https://keywords.nyupress.org/environmental-studies/essay/queer-ecology.

———. "Wild Democracy: Ecofeminism, Politics, and the Desire Beyond." *Frontiers: A Journal of Women Studies* 18, no. 2 (1997): 135–56. https://doi.org/10.2307/3346970.

Schindler, Kristine, and Jennifer Kraus. *Estimating the Carbon Footprint of Mountaineering Expeditions*. Source 44 Technical White Paper, November 11, 2011. https://www.sourceintelligence.com/userfiles/file/Expedition%20Footprinting_White_Paper.pdf.

Schooler, Lynn. *Walking Home: A Journey in the Alaskan Wilderness*. New York: Bloomsbury, 2010.

Schrepfer, Susan R. *Nature's Altars: Mountains, Gender, and American Environmentalism*. Lawrence: University Press of Kansas, 2005.

Schultheis, Rob. *Bone Games: Extreme Sports, Shamanism, Zen, and the Search for Transcendence*. New York: Breakaway Books, 1996.

Schulz, Brad, dir. *Black Hiker with Blair Underwood*. Funny or Die, November 24, 2009. https://www.funnyordie.com/2009/11/24/18021000/black-hiker-with-blair-underwood.
Segal, Robert Alan. *Theorizing about Myth*. Amherst: University of Massachusetts, 1999.
Shepard, Paul. *Nature and Madness*. Athens: University of Georgia Press, 1998.
Simon, Alvah. *North to the Night: A Spiritual Odyssey in the Arctic*. New York: Broadway Books, 1999.
Simpson, Sherry. *The Accidental Explorer: Wayfinding in Alaska*. Seattle: Sasquatch Books, 2008.
Sinha, Sanskrity. "8 Tons of Trash Cleared Off Mt. Everest; 50 More Remain at Top." *International Business Times*, June 3, 2011. https://www.ibtimes.com/8-tons-trash-cleared-mt-everest-50-more-remain-top-288149.
Slemon, Stephen. "Climbing Mount Everest: Postcolonialism in the Culture of Ascent." *Canadian Literature* 158, no. 9 (Autumn 1998): 15–35.
Soholt, Rennik, dir. "Swamped." Season 1, episode 6, of *Dual Survival*. Aired July 16, 2010, on Discovery Channel.
Spitzer, Nick. "The Story of Woody Guthrie's 'This Land is Your Land.'" *National Public Radio*. February 15, 2012. https://www.npr.org/2000/07/03/1076186/this-land-is-your-land.
Spivak, Gayatri Chakravorty. "Can the Subaltern Speak?" In *Marxism and the Interpretation of Culture*, edited by Cary Nelson and Lawrence Grossberg, 271–313. Urbana: University of Illinois Press, 1988.
Stabile, Carol A. "'A Garden Inclosed Is My Sister': Ecofeminism and Eco-Valences." *Cultural Studies* 8, no. 1 (1994): 56–73. https://doi.org/10.1080/09502389400490041.
Stark, Peter. *Last Breath: Cautionary Tales from the Limits of Human Endurance*. New York: Ballantine Books, 2001.
Stein, Rachel. "Introduction." In *New Perspectives on Environmental Justice: Gender, Sexuality, and Activism*, edited by Rachel Stein, 1–18. New Brunswick, N.J.: Rutgers University Press, 2004.
Stockwell, Peter. *Cognitive Poetics: An Introduction*. New York: Routledge, 2005.
Stoddart, Mark CJ. "Constructing Masculinized Sportscapes: Skiing, Gender and Nature in British Columbia, Canada." *International Review for the Sociology of Sport* 46, no. 1 (March 2011): 108–24. https://doi.org/10.1177/1012690210373541.
Storey, Gail D. *I Promise Not to Suffer: A Fool for Love Hikes the Pacific Crest Trail*. Seattle: Mountaineers Books, 2013.
Stowe, William. *Going Abroad: European Travel in Nineteenth-Century American Culture*. Princeton: Princeton University Press, 1994.
Strayed, Cheryl. *Wild: From Lost to Found on the Pacific Crest Trail*. New York: Alfred A. Knopf, 2012.
Streep, Abe. "Dave Morton Is Quitting Everest. Maybe. (It's Complicated.)." *Outside Online*, April 4, 2016. https://www.outsideonline.com/2064481/david-morton-and-ghosts-everest.
Sundeen, Mark. *The Man Who Quit Money*. New York: Riverhead Books, 2012.
Tam, Kim-Pong, Sau-Lai Lee, and Melody Manchi Chao. "Saving Mr. Nature: Anthropomorphism Enhances Connectedness to and Protectiveness toward Nature." *Journal of Experimental Social Psychology* 49, no. 3 (May 2013): 514–21. https://doi.org/10.1016/j.jesp.2013.02.001.

Taylor, Bron. *Dark Green Religion: Nature Spirituality and the Planetary Future*. Berkeley: University of California Press, 2010.

Taylor, Dorceta E. "Highlights: The State of Diversity in Environmental Organizations: Mainstream NGOs, Foundations and Government Agencies." Green 2.0, July 2014. https://www.diversegreen.org/the-challenge.

———. *The Rise of the American Conservation Movement: Power, Privilege, and Environmental Protection*. Durham, N.C.: Duke University Press, 2016.

"Temoa Adventures." *Temoa Journal* (blog of NativesOutdoors). March 28, 2018. https://natives-outdoors.com/blog/2018/3/28/the-temoa-adventure-journal. Accessed August 30, 2018.

Terry, Macy, and Daniel Hart, dirs. *White Shamans, Plastic Medicine Men*. 1995; Bozeman, Mont.: Native Voices Public Television Workshop, 1995.

Than, Ker. "Everest Climb Successful, Despite Crowds, Unrelenting Winds." *National Geographic News*, May 26, 2012. https://news.nationalgeographic.com/news/2012/05/120526-mount-everest-mt-summit-world-science-crowds-climbers.

Thomson, Rosemarie Garland. *Extraordinary Bodies: Figuring Physical Disability in American Culture and Literature*. New York: Columbia University Press, 1997.

Trombold, John. "High and Low in the Himalayas: Jon Krakauer's *Into Thin Air*." *Popular Culture Review* 10, no. 2 (1999): 89–100.

Twight, Mark. *Kiss or Kill: Confessions of a Serial Climber*. Seattle: Mountaineers Books, 2002.

Vance, Linda. "Ecofeminism and Wilderness." *NWSA Journal* 9, no. 3 (Autumn 1997): 60–76.

van Dooren, Thom, and Deborah Bird Rose. "Storied-Places in a Multispecies City." *Humanimalia: A Journal of Human/Animal Interface Studies* 3, no. 2 (Spring 2012): 1–27.

Vanreusel, Bart. "From Bambi to Rambo: Towards a Socio-Ecological Approach to the Pursuit of Outdoor Sports." In *Sport in Space and Time*, edited by Otmar Weiss and Wolfgang Schulz, 273–82. Vienna, Austria: WUV-Universitätsverlag, 1995.

Vivanco, Luis A. "The Work of Environmentalism in an Age of Televisual Adventures." *Cultural Dynamics* 16, no. 1 (July 2004): 5–27. https://doi.org/10.1177/0921374004042753.

Wagner, Karin. "A Lesson to Be Learned or 'Take a Walk on the Wild Side.'" *Visual Communication* 7, no. 4 (November 2008): 477–502. https://doi.org/10.1177/1470357208096211.

Wallace, Molly. *Risk Criticism: Precautionary Reading in an Age of Environmental Uncertainty*. Ann Arbor: University of Michigan Press, 2016.

Warshaw, Matt. "Environmentalism and Surfing." In *The Encyclopedia of Surfing*, 186–87. Orlando, Fla.: Harvest, 2005.

Weihenmayer, Erik. *Touch the Top of the World*. New York: Dutton, 2001.

Weiss, Miranda. *Tide, Feather, Snow: A Life in Alaska*. New York: Harper Perennial, 2010.

Welling, Bart H. "On the 'Inexplicable Magic of Cinema': Critical Anthropomorphism, Emotion, and the Wildness of Wildlife Films." In *Moving Environments: Affect, Emotion, Ecology, and Film*, edited by Alexa Weik von Mossner, 81–101. Waterloo, Ont.: Wilfrid Laurier University Press, 2014.

Wenzel, Michael, Tyler G. Okimoto, Norman T. Feather, and Michael J. Platow.

"Retributive and Restorative Justice." *Law and Human Behavior* 32, no. 5 (October 2008): 375–89. https://doi.org/10.1007/s10979-007-9116-6.

Weyland, Jocko. *The Answer Is Never: A Skateboarder's History of the World*. New York: Grove Press, 2002.

Wheaton, Belinda. "Introduction: Mapping the Lifestyle Sport-Scape." In *Understanding Lifestyle Sports: Consumption, Identity and Difference*, edited by Belinda Wheaton, 1–28. New York: Routledge, 2004.

———. "'New Lads'? Competing Masculinities in the Windsurfing Culture." In *Understanding Lifestyle Sports: Consumption, Identity and Difference*, edited by Belinda Wheaton, 131–53. New York: Routledge, 2004.

Wheeler, Elizabeth A. "Don't Climb Every Mountain." *ISLE: Interdisciplinary Studies in Literature and Environment* 20, no. 3 (Summer 2013): 553–73. https://doi.org/10.1093/isle/3.1.7.

White, Lynn, Jr. "The Historical Roots of Our Ecologic Crisis." *Science*, n.s., 155, no. 3767 (March 10, 1967): 1203–7. https://doi.org/10.1126/science.155.3767.1203.

Whitman, Walt. *Leaves of Grass: Poems of Walt Whitman*, edited by Lawrence Clark Powell. New York: T. Y. Crowell, 1986.

Whittaker, Tom, and Johnny Dodd. *Higher Purpose: The Heroic Story of the First Disabled Man to Conquer Everest*. Washington, D.C.: Lifeline Press, 2001.

Wilderness Act of 1964. Pub. L. No. 88-577, 16 U.S.C. §§ 1131–1136 (1964).

Williams, Terry Tempest. "The Erotic Landscape." In *Literature and the Environment: A Reader on Nature and Culture*, edited by Lorraine Anderson, Scott P. Slovic, and John P. O'Grady, 28–30. New York: Longman, 1999.

Willis, Clint, ed. *Epic: Stories of Survival from the World's Highest Peaks*. New York: Thunder's Mouth Press, 1997.

———, ed. *High: Stories of Survival from Everest and K2*. New York: Thunder's Mouth Press, 1999.

———, ed. *Ice: Stories of Survival from Polar Exploration*. New York: Thunder's Mouth Press, 1999.

———, ed. *Kennedys: Stories of Life and Death from an American Family*. New York: Thunder's Mouth Press, 2001.

———, ed. *Mob: Stories of Death and Betrayal from Organized Crime*. New York: Thunder's Mouth Press, 2001.

———, ed. *Rough Water: Stories of Survival from the Sea*. New York: Thunder's Mouth Press, 1999.

Willis, Clint, and David Roberts, eds. *Climb: Stories of Survival from Rock, Snow and Ice*. New York: Thunder's Mouth Press, 1999.

Wilson, Erica, and Donna E. Little. "Adventure and the Gender Gap: Acknowledging Diversity of Experience." *Loisir et Société/Society and Leisure* 28, no. 1 (April 2005): 185–208. https://doi.org/10.1080/07053436.2005.10707676.

"Woman's Solo Hiking Trip Shockingly Doesn't Have to Do with Inner Journey or Anything." *The Onion*, March 15, 2019. https://local.theonion.com/woman-s-solo-hiking-trip-shockingly-doesn-t-have-to-do-1833329867.

Woodlief, Jennifer. *A Bolt from the Blue: The Epic True Story of Danger, Daring, and Heroism at 13,000 Feet*. New York: Atria, 2012.

Woodward, Forest, Anna Callaghan, and Marie Sullivan, dirs. *Sacred Strides*. Boulder, Colo.: Outside, 2018. Posted in "Culture," *Outside Online*, August 6, 2018. https://www.outsideonline.com/2333331/sacred-strides.

Zinn, Jens Oliver. "Living in the Anthropocene: Towards a Risk-Taking Society."

Environmental Sociology 2, no. 4 (October 2016): 385–94. https://doi.org/10.1080/23251042.2016.1233605.

Zuckerman, Peter, and Amanda Padoan. *Buried in the Sky: The Extraordinary Story of the Sherpa Climbers on K2's Deadliest Day*. New York: Norton, 2012.

INDEX

180° *South* (film), 8, 22

Abbey, Edward, 99, 142, 172, 209
Abram, David, 126, 162, 229, 241n57
accidents, 18, 27, 70, 101, 183, 185. *See also* risk
Ackerman, Diane, 35, 126, 263n60
activism. *See* environmental awareness; environmental justice; environmental movement; feminism; social justice
adrenaline junkie. *See* adrenaline madness
adrenaline madness, 26, 87, 213; audience appeal, 2, 9–11, 33–36, 85, 168–69; environmental benefit, 141, 224; environmental danger, 199; nature's unique appeal, 112; participant appeal, 2, 6–7, 56, 59–60, 82, 84, 91–92, 99, 128, 169, 174–83, 191. *See also* adventure; audience; death; risk
adrenaline narrative. *See* American adrenaline narrative
adventure: charity tie in, 48, 84–85, 218–19, 228, 249n130; corporate sponsorship, 46–47, 49–50, 84–85, 94–95, 145, 151, 186, 246n32; environmental impact of, 71, 86, 151, 164–65, 204–7, 218–19, 221, 246n26; expedition/prize economics, 46, 49–50, 80, 218, 246n31; family impact on, 27–28, 53–54, 78–79, 96, 102–3, 185–86, 217, 220, 224. *See also* adrenaline madness; adventure film; adventure gap; adventure porn; adventure television; adventure travel; armchair adventurer; authenticity; body: adventurous; exploration; extreme; heroic masculinity
—environmental movement's connection to, 2–3, 10–11, 23, 148, 151, 218, 222–24, 229, 231; conquering goals shared, 82–85, 86; in erotic desire, 121–23, 139, 141–42, 144, 154; in risky desire, 169–72, 199–213; in spiritual desire, 101, 103–4, 118, 120, 130
adventure film, 15, 18, 21, 32, 242n72; adaptations, 4–5, 8; African Americans, 29; documentary films, 8; Everest, 4, 22, 23; exoticism in, 57; free solo climbing, 47–48; Native Americans, 221–22; Treadwell, Timothy, 150; wildlife, 155
adventure gap, 30–31, 186; gender, 50, 51, 192; historical exclusion, 22–23; race/ethnicity, 53–56, 72, 145, 220, 222, 224n137
adventure marketing, 1–2, 7; adrenaline term/lifestyle, 17, 211; advertising, 51, 172–73, 228–29, 244n137; athletes, 48; best sellers, 25; North Face, 2, 227–28, 244n129; Sundance, 2, 239n3. *See also* extreme: branding
adventure porn, 67, 123, 173, 205, 227, 230. *See also* adrenaline madness
adventure television, 8, 15, 28, 242n72, 247n85. *See also* survival: television and media; *and specific television shows*
adventure travel, 3, 15, 197, 206, 239n7, 265n183; alternative routes, 12, 13, 217, 224–25, 229, 257n46; frontier travel, 21–22, 64
advertising. *See* adventure marketing
Aebi, Tania, 85, 201, 202–3
African Americans, 168, 201, 222, 227, 244n137, 247n85; American identity, 191, 220; Black Lives Matter, 172; Black Power, 172, 269n85; Expedition Denali, 168, 219–20, 244n129; Johnson, Shelton, 219–22, 227; lynching, 193–94, 195; National Parks Event, 195; ownership of nature, 69;

African Americans (*continued*)
Pinkney, William, 50, 176, 194–95; risk, 53, 193–96; trailblazers, 5–6, 29, 30, 50–51, 145–46, 187, 194–95. *See also* Danenberg, Sophia; Haile, Rahawa; Harris, Eddy L.; Mills, James Edward

Alaimo, Stacy, 133, 137; cyborg, 125; transcorporeality, 20, 125–26, 127, 132–33, 140, 155, 158

Alaska, 28, 67; environmental impact on, 71, 86, 158–59, 198, 202, 204–5, 218, 266n220; frontier mythology, 103, 203, 205, 208; pilgrimage destination, 103, 180, 214; risky setting, 27, 65, 100, 140, 149–50, 160, 190

Allison, Stacy, 15, 25, 34, 116, 186; Everest significance of, 82, 89–90, 96, 98

Alone on the Wall: Alex Honnold (film), 47–48

American adrenaline narrative: archetypal characteristics, 3, 11, 115, 124, 166, 211; footsteps travel writing relationship to, 21–22, 242n86; genre defined, 2–3, 7, 12–36, 53, 59, 140, 200, 223, 230, 241n68, 242n72, 242n102; irony in, 107, 137–38, 156, 165, 196; literary style and tone, 16, 25–29, 87, 167, 169, 174, 196, 210, 227; popularity, 1–3, 9–13, 32–36, 168–69, 231; pre-1970 precursors, 3–8; protagonists, 5, 29–33, 43, 161–62. *See also* adrenaline madness; adventure film; adventure television; animals; armchair adventurer; audience; authorship; body; class; desire; environmental imagination; gender; heroic masculinity; plot; race; setting; tragedy

American dream, 33–36, 85–86, 215

American identity, 2, 8, 54, 213, 215–16, 220; heroic masculinity, 4, 5, 43, 85, 228. *See also under* African Americans; frontier; masculinity; risk; wilderness

American myth, 33, 211; challenges to, 122; exceptionalism, 3–4; freedom, 88, 144, 167, 204; frontier, 5, 33, 43, 85–86, 139, 203, 222; westering, 55. *See also* frontier; heroic masculinity; manifest destiny; Protestant work ethic

Anderson, Douglas, 116

Anderson, Lorraine, 142

androcentrism, 20, 122, 137, 156

animals: bears, 73, 110, 149–51, 157, 158–59, 160–62, 180–81, 188, 197, 204, 206, 215; birds, 110, 120, 130, 153, 158, 163, 197, 209; cruelty free label, 9; domesticated, 166, 215; emotion of, 157–58, 162; fish, 155–56, 159–60, 165–66, 197; fox, 109–10, 197; planning by, 225–26; prairie dogs, 109;

representation in adrenaline narratives, 120, 146, 158, 188; self/other distinction, 11, 28, 124, 128–29, 132, 144, 150, 151–53, 155, 158, 160–62, 256n28; as teachers, 90, 109–10. *See also* anthropomorphism

animal studies, 151. *See also* animals; anthropomorphism

Anker, Conrad, 68, 197

Anthropocene, 37, 152, 170, 171; adventure in, 14, 38, 196–205; definition of, 38

anthropocentrism, 119, 130, 156, 199, 208, 217; challenge to, 120, 122, 123–24, 126, 128, 141, 154; environmental impact, 138, 148, 165, 207, 226

anthropomorphism, 127, 137, 151, 152–62, 164; blurred, 125, 127, 133, 155, 157, 158, 160–61, 162–66; cinematic, 155; critical, 123, 130, 151–58, 160, 162, 164; liminal, 124, 125, 126, 127, 133, 134, 154–58, 160–62, 164, 205; queer, 161–62

apocalypse, 2, 9, 36, 206; post-apocalypse, 247n85

Appalachian Trail, 31, 38, 105, 106, 187, 191; Appalachian Mountain Club Library and Archives, 7. *See also* Davis, Jennifer Pharr; Haile, Rahawa

armchair adventurer, 4, 29, 33; (re-)connect with nature, 10, 34, 67, 183, 224; responsibility of, 231; superior intelligence, 98, 100, 183. *See also* adrenaline madness; audience

Armstrong, Philip, 152

Arnesen, Liv: discrimination, 79, 81; relationship impact, 76–77; spiritual desire, 104, 109; team's journey, 93

Asian Americans, 53–54, 79; Outdoor Asian, 222. *See also* Pham, Andrew X.

Atherton, John (Michael), 122, 163–64

audience, 20, 40, 76; appeals to, 25, 28, 33–36, 175, 177; assumptions, 59; judgments by, 185, 201, 202; mainstream, 43; responsibilities of, 13, 231; touristic gaze, 57; wilderness readers, 251n19. *See also* adrenaline madness; armchair adventurer
—adrenaline narrative impact on, 224; via anthropomorphism, 154, 155, 164; via climate crisis education, 207, 212; via heroic masculinity, 58, 60–61; via spiritual transformation, 88, 89, 93, 98, 116, 215

Austin, Mary, 142, 145

authenticity, 205; adventure, 13, 21, 45–52, 101, 151, 229; Disney contrast with, 102–3, 246n24; elite status marker, 83, 99, 106; fragility of, 155; Indigeneity characteristic

INDEX   293

of, 57, 109; setting characteristic of, 111, 112, 198. *See also* desire
authorship, 58, 138-39, 175, 212; class, 45; climate crisis priority, 205, 222; gender differences, 77, 96-97; niche, 105; scope in adrenaline narratives, 2, 13, 15-17, 25-33, 53-56; underrepresented, 72. *See also* American adrenaline narrative: protagonists; body; class; gender; race; sexuality

Balf, Todd, 16, 166-67; adrenaline appeal, 8; adrenaline scale, 26, 139-40; corporate expeditioning, 46
Balmain, Melissa, 184
Bancroft, Ann: conquering, 68; debt, 49-50; discrimination, 79, 81; footsteps narrative, 22; motivation, 84, 90; partner, 31; team's journey, 93
Barcott, Bruce, 25, 241n69, 244n129
Barnes, Barbara A., 217, 220-22
Barnes, David M., 105
Barthes, Roland, 59, 60, 97-98, 252n57
Bates, Robert H. Mountaineering Collection, 6
Baudrillard, Jean, 102
Bayers, Peter L., 41, 63, 244n137
Baym, Nina, 114
Beck, Ulrich, 255n4; risk assessment, 182; risk sharing, 218; risk society, 35, 38, 170-71, 210; social status, 183-84. *See also* risk
Beedie, Paul, 68-69
Berman, Tao, 38; risk, 100, 101, 177-79, 181, 182; sport's gender disparity, 32
Beyond Survival (television show), 57
biking, 16, 18, 54, 84; mountain, 61-62, 64, 227; risk, 26, 28, 188, 211
biocentric, 156, 207, 226. *See also* ecocentric
Bird, Isabella, 142
Birrell, Susan, 184; Everest narrative, 21, 26, 56, 58, 99, 117
black Americans. *See* African Americans
Black Hiker with Blair Underwood (video), 30
Blanchard, Barry, 60
Bledsoe, Lucy Jane, 31, 100
Blehm, Eric, 16, 232
Blum, Arlene, 186; all-female expedition, 75; gender disparity, 77, 78, 79, 80-81; second-wave feminism, 135
Blum, Hester, 4
Blumenburg, Hans, 65
body, 36, 42, 66; adventurous, 48, 73-82, 92, 169, 222-25, 231; dead, 26, 68, 163, 198, 201-2; disabled, 29-30, 31, 216, 244n131;

disembodiment, 164; entanglement, 133, 257n71; female/feminine, 44, 57-58, 59-60, 67, 73, 81, 117, 121, 135, 166, 185, 187-91; male/masculine, 73, 75, 103, 121-22, 135, 165-66, 223, 247n85; mind/body split, 133, 146, 224; normate, 30, 150, 216, 222, 228-29; porous, 125-26, 160-61, 219. *See also* animals; death; disability; femininity; intersectionality; masculinity; trans-corporeality
Booth, Douglas, 181
bootstrap mentality. *See* Protestant work ethic
Boston, Elliot, 51, 244n129
Bott, Esther, 57, 173
Bourdieu, Pierre, 75
Bowley, Graham, 46, 83, 104-5, 106, 115-16
Braverman, Blair, 31, 38, 188-93, 218 251n12
Breivik, Gunnar, 206, 210
Bridgers, Lee, 61-63, 66, 248n103
Brown, David, 42-43, 75
Brymer, Eric: dancing with nature, 130; ecocentric transformation, 141, 142, 156, 162, 223; environmental impact, 199; participation rates, 8; risk, 168, 175-77, 182-83
Bryson, Bill, 8, 26
Buell, Frederick, 170, 197
Buell, Lawrence, 12, 13, 200, 203. *See also* environmental imagination
Bullis, Connie, 257n46
Burkard, Chris, 227-28, 269n72
Burke, Shaunna A., 245n7
Burroughs, John, 215
Buxton, Ryan, 217
Byers, Alton, 198-99
Byl, Christine, 164; environmental impact and responsibility, 202-6, 209, 210; gender inclusion, 187, 224-25; wildness, 128-29, 144-45

Cabeza de Vaca, Álvar Núñez, 4
Callaghan, Anna, 199, 221; *Sacred Strides*, 221-22
Callahan, Steven, 37; environmental ethic, 101, 119, 165-66, 196, 202; self/other, 137-38, 154, 155-57; spiritual desire, 95, 99-100, 104, 108, 109
Campbell, James, 100
Campbell, Joseph, 85
Canebrake Archive, 7, 240n26
Canterbury, Dave, 110-11, 150, 250n166. *See also Dual Survival*
Cape Fear Surfing Archive, 7, 240n26
carbon footprint, 68, 231, 249n130

Carman, Colin, 149, 150, 161
"Carrie Cooper: 39 Weeks" (YouTube video), 185
Carson, Rachel, 142, 172, 209
Chagani, Fayaz, 152, 158, 260n169
Chao, Melody Manchi, 153, 154, 155
Chavez, Tazbah, 230–31
Chin, Jimmy, 48
Chisholm, Dianne, 44
chremamorphism, 160, 257n74
Christensen, Doug, 200, 229, 231
Clare, Eli, 31
class, 10, 53, 56, 153, 155, 193; athletes, 11, 32, 33, 114, 117, 194; dirt bag, 32, 47, 114–15; exploitation, 109, 246n26; extremes, 172; heroic masculinity, 22, 45–50, 58, 74; middle class, 3, 70; nonmaterial wealth, 48, 101, 107; poverty, 126, 184, 197, 201; prize money, 49–50. *See also* intersectionality
climate change. *See* climate crisis
climate crisis, 12–15, 35, 84, 88, 213; denial, 36, 68, 218; impact, 196–202, 212, 221, 215, 249n130; overpopulation, 197; poverty, 197; response to, 23, 37, 38, 139, 169–74, 179, 182–83, 225; thinking, 207. *See also* conservation; environmental awareness; environmental movement; environmental protection; pollution
Coffey, Maria, 31, 218; appeal of extreme adventure, 43, 74, 83, 87, 112, 118; family-minded adventurer, 186; gender disparity, 51, 79; magical nature, 157; motivating mountaineer, 84–85
Cohen, Michael P., 20, 130
Cohen, Tom, 196, 265n162
colonialism, 70, 82, 88, 123, 209, 211; American adrenaline narrative, 30, 32, 61, 141, 167, 212, 242n102, 244n137; animal studies, 152; fantasy, 19; heroic masculinity, 31, 40, 43, 59, 245n11; neo-imperialism, 46; (pre-)colonial America, 4, 5, 28, 37, 41–42, 53–54, 55–57, 110–11; restorative desire, 229. *See also* postcolonialism
Colony, The (television show), 247n85
Connell, R. W., 42, 245n10
conquering desire, 40–86, 242n102; complication/rewriting of, 4, 7, 123–24, 138, 147, 219; control characteristic of, 3, 24, 37, 41–42, 56–82, 126, 127; dominate desire, 31, 32, 37, 40–41, 45, 58; erotic desire relation to, 70, 88, 121–23, 136, 138–43, 146–49, 166–67; goals of, 61, 82–85, 90, 140, 193, 195, 200, 220, 227, 228; hyperbole in, 56, 68–69, 176; military influence on, 3, 32, 61, 68–69, 75, 105, 110–11; ownership/naming of nature in, 57, 68–71, 110, 113, 140, 143, 146; restorative desire relation to, 230; sexual metaphor use of, 59–68; spiritual desire relation to, 37, 40–41, 47, 82, 85, 88, 90–92, 93–95, 99, 110–11, 117, 119; suffering (secular), 27, 58, 64, 69, 71–72. *See also* adventure; desire; ecofeminism; heroic masculinity; journey; Krakauer, Jon; manifest destiny; mountaineering; patriarchy; postcolonialism; sexuality
—exploitation of: environment, 35–36, 88–89, 136, 153, 165, 171–72, 209, 211, 225, 227; Indigenous people, 110, 153, 231; Sherpa labor, 246n26; women, 60, 153
—risky desire relation to, 70, 82, 174–75; authenticity, 47–48, 84, 198; environment, 67, 200; gender and race, 52–56, 59, 63, 69, 72–79, 85–86, 192–93, 195
conservation, 12, 35, 61, 206–7, 222; behavior, 154, 165, 209; heroic masculinity, 209; models of, 38, 62; service corps, 228. *See also* climate crisis; environmental awareness; environmental movement; environmental protection
conservatism, 81; environmental imagination, 33; risk, 12, 114, 186. *See also* counterculture
Conway, Eustace, 106, 109, 114, 208, 209. *See also* Gilbert, Elizabeth
Copeland, Sebastian, 22
Counter, S. Allen, 6
counterculture, 8; alternative routes, 12, 13, 217, 224–25, 229, 257n46; extreme lifestyle, 16, 28, 33, 81; extreme sports, 18, 61, 184, 206, 240n37; risk narrative, 172. *See also* conservatism
Cox, Lynne, 201–2
Crane, Cason, 31
Crenshaw, Kimberlé, 14
Cronon, William, 20, 130, 147, 225–26, 269n64
Crouch, Geoffrey I., 21–22, 44–45, 64
Crouch, Gregory, 37, 247n46; nature representation of, 63–64, 65, 66, 68, 86, 99, 112, 113, 229; pilgrimage, 89; risk, 26, 70, 95–96, 114, 118–19, 175; success, 48–49, 83
Csikszentmihalyi, Mihaly, 177
Cuomo, Chris, 14, 66, 256n13
cyborg, 125–26

Danenberg, Sophia, 29, 30, 51, 145–46, 244n138
Darwin, Charles, 142
Davis, Jennifer Pharr, 52, 105, 155, 191
Davis, Steph, 176

INDEX 295

death, 4, 66, 71, 164; adventurers, 16, 18, 25, 27, 68, 105, 198, 217; camp, 53; defying, 26, 28, 35–36, 47–48, 65, 72, 73, 89, 93, 119, 173; double-standard, 78, 184, 185; drive, 210; environment, 66, 151, 163, 197, 201–2, 203; lynching, 193–94; plot point, 21, 33–34, 100–101; risk as "little death," 59–60; as transformative risk, 99, 141, 156, 165–66, 170, 175–76; Treadwell views of, 149–51, 160, 180–81; wish, 82, 178–79; zone, 81, 140, 199. *See also* adrenaline madness; risk; tragedy
d'Eaubonne, Françoise, 256n13
de Crèvecoeur, J. Hector St. John, 4, 13
deep play. *See under* play
de Gennaro, Mara, 133, 152, 159
Deloria, Philip J., 111
democracy, 61, 213, 219; wild, 144–45, 231
Denali, 71–72, 73, 93, 100–101; Expedition Denali, 29–30, 168, 219–20, 244n129
desire: adventurous, 1–2, 10, 12, 24–25, 36–39; five desires origin of, 242n102; five desires relation to each other, 2, 24, 27, 36, 38, 40, 129–34, 166–67, 175, 210, 212, 216–17. *See also* adrenaline madness; authenticity; conquering desire; erotic desire; restorative desire; risky desire; spiritual desire
Diamond, Irene, 256n13
Dillard, Annie, 26, 142
disability, 29–30, 31, 216, 244n131; Supercrip, 30, 216. *See also* body; intersectionality
discovery. *See* exploration
Disney, 47, 102, 246n24
Diversify Outdoors, 222, 223
diversity. *See* intersectionality
Doomsday Preppers (television show), 8
Dougherty, Alan P., 151, 205
Douglas, Mary, 29, 170
Downey, Greg, 199
Dual Survival (Canterbury, Lundin, and Teti television show), 8, 75, 110–11, 119
Dude, You're Screwed (television show), 247n85
Dufresne, John, 34
Dwyer, June, 150, 256n28

Earth Day, 2, 7, 55
Earth First!, 9, 172
Earth Liberation Front, 172
Ebert, Philip A., 206–7, 208
ecocentric, 141, 156, 223. *See also* biocentric
ecocriticism, 12, 151–52, 169, 216, 232, 257n71
ecofeminism, 170, 257n46; conquering desire, 56, 58, 59–60; erotic desire, 24, 62, 119, 122–23, 129, 133, 134, 256n13; essentialism, 66, 249n123; methodology, 14, 36–37, 41, 151; self/other, 123–27, 136, 138, 143, 153; wilderness, 122, 139–45, 211–12. *See also* feminism
eco-imaginary, 13–14. *See also* environmental imagination
ecological footprint, 14, 68, 203, 205, 231, 249n130
ecological Indian, 111, 156, 230. *See also* Native Americans
ecology, 38, 90, 116, 151, 226; bankrupt, 37, 119; dark, 19, 24; deep, 24, 125; restoration, 24, 215, 229; queer, 132, 161–62
eco-terms, 9, 240n38
Edelman, Lee, 210, 267n249
edgework, 186, 223. *See also* risk
Ehrlich, Gretel, 142
Ellis, Reuben J., 244n137
Else, Liz, 136
endurance. *See* survival
entanglement, 133, 257n71. *See also* body
environment: gift economy, 119, 225–26; natural/unnatural definition, 1, 5, 9, 11, 16, 17–19, 23, 26, 76, 103, 110, 112; race and, 54, 187, 193–96; stewardship of, 67, 117. *See also* climate crisis; desire; environmental protection; nature; setting; sustainability; wilderness
environmental awareness: art installation as, 218; in / effect of extreme adventure, 84, 88, 120, 135, 141, 159, 176, 200, 204, 221, 223–24, 255n4; greenwashing, 38, 205–10; products, 9. *See also* green; sustainability
environmental ethics, 14, 101, 102, 138–39, 200, 205, 207–8, 210; children as motivation, 209–10; ecological Indian, 111, 156, 230; erotic, 164–67; greenwashing, 38, 205–10; Indigenous, 163, 167; kinetic empathy, 223–24; leave no trace, 164–65, 203, 208; pragmatism, 205–10; risky, 206; simple life, 205–8. *See also* authenticity
environmental humanities, 12
environmental imagination: definition of, 12–15, 23–25, 36–38, 115–16, 219–20, 223, 227, 231; paradoxical relationship to nature, 10, 19, 35–36, 71, 86, 170, 196, 203, 205, 208, 224, 227; risk, 170, 178; schizophrenic relationship to nature (Jacobs), 35, 88, 170, 211; spirituality in, 89; white (heroic) masculinity, 29–33, 58, 67, 122. *See also* Buell, Lawrence
environmental justice, 193; adventure characteristic of, 84, 183, 199, 210, 211–12, 220, 223–24, 228, 230–32; Anthropocene,

environmental justice (*continued*)
37; anthropomorphism, 152, 164; environmental racism, 111, 201. *See also* environmental awareness; environmental movement; feminism; social justice

Environmental Life Force (ELF), 172

environmental movement: activism, 12, 38, 54, 172, 200, 204, 205-10; American, 2-3, 7, 9, 24, 29, 38-39, 67, 242n98; direct action, 9, 172; representation of, 61-62, 208-9; spiritual connection to, 104-5, 110, 112-13, 130; wildness role of, 144-45. *See also* conservation; environmental awareness; environmental ethics; environmental justice; environmental protection; feminism; green; National Geographic; social justice; sustainability

—adventure's connection to, 2-3, 10-11, 23, 24, 148, 151, 218, 222-24, 229, 231; conquering goals shared, 82-85, 86; in erotic desire, 121-23, 139, 141-42, 144, 154; in risky desire, 169-72, 199-213; in spiritual desire, 101, 103-4, 118, 120, 130

—organizations: Earth First!, 9, 172; Earth Liberation Front, 172; Environmental Life Force (ELF), 172; Orangutan Foundation International (OFI), 207; Sierra Club, 61; Surfrider, 206; Twenty-first Century Conservation Service Corps, 228

environmental protection, 205-7, 209-10, 221, 224; failure, 116-17; gender, 52, 67-68; paradox, 35, 88-89, 124, 171-72; wilderness, 139. *See also* conservation; environmental awareness; environmental movement

epic, 16, 114, 211

epiphany. *See* spiritual desire

Ericson, Katherine, 231-32

erotic desire, 27, 121-167; companion species, 120, 126, 148, 156, 158, 256n28; conquering desire relation to, 70, 88, 121-23, 136, 138-43, 146-49, 166-67; dancing, 101, 127-39; deep play, 35, 126, 137, 175, 176, 178-79, 183, 216, 228; definition of, 24, 36, 256n13; egalitarian, 60, 61, 129; goals of, 129, 138, 140-41, 157-58, 167; heroic masculinity, 122-23, 131-32, 136-37, 139-43, 145-51, 162, 164; liminal intimacy, 124-27, 133-34, 154-58, 160-62, 164, 205; mystery/ magic, 137, 144, 157; participatory, 123, 126, 127, 138, 148; pornographic contrast to, 123, 131, 138; restorative desire relation to, 219, 223, 226-27, 229, 231; risky desire relation to, 126-27, 141, 149-50, 152, 167, 173, 205; self/other, 123-29, 130-31, 134, 138, 143, 148, 158, 166; significant otherness, 125-27, 158, 164; spiritual desire relation to, 88, 119-23, 136, 137, 139-42, 144, 146-49, 156, 163-64; sustainability, 173, 205, 223, 226; voice (human), 138, 142-43, 231; voice (nature's), 70, 123, 144, 151-53, 158-59, 167, 222; wilderness, 20, 122-27, 129, 130, 133-34, 138-45, 147, 155, 157-58, 163-66. *See also* anthropomorphism; desire; mutuality; trans-corporality

ethnocentric, 20, 117, 122

Everest, 89-90, 96, 112, 239n1, 239n5; deaths, 25, 26, 31, 41, 50, 68, 98-99, 198, 202; disabled climbers of, 29-30, 244n131; ethics, 28, 82-83, 121, 217-19, 267n14; expense, 46; films, 22, 23; marketing, 25, 173; narratives, 21, 26, 40-41, 56, 58, 117, 139; pollution, 68, 116-17, 198-99, 223, 265n178; race, 29, 51, 145-46, 244n129; risk, 4, 26, 28, 79, 148-49, 176, 180, 214-15; suffering, 87; tourism, 1-2, 18-19, 72, 203. *See also* adventure film; Sherpas

Ewert, Alan, 174

Expedition Denali, 168, 219-20, 244n129

exploration, 113, 232; adrenaline narrative origins in, 4-7, 16-18, 85-86; American, 37, 41; excessive, 83; gender/race challenges, 31, 55, 59-60, 64, 79; retracing, 22; self, 89-90, 91, 109, 129, 168, 175, 191-92; wayfinding contrasted to, 140-41. *See also* adventure; colonialism

extreme, 59, 108, 215, 230; alternative lifestyle, 17, 19, 33, 47, 61, 81, 107, 205, 208, 225; branding, 1-2, 7, 17, 48, 51, 172-73, 211, 227-28; cultures of, 3-14, 28-29, 32-36, 170-74, 198; definition of, 8; mainstreaming of extreme cultures, 7-9, 43, 172-74; as new normal, 70, 173-74, 182; normal contrasted to, 9, 28-29, 89, 103, 114, 150-51, 179, 183, 186, 191; risky lifestyle and appeal, 2, 12, 16, 23, 27, 172-73, 174-81, 204, 210-12; weather, 9, 29, 173. *See also* adrenaline madness; adventure; audience; counterculture; environmental imagination; extreme sports; risk; setting

extreme sports, 2, 3, 23, 130; adrenaline narrative focus, 12, 16-19, 227; alternative lifestyle of, 61, 81; heroic masculinity in, 42-43, 63; mainstreaming of, 7-9, 11; male dominance of, 30, 32, 43, 49-50, 53, 72, 172, 174; nationalism in, 83; risk in, 83, 170, 172, 175-85, 196-200, 210-11, 218; spiritual calling/transformation, 90, 92-93, 105, 116, 119, 141, 223-24. *See also* biking; hiking; kayaking; mountaineering; rafting; running; sailing; skiing; surfing; swimming

Faludi, Susan, 241n52
family. *See* adventure: family impact on
femininity, 68; athletic, 31-32, 73, 110-11, 122, 150, 145-46, 223, 224; dependency, 76-77, 81-82, 85, 93-94, 96; domestic, 74; emotion, 70; irrationality, 137; nature, 45, 56, 58, 59, 64, 66, 74, 115, 119, 134-36; nurturing, 142. *See also* gender; *jouissance*
feminism, 9, 43, 62, 133, 151, 224; activism, 135; complaint, 44; crisis in white masculinity connection to, 210; environmental movement connection to, 213; essentialist, 14, 66, 126, 135, 249n123; French, 124, 256n13; Indigenous, 256n13; liberal, 135, 192; male gaze, 138, 190; #MeToo, 172, 191; *parler-femme*, 124; radical, 123, 172; second wave, 58, 75, 135; self/other relationship, 123-27; third wave, 256n34. *See also* ecofeminism; environmental justice; environmental movement; social justice
Fern, Richard L., 129-30
Field, Terri, 126
film. *See* adventure film
Finney, Carolyn, 193, 195
FitzGerald, Holly Conklin, 100
Five Elements of Adventure, The (film), 57, 248n86
flow. *See* play
Fondren, Kristi M., 51
Ford, Nick, 42-43, 75
Francis, John, 130, 139
Franklin, Adrian, 248n88
Fredston, Jill, 37, 141; Alaska, 27; climate crisis, 111, 197-98, 202, 203, 209-10; gender, 79-80; leave no trace, 165; nature, 65, 132, 133, 158-60, 222; risk, 182; spiritual-erotic desire, 108, 113, 120, 163; sport as lifestyle, 92, 94-95, 102, 172-73, 208
Freer, Luanne, 217-18
Free Solo (film), 48
Freud, Sigmund, 65
Frohlick, Susan, 43, 72, 246n26
Fromm, Pete, 16, 26
frontier: Alaska as last frontier, 103, 203, 205; American identity, 54, 114, 209; American myth, 16, 43, 85-86, 203, 211, 222; closing of, 5, 213; popularity/nostalgia, 6, 10, 34, 145, 215; travel narrative, 21-22, 33, 44, 69. *See also* Alaska; American myth; heroic masculinity
Frontin, Glenn, 105

Gaard, Greta, 122-27, 134, 136, 199; environmental justice, 201; wilderness, 20, 188, 189, 203, 212, 213, 223, 257n46
Gardner, Renne, 244n129
Garrard, Greg, 11
Gates, Barbara T., 256n113
gender, 22, 53, 139, 174, 228-29; American dream, 85; authentic adventure, 51-52; binary, 133, 135-37; cultural construction, 9, 54, 56-59, 82, 95-96, 135-36, 193, 196, 224; filter, 146, 187-90; inequality, 29, 30-31, 41, 43, 49, 56, 73-82, 135, 184, 186, 213; risk, 11, 72-82, 169-70, 180, 183-93; wilderness, 10, 19. *See also* femininity; gendered space; intersectionality; masculinity; nature; sex-based violence; wilderness
gendered space, 44, 67, 74, 94, 187
gender performance, 31-32, 40-41, 44, 68, 72-77; in *Dual Survival*, 110-11; Treadwell, Timothy, 150, 161. *See also* gender: cultural construction
genre. *See* American adrenaline narrative
Gersdorf, Catrin, 242n102
Gessner, David, 9
Gilbert, Elizabeth, 16, 38; American dream, 33, 85-86; environmental ethic, 208; masculinity, 209; spiritual desire, 106, 109, 114
Gilbertson, Ken, 174
Girl Scouts, 51
Giulianotti, Richard, 174-75, 177
Glave, Dianne D., 244n137
Glick, Daniel, 10-11, 197, 207
global warming (and extreme weather): 9, 29, 173. *See also* climate crisis
god, 35, 100, 104-9, 211; given right, 214, 220; goddess, 116-17, 128, 129; nature, 64-65, 93, 99, 114, 115, 147, 148, 212; sin against, 118-19. *See also* religion; soul; spiritual desire; spirituality
Gonzales, Laurence, 15, 101, 178, 181-83
Gordon, Jon F., 246n43
Gram, Margaret Hunt, 210
Gray, Tonia: dancing with nature, 130; ecocentric transformation, 141, 142, 156, 162, 199, 223; risk, 175
green: adventure, 205, 210; ceiling, 29; fire, 128; greenwashing, 38, 205-10; practices,

green (*continued*)
172; products, 9, religion, 37, 88, 105, 109. *See also* sustainability
Green, Martin, 74
Green 2.0, 29
Greenfield, Rob, 84, 85
Greenpeace, 9
greenwashing, 38, 205–10. *See also* environmental ethics
Gregory, Derek, 76
Griffin, Susan, 60, 66, 124, 242n102, 249n123
grit. *See* heroic masculinity; Protestant work ethic; survival
Grizzly Man (film), 150, 259n156
Grothjan, Sarah, 52
Guthrie, Woody, 227–28, 269n72

Hahn, Jennifer, 16, 26, 27, 38; journey, 90; nature, 155, 158, 159–60, 163–64; ritual, 110; spiritual-erotic desire, 120
Haile, Rahawa: adrenaline narrative (forthcoming), 31; Appalachian Trail, 38, 187, 188, 191, 192, 195
Haraway, Donna, 125–26, 127, 158
Hargreaves, Alison, 78, 79
Harman, Graham, 19
Harris, Deborah A., 51
Harris, Eddy L., 15, 37, 138; heroic masculinity revision, 131–32, 136–37, 140, 146–49; nature's gifts, 119, 166; ownership of nature, 69; pollution, 200–201; spiritual desire, 99, 105, 107, 108, 109; sportscape, 139; voice, 159; wilderness as raced space, 53, 55, 194, 195
Hart, Daniel, 111
Hawk, Tony, 19
Hediger, Ryan, 150–51, 161
hegemonic masculinity. *See* heroic masculinity
Heise, Ursula K., 169–70, 182, 183–84, 200, 211, 265n166
Heller, Chaia, 242n102; ecofeminist desire as revolutionary, 129; erotic desire, 119; self/other, 124–25, 126, 127, 158
Henderson, Philip, 29, 244n129
Henson, Matthew A., 5–6, 22
heroic masculinity, 68, 182, 215; adrenaline narrative investment in, 22, 72; class, 45–50; definition, 3, 5, 41–45, 94–95, 175, 199–200, 216, 228–29; gender, 51–52, 73, 77–82, 136–37, 162, 180–81; myth, 65, 85; race, 50–51, 53–56, 209, 219–22; resistance to, 90, 122–23, 131–32, 139–43, 145–51, 164,
193, 217, 219–22, 223. *See also* American identity: heroic masculinity; authenticity; masculinity
Herr, Patricia Ellis, 184
Herzog, Werner, 94, 150–51, 259n156
heteronormality, 210, 267n249; adrenaline narrative, 31, 32, 192–93; destabilization of, 132; gendered expectations of, 76. *See also* intersectionality
Heywood, Leslie, 200, 206
High and Hallowed (film), 22
hiking, 2, 18, 84, 112; adrenaline narrative role in, 7, 16; class, 45; climate crisis, 212; family, 27–28, 102–3, 184; gender, 52, 133, 141–42, 186–88, 191–92; nature/culture, 166; normate privilege, 216; popularity, 6; race, 30, 31, 187, 192, 195, 229–31; spiritual desire, 95, 105, 157
Hill, Diana Ellis, 57, 248n86
Hill, Lynn, 44, 90; authenticity, 46–47; conquering, 83; El Capitan, 28, 243n122; gender disparities in sport, 31–32, 49, 186
Hogan, Linda, 142
Honnold, Alex, 47–48, 228; Honnold Foundation, 204
hooks, bell, 74
Hornbein, Tom, 51, 112, 113, 118
Howkins, Heidi: abusive relationship, 251n12; erotic desire, 121–22, 124, 133, 158; gender dynamics, 31–32, 78–79, 80; nature, 65–66; risk, 26, 83, 92; spiritual desire, 106, 107, 109
Huckleberry Finn, 74, 114–15
Hudson, Henry, 55
Huggan, Graham, 241n68
Huguenard, Amie, 180
Humberstone, Barbara: hegemonic masculinity, 42, 122; nature, 134, 153, 165, 176; participation in extreme sports, 122, 135, 184, 223–24; popularity of extreme sports, 8

Ilgunas, Ken, 84
imperialism. *See* colonialism
Indigenous people: ancestry claim, 156–57; environmental ethic, 167; erasure/subjugation of, 20, 212; feminism, 256n13; guides, 46; local color status, 57; religion, 88, 106, 109–11, 123, 130, 161, 162–63; storytelling, 3. *See also* Native Americans
Indigenous Women Hike, 229–31
Inglis, Mark, 244n131
intersectionality, 14–15, 74, 135, 180, 213

See also class; disability; gender; heteronormality; race; sexuality
Into the Cold (film), 8, 22
Into the Wild (Krakauer book): appeal, 8, 34, 103, 214–15; conquering desire, 59–60, 61; risk, 149, 168; survival narrative, 16, 27
Into Thin Air (Krakauer book): adrenaline scale, 15, 26, 28; appeal, 1, 33, 35, 214–15; authenticity, 46–47, 48, 77, 246n31; climate crisis, 255n165; conquering desire, 40–41, 82, 86; gender, 49, 79, 186; heroic masculinity, 40–41, 63, 71, 149, 151, 245n7; nature, 139, 148–49; risk, 98; Sherpas, 116–17, 121, 246n26; spiritual desire, 87, 92, 97, 119, 176
Irvine, Amy, 16, 105, 144

Jacobs, Jane, 35, 88, 170, 211
James, Erin, 12
Jans, Nick, 38, 149–50, 160–61, 179–80, 259n156
Jewett, Sarah Orne, 209
John Muir Trail. *See* Muir, John
Johnson, Mat, 30
Johnson, Shelton, 219–22, 227
Jordan, Jennifer: climate crisis, 197; gender disparity, 77, 78, 80, 81; Krakauer critique, 49, 246n27
Jorgenson, Andrew K., 14
jouissance, 59–60, 97, 124, 252n57
journey: adrenaline narrative plot structure as, 18, 21–22, 25, 88; archetypal, 3, 22; authentic, 13; cathartic, 34; conquering, 63, 85, 140–41, 199–200, 214; pilgrimage, 89–98, 102–3, 104, 108–10, 112, 113–16, 119, 120, 167; revised, 55–56. *See also under* Hahn, Jennifer; Kocour, Ruth Anne; plot; rite of passage; soul

K2, 31, 121, 240n22, 241n71; appeal, 106, 115; deaths, 78, 104–5; Everest shared problems, 46. *See also* Bowley, Graham; Howkins, Heidi; Jordan, Jennifer
Kane, Joe, 16; climate crisis, 197; military language, 69; nature, 57, 64, 137, 146; risk, 98–99
Karnazes, Dean, 228
kayaking, 16, 31, 227; nature, 64, 120, 137, 163; participation, 32, 69, 112; risk, 177
Keen, Suzanne, 268n53
Keirstead, Christopher M., 242n86
Kerr, John H., 262n24
Kimmel, Michael, 241n52
Kipnis, Laura, 255n8
Kocour, Ruth Anne, 37; appeal, 28, 174, 177;

climate crisis, 198; control, 137; family, 73; gender, 67, 77; journey, 91–92, 93; nature, 65, 68, 70, 71–72, 146; risk, 82, 100–101; spiritual desire, 107, 113
Kodas, Michael, 265n178
Kollin, Susan, 45–46
Kolodny, Annette, 124, 134
Krakauer, Jon: adrenaline scale, 15, 26, 28; appeal, 1, 8, 33, 34, 35, 103, 214–15, 231–32; authenticity, 46–47, 48, 77, 246n31; climate crisis, 255n165; conquering desire, 37, 40–41, 59–60, 61, 66, 82, 86; gender, 49, 79, 186; heroic masculinity, 40–41, 43, 63, 71, 149, 151, 217, 245n7; nature, 139, 148–49; risk, 98, 149, 168; Sherpas, 116–17, 121, 246n26; spiritual desire, 87, 92, 97, 119, 176; style, 25, 36, 61; survival narrative, 16, 27. *See also Into the Wild*; *Into Thin Air*
Kraus, Jennifer, 249n130
Krein, Kevin: on Bridgers, 61, 62–63, 248n103; extreme sports definition, 18; nature, 126, 138; risk, 167, 177, 178, 179, 196
Kull, Robert: alternative narrative, 122, 124, 129, 140, 141, 146; spiritual desire, 112–13
Kusz, Kyle, 8, 11, 43, 172, 210

Lacan, Jacques, 60, 124
LaDuke, Winona, 209
Laing, Jennifer H., 21–22, 44–45, 64
Lane, Belden C., 187, 251n19
Langlois, Krista, 188
Laurendeau, Jason, 186, 192
Least Heat-Moon, William, 37, 54–56
Lecomte, Benoît, 84
Lee, Sau-Lai, 153, 154, 155
Leopold, Aldo, 10, 67, 128–29, 132, 147
Lévy-Bruhl, Lucien, 162
Lewis and Clark, 55
Lianos, Michaelis, 29
Lieu, Charlie, 52, 188
Lightner, Kai, 196
Little, Donna E., 192–93, 216, 224, 226–27
Littlebear, Alicia, 221
local color. *See under* setting
Lopez, Barry, 12, 163
Lord, Nancy, 153, 162–63, 215
Love, Glen, 12
Lundin, Cody, 75, 111, 250n166. *See also Dual Survival*
Luo, Yuan-Chun, 174

Macfarlane, Robert, 3–4, 6–7, 12
Mack-Canty, Colleen, 256n34

male gaze, 138, 190. *See also* feminism
Malusa, Jim, 26–27
Man, Woman, Wild (television show), 8
manifest destiny, 4, 43, 55, 114, 139
Manning, Peter K., 169
Manos, Jarid: frontier literature, 22–23; heroic masculinity, 55; nature, 66; spiritual desire, 97, 108–9; urban adventure, 54
Marchetti, Gina, 242n72
marketing. *See under* adventure
Martin, Derek Christopher, 51, 244n137
masculinity, 117, 134–36, 142, 166; adventure, 52, 74–77, 103–4; alternative, 47, 63, 111, 150, 186, 206; American environmental imagination, 14; American identity, 85–86, 114; crisis, 11, 43, 172, 210, 241n52; fatherhood, 10–11, 53–54, 78–79, 128, 184, 186; hardness quality of, 44–45, 65, 69, 74, 78–79, 96, 192–93; heterosexual desire, 59–60; rationality quality of, 56, 58, 66, 70, 79, 94, 137, 161, 178, 182; test characteristic of, 3, 56, 65, 73, 81–82, 95–96, 149, 168–69, 175, 213; white, 3, 11, 29, 31–33, 43, 45, 66, 72–73, 81–82, 103, 172, 210; white privilege, 135, 187, 192; wilderness, 67–70. *See also* gender; heroic masculinity; rite of passage
Mattessich, Stefan, 259n156
Mazzolini, Elizabeth, 198, 218, 265n178
McCairen, Patricia, 15, 16, 38; appeal, 34; dependency, 76, 93; erotic desire, 127–28, 129, 132–33, 134, 154, 155, 166; gender disparity, 73–74; spiritual desire, 96–98, 119; style, 25, 139
McCandless, Chris, 16, 27, 149, 168, 214. See also *Into the Wild*
McCarthy, Anne C., 3
McCarthy, Jeffrey: adrenaline narrative pedagogy, 23; nature, 34, 69, 117–18, 126, 133, 242n102
McClure, Tori Murden, 77, 80, 93–94, 95, 176
McConnell, Robert M., 265n183
McDougall, Christopher, 52
McKibben, Bill, 8
McNiel, Jamie N., 51
McQuillan, Gene, 253n66
Medred, Craig, 180
Meeker, Joseph W., 241n57
memoir, 10, 16, 30, 31, 188
Merchant, Carolyn, 242n102
Messerschmidt, James W., 245n10
Messner, Reinhold, 8, 47
Mills, James Edward, 29, 224; African American participation in outdoors, 6, 30, 145–46, 168, 194, 196, 220–22, 227

Mitchell, Timothy, 260n169
Monahan, Erin, 47
Montgomery, Mark, 200, 206
Morton, David, 22, 217–19
Morton, Timothy: dark ecology, 19, 125, 211; mesh, 20, 127, 132, 133, 155
Moser, Susanne C., 182
Moulton, Sam, 228
Mountain (film), 4
mountaineering, 22, 23, 49, 58; alternative climbing method, 121, 137; authenticity, 46–47, 82–83, 246n43; climate crisis, 197–99, 202, 249n130; conquering, 69–70, 71–72, 228; environmental thinking, 23; gender, 67, 73–74, 77–79, 80, 135; genre, 15–16, 17, 18, 25, 26–27, 31, 43, 241n69, 242n102; history, 3–4, 6–7, 8, 60–61, 243n104; motivating mountaineer, 84–85; nature, 63–64, 65, 126, 132, 139, 214; participation in, 50–51, 174, 177, 180, 194, 216–20, 244n137; risk, 27, 56, 87, 168, 186, 208; spiritual desire, 89–90, 91–92, 93, 98–102, 103, 105–6, 107, 112, 115–18. *See also* Everest; *Into Thin Air*; Sherpas
Mozingo, Joe, 50–51, 244n129
Muir, John, 10, 142–43, 223, 230; John Muir Trail (JMT; Nüümü Poyo), 188, 195, 229–31
mutuality, 173, 225, 226, 242n102; adrenaline narrative examples, 128, 129, 147, 156; animism, 162; ecofeminism, 122–23, 124–26, 135–37, 138, 143; erotic desire characteristic, 24, 36, 37, 62, 122–23, 125, 158, 164, 227. *See also* erotic desire
myth: epic, 16, 114, 211; heroic masculinity, 65, 85; mystery/magic and erotic desire, 137, 144, 157; mythical settings, 63–65. *See also* American myth; nature: magical/mythic; spiritual desire: magic and mystery

Naked and Afraid (television show), 48
Nash, Roderick Frazier, 10, 20, 139, 165, 215
National Geographic, 81; Everest, 239n5, 244n129; extreme photo, 8, 240n36
National Geographic Society, 239n5, 246n32
National Parks, 11; American environmental imagination, 35, 209; climate crisis, 203; Glacier, 204; National Archives, 7; race, 195; sexual harassment in, 52; Yosemite, 28
Native Americans, 71, 109–11, 167, 201, 225–26, 228–31, 269n64; adrenaline narrative impact on, 3, 4, 5; Ahwahnechee, 230; ecological Indian stereotype, 111, 156–57, 230; Inuit, 109–10; Koyukon, 163; land claims, 221–22; Least Heat-Moon, William, 37, 54–56; white shaman, 110, 111. *See*

INDEX 301

also adventure film; Indigenous people; religion: Indigenous/shamanism
NativesOutdoors, 222
Native Women's Wilderness, 222
nature: alienation from, 33–36, 89, 103, 156, 173, 188–89, 200–201, 212, 229; as character, 120, 128–29, 147, 148, 151–58, 163–64; control of, 3, 24, 37, 41–42, 56–73, 110–11, 113, 123, 127, 136–38, 140, 167; as escape, 10–11, 34, 74, 94, 102, 174, 179, 187, 194, 195, 204, 205; feminist reworking, 120, 123–24, 129, 131, 133–35, 138, 140–41, 143–47, 153, 164; indifferent, 63, 64–65, 70, 128, 154, 161; listening to, 70, 123, 138, 143–44, 147, 152, 157–64, 165–66, 167, 217–18; magical/mythic, 34, 59–60, 63–65, 102, 108, 113, 137, 144, 157, 202; mother nature, 29, 136, 154, 166, 178, 209; natureculture, 127, 167, 256n37; as teacher, 56, 90, 109–10, 119. *See also* desire; environment; god; pollution; setting; soul; sublime; wilderness
—as other, 28–29, 37, 70, 102, 117, 151, 199, 201, 226; exotic/feminized, 15, 28, 54, 56–67, 113–14, 124, 128–29, 134, 154, 211; rejection/revision of, 3, 123–31, 133–34, 137–38, 142–43, 148, 223
—(re)connection to, 10–11, 20, 173; in conquering desire, 49, 69–70; in erotic desire, 36, 125, 132–34, 137–44, 146, 152–59; in restorative desire, 221–23, 226–29, 231; in risky desire (deep play/flow), 175, 176, 178–79, 183, 199, 206, 208–9, 213, 216, 228; in spiritual desire, 47, 88–90, 93, 99, 101–4, 106–10, 112–16, 119, 215
nature writing, 16, 17, 18, 21, 26
Nelson, Richard, 27
neoliberalism, 217
Nichols, Peter, 81–82, 95, 96, 154
Nimmo, Richie, 124, 152, 153, 154–55, 157, 162
Norgay, Jamling Tenzing, 23, 240n22
normate. *See under* body
North Face, 2, 227–28, 244n129
Norton, Jake, 22
nostalgia. *See* frontier: popularity/nostalgia
Nouzeilles, Gabriela, 13, 102, 247n46
Nunley, Vorris L., 196, 265n158
Nüümü Poyo, 229–31. *See also* Muir, John

Oates, Joyce Carol, 211
O'Connor, Flannery, 96
Oliver, John, 217
Olivier, Steve, 199, 201, 261n4
O'Neill, Hilaree, 228
Orangutan Foundation International (OFI), 207

Ortner, Sherry B., 61, 240n22, 256n26
Ostman, Cami, 93
other, exotic, 28. *See also* animals: self/other distinction; ecofeminism: self/other; nature: as other; risky desire; setting: local color
Out of the Wild (television show), 8
Ozturk, Renan, 228

Pacific Crest Trail, 133, 166, 186, 212; Strayed on, 8, 20, 186. *See also* Storey, Gail D.
Pagh, Nancy, 75, 134–35
Palmer, Catherine, 172, 173, 187, 210–11
Park, Sowon S., 152–53, 164
parler-femme, 124
pastoral, 65–66, 109, 114, 200. *See also* nature
Patagonia: company, 2; region in South America, 22, 48–49, 63–65, 68, 89, 99, 112–13, 175
patriarchal masculinity. *See* heroic masculinity
patriarchy, 19, 41, 156, 167, 190; control, 61, 69; erotic desire, 129, 132, 135, 138, 142, 147; fantasy, 19, 148; Griffin, Susan, 60, 66; homosocial, 94; hooks, bell, 74; imperialism/colonialism, 30, 31, 32, 54, 56, 59, 61, 110, 117, 123, 211–12; logic/norms, 52, 58, 60, 66–67, 75, 81, 135–36, 164, 186, 205, 216, 231; masculinity, 33, 40, 42, 45, 63, 72, 75, 85, 162; neo-patriarchy, 82–85; objectification, 59–60, 119, 122, 123, 144; restorative desire, 229. *See also* conquering desire; heroic masculinity
Peary, Robert E., 5–6, 22
Peisner, David, 250n166
Perrow, Charles, 183
Pfeil, Fred, 241n52
Pham, Andrew X., 37, 53–54, 55, 79, 97
Phillips, Richard S., 74
pilgrimage. *See* journey; spiritual desire
Pinkney, William, 50, 176, 194–95
Pioneer Climbing Expedition Team, 50, 244n129
Pittman, Sandy Hill, 46, 49, 79, 246n27
plaisir, 59
play, 21, 35–36, 62, 101; deep, 35, 126, 137, 175, 176, 178–79, 183, 216, 228; environment as playground/playmate, 10, 200, 227; erotic desire, 127; socially redeemable, 181; spiritual desire, 106, 109; sustainable, 86
plot, 16, 114, 117, 169; journey, 18, 21–23, 25, 88, 140–41; revised, 139–43; risk structure, 210; tragic, 36. *See also* journey
Plumwood, Val, 138, 143

pollution, 89, 109, 145, 197, 200–204, 218; Everest, 68, 116–17, 198–99, 202; gendered, 57, 63–64; pastoral disruptions, 200; risk society, 10, 170–71; spiritual, 116–20, 121–22; water, 84, 111, 171, 196, 200–203, 209–10. *See also* climate crisis; environmental ethics; environmental movement; nature
postcolonialism: anthropomorphism, 151–52; conquering desire, 53, 56, 88; mountaineering, 244n137; nature critique, 37, 41–42. *See also* colonialism
posthumanism, 125
Potter, Will, 172
prAna, 185
Primal Quest, 18
Protestant work ethic, 35, 44, 49, 216–17
Purdy, Jedediah, 61–62; imagination, 24, 38, 227; nature, 215, 219, 226
Putnam, Walter, 260n169

queer, 31, 42, 132, 161–62, 267n249; homosocial desire, 94

race, 10, 46, 59, 103, 153, 247n85; Asian Americans, 53–54, 79, 222; exclusion, 22–23, 29–31, 43, 56–57, 109, 222, 227–28, 244n137; heroic masculinity, 5–6, 22, 42–44, 50–51, 53–56, 72, 74–75, 146; patriarchy, 60; racial justice, 220; risk, 11, 169–70, 180, 183, 184, 186, 187, 191–96, 201, 213; white privilege, 135, 187, 192. *See also* African Americans; intersectionality; Native Americans; nature; racism
racism, 60, 153, 194, 195, 229; environmental, 111; heroic masculinity, 4, 44. *See also* colonialism; postcolonialism; race
rafting, 28, 139, 227, 228; solo, 16, 25, 96–98
Rak, Julie, 60–61, 70, 73, 94, 115, 135
Ralston, Aron, 15, 26, 37, 60; catharsis, 92; environmentalist characterization, 209; ownership of nature, 69, 70, 71
Randall, Cassidy, 186
Raskin, Jonah, 144
reader. *See* audience
regionalism. *See under* setting
religion, 35, 87–88, 104–6, 108, 109; agnosticism, 87, 104, 105, 108, 111, 144; Christianity, 105, 107, 109, 187, 251n19; dark green, 88, 105, 109; Indigenous/shamanism, 105, 106, 109–10, 111, 123, 130, 157, 161, 230; Mormonism, 105; pantheism, 106; religious naturalism, 129–30; religious writing, 5, 17, 24, 105. *See also* god; soul; spiritual desire; spirituality; transcendentalism
restoration ecology, 24, 229
restorative desire, 38, 213, 214–32; conquering desire relation to, 230; definition, 24, 36, 37, 214–15, 229–31; erotic desire relation to, 219, 223, 226–27, 229, 231; risky desire relation to, 214–18, 223–24, 226, 230; spiritual desire relation to, 215, 219, 222, 225, 229–31. *See also* desire
risk, 24; American identity, 4, 5, 13, 23, 53–54, 83–84, 213; assessment, 179, 182, 184, 216–17; culture/society, 34–35, 38, 169, 170–74, 182, 183, 196, 207, 210, 213, 216, 218; dangerous limits / natural extremes, 9, 26–29, 178–81; management, 14, 37, 67–68, 70, 72, 100–101, 152, 169–72, 176–77, 181–97; narrative, 15, 169, 172; professions, 32; regimes, 186–93; theme of, 16, 29, 97, 169, 174, 184, 188, 211; tone, 25–29, 169, 210; truth relationship to, 15. *See also* accidents; adrenaline madness; Beck, Ulrich; climate crisis; death; gender; heroic masculinity; race; risk aesthetic; risky desire; setting; sex-based violence; survival
risk aesthetic, 25, 29, 38, 112, 168–70; appeal, 174–81; context, 170–74; embodiment and management, 181–96; implications of, 178–79, 182–83, 205–10, 213; setting, 196–205. *See also* risk; risky desire
risky desire, 24, 38, 168–213, 216, 226; appeal, 101, 174–81; conservatism, 12, 33, 114, 186; control, 181–83; environmental movement, 67–68, 152, 172, 205–13, 216–17; erotic desire relation to, 126–27, 141, 149–50, 152, 167, 173, 205; gender, 73–77, 79, 146, 183–93; race, 53–55, 72, 193–96; restorative desire relation to, 214–18, 223–24, 226, 230; risk society, 170–74; setting, 7, 113, 168–69, 173, 211; spiritual desire relation to, 91–93, 97–101, 112–16, 118–20, 187, 200, 205. *See also* adrenaline madness; climate crisis; death; desire; risk; risk aesthetic; rite of passage; setting; sex-based violence
—conquering desire relation to, 70, 82, 174–75; authenticity, 47–48, 84, 198; environment, 67, 200; gender and race, 52–56, 59, 63, 69, 72–79, 85–86, 192–93, 195
rite of passage, 34, 89, 90–93, 97–101, 168–69, 196–205, 210; ritual, 21, 34–35, 58, 74, 96, 98, 110; as test, 3, 18, 56, 65, 73–74, 82, 95–96, 149, 175, 211, 213. *See also* journey
ritual. *See* rite of passage

INDEX 303

Roberts, Suzanne, 37, 145, 146; anthropomorphism, 153; class, 45; climate crisis, 203-4; gender, 75-76, 138, 141-43, 188, 189, 192, 195
Robertson, Simon, 206-7, 208
Robinson, Victoria, 179
Romanticism, 3, 88, 149; ecofeminist revision, 123, 124-25, 128; mountaineering, 61, 115
Rose, Deborah Bird, 159
Rose, Patricia, 88
Rosen, Nick, 47-48
Ross, Cindy, 119; family, 27-28, 96, 102-3, 246n24; nature, 99, 105, 106, 109, 159
running, 52, 227; endurance, 16, 18, 228, 250n206; marathon, 93; prayer, 221-22, 230
Ryan, Sean, 7, 164-65
Ryman, Dale, 2

Saatchi, Anaheed, 53
sacred space, 113-14, 116. *See also* setting; spiritual desire; spirituality
Sacred Strides (film), 221-22
sailing, 4, 28, 227; climate crisis, 201, 202, 203; self-discovery, 82, 95, 154, 194; solo, 50, 85, 176
Sandilands, Catriona, 60, 132, 143-45, 226, 231, 256n13
Savran, David, 241n52
Schindler, Kristine, 249n130
Schooler, Lynn, 100
Schrepfer, Susan R., 10, 243n104
Schultheis, Rob, 225; animism, 163-64, Everest, 198; shamanism, 105; spiritual desire, 109, 113
setting, 21, 93, 103, 155, 176; distinct character, 120, 123-34, 158, 217-18; gender and race impact on, 52-53, 135; local color (exotic), 15, 28, 57, 113, 153, 211; mythical, 63-65; regionalism, 7; risky, 16-21, 24, 26, 29, 140-41, 148-49, 169, 175, 196-205, 210, 216; sportscape, 76; sublime, 88, 89, 100, 103-4, 116, 123, 147; transformative, 93, 106, 112-20, 222-23; wild, 10, 13, 15, 17-21, 34, 73, 113. *See also* Alaska; authenticity; nature; wilderness
—sacred: destination, 93, 103; Indigenous land as, 221; nature representation as, 37, 88, 98-99, 105, 108, 112-14, 116, 119, 130, 144; spiritual territory, 85
Seven Summits, 27, 29, 31, 50, 244n129
sex-based violence, 51-52, 89, 188-92, 251n12; landscape, 52, 58, 62, 65, 116-17, 121; rape culture, 52, 188-93. *See also* risk

sexism. *See* patriarchy
sexuality, 11, 74, 132, 153, 192-93; heterosexuality, 31, 59, 61, 74, 132; homophobia, 42, 43; homosexuality, 31; homosocial desire, 94; LGBTQIA, 222. *See also* heteronormality; intersectionality; queer
Shackleton, Ernest, 90
Sharara, Nancy, 192
Shepard, Paul, 34-35, 241n57
Sherpa (film), 23, 240n22
Sherpas, 81, 217, 218; adrenaline narrative about/by, 6, 23, 33, 50, 240n22, 247n55; authenticity, 41, 83; pay disparity, 46, 246n26; Sherpa orphan, 116-17, 121
Sierra Club, 61
Simmel, George, 28, 31
Simon, Alvah, 37, 94; anthropomorphism, 73, 157, 162; authentic adventure, 13, 96, 103; climate crisis, 197, 207-8, 209; erotic desire, 140, 141; risk, 100, 101, 175-76; spiritual desire, 106-8, 109-10, 113-14
Simpson, Sherry, 37, 140-41
skiing, 63, 90; backcountry, 16, 227; climate crisis, 218; extreme, 8, 180, 240n34; gender, 67, 73, 81, 103-4, 188; resort, 19
Skog, Cecilie, 104-5
Slemon, Stephen, 245n1
social justice, 210, 211, 218, 223, 231-32; anthropomorphism, 164; heroic masculinity, 7; radical, 172; restorative desire, 36, 37, 221-22, 230; risk, 183, 213; spiritual desire, 108-9. *See also* environmental justice; environmental movement; feminism
soul, 118; journey to/for, 94, 96, 108, 113; nature's impact on, 73, 99, 103, 114, 115, 116, 131; nature's soul/spirit, 121, 137, 163; searching, 40; surfer, 206. *See also* spiritual desire
Sparkes, Andrew C., 245n7
spiritual desire, 87-120; conquering desire relation to, 37, 40-41, 47, 82, 85, 88, 90-92, 93-95, 99, 110-11, 117, 119; definition, 10, 36, 47, 87-86, 88, 140, 242n102; epiphany, 10-11, 88-89, 96-111, 116, 133, 139, 140, 204, 215, 216, 229; erotic desire relation to, 88, 119-23, 136, 137, 139-42, 144, 146-49, 156, 163-64; magic and mystery, 34, 56-57, 63-65, 102, 104, 108, 113, 137, 144, 157, 202; nature as spiritual teacher, 90, 116; pollution of, 116-20, 121-22; restorative desire relation to, 215, 219, 222, 225, 229-31; risky desire

spiritual desire (*continued*)
  relation to, 91–93, 97–101, 112–16, 118–20, 187, 200, 205; self-centered, 118; suffering (sacred), 86, 87, 92, 95, 99–101, 108–9, 208, 216, 230. *See also* adventure: authenticity; desire; god; religion; rite of passage; romanticism; setting: sacred; setting: sublime; soul; spirituality; spiritual writing; sublime
spirituality, 114; contemporary culture absence, 10, 34–35, 112–13; definition, 88–89, 104, 107, 146; exotic other, 28; extreme as calling, 92, 114; green, 88; Indigenous, 88, 106, 109–10, 130, 157, 162–63, 167, 222; intraspecies, 149; polluted, 116–20; pure, 147, 164; spiritual seekers, 94, 103, 106, 122; transformative, 85, 215, 253n87; wilderness reading as spiritual practice, 187, 251n19. *See also* god; religion; soul; spiritual desire
spiritual writing, 17; autobiography, 5; narrative, 93, 96, 118
Spivak, Gayatri Chakravorty, 151–52, 159
Stabile, Carol, 249n123
Stark, Peter, 126–27
Stein, Rachel, 192–93
Stockwell, Peter, 224
Stoddart, Mark CJ, 67, 73, 76, 103, 204
Storey, Gail D., 38; climate crisis, 212; entanglement, 133–34, 257n74; risk, 177; transformation, 141, 166
Stowe, William W., 5
Strayed, Cheryl, 8, 20, 186
Streep, Abe, 217–19
Stroud, Les, 57
sublime, 40, 113, 115–16, 117, 216; conquering desire, 60; Red Bull, 3; setting, 88, 89, 100, 103–4, 116, 123, 147. *See also* nature; wilderness
Suelo, Daniel, 107, 225–26
Sundance, 2, 239n3. *See also* adventure marketing
Sundeen, Mark, 16, 107, 139, 225
surfing, 16, 63; archives, 7; big-wave, 42–43, 83, 179, 181; climate crisis, 200, 204; pragmatic soul surfer, 206; World Surf League prize, 49
Surfrider, 206
survival, 2, 140; choice, 71–72, 77, 82, 92; class, 46, 54; climate crisis, 108–9, 201, 208, 217; endurance, 16, 18, 44, 54, 79, 82, 87–88, 92, 110, 175–76; gender stereotypes, 81, 194; guilt, 77; Krakauer, Jon, 1, 214; narrative, 16, 17, 27, 30, 31, 53–54, 56, 65, 82, 85, 200, 231; species, 161; strategy/skill, 70, 101, 132, 152, 155–57, 169–70, 178–83, 187–90, 195, 226; television and media, 8–9, 28, 48, 57, 75, 110–11, 119, 247n85; triumph, 83, 196; voyage, 95. *See also under* wilderness
Survivor (television show), 8
Survivorman (television show), 8
sustainability, 9, 23, 30, 63, 231; behavior, 14, 24, 41, 67–68, 101, 173, 179, 199–200, 207, 216–18; environmental, 2, 84, 102, 112, 135–36, 166, 167, 174; expedition, 84–85; future, 24, 39, 179, 226; greenwashing, 38, 205–10; restorative desire, 24, 36, 230; risky desire, 170, 176, 210–13; spiritual desire, 119. *See also* environment; environmental awareness; environmental movement; green
sustainable play, 36; adventure, 205
swimming, 16, 84, 201–2, 250n206

Tam, Kim-Pong, 153, 154, 155
Taylor, Bron, 37, 88, 104–5, 109
Taylor, Dorceta E., 88, 116, 242n98
television. *See* adventure television; *and specific television shows*
Temoa Adventures, 222
Teti, Joseph, 110–11, 250n166. See also *Dual Survival*
Than, Ker, 244n129
Theberge, Nancy, 184
Thompson, Charis, 268n36
Thoreau, Henry David, 13, 106, 142, 144, 205; self-reliance, 49, 204–5
Title IX, 51
touristic gaze, 57, 248n88
tragedy: adrenaline narrative relationship to, 3, 8, 21, 114, 173, 180–81, 199–200; catharsis, 22, 34, 87, 89, 90, 92, 97–98, 180; climate crisis distraction, 35–36; Everest, 26, 34, 41, 98, 121, 253n66; heroic masculinity, 149–51. *See also* death
transcendentalism, 88, 123, 125, 128; conquering desire, 147; spiritual desire, 24, 175; transcendent experience/nature, 99, 115, 119, 129, 148. *See also* sublime
trans-corporeality, 20, 132–33, 164; adventurers, 143, 159–61; cyborg/companion species compared to, 125–26, 158; liminal intimacy compared to, 155; natureculture, 127. *See also under* Alaimo, Stacy
travel. *See* adventure travel
Treadwell, Timothy, 149–51, 155, 160–62, 179–81, 259n156
Treinish, Gregg, 206
Trombold, John, 33–34, 246n27

Twain, Mark. *See* Huckleberry Finn
Twenty-first Century Conservation Service Corps, 228
Twight, Mark, 26

Vance, Linda, 173; liminality, 124, 125, 127, 143; wilderness, 139, 145, 164, 211-12
Van Dooren, Thom, 159
Vanreusel, Bart, 161, 206, 208, 218
Varela, Jolie, 231
viewer. *See* audience
Vivanco, Luis A., 10, 28-29
Voight, Alison, 174
Vouillamoz, Phillipe, 218

Wagner, Karin, 63
Walker, Matt, 57, 248n86
Wallace, Molly, 171, 196
Weihenmayer, Erik, 244n131
Weiss, Miranda, 26; climate crisis, 86, 197, 203, 204-5; ownership of nature, 71; risky desire, 27, 28
Welling, Bart, 155
Wenzel, Michael, 230
West (American), 97, 105, 115, 222; expansion, 7, 22-23, 55, 86; heroic masculinity, 54; National Archives photographs, 5. *See also* frontier
Western culture, 3-4, 20, 22; climate crisis, 199, 203; heroic masculinity, 54, 75, 125; mountaineering, 6-7, 23, 50, 83; nature, 35, 115, 164, 257n46; religion, 88, 108, 109, 111
Weyland, Jocko, 19
Wheaton, Belinda, 42, 240n37
Wheeler, Elizabeth, 30, 31, 216-17, 219
White, Lynn, 88
white privilege, 135, 187, 192. *See also* masculinity
White Shamans, Plastic Medicine Men (film), 111

Whitman, Walt, 4, 146-47
Whittaker, Tom, 244n131
wild, 33, 96; definition of, 20-21; democracy, 144-45; environmentalism, 9; fear of, 24; feminization of, 40, 42, 52, 56-59, 63-64, 66-67, 123, 129; identity, 109, 141-43, 156, 225; nature qualities of, 9-11, 20, 66-67, 102, 166; violent indifference, 65. *See also* environment; nature; wilderness; Wilderness Act of 1964
wilderness, 67-68; American identity, 10, 16, 33, 51, 55, 195, 211-13, 215-29; definition, 20-21, 130, 241n50; as empty space, 10, 19-20, 34, 57, 116, 132, 145, 155, 212, 215, 217; feminist reworking, 122-27, 129, 133-34, 138-45, 147, 158, 166, 219, 222, 229, 232, 257n46; literature, 10, 15-16, 35; reading, 187, 251n19; spiritual transformation, 100-104, 106, 112-13, 119, 122, 134, 212; survival, 9, 16, 30, 110, 157, 190; untrammeled, 19, 34, 57, 139, 165, 203, 208; violence in, 51-53, 186-96; virgin, 21, 34, 45, 57, 61-64, 123, 139, 145, 164-65, 219, 227. *See also* environment; nature; setting; sublime; wild; Wilderness Act of 1964
Wilderness Act of 1964, 19, 20, 57, 116, 139
Williams, Terry Tempest, 36, 123, 142
Willis, Clint, 241n71
Wilson, Erica, 192-93, 216, 224, 226-27
Woodlief, Jennifer, 176

X Games, 17, 18, 242n72

Zerain, Alberto, 105, 106, 115
Zinn, Jens Oliver, 171-72
Žižek, Slavoj, 29, 136-37, 149, 151
zoomorphism, 160
Zuckerman, Peter, 240n22